American Economic Development
in Historical Perspective

American Economic Development in Historical Perspective

Edited by
Thomas Weiss and Donald Schaefer

STANFORD UNIVERSITY PRESS
STANFORD, CALIFORNIA 1994

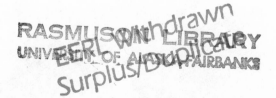

Stanford University Press
Stanford, California
© 1994 by the Board of Trustees of the
Leland Stanford Junior University
Printed in the United States of America

CIP data appear at the end of the book

Stanford University Press publications
are distributed exclusively by Stanford
University Press within the United
States, Canada, and Mexico; they are
distributed exclusively by Cambridge
University Press throughout the rest of
the world.

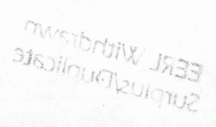

❧ Preface

THIS VOLUME had its origins in a conference held at Loyola College in Baltimore, Maryland, in honor of Robert Gallman, whose work is an example *par excellence* of the fruitful connection between economic development and economic history.[1] Following in the tradition of Simon Kuznets, his mentor, Gallman has focused his work on the great issues of long-term economic development, bringing economic analysis and careful quantification to bear on this broad subject. Like Kuznets, Gallman has shown in his quantitative work a thorough understanding of the actual history from which the data derive.

Kuznets made extensive use of cross-sectional evidence and employed long-term statistical series to describe the aggregate performance over time of each sector and nation. While focusing on the common elements, he also emphasized the great diversity among countries. Much was to be learned, he thought, from the details of how the growth process worked out in each nation. The reliability of any international comparisons, he taught, must rest on the accuracy of the evidence for the individual countries.

Gallman, too, has devoted a lifetime to identifying and understanding general patterns of long-term economic change. Rather than examine the growth process displayed across a broad set of countries, he has focused on the economic history of the United States. His work has given a deeper, more detailed understanding of one successful case of development—for a long time the most successful one. To this end, he first extended the statistical series on national income and wealth, and its distribution across regions and industries. Then, using these expanded series, he addressed himself to measuring the pace and timing of U.S. growth, interpreting the data and phenomena in historical context. His work makes clear that a full understanding of a record of sustained increases in national income and income per capita over a very long period rests on the details of how, and how well, institutions and markets performed, and how they changed over time.

No study of the pace and pattern of American economic growth, of the sources of that growth, its structural changes, and the changing distribution of income and wealth can proceed without making use of Gallman's research. It has been of major importance in the examination of U.S. economic development and in the establishment of the empirical record of that performance. Combined with the work of Kuznets, the estimates prepared by Gallman extend our national income statistics back quite firmly to around 1835. His magisterial essay on American economic growth for the *Encyclopedia of American Economic History* gives a careful and commanding view of his findings and his methods.

Gallman, along with several other contributors to the present volume, was among the pioneers of "new" economic history—now more commonly known as "cliometrics."[2] Cliometricians have analyzed a variety of issues over the years, but early on the issues related to growth and development were paramount, and they have remained Gallman's major interest. Gallman, perhaps more than the others, has kept to the original course—with occasional forays into colonial economic history, population growth, and the issues related to antebellum plantation slavery.

Gallman has inspired others to follow his course. His graduate courses at the University of North Carolina have remained among the most demanding and challenging in the curriculum. Geared up and excited about the latest advances in theory and econometrics, students initially were puzzled as to why the course in economic history was required, and unhappy that it was always scheduled for late afternoons, when enthusiasm for economics was waning for the day. Yet in the long run, this experience proved to be very rewarding for most students, regardless of their areas of specialization. His course even prepared us for the staple of academic life, the late afternoon seminar. For some of us, the value of his teaching was immediate and obvious, as well as long lasting. To have participated in his work, to have begun our own work under his kindly but exacting eye, and to have shared professional experiences with him has been most rewarding.

Robert Gallman has also taught any number of his peers a thing or two: the subtle but correct interpretation to be put on certain pieces of evidence, and the shortcomings as well as the importance of historical data. His essays have been models of graceful writing. Though not always legible in manuscript draft, his writing is a work of art—done with such apparent ease that one forgets how difficult it is to write well. When necessary, Bob could also explain why the North Carolina basketball team was struggling, and he was well posted on the home schedule of UNC baseball.

Without realizing it or working at it, Bob has been one of the best role models for graduate students and young faculty, and even for older faculty who admire his collegiality, his professionalism, and his dedication. The list of his accomplishments holds out the sort of career a student strives for. He was awarded a doctorate in economics by the University of Pennsylvania in 1956, and taught at Ohio State University from 1954 to 1962. He has been a member of the faculty of the University of North Carolina at Chapel Hill since 1962, with visiting positions at Stanford University (1967–68), Nuffield College, Oxford University (1972–73), and the National Bureau of Economic Research (1989–90). He has served as president of the Economic History Association and of the Southern Economic Association, and editor of the *Journal of Economic History* and the *Southern Economic Journal*; has been a Guggenheim Fellow, a research associate of the National Bureau of Economic Research and a member of its Conference on Research in Income and Wealth; and is the author of over 30 articles, and editor or coeditor of several volumes of essays on American economic history. It is not just by doing his own thing that he sets a shining example. His genuine and unending enthusiasm for the pursuit of knowledge in all directions has excited students, and convinced some of us to choose economic history for our life's work. He is one of those rare scholars whose sincere interest in the work of colleagues makes for a productive environment for both a faculty and a profession. He has always been, and still is, where the action is—actively engaged in research and at the cutting edge of his subject.

The papers in this volume presented at the Loyola-Baltimore conference have been revised extensively, both individually and as a group, to form a coherent and substantial explanation of the interconnections between the academic study of economic history and economic development in the American experience. The reviewing, refereeing, and editing could not have been carried out without the assistance of many people, all of whom were eager to help honor Bob. Each of the contributing authors acted as an outside referee for at least one other paper. Each paper was also reviewed by someone outside the group of authors. Those who helped the authors and the editors in this task include the following scholars: Lou Cain, Charlie Calomiris, John Clark, Wayne Joerding, Maurice Joy, Robert McGuire, Cynthia Taft Morris, Kerry Odell, Josh Rosenbloom, Ken Sokoloff, Rick Steckel, and John Wallis. Our special thanks are due to them.

T.W.

D.S.

❧ Contents

❧ Contributors

Colleen Callahan is Assistant Professor of Economics, Lehigh University. She completed her Ph.D. at the University of North Carolina in 1987, with a dissertation called "Movements in Aggregate Price Uncertainty in the United States, 1884–1981." She has written articles on the self-sufficiency of the South, the financial history of the United States, and international trade.

Lance E. Davis is Mary Stillman Harkness Professor of Social Science, Division of the Humanities and Social Sciences at California Institute of Technology, and a research associate of the National Bureau of Economic Research. He is one of the founding fathers of the "new economic history" and a past president of the Economic History Association. His publications include *Institutional Change and American Economic Growth* (Cambridge, 1971), written with Douglass North; *Mammon and the Pursuit of Empire* (Cambridge, 1986), written with Robert Huttenback; and numerous articles on American economic history.

Stanley Engerman is Professor of Economics and History, Department of Economics, University of Rochester, a research associate of the National Bureau of Economic Research, and a past president of the Economic History Association. He has written about slavery in the United States and the West Indies as well as about U.S. economic growth. With Robert Fogel he is coauthor of *Time on the Cross* (Boston, 1974); coeditor of *The Reinterpretation of American Economic History* (New York, 1971); and coeditor (with Robert Gallman) of *Long-Term Factors in American Economic Growth* (Chicago, 1986).

Robert Fogel is the Charles R. Walgreen Professor of American Institutions and Director of the Center for Population Economics, University of Chicago, and a research associate of the National Bureau of Economic Research. He has served as president of both the Economic History Association and the Social Science History Association, and as director of the National Bureau of Economic Research's Program on the Development of the American Economy. He has written extensively on the issues of slavery and American economic growth. His publications include *Time on the Cross* and *The Reinterpretation of American Economic History* (written with Engerman); *Railroads and American Economic Growth* (Baltimore, 1964); and *Without Consent or Contract* (New York, 1989).

Louis Galambos is Professor of History, The Johns Hopkins University, past president of the Economic History Association, former editor of the *Journal of Economic History*, and editor of *The Papers of Dwight David Eisenhower*. He has written extensively in the area of U.S. business history, including *The Public Image of Big Business in America, 1880–1940* (Baltimore, 1975); *The Fall of the Bell System: A Study in Prices and Politics*, with Peter Temin (New York, 1987); and *The Rise of the Corporate Commonwealth: United States Business and Public Policy in the Twentieth Century*, with Joseph Pratt (New York, 1988).

J. Matthew Gallman is Associate Professor of History, Loyola College, Baltimore. He is the author of *Mastering Wartime: A Social History of Philadelphia During the Civil War* (Cambridge and New York, 1990).

Robert Gallman is Kenan Professor of Economics and History, chair, Department of Economics, University of North Carolina at Chapel Hill, and a research associate of the National Bureau of Economic Research. He has served as president of both the Southern Economic Association and the Economic History Association, and as editor of the *Journal of Economic History*. His extensive research has provided the empirical basis for much of our knowledge of the nineteenth-century economy of the United States.

Claudia Goldin is Professor of Economics, Harvard University, and director of the National Bureau of Economic Research's Program on the Development of the American Economy. She is a former editor of the *Journal of Economic History* and has written numerous articles on labor history. Her publications include *Urban Slavery in the American South, 1820 to 1860* (Chicago, 1976); *Understanding the Gender Gap: An Economic History of American Women* (Oxford, 1990); and *Strategic Factors in Nineteenth-Century American Economic History* (edited with Hugh Rockoff) (Chicago, 1992).

Teresa Hutchins is Assistant Professor of Economics, Department of Economics, Ramapo College of New Jersey. Her dissertation, "The American Whale Fishery, 1815–1900," was written at the University of North Carolina under the direction of Robert Gallman. She has collaborated with Gallman and Davis on numerous articles about the economics of the U.S. whaling industry, including "The Structure of the Capital Stock in Economic Growth and Decline: The New Bedford Whaling Fleet in the

Nineteenth Century," in P. Kilby, ed., *Quantity and Quiddity: Essays in U.S. Economic History* (Middletown, Conn., 1987).

Charles P. Jones is Edwin Gill Professor of Finance, North Carolina State University. He is the author of *Investments: Analysis and Management* (New York, 1985; 3d ed., 1991), *Introduction of Financial Management* (Homewood, Ill., 1992), and many articles on financial economics.

Douglass North is Professor of Economics and director of the Center in Political Economy at Washington University in St. Louis. He is a former editor of the *Journal of Economic History*. His publications include *The Economic Growth of the United States, 1790–1860* (Englewood Cliffs, N.J., 1961); and *Institutions, Institutional Change and Economic Performance* (Cambridge, 1990).

William Parker is Phillip Golden Bartlett Professor of Economics and Economic History, Emeritus, Yale University. He has served as president of both the Agricultural History Society and the Economic History Association, and as editor of the *Journal of Economic History*. His work has encompassed not only empirical investigations of the United States but the broader issues of U.S. and European history, exemplified by his two-volume work *Europe, America, and the Wider World* (Cambridge, 1984 and 1991). He is editor of *Trends in the American Economy in the Nineteenth Century* (Princeton, 1964), and *Economic History and the Modern Economist* (Oxford, 1986).

Barry Poulson is Professor of Economics, University of Colorado at Boulder. An expert in both economic history and economic development, he has published *Value Added in Manufacturing, Mining, and Agriculture in the American Economy from 1809 to 1839* (New York, 1975); *Economic History of the United States* (New York, 1981); and a number of books and articles on economic development in Latin America and the Middle East.

Donald Schaefer is Professor of Economics, Washington State University. He has written on a variety of topics in the economic history of the United States, including slavery, migration, and railroads. His publications include *A Quantitative Description and Analysis of the Growth of the Pennsylvania Anthracite Coal Industry, 1820–1865* (New York, 1977).

Richard Sylla is Henry Kaufman Professor of the History of Financial Institutions and Markets and Professor of Economics, New York University, and research associate of the National Bureau of Economic Research. A former editor of the *Journal of Economic History*, he has written extensively on the topic of financial economic history. His publications include *The American Capital Market, 1846–1914* (New York, 1975); *The Evolution of the American Economy* (New York, 1979; 2d ed., 1993), written with Sidney Ratner and James Soltow; and *A History of Interest Rates,* 3d ed. (New Brunswick, N.J., 1991), with Sidney Homer.

Thomas Weiss is Professor of Economics, University of Kansas, research associate of the National Bureau of Economic Research, and former editor of the *Journal of Economic History.* He is author of *The Service Sector in the United States, 1839 through 1899* (New York, 1975); coauthor (with Fred Bateman) of *A Deplorable Scarcity* (Chapel Hill, 1981); and author of many articles on the U.S. labor force in the nineteenth century.

Jack W. Wilson is Professor of Economics and Business at North Carolina State University. He has published a number of articles on financial history, including "Financial Market Panics and Volatility in the Long Run, 1830–1988" (with Sylla and Jones), in E. White, ed., *Crashes and Panics: The Lessons from History* (Homewood, Ill., 1990); and "A Comparison of Common Stock Returns, 1871–1925 with 1926–1985," *Journal of Business* (April 1987).

American Economic Development
in Historical Perspective

Introduction

SINCE 1950, so-called underdeveloped nations and regions have been the focus of concern and attention for many American and European economists. These less-advanced countries all seemed to aspire to the same goals as the more-advanced nations, and it seemed obvious that the latters' histories should be examined for the keys to success. In the 1960 presidential address to the U.S. Economic History Association, Carter Goodrich said, "The strength and significance of work in economic history has always depended on the degree to which it was related to economic generalizations, to the great issues of organization and policy. Today there appears to be something of a consensus within our profession that the question of economic development offers the most stimulating central theme . . . the largest possibility that economic historians may make a useful contribution toward the improvement of public policy."[1]

Studies of the development process took a variety of forms, from the broad, cross-sectional, and historical analyses of Simon Kuznets, which made extensive use of national income data and other indicators of aggregate economic performance, to the many detailed examinations of industrialization and structural change in specific countries. Economists studied the aggregate performance of the American economy and its constituent elements—the growth of individual companies and industries, the behavior of prices and wages, the performance of specific markets, and the variations across regions. Studies of the long-run growth of various economic sectors were carried out by the National Bureau of Economic Research. The bureau was a critical source of data, as well as a stimulus to analysis of the country's economic performance. The focus on development in the United States was also evident in the "new economic history" that was taking root in the United States and flourishing to a far greater extent there than elsewhere. The greater preponderance of work on U.S. development reflected as well the success of the economy. The devastation of World War II had left the United States standing virtually alone as a model of economic success, a success well grounded by a long and steady record of growth.

The nineteenth century, the period of U.S. history most pertinent to the less-developed countries, was a time of substantial economic growth and structural change. Although the data are subject to some uncertainty, it appears that over the course of the century, real output per capita more than tripled, rising from around $900 in 1800 to about $3,000 in 1900 (expressed in constant 1980 dollars). This was accomplished in the face of rapid population growth, a phenomenon that was viewed as immiserizing in the less-developed countries after World War II. The century was also marked by war, including a devastating civil war, business cycles, periodic crises, and substantial institutional change; yet the American economy forged ahead steadily. That enviable record beckoned researchers; U.S. history was and is a valuable laboratory for those interested in the process of economic development.[2]

The keys to the American success are to be found in its long-term performance, and the essays in this volume explore that record in great detail. All the essays are concerned with development as seen through the prism of history, but they do so in different ways. Some improve and extend the statistical data base, in particular the national output series, the yields on common stocks and bonds, the interregional pattern of migration, and the industrial distribution of the labor force. Others try to understand how the various parts and factors, such as labor and capital markets, contributed to the nation's sustained economic success. While they identify some forces contributing to the country's success, and show how the flexibility and adaptability of institutions helped the process along, they also demonstrate the difficulties of recognizing and measuring all the pertinent variables. Several essays provide interpretations of the interplay between economic change and other historical events. The essays explore how growth began, as well as how it has been sustained for such a long time.

The first set of essays deals with the meaning and measurement of economic growth and development. Two of these touch directly on the subject of the pace and pattern of U.S. growth during the nineteenth century, and provide a revised view especially of the period before the Civil War.

One of the paradigms that has driven research into the American growth record is W. W. Rostow's "stages of economic growth," which postulated a sharp increase in the growth rate of product per capita in the United States during the period from 1843 to 1860.[3] Thomas Weiss deals directly with this issue by using new estimates of the labor force to produce a set of revised figures describing the level and rate of growth of gross domestic product per capita over the antebellum period. He finds little evidence to support a takeoff at any time before the Civil War. This result greatly reinforces Paul David's conclusion that no sharp acceleration had taken place in that period. David's evidence directly confronted Rostow's dating of an American takeoff in the 1840's, but left open the possibility that it had occurred earlier. Weiss finds even more clearly a gradual acceleration in the growth of output per capita before the Civil War, removing the last vestiges of support for the takeoff thesis.

Richard Sylla, Jack Wilson, and Charles Jones examine the pace and pattern of U.S. growth indirectly through the long-term behavior of financial variables. Their data on stock and bond yields extending back to the late eighteenth century are valuable in their own right, but may also shed light on U.S. growth over a longer period than can be found in extant time series on real economic variables. These authors suggest that the transition to a higher, modern rate of growth may have occurred around 1815, a bit earlier than indicated by Weiss's evidence on real product per capita, and it may have been more abrupt. As they point out, however, their evidence may be more indicative of industrialization in the Northeast, and although that was crucial to growth, the nation's performance was influenced by changes in other regions and by progress in agriculture.

Their data also permit examination of the determinants of the savings rate, an important constraint on capital investment, and thus on growth. Knowledge of how successful nations provided for capital formation is important for a full understanding of how growth came about. The U.S. savings rate may have been low for much of the nineteenth century compared with that in the newly industrializing countries today, but its increase was crucial to the long-term sustenance of growth. In spite of the importance, a full explanation of the determinants of the level of saving and its increase has not materialized. Sylla, Wilson, and Jones suggest that previous explanations have stumbled by focusing just on interest rates and bond yields, when the total return—the yield plus capital gains—may be a more appropriate gauge of the incentive to save.

How economic growth is brought about remains a mystery. Economists most often look to the real side of the economy for the sources of growth, examining the quantities of economic inputs, such as labor and capital, and the output per unit of input. Although it is readily understood how some items contribute to growth in conventional ways—an increase in the number of workers or the number of hours worked per year, for example, should make for some increase in output—the effects of changes in other identifiable forces, such as education, are not so obvious and certainly are difficult to measure. Moreover, some factors that contributed to growth have yet to be identified. There is still a large residual amount of economic growth that cannot be attributed to sources identified so far.

Immigration is one factor whose exact contribution to growth is not clear. Its full ramifications have not been completely understood, and the data have been highly imperfect. Immigration's impact is pervasive yet subtle, and is seen as a mixed blessing to the receiving country. On the one hand, immigrants generally have increased the labor supply disproportionately because of an age distribution favoring those in the prime working ages. This greater participation in the labor force strengthens the economy in the aggregate, but certain workers, usually the least skilled, feel its competition more than others. Some immigrants enhance the capital stock, at least indirectly and unconventionally, by virtue of the education and skills they acquired in their home countries. Furthermore, immigrants have not arrived on a broad front at an even rate; their flow has had its ups and downs, and the stream tends to enter through a handful of ports and concentrate in a few locations. The uneven impact, then, has had differential consequences for the growth of regions and industries. The essay by Donald Schaefer takes up this uneven impact. He provides revised measures of the immigration to the United States during the 1850's and its dispersion to the various regions. Eventually these improved estimates will permit greater understanding of the changes in labor quality and of the changes in industrial structure fostered by the different rates of regional settlement by international migrants.

In a recent article, A. K. Cairncross stressed "that change and development, which lie at the root of economic growth, are historical processes that can be understood and analyzed only in historical terms."[4] Barry Poulson addresses directly this juxtaposition of economic history and development. He contrasts the analyses of long-term change conducted by those with a historical perspective, such as Simon Kuznets and Robert Gallman, with other studies of development that lacked that dimension. He argues that some seemingly novel results of the development studies and the surprising outcomes that materialized when policies were implemented on the basis of those studies could have been foreseen if greater attention had been paid to the histories of countries that had experienced economic success for some time. Efforts by the less-developed countries to catch up with the developed nations proceeded without sufficient regard for how far the advanced countries had come, how long it had taken, and what changes had occurred along the way.

Perhaps this lesson is being learned now that the Asian giants have offered what appear to be even more successful models of development. What seem to be important elements in Japan's postwar growth clearly had their origins much earlier, as far back as the late nineteenth century. What appears to the public to be Japan's takeoff after World War II was in fact the resumption of a long-term upward trajectory, albeit at a quicker pace. Countries that wish to emulate Japan, then, must look beyond and beneath the recent record for guidance.

The second group of essays examines the influence of institutional changes on American economic growth. Douglass North takes a broad and generic view of how institutions shape the economy's direction and performance. He argues that in the real world, economic agents are guided by procedural rationality, the idea that individuals make decisions in a reasonable way given the limitations on their knowledge and computational ability, rather than by the nearly flawless instrumental rationality of economic theory. As a consequence, ideas, ideologies, and institutions matter. Historically they helped to shape the patterns of exchange that emerged to cope with economic activity. In the American case, what emerged was an environment that not only was hospitable to efficient economic behavior, but also could be altered by that behavior in ways favorable to further growth. In his view, the adaptability of that institutional matrix was essential to sustaining growth.

The labor market and its myriad of implicit and explicit contractual arrangements is at the heart of the economy's efficient use of resources— guiding workers to their most productive uses and influencing their productivity. Over time, changes in the arrangements alter labor's allocation among occupations and industries, its efficiency, and its impact on growth. Stanley Engerman and Claudia Goldin look at the changes in one such arrangement, the seasonality of employment, a much-neglected factor contributing to increased output. In the nineteenth-century United States, there was much unutilized time in the labor markets. Engerman and Goldin estimate that had all that time been fully exploited, national income might have increased by more than 30 percent. They show how the seasonal workers were absorbed more fully into the growth process as the years progressed. Unutilized time dwindled due to the reduction in seasonality within industries and the faster growth of less-seasonal ones.

Another example of evolution in the institutional arrangements of labor markets is found in the essay by Lance Davis, Robert Gallman, and Teresa Hutchins. They examine the elaborate arrangements for paying the crews of whaling ships. Whaling was an industry with some great, and very unusual, risks and rewards, and so could not simply adopt the same wage-payment schemes that had worked well in other industries. These authors conclude that, despite some negative aspects for the crew, the arrangements that were established worked to bring about the cooperation necessary to the success of the whaling voyages. Moreover, the system was flexible enough to adjust to changes in productivity and technologies.

Financial institutions also play a critical role in the development process, serving to raise the share of output that can be devoted to capital investment and to allocate it among its competing uses. The ability of modern financial institutions to carry out these roles seems assured, but in much earlier stages of development the arrangements were much different. This earlier capital formation and its finance are taken up by William Parker. He argues that during the nineteenth century, on midwestern farms and in industrial establishments, self-finance with a family's own labor or by reinvestment of profits was a major, even dominant, source of continued real capital formation. In transportation and urban construction, as well as in mercantile trade and short-run finance, financial markets and intermediaries were important. Parker points to monetary and credit inflation and to deflation of the price level as major sources of "forced" saving and dissaving, particularly in the face of rising productivity.

The economy, of course, does not work in a vacuum. The smooth, frictionless, instantaneous working of the perfectly competitive market gives way to the messier interplay of a variety of forces, perhaps most importantly the interaction between economics and politics. In this political economy, the competing behaviors of rational economic agents are shaped and battered by many things; at the same time, the influence of their behaviors extends beyond the pure economic calculus. The essays of the third section examine events in the political economy of U.S. development.

Slavery and the Civil War of 1861–65 were prominent examples of the political economy of the nineteenth-century United States. Southern slavery, according to some, bred a noncapitalist class of economic actors—the slaves and their masters—that acted to retard industrialization and economic development in the region. The North's victory in the Civil War, according to the Beard-Hacker thesis, helped to create a favorable industrial environment and set the stage for the economic success that the nation enjoyed thereafter.

The Civil War and slavery lie at the root of Robert Fogel's essay, as he explains the political realignment of the 1850's that led to the election of Abraham Lincoln. Fogel makes clear that the dynamic interaction between the economy and the polity was important in the American past, but the impact of the economy must be drawn carefully. Although the period from 1840 to 1860 may have been robust overall, suggesting little inducement on average for voters to shift political affiliation, the variations in economic conditions within the period, and the uneven impact of those changes across regions, demographic groups, and economic classes, did influence voting behavior, the outcome of which had feedback effects on the economy. In the case of the United States, there was one extreme result: the political change that led to the abolition of slavery.

The macroeconomic effects of the Civil War have been widely examined, and as a result largely of Robert Gallman's national income estimates, its impact on the aggregate economy has been downplayed. Less attention has been paid to the war's immediate microeconomic effects on specific industries and firms. Matthew Gallman's essay examines the war's effect on the economic fortunes of Philadelphia's entrepreneurs, only some of whom entered into government contracts to supply war materiel. He concludes that the war contractors typically had a more volatile economic experience than those companies which did not enter into such contracts, but that the long-term consequence of the war on the local economy was not great.

Political controversy can influence the economy's performance by creating uncertainty about the rules of the game. Colleen Callahan analyzes the behavior of prices before the establishment of the Federal Reserve system in this vein. That period relied on the traditional gold standard, which is typically thought to foster stability of prices. Callahan, however, finds a surprising amount of price instability in that era, much of which she attributes to political controversy over a return to bimetallism, and the uncertainty created by the strength of the silver movement. The essay's focus is on monetary issues, but it has an important bearing on economic development as well. As Callahan says, money matters—real economic growth was influenced by the behavior of monetary forces. Individual decisions about real economic variables, such as investment, are shaped by expectations, particularly expectations about prices.

Louis Galambos interweaves institutional change and political force in his analysis of the "triumph of oligopoly." Dissatisfied with existing explanations for the rise of oligopoly, he argues that although the first movers in an industry were able to master the economies of scale and scope and to establish their market dominance, they became politically vulnerable. Public opinion and reaction led to the rise of oligopoly. In the long run, this form of industrial structure proved beneficial to the corporations because it provided security and greater profits than would have occurred in atomistic competition, and it proved valuable to society as a whole by providing more competition than would have prevailed under monopoly. The competition induced the firms to invest the greater profits in research and development, to innovate and foster the economic growth of the nation.

The U.S. record makes clear that economic growth is a long-term affair, a continuing process that has been unfolding in the United States for well over 150 years. The proper perspective from which to understand it is historical. These essays do just that—they explore how the economy persisted on its upward trajectory in spite of perilous times and events, and occasional political crises. The sum of the essays is to show how complex the experience was, how many bits and pieces went into starting the process and sustaining it, how fluid and fragile the process can be. Its continuance cannot be taken for granted. The United States, however, is one of the handful of countries that can offer evidence on how—or whether—growth may be sustained over the foreseeable future in other nations of the world.

PART ONE

*Economic Growth
and Its Measurement*

CHAPTER ONE

✄ Economic Growth Before 1860: Revised Conjectures

Thomas Weiss

ECONOMIC HISTORIANS have long been interested in determining when modern economic growth began in the United States, whether the shift to a high rate of growth was a sudden or a gradual affair, and what caused growth to proceed at a faster pace. It is generally accepted that the transition occurred before the Civil War, but there is disagreement whether this took place before or after 1840.[1]

A leading proponent of the view that modern growth began in the last two decades of the antebellum period is W. W. Rostow, whose "stages of growth" thesis was one of the broader and bolder attempts to date and explain the start of growth.[2] In that scheme, the "takeoff" was an abrupt transition to modern growth, with a substantial increase in per capita output being achieved over a fairly short period of time, roughly twenty years. Rostow did not specify exactly how large an increase in per capita output was necessary, only that there be a "distinct rise."[3] He further delineated some necessary conditions for the takeoff; in particular, he stipulated an increase in the investment share of national output, the emergence of a leading sector, and the development of political and social institutions conducive to growth.[4]

The more recent, and more widely accepted, view is that modern growth began before 1840 in the United States, although the exact dating is not known.[5] The current statistical picture of the transition is based on

The research reported here is part of the National Bureau of Economic Research's Program on the Development of the American Economy. Any opinions expressed are those of the author and not those of the NBER. This paper has benefited from discussions with the participants of the NBER's Summer Institute on the Development of the American Economy. Earlier versions were presented at the Second World Congress of the Cliometrics Society and at the Universities of Chicago, Indiana, Illinois, Northwestern, and Stanford, and at Lake Forest College. I would also like to thank Jeremy Atack, Lou Cain, Gregory Clark, John Clark, Stan Engerman, Betsy Field, Claudia Goldin, John Komlos, Barry Poulson, Joshua Rosenbloom, Donald Schaefer, Peter Temin, and John Wallis for helpful comments. The work has been funded by the University of Kansas and the National Science Foundation (grant no. SES8308569).

the controlled conjectures of per capita output made by Paul David.[6] For the period from 1800 to 1840, his figures reveal an average annual growth rate of between 1 and 1.5 percent: an enviable performance, albeit not quite as good as the rates achieved after the Civil War.[7] For longer-term changes, those of twenty years or more, he found that "no significant acceleration of the secular trend in real GDP per capita took place within the period of our national history that preceded the Civil War."[8] Instead, he concluded that "the acceleration of per capita real income growth to a higher secular rate was a much more gradual affair."[9]

David acknowledged that the performance before 1840 was not steady, and that "most of the net gain between 1800 and 1840 was thus a consequence of an impressively rapid rate of advance achieved after 1820." This is quite evident in his figures, reproduced in Table 1.1. The average annual rate of growth was a scant 0.27 percent per year in the opening twenty years of the century, and then rose to nearly 2 percent per year in the next two decades.[10]

According to these data, the economy's performance before 1840, and especially between 1820 and 1840, was impressive. That accomplishment has raised some questions, however. Robert Gallman has expressed doubts about the conjectures on two occasions.[11] He first questioned the low levels of per capita output in the years 1800 through 1820 because they implied low nonperishable output. He subsequently indicated skepticism about the pattern of agricultural productivity advance that lay behind the growth figures, because it suggested that farm productivity increased at the same rate in the first and second halves of the century. In both cases he argued that there were some problems with the farm labor-force figures.

I have revised those labor-force figures and used them to produce a new set of conjectures about per capita output before 1840. The new conjectures, which I call the base case, present a much different picture of U.S. growth and its sources. A comparison between these figures and those of David yields valuable insights into the impact of the alterations to the labor force and allows some assessment of the new figures. It highlights the sources of growth that are driving these conjectures as well. I have also made use of information that was unavailable when Paul David constructed his conjectures in order to produce a more refined set of estimates. These refined measures show the more likely path of U.S. growth before the Civil War and are more pertinent for assessing the likelihood of a takeoff.

The base case figures on the levels and changes in per capita output produced by the new labor-force series are presented in Table 1.1, along with David's original estimates. The levels of per capita product implicit in my conjectures are above David's in each year, and in particular are

TABLE I.I

Comparison of Conjectural Estimates of Per Capita Product, 1800 to 1860

(1840 dollars)

Year	Growth index (1840 = 1.000)		Per capita product		Nonperishable residual	
	David	Weiss	David	Weiss	David	Weiss
1800	0.644	0.801	$58	$73	$16	$31
1810	0.619	0.826	56	75	13	32
1820	0.676	0.846	61	77	18	34
1830	0.840	0.913	77	83	32	39
1840	1.000	1.000	91	91	46	46
1850	1.099	1.099	100	100	53	53
1860	1.374	1.374	125	125	70	70
			Average annualized rate of change			
1800–1820			0.27%	0.28%	0.67%	0.48%
1820–1840			1.96	0.84	4.77	1.49
1840–1860			1.60	1.60	2.12	2.12
1800–1840			1.13	0.56	2.70	1.00
1800–1860			1.29	0.90	2.51	1.37

S O U R C E: David, "Growth of Real Product," table 8; Gallman, "Statistical Approach," table 1.

N O T E: The growth index is the product of an index value for three variables: the participation rate, farm output per worker, and the effect of the shift to nonfarm employment. These indexes are presented in Table 1.4.

The 1840, 1850, and 1860 per capita product figures are based on Gallman's direct estimates of output for those years. The conjectural figures would be $103 and $126 in David's series, and $100 and $131 in mine. Values for earlier years were obtained by extrapolating the 1840 base-year figure on the growth index. The product figures are intended to represent gross domestic product, exclusive of the value of home manufacturing and farm improvements.

The value of perishable consumption (food and firewood) deducted in order to derive the nonperishable residual was $42 in 1800, $43 in 1810 and 1820, $44 in 1830, $45 in 1840, $47 in 1850, and $55 in 1860 (Robert Gallman, "Gross National Product in the United States, 1834–1909," in Dorothy Brady, ed., *Output, Employment, and Productivity in the United States after 1800* (New York, 1966), tables A-1 and A-2.

roughly 25 percent higher in the years 1800 through 1820.[12] In my base case, growth was slower over the entire antebellum period, but the difference rests entirely on the subperiod 1820 to 1840. There is no difference between the two series regarding the growth of per capita output between 1840 and 1860, or between 1800 and 1820. The levels of output per capita differ in that earliest period, but the rates of growth are equal and low. Finally, as will be shown below, the sources of growth are now different. Advance in agricultural productivity was slower and of less importance before 1840, especially between 1820 and 1840.

The different behavior of the economy described by the two series can be traced in one way or another to the labor-force estimates, especially the farm figures.[13] The importance of the labor-force figures can be seen in Paul David's conjectural estimating equation for that early period,[14]

$$O/P = LF/P \, [S_a(O/LF)_a + S_n k(O/LF)_a].$$

According to this, output per capita (O/P) in any year is equal to the product on the right-hand side of the equation, the participation rate times the weighted average output per worker. In this scheme, only three factors bring about *changes* in output per capita: changes in the participation rate (LF/P), changes in agricultural output per worker (O/LF)$_a$, and shifts in the distribution of the labor force between agriculture (S_a) and nonagriculture (S_n). The labor-force estimates affect each of these factors. The total labor force determines the participation rate, whereas the size of the farm labor force has an obvious and direct effect on farm labor productivity.[15] At the same time, estimates of the changes in the industrial allocation of the labor force have an effect on the overall level of productivity because of the differences in the levels of output per worker in the farm and nonfarm sectors.[16]

Estimation of the Labor Force

For the most part, my estimation of the labor force follows the procedures laid out by Stanley Lebergott but is executed at the state and regional level.[17] In concept and coverage, the new total and farm labor-force series are similar to those of Lebergott.[18] In practice, the levels and changes in the total labor force are nearly identical in the two series.[19] The farm figures, which differ more, are based largely on the existing census statistics in both cases. Though imperfect, these census counts were collected at specific dates during the antebellum period, and so represent the actual state of affairs at that time.[20]

Lebergott and I both assessed and revised the census data for 1820, 1840, 1850, and 1860.[21] Lebergott focused primarily on the national totals, whereas I examined each state, and was concerned as well with the accuracy of the major demographic components of each state's labor force. My work has produced a clearer picture of the age-sex coverage of each of those censuses, which in turn has permitted a more reliable revision of the labor-force data.[22] In addition, for 1820 and 1840, it was possible to use the revised census data to estimate the number of slaves engaged in farming, and to derive the urban and rural labor forces in several industries. All these improvements in accuracy and detail provided a better statistical base with which to estimate the farm labor force in 1800, 1810, and 1830.

There are three aspects of my estimation that differ substantially from the earlier work of Lebergott, Easterlin, and David.[23] In all years, the new estimates incorporate a smaller number of slaves in farming, roughly 75 percent of the rural slave population of working age as opposed to the previous estimate of nearly 90 percent. In 1850 and 1860, these lower slave counts are more than offset by the addition to farming of workers who had reported their occupation as "laborer, not otherwise specified." Previous estimates had placed all these workers in nonfarm industries, but careful examination of the state data, and the location of many of these workers in rural areas, argues for the assignment of many of them to farming. In 1820 and 1840, the new estimates differ from the older ones because of varying judgments about how to correct the census deficiencies.[24] In 1840, I raised the census count of farm workers by about 5 percent, whereas Lebergott reduced it by about the same margin. For 1820, we both increased the census count of the total labor force by approximately the same amount, but Lebergott allocated nearly twice as many of these added workers to agriculture. Since the original census count was low primarily because of the exclusion of workers in the service industries, a large allocation to farming seems inappropriate.[25]

Although the new estimates of the farm labor force were constructed at the state and regional level, a by-product of that detailed estimation has been, I believe, an improvement in the accuracy of the national totals. The new estimates are presented in Table 1.2, along with the Lebergott series for comparison. As can be seen readily, the total labor-force figures differ very little, the Lebergott series being slightly below mine in most years. The farm figures differ much more, and the variations are not all in the same direction.

The new farm figures are higher than the previous ones in 1840, 1850, and 1860, by a fairly uniform percentage: 7 percent in 1840, 8 percent in 1850, and 6 percent in 1860. Though the levels of the two series differ, they show roughly the same growth over this subperiod, as well as over each of the two decades. In sharp contrast, the new figures for 1800 through 1820 are below the previous estimates by approximately 10 percent in 1800 and 1820, and by 15 percent in 1810. In spite of these disparities, the two series show very similar rates of change over the earliest twenty-year period.[26] The most notable consequence of these revisions occurs over the twenty-year period from 1820 to 1840, over which time the new series shows an increase of 72 percent (2.77 percent per year), in contrast to a rise of only 45 percent (1.86 percent per year) in the old series.

The two alternative series can be assessed by comparing the rate of decline of the farm labor-force share to that of the rural population share.[27] As can be seen in Table 1.2, the farm share declined at about the same rate

TABLE I.2

Estimates of the Total and Farm Labor Force in the United States, 1800 to 1860

Year	Total labor force (thousands)		Farm labor force (thousands)		Farm shares (%)	
	Lebergott	Weiss	Lebergott	Weiss	Lebergott	Weiss
1800	1,700	1,712	1,406	1,274	82.6%	74.4%
1810	2,330	2,337	1,950	1,690	83.7	72.3
1820	3,165	3,150	2,500	2,249	78.9	71.4
1830	4,200	4,272	2,965	2,982	70.6	69.8
1840	5,707	5,778	3,617	3,882	63.4	67.2
1850	8,250	8,192	4,520	4,889	54.8	59.7
1860	11,180	11,290	5,950	6,299	53.2	55.8
	Average annualized rate of change					
1800–1820	3.16%	3.10%	2.92%	2.88%	−0.23%	−0.19%
1820–1840	2.99	3.08	1.86	2.77	−1.09	−0.32
1840–1860	3.42	3.41	2.52	2.44	−0.87	−0.93
1800–1840	3.07	3.09	2.39	2.82	−0.66	−0.25
1800–1860	3.19	3.19	2.43	2.70	−0.73	−0.48

SOURCE: David, "Growth of Real Product," app. table I. The construction of the Weiss estimates is described briefly in the text. More detailed descriptions of the procedures may be obtained from the author.

NOTE: For consistency with the exposition in the text, I have labeled these "the Lebergott series," although the figures are in fact David's. Lebergott developed the estimation procedures and produced the initial estimates, whereas David revised some of the figures, especially that for 1800. I have used David's figures because they are more pertinent to the subsequent discussion of conjectural growth. There are now few differences between the two. David's estimates are identical to Lebergott's in 1810, 1830, and 1850. For 1800, Lebergott's original estimates were 1.9 million workers in total, and 1.4 in farming, but now he puts the total at 1.68 million workers and leaves the farm figure unchanged (Stanley Lebergott, The Americans [New York, 1984], p. 66). In other years, the differences between the two series are quite small. Lebergott's total labor-force estimates are 3.135 million in 1820, 5.66 million in 1840, and 11.11 million in 1860; the farm figures in those respective years are 2.47, 3.57, and 5.88 million (Lebergott, "Labor Force," table 1).

in both series over two of the twenty-year subperiods, 1800 to 1820 and 1840 to 1860. During those intervals, the rural share of the population declined at annual rates of 0.06 and 0.57 percent, slower than the decline in the farm share in either labor-force series. In the period 1820 to 1840, however, the series diverge noticeably. The rural population share declined by 0.20 percent per year in that subperiod, and although the farm share in my series declined slightly faster, at 0.32 percent per year, continuing the pattern that prevailed in the other subperiods, the farm share in Lebergott's series declined by 1.09 percent per year. The greater conformity between changes in the rural population and changes in the farm labor force in my series provides some confidence in the new figures.[28]

Productivity and Sources of Growth

Labor productivity in the antebellum period, as determined by the two different labor-force series, is summarized in Table 1.3. Two measures of productivity are shown. One describes the path of agricultural productivity advance; the other, total output per worker, measures the combined effect of intrasectoral productivity advance and the intersectoral shift of workers toward the more productive nonfarm sector.[29] The most obvious consequences of the new labor-force estimates are to raise the levels of output per worker in farming in the opening decades of the century and to lower them in the late antebellum period.

In spite of these adjustments, the two series show similar growth in two

TABLE 1.3

Participation Rates and Estimates of Output per Worker, 1800 to 1860

Year	Participation rates		Output per worker (dollars)			
			Agriculture		Total	
	David	Weiss	David	Weiss	David	Weiss
1800	0.322	0.323	$134	$147	$179	$225
1810	0.323	0.324	129	148	172	231
1820	0.329	0.328	134	149	185	234
1830	0.325	0.331	158	157	233	250
1840	0.333	0.338	175	163	272	268
1850	0.355	0.352	175	161	282	284
1860	0.355	0.358	213	201	351	348
	Average annualized rate of change					
1800–1820	0.11%	0.06%	0.02%	0.06%	0.17%	0.20%
1820–1840	0.06	0.13	1.35	0.47	1.94	0.69
1840–1860	0.32	0.30	0.97	1.05	1.27	1.31
1800–1840	0.08	0.10	0.68	0.27	1.05	0.44
1800–1860	0.16	0.18	0.78	0.53	1.12	0.73

SOURCE: See Tables 1.1 and 1.2; David, "Growth of Real Product," tables 2, 5, and 6.

NOTE: Output per worker is valued in 1840 prices. Agricultural output per worker is farm gross product divided by the number of workers in farming. The farm gross product figures were constructed from farm output and output indexes presented in David ("Growth of Real Product," tables 2, 5, and 6). The original output figures, from Towne and Rasmussen ("Farm Gross Product"), exclude the value of home manufacturing and farm improvements, and were revised slightly by David. The labor-force figures are presented in Table 1.2 above.

Total output per worker is the value implicit in the growth-index calculations presented in Table 1.1. It is derived for each year by dividing the estimated output per capita by the participation rate.

of the twenty-year subperiods, 1800 to 1820 and 1840 to 1860. In the remaining subperiod, however, productivity growth is much more rapid in the David series. As a consequence, over longer time spans that encompass this subperiod, the older labor-force series produces a noticeably faster rate of productivity growth than does the new one: for example, 0.78 percent versus 0.53 percent average annual increases between 1800 and 1860. The higher rate means a cumulative rise of 59 percent, in contrast to an increase of only 36 percent in the Weiss series.[30]

The sources of growth in per capita output are now slightly different from those that generated David's figures (see Table 1.4). In both series, the rise in the participation rate is the least important source, except for the earliest twenty years, when little growth took place. For the entire period, this factor is relatively more important in the new series, reflecting the nearly equal rise in the participation rate in both series, whereas the new series shows a smaller increase in output per capita. The effect of the labor-force redistribution is roughly the same in the two series, a consequence of two offsetting forces. My series has lowered the farm share of the labor force in the earliest years, raised it slightly after 1830, and as a result shows a smaller shift of the work force out of farming (19 percent versus 29; see Table 1.2). This works to reduce the impact of the intersectoral shift of the labor force on worker productivity. The net effect of the redistribution of the work force is about the same in the two series because the weight given to the redistribution is greater in my conjectures.[31]

The most important source of growth in both series is labor productivity. In this regard, there is little disparity between the two series over the entire antebellum period or over the years 1840 to 1860. In the earliest twenty-year period, 1800 to 1820, intrasectoral productivity advance is a more important source of growth in my series, but more noticeable is that the average rates of productivity are low in both series and are relatively unimportant sources of growth as well.

In the middle twenty years, however, the differences are glaring, and they give rise to dissimilar results for the longer period of 1800 to 1840. In this critical twenty-year period, the new series shows a much slower growth rate (0.47 versus 1.35 percent per year), stemming from the faster growth of the farm labor force evident in the new series (2.77 versus 1.86 percent per year), and the corollary phenomenon of a smaller decline in the importance of the farm labor force (see Table 1.2).[32] The latter is no minor matter, because in David's series the work-force shift over this period generated more growth of per capita product than occurred in total in my series. Even so, the productivity advance was the dominant source of growth in David's series, accounting for nearly two-thirds of the growth

TABLE I.4

Comparison of Input Indexes, 1800 to 1860

($1840 = 1.000$)

Year	Output/labor		Participation rate		Intersectoral shift effect	
	David	Weiss	David	Weiss	David	Weiss
1800	0.762	0.899	0.967	0.956	0.864	0.931
1810	0.736	0.907	0.970	0.959	0.856	0.953
1820	0.765	0.910	0.988	0.970	0.890	0.961
1830	0.901	0.958	0.976	0.979	0.948	0.976
1840	1.000	1.000	1.000	1.000	1.000	1.000
1850	0.995	0.988	1.066	1.041	1.039	1.071
1860	1.213	1.232	1.066	1.059	1.062	1.054
	Average annualized rate of change					
1800–1820	0.02%	0.06%	0.11%	0.08%	0.15%	0.14%
1820–1840	1.35	0.47	0.06	0.15	0.59	0.21
1840–1860	0.97	1.05	0.32	0.29	0.30	0.26
1800–1840	0.68	0.27	0.08	0.11	0.37	0.17
1800–1860	0.78	0.53	0.16	0.17	0.34	0.20
	Relative contribution to per capita growth					
1800–1820	6%	20%	42%	25%	52%	55%
1820–1840	66	56	3	19	31	25
1840–1860	63	67	19	17	18	15
1800–1840	58	47	8	21	34	32
1800–1860	60	60	13	18	26	22

S O U R C E : The indexes for the participation rate and output per worker can be calculated from the data in Table 1.3.

N O T E : The intersectoral shift effect equals $S_a + kS_n$, where S_a and S_n are the labor-force shares in farm and nonfarm industries, and k is the 1840 ratio of nonfarm to farm productivity. The 1840 base-year values for the intersectoral shift effects are 1.35 and 1.43 for the David and Weiss series respectively. The values of k are 1.97 for David and 2.31 for Weiss. The shift effect for 1850 and 1860 is based on the actual values, not the hypothetical results that would be derived holding k constant.

The relative contribution to growth is measured here as that variable's share of the sum of the changes in all the indexes over the given time period. Details of the relative contributions may not add to one hundred percent due to rounding.

between 1820 and 1840, and three-fifths between 1800 and 1840. In both instances, its importance is noticeably greater than in my series.

The reason for these differences has to do with the behavior of farm labor productivity. In particular, David's series shows a much more rapid growth in productivity between 1820 and 1840 than does mine, and a far superior performance in that period than occurred in the subsequent twenty years.[33] Given the time pattern of advance in the two series, at issue is whether agricultural productivity grew faster in the twenty years before 1840, as in David's series, or in the twenty years after, as implied in my estimates.

The absence of data on productivity requires that we form an opinion on less direct evidence. David turned to wage data to assess his estimated index of farm productivity, and found "a fair resemblance . . . between the magnitude and timing of the changes" in the two series.[34] That evidence showed average annual wage-rate increases between 1818–20 and 1840 that corresponded roughly to the change in his growth index. The evidence also revealed an acceleration in real wage increases, however, from 1.84 percent per year before 1840 to 2.01 percent over the next two decades, implying that labor productivity increased more rapidly after 1840 than before.

This shred of quantitative evidence is fortunately consistent with what Gallman termed "the burden of the narrative histories of the period" and with other scraps of descriptive information.[35] Perhaps most importantly, that more tangible evidence suggests that there was far greater mechanization after 1840. According to Towne and Rasmussen, "The rate of real investment in implements and farm machinery increased markedly in 1845–55 from an average of $11 million a year (in 1910–14 dollars) to $23 million. . . ."[36] Their figures for *real* farm improvements show a 61 percent increase between 1840 and 1860, compared with only 42 percent in the preceding twenty years.[37] Even Cooper, Barton, and Brodell, who paint a favorable view of the period before 1840, contended that "the year 1840 marks the beginning of worth-while results by inventors and experimenters who had been making persistent trials and studies throughout 50 years."[38] Leo Rogin's narration of the development of farm machinery makes the same point in exquisite detail.[39]

Institutional developments also argue for more rapid advance in the later decades. There were more agricultural periodicals after 1840, and increased readership; state agricultural societies, whose purposes were to improve technology and diffuse knowledge, "did not attain widespread importance until the 1840's."[40] Moreover, there were no commercial sales of fertilizer until 1843.[41]

Variations on a Theme

The preceding comparison of the two conjectural estimates of per capita output was intended to show the impact of the labor-force revisions, and so retained the estimating procedure and equation laid out by David. Both variants made use of the assumption that productivity in the nonfarm sector grew at the same rate as that in farming. David made the assumption in an effort to bias the growth rate downward before 1840 and thus provide a stronger test of the hypothesis that there was a takeoff after that date. The intuition that the bias ran this way, that nonfarm productivity must have grown faster than that in farming, seemed plausible, particularly if nonfarm output were taken to be largely manufacturing, an industrial sector that featured the growth industries of the time. That intuition is misleading, however, for other nonfarm industries. Although technological progress and other favorable conditions in these growth industries served to push up the rates of growth of worker productivity in manufacturing, the same forces were not at work in some service industries important at the time.

Engerman and Gallman have stressed this very point, that productivity growth for the entire nonfarm sector probably did not exceed that of farming.[42] In fact, such was not the case in the period 1840 to 1860, when we have some direct estimates by which to judge the two sectors' performances. The figures in Table 1.5 show the percentage increases in output per worker over the period for the two broad sectors. It does not matter which labor-force series is used; output per worker in farming increased faster, the difference being greater using the Weiss labor-force statistics. Part of the reason for this relative performance is that nonfarm output includes the value of shelter, a product that cannot easily be ascribed to either sector's labor force and that increased only about as fast as population did after 1840. Its inclusion in the nonfarm sector biases downward the growth of that sector's output, and the effect on the productivity calculations can be seen in Table 1.5.[43] The narrowly defined nonfarm output per worker increased faster than the broader measure, by about 9 percentage points.

Beyond the bias introduced by the inclusion of the output of shelter, it is debatable whether output per worker in the remainder of the nonfarm sector could have consistently increased faster than output per worker in farming. The evidence in Table 1.5 sheds some light on this, but it is far from conclusive. With the value of shelter removed, output per worker in the more narrowly defined nonfarm sector grew slightly faster than output per worker in agriculture using the David labor-force series, but still somewhat slower using the Weiss figures. Even for this later part of the antebellum period, when technological progress in manufacturing and transportation must have had a stronger impact than in earlier years, the verdict is not so clear. Before 1840, the behavior of productivity in the other service industries would have had a greater influence, and may have slowed down the growth of output per worker for the entire nonfarm sector so that it lagged behind that in agriculture.

TABLE 1.5

Comparison of Farm and Nonfarm Productivity, 1840 to 1860

Variable	1840	1860	Increase (%)
Gross domestic product	$1,553,000	$3,930,000	
Farm sector			
Gross product	634,000	1,266,000	
Output per worker			
Weiss	163	201	23.3%
David	175	213	21.7
Nonfarm sector (broad measure)			
Product	919,000	2,664,000	
Output per worker			
Weiss	485	534	10.1
David	440	509	15.7
Nonfarm sector (narrow measure)			
Product	753,000	2,352,000	
Output per worker			
Weiss	397	471	18.6
David	360	450	25.0

SOURCE: The gross domestic product and farm gross product figures for 1840 come from David, "Growth of Real Product," table 5. The 1860 GDP figure was obtained by multiplying the 1840 figure by the index of real GNP in 1860 prices (Gallman, "Gross National Product," p. 26). The farm gross product figure for 1860 was obtained by extrapolating the 1840 figure on an index of real farm output in 1879 prices, estimated following the procedures outlined by David ("Growth of Real Product," table 2).

The labor-force figures used in the calculations come from Table 1.2 above.

NOTE: The gross domestic product and farm gross product figures are valued in 1840 prices, and exclude farm improvements and the value of home manufacturing.

The value of shelter included in the broad measure of nonfarm product (in 1840 prices) was $166 million in 1840 and $312 million in 1860 (Robert Gallman and Thomas Weiss, "The Service Industries in the Nineteenth Century," in Victor Fuchs, ed., Production and Productivity in the Service Industries [New York, 1969], pp. 292 and 330).

My refined conjecture, presented in Table 1.6, drops the assumption of equal rates of productivity growth, an exercise made possible for the years after 1820 by the recent availability of evidence regarding productivity growth in manufacturing. In this version, the nonfarm sector has two parts, manufacturing and all other industries, with different rates of productivity advance in each. Furthermore, I have treated the value of shelter output separately from the product of either industrial sector, and added an independent estimate of its value to the output of those two sectors in order to obtain gross domestic product.[44] For the earliest twenty years, 1800 to 1820, a lack of evidence on nonfarm productivity forced me to retain the assumption that productivity of the nonfarm workers, including those in manufacturing, increased at the same rate as that of farm workers. For the period from 1820 to 1840, I assumed that manufacturing productivity grew at 2.3 percent per year.[45] For all other nonfarm workers, however, I kept the original assumption that output per worker grew at the same rate as that for farming.[46] The weighted average rate of nonfarm productivity growth is calculated to have been 0.93 percent per year for this subperiod.[47] Finally, the refined figures include some minor revisions to the underlying farm gross product series.[48]

The chief alterations resulting from the relaxation of the assumption of equal productivity advance are, by construction, concentrated in the middle twenty years. The David series showed an annual growth of per capita income of only 0.27 percent between 1800 and 1820, then a more substantial increase of 1.96 percent over the subsequent twenty-year period, followed by a slightly slower rise of 1.60 percent over the years 1840 to 1860 (see Table 1.1). In my base case, in which only the labor-force figures were revised, the calculated conjectural growth was also very small in the opening twenty years of the century, then accelerated in each of the subsequent twenty-year periods. In the refined series, the pattern of acceleration still prevails, with a more noticeable quickening of the rate after 1820. Even so, the revised pace of 1.19 percent per year is well below David's figure, and the rate in each twenty-year period exceeds that of the preceding two decades.

The refined estimates reflect a pattern of labor productivity growth different from those in David or in my base case. From 1800 to 1840, the growth of output per worker, capturing both intrasectoral advances and the effect of the redistribution of the labor force, was 0.62 percent in the refined series—slightly faster than in my base case (0.44 percent), but noticeably below the 1.05 percent figure in David's series (see Table 1.3). A similar result prevails for the years 1820 to 1840; the refined figure of 0.93 percent per year reflects faster growth than does my base figure (0.69 percent), but still much slower growth than David's (1.94 percent). Moreover, the source of the acceleration evident in the refined series is fundamentally different from that propelling David's figures. In his series, the acceleration of total output per worker required a sharp rise in agricultural productivity growth, from virtually 0 percent per year to 1.35 percent, and a substantial effect from the shift of labor toward the more productive nonfarm industries (see Tables 1.3 and 1.4). Now the overall acceleration is accomplished with only a mild increase in the rate of agricultural productivity advance, from 0.17 to 0.52 percent per year, and it rests more on the speeding up of productivity advance in manufacturing.

Let me now drop the base case, and focus just on the refined series and how its picture of U.S. growth differs from the view evident in David's estimates. First, the refined conjecture depicts a standard of living somewhat higher than what is shown in David's figures. The refined per capita figures are 12 to 21 percent above David's in the years 1800 through 1820. These slightly higher levels seem more reasonable because they contain

TABLE 1.6
Output per Worker and per Capita, *1800 to 1860, Refined Conjecture*

Year	Output per worker			Output per capita	Composition of refined estimate		
	Agricultural	Nonagricultural	Total		Value of shelter	Perishables	Non-perishable residual
1800	$142	$319	$188	$66	$5.50	$42.00	$18.50
1810	146	327	196	69	5.80	43.00	20.50
1820	147	330	200	72	6.30	43.00	22.35
1830	153	357	215	79	7.80	44.00	27.00
1840	163	397	240	91	9.70	45.00	36.00
1850	161	402	258	100	9.00	47.00	44.00
1860	201	470	320	125	9.90	55.00	60.00
				Average annualized rates of change			
1800–1820	0.17%	0.17%	0.31%	0.41%	0.68%	0.12%	0.94%
1820–1840	0.52	0.93	0.93	1.19	2.18	0.23	2.41
1840–1860	1.04	0.85	1.45	1.60	0.10	1.01	2.56
1800–1840	0.34	0.55	0.62	0.80	1.43	0.17	1.68
1800–1860	0.58	0.65	0.89	1.06	0.98	0.45	1.97

more plausible values of the implicit flow of nonperishable consumption and investment spending.[49]

Second, the new, refined series offers a much different perspective on the course of American economic growth. David's figures indicated that for much of the period before the Civil War, per capita output grew nearly as fast as it did after the war. The nation had reached its modern rate of growth long before the war; from 1820 onward, the antebellum record was nearly identical to the postbellum, doubling every 40 years. In the new series, growth is slower overall during the antebellum period, and there is a greater distinction between the ante- and postbellum records.

Moreover, within the antebellum era it seems quite clear that the United States experienced a gradual acceleration in the growth of per capita output, rather than a sudden increase. To be sure, there were sharp differences in growth from decade to decade; the 1850's, for example, witnessed growth in excess of 2 percent per year, double that of the 1840's. If we look at twenty-year periods, thereby abstracting from the influence of the long swings in the economy, we find a pattern of gradual but consistent acceleration, with the rate of growth in each twenty-year period exceeding that of the preceding two decades (see Table 1.6). The rates of growth in overlapping twenty-year periods show this even more clearly: 0.41 percent between 1800 and 1820, 0.65 from 1810 to 1830, 1.19 from 1820 to 1840 and from 1830 to 1850, and 1.60 between 1840 and 1860. There was a smooth but persistent transition from the slow pace of the colonial era to the modern rate of advance that materialized fully after 1840.[50]

Third, although the two series imply dissimilar stories about the entire antebellum period, the difference rests entirely in the subperiod from 1820 to 1840. There is no difference between the two series regarding the growth of per capita output between 1840 and 1860, because both series are based on Gallman's direct measures of output; and there are similar, but not identical, results for the earliest twenty-year period, 1800 to 1820. The levels of output per capita differ, but the rates of growth are close and low. The differences in the period 1820 to 1840 are striking, and show up in both output per capita and farm output per worker—to a large extent because the latter heavily influences the former.

Conclusions

The new estimates of output per capita reveal a different pace and pattern of economic growth in the period before the Civil War than what prevails in the extant view. The differences arise primarily from the use of a new set of labor-force figures that alter the measured course of agricultural productivity and the timing of the economy's shift away from agriculture. Per capita output and the timing of its acceleration are influenced as well by the assumption of a more rapid productivity growth in manu-facturing after 1820 than was used in David's conjectures.

In the revised version, the levels of per capita product are above those derived by David for the years 1800 through 1830, and growth is slower over the entire antebellum period. The nation had not quite reached its modern rate of growth before 1840, and the antebellum record was overall more distinct from that of the postbellum period. The most noteworthy revision to the series shows up in the subperiod 1820 to 1840.

The new labor-force figures have also caused the series on agricultural output per worker to be revised. These new productivity figures are, of course, the driving force behind the new conjectural values of per capita output, but they also give a different picture of the sources of growth. In particular, agricultural productivity advance was a slower and less impor-tant source of growth before 1840, especially between 1820 and 1840.

These differences should not distract us from one common point: there is little evidence of a takeoff, in the Rostovian sense, in any of these con-jectural figures. David delivered the coup de grace to the idea of a sharp acceleration after 1840. His estimates did show much more rapid growth from 1820 to 1840 than from 1840 to 1860, which David saw as a long swing fluctuation in economic activity. That surge could have reflected a takeoff that had occurred earlier than Rostow had postulated, however. My revised conjectures remove that last vestige of support for a take-off. Although there was substantial variation from decade to decade, the twenty-year periods reveal a more gradual acceleration. The absence of a takeoff is especially evident when the data are viewed in overlapping dec-adal fashion.

The failure to locate a takeoff should not detract from the importance of much of the antebellum period to the sustained economic growth that occurred in subsequent years. The growth between 1800 and 1820 of only 0.41 percent per year looks very much like the record for the colonial pe-riod, but the subsequent gradual acceleration indicates that something was stirring, important transformations were under way. One of the more prominent changes was the economy's shift toward industry that began in this period, with the farm share of the labor force declining noticeably after 1820. The results of those stirrings were to materialize more fully in the last decade or two of the period, and all the more so after the Civil War, but the period 1800 to 1840 set the stage.

CHAPTER TWO

U.S. Financial Markets and Long-Term Economic Growth, 1790-1989

Richard Sylla, Jack W. Wilson, and Charles P. Jones

OUR CURRENT understanding of the long-term performance of the U.S. economy since colonial times is grounded in analysis of the real sector: the measurement of inputs and outputs, the composition of GNP and capital formation, and the sources of growth in different eras. That analysis rests on the research of Simon Kuznets, Robert Gallman, Paul David, and others, who carried out fundamental work on GNP and its components between 1839 and 1909, which uncovered striking results on savings and capital formation rates in the nineteenth century; examined similarities and differences in the pace, pattern, and sources of economic growth during the nineteenth and twentieth centuries; and explored the quantitative dimensions of economic growth in the statistical dark age before 1840.[1] Here we explore these same issues from a different vantage point, that of the financial sector. We have developed long-term series on nominal and real interest rates, stock prices, and bond and stock returns, sometimes annual but often monthly, that reach back to the end of the eighteenth century. The data allow us to study the levels, trends, and variability of financial returns throughout U.S. history, including the pre-1840 period before reliable GNP data became available, and the Civil War era, which left a gap in the GNP data.

Financial economists generally accept the proposition that the financial sector reflects what is happening in the real economy. Major cyclical and secular changes in interest-rate levels and in debt and equity returns are related to underlying economic growth and development. To be sure, there are a host of complications that make it difficult to sort out the precise relationships between financial developments and real economic growth. For example, do high or rising interest rates indicate a high or

We acknowledge the helpful comments of the editors of this volume and two anonymous readers, as well as those of Lance Davis, Stanley Engerman, Robert Gallman, Paul Wachtel, and the members of the Columbia University Economic History Seminar, the Research Triangle Economic History Workshop, and the Rutgers University Financial History Workshop.

increasing demand for capital during a growth surge, or are they a sign of stress or underdevelopment on the supply side of the capital markets?

Another complication is that the costs of capital to borrowers and investors are different from the returns reaped by lenders and savers. There are always transactions costs involved in bringing investors and savers together; that is, there is a spread between rates paid and rates received. Students of the history of financial intermediation have noted a further complication: the rates of interest paid by borrowers may move in the opposite direction from rates received by savers if the development of financial intermediaries reduces the transactions-cost spread. In that case, which was possibly of great significance as financial institutions and markets developed historically, the cost of capital to investors may fall even as returns to savers rise.

A final complication, one that we emphasize in this paper, is that the return to saving is itself a complex concept. Usually it is taken by economic historians as simply the interest rate, or, more precisely, the interest rate received by the saver or the yield on a bond at the time of purchase. But if there are capital gains or losses on the asset during the period it is held, the true return to the saver will differ from the interest rate or bond yield. Equity investors have long been aware of this distinction. To them, the current dividend paid by an equity share of stock in a firm is only one consideration, for the firm's earnings not paid out as dividends will be reinvested in the firm, whose growth may then be reflected in a higher share price in the stock market. Only a part of the total return comes from the dividend; the rest takes the form of a change in the price of the firm's stock.

These complications imply that it is far from easy to infer from trends in financial variables what was, or may have been, happening in the real economy in periods before comprehensive GNP and other macroeconomic estimates are possible. Nonetheless, since our financial data also cover a much longer period after 1840, when much more is known about the behavior of the real economy, the data may offer some insights into pre-1840 real trends. If, for example, the pattern of movement of financial variables in the pre-1840 period is similar to the pattern in a later period when we know something about underlying real growth, it may not be unwarranted to assume a similar real-growth behavior in the earlier period.

Our data also shed additional light on Davis and Gallman's finding of a notable rise in the U.S. savings rate that occurred during the Civil War era. They indicate that returns to savers after the war rose substantially even as the interest rates paid by borrowers and investors were falling.

Our comparison of financial returns and their variability in the nineteenth and twentieth centuries, like Gallman's comparison of economic growth in the two centuries, poses a number of problems relating both to the coverage of the data and to the relative economic importance over time of the markets we study, in our case the financial markets. Nonetheless, such comparisons are useful in a tentative way for isolating both similarities and differences in the behavior of financial markets in the two centuries.

The Data Base

Stock price and dividend data are available for a broadly representative sample of U.S. firms and industries from 1871 to the present.[2] Before 1871 the data are less representative of the corporate economy because the coverage is confined to a few industries such as banks and railroads in which active stock trading occurred. Fortunately, such industries are likely to reflect trends in the economy as a whole. An innovation of this paper is to extend the stock returns data back to 1802 in a form that leads to a continuous series from that date to the present. Another series allows us to add stock returns for the period 1789–1801, but these data must be used with caution.

Monthly bond price data are available for U.S. Treasury bonds from 1795 to 1820, and for railroad and, later, corporate bonds from 1857 to the present. Annual data on U.S., state, and municipal bond prices and yields are available for the intervening period, 1821–56. Such data are less than ideal for calculating annual holding-period returns from bond investment, but nonetheless allow rough estimates of such returns, as discussed in the appendix to this chapter. Monthly commercial paper rates are available from 1831 to the present.

Another innovation of this paper is the presentation and analysis of nominal and real *returns* from stocks, bonds, and commercial paper. Much of the literature of financial and economic history has dealt with observable financial variables such as interest rates, bond yields, and dividend rates on stocks. For some issues of economics and history this is appropriate, and we shall discuss interest rate and bond yield trends here. But for others, such as the incentives to save or the actual outcome of saving activities over various periods, data on returns to saving are more appropriate. Returns from stocks and bonds can be quite different, and can even move in the opposite direction, from interest and dividend rates and bond yields. Economists and economic historians are aware, for example, that as bond yields rise, the capital values of outstanding bonds fall, so that the return from owning a bond can be less than its yield, possibly even negative. Yet this insight has been applied infrequently to economic history, even though it is potentially relevant to such questions as why savings rates have varied historically.

Economic Growth Before 1860

There is still much disagreement about the pace and pattern of U.S. economic growth before the Civil War. As Poulson notes in this volume, Robert Gallman's work extending GNP estimates back to 1839 essentially answered the question for the last two antebellum decades, 1839–59.[3] Gallman found that both output and output per capita grew at rates quite similar to subsequent rates. These findings were consistent with Rostow's dating of the U.S. takeoff in the period 1843–60.[4] But the lack of data for the period before 1839 meant that one could not be sure that the 1840's marked a watershed between the premodern economy and modern economic growth.

Paul David was among the earlier investigators (most of whom are cited by Poulson) to tackle the problem of U.S. economic growth before 1840.[5] David's conjectural estimates indicated a rate of per capita output growth for the period 1800–1840 (1.13 percent per year) that was only moderately lower than the rate Gallman found for 1840–60 (1.60 percent). The lower growth rate was the result of a negligible growth rate in the period 1800–1820 (0.25 percent per year), and a rate from 1820 to 1840 (1.96 percent) that was actually above the rate for 1840–60. This finding was inconsistent with Rostow's dating of the takeoff. If such a takeoff occurred, it would have to be placed in the 1820–40 period. But David preferred to regard his estimates as indicating a gradual and uneven quickening of growth rather than a takeoff dated earlier than Rostow's.

The most recent study of the growth-before-1840 question is that of Thomas Weiss in this volume.[6] Weiss follows David's methods but uses labor-force statistics that are revisions of those used by David as well as new estimates of productivity in manufacturing that were unavailable to David. Weiss's refined conjectural estimates of the rate of growth of per capita output are similar to David's for the period 1800–1820, but considerably lower for the period 1820–40. Whereas David had estimated output growth at an average annual rate of 1.96 percent in this period, Weiss estimates the rate to be 1.19 percent. Weiss, in contrast to David, thus finds an acceleration of growth from the 1820–40 to the 1840–60 period. Indeed, Weiss's refined estimates show a growth acceleration throughout the three twenty-year periods before 1860. The change in growth rates from period to period was largest between 1800–1820 and 1820–40, which is broadly consistent with David's findings and inconsistent with a Rostovian takeoff in the period 1843–60. Still to be resolved is whether U.S. growth before 1840 is best characterized as a gradual acceleration or as something akin to a takeoff in the two to three decades before 1840.

Trends in U.S. financial markets shed some light on this issue. Table 2.1

TABLE 2.1

Decadal Geometric Means and Standard Deviations for Common Stocks: Nominal Returns, CPI Changes, and Real Returns, 1790–1989

Decade	Nominal return (%)	Standard deviation for nominal return (%)	CPI (%)	Standard deviation for CPI (%)	Real return (%)	Standard deviation for real return (%)
1791–1800	10.2485	13.8758	3.1471	4.7089	6.8847	13.7458
1796–1805	3.1419	20.3597	-0.7334	3.7948	3.9039	19.1871
1801–1810	1.5252	16.0809	0.0656	3.9226	1.4587	14.8164
1806–1815	5.6904	6.6529	2.0848	6.6214	3.5320	9.4853
1811–1820	5.2327	8.6070	-0.9907	7.7344	6.2857	12.2465
1816–1825	6.8258	6.6909	-3.8925	3.1776	11.1524	7.7533
1821–1830	6.8075	4.0734	-2.5020	3.0122	9.5483	5.3802
1826–1835	9.0004	4.3065	-0.8739	2.5686	9.9614	4.5045
1831–1840	6.8330	7.2987	-0.2826	2.8971	7.1358	8.0033
1836–1845	9.0050	16.7050	-1.7349	3.3571	10.9295	17.1540
1841–1850	12.2370	16.6431	-1.1591	3.5005	13.5532	17.1678
1846–1855	4.5730	15.9813	1.1909	2.6710	3.3423	18.2371
1851–1860	2.0187	15.8191	1.0265	2.3957	0.9820	17.5319
1856–1865	14.4812	18.5254	6.5085	8.6870	7.4855	11.8643
1861–1870	17.9701	16.4171	3.9682	10.7410	13.4675	10.8709
1866–1875	8.0116	10.9445	-3.8625	1.2649	12.3511	10.9963
1871–1880	10.2869	18.5983	-2.0947	1.8961	12.6466	16.9422

1876–1885	7.6770	20.3905	−1.2995	1.5758	9.0947	19.1383
1881–1890	1.3671	10.5053	−1.2011	0.9034	2.5994	10.5989
1886–1895	2.0737	11.3778	−1.2467	1.1595	3.3623	10.9659
1891–1900	8.7333	13.8208	−0.7104	1.3151	9.5112	12.8624
1896–1905	13.0950	12.8653	0.5788	0.8343	12.4443	13.3605
1901–1910	7.0406	22.7285	1.1682	1.3200	5.8047	23.8056
1906–1915	5.0017	22.4651	1.5253	1.2811	3.4241	23.1584
1911–1920	3.1089	18.2196	7.4061	6.9994	−4.0009	19.0997
1916–1925	9.5908	18.3202	5.6480	9.3840	3.7320	23.3058
1921–1930	12.0840	22.4403	−1.8135	4.1842	14.1542	21.8614
1926–1935	4.0722	37.6156	−2.5678	4.6879	6.8149	33.4667
1931–1940	2.3093	37.6790	−1.3410	4.9436	3.7000	35.1611
1936–1945	8.9965	24.7667	2.7873	3.6440	6.0407	26.1265
1941–1950	13.3745	14.6353	5.9051	5.1247	7.0529	18.9323
1946–1955	14.9207	14.4690	3.9647	5.4146	10.5382	18.4971
1951–1960	15.2784	16.6563	1.7740	1.6706	13.2689	17.2716
1956–1965	11.4721	15.2338	1.7254	0.6805	9.5815	15.5251
1961–1970	8.2148	14.1767	2.9215	1.7942	5.1431	15.2083
1966–1975	3.1143	20.9840	5.7145	2.6397	−2.4596	23.1768
1971–1980	9.0517	21.7579	8.0533	3.2807	0.9240	22.9912
1976–1985	15.2256	12.4579	7.0086	3.2751	7.6789	13.0317
1981–1989	16.7949	10.8087	5.0910	2.8608	11.1370	11.2038

SOURCE: See appendix to Chapter 2.

presents overlapping decade averages of annual returns on common stocks from 1791 through 1989, given in both nominal and real (price-level-adjusted) terms. Also included are CPI changes and standard deviations of returns and CPI changes. Figure 2.1, Panel A, portrays the real stock returns in the form of ten-year moving averages. Tables 2.2 and 2.3 present the overlapping-decade average yield, returns, and variability data for bonds (back to 1796) and commercial paper (back to 1831). Panels B and C of Figure 2.1 also present the real returns of bonds and commercial paper.[7]

The stock and bond data indicate that something like a financial watershed occurred around 1815. The break with the past is most evident in the stock market, where both nominal and real returns to stocks were substantially greater in the period 1815–50 than they had been earlier. Stock returns fell in the later 1830's, but still remained above the levels typical before 1815. The later 1830's and early 1840's were in the nature of a pause in a great bull market in stocks that lasted for approximately three-and-a-half decades. It appears to have been the longest bull market in stocks in two centuries of U.S. financial history. During much of this bull market, moreover, the variability of stock returns, as measured by their standard deviation, was at its lowest level in U.S. history. (Variability of returns is discussed further below.) It is possible, of course, that the combination of high stock returns and their low variability (especially from 1815 to 1840) is the result of limited coverage—the data are mostly for bank stocks. An alternative historical hypothesis is also intriguing: the Second Bank of the United States dominated the U.S. financial system for much of the period from 1815 to 1840, and we are not the first to provide evidence that it may have exerted a stabilizing effect on the economic and financial affairs of the young republic in these years.[8]

Investors in the bond market after 1815 also fared well. Nominal interest rates (bond yields), charted in Figure 2.2 with representative data given in Table 2.2, declined sharply from pre-1815 levels between 1815 and the early 1820's, and they remained at the new lower levels until the Civil War. Real bond interest rates, in contrast, averaged higher from 1815 to 1850 than they had averaged before 1815, mostly as a result of high real rates from 1815 to 1830. Real bond returns, a better indication than real bond interest rates of how investors actually fared in any period, were above but followed the pattern of real interest rates between 1815 and 1850 (see Panel B of Figure 2.1). In the 1850's, however, real bond returns remained high even as real interest rates fell. In that decade of California gold production, a rising price level converted falling nominal rates into even lower real rates, but the capital gains on bonds resulting from falling nominal rates offset the effects of a rising price level and maintained real returns to bondholders.

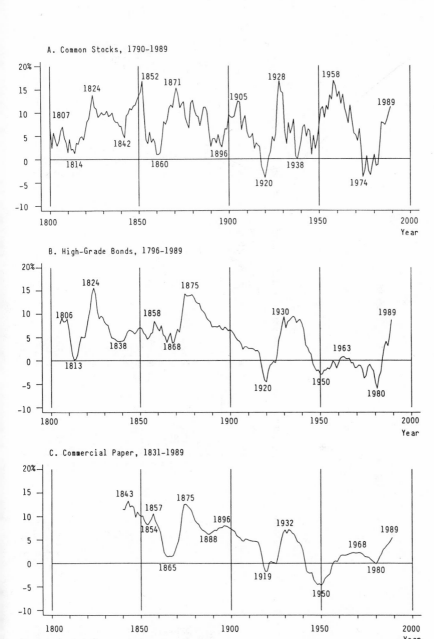

Fig. 2.1. Real returns of common stocks, bonds, and commercial paper, 1789–1989 (ten-year moving averages). See appendix for sources. Since the data charted are ten-year moving averages, the initial dates of the charted series are 1800 for stocks, 1805 for bonds, and 1840 for commercial paper. Dates of major peaks and troughs are noted on the charts.

TABLE 2.2

Geometric Means and Standard Deviations for Twenty-Year Bonds: Nominal and Real Returns and Yields, by Decade, 1796–1989

Decade	Nominal return (%)	Standard deviation for nominal return (%)	Real return (%)	Standard deviation for real return (%)	Nominal yield (%)	Real yield (%)
1796–1805	7.1466	6.1801	7.9382	8.5265	6.8131	7.6759
1801–1810	6.8930	4.0699	6.8230	7.6501	6.1140	6.1260
1806–1815	3.4247	4.8138	1.3125	9.7101	6.3160	4.3797
1811–1820	5.9381	10.1185	6.9981	16.2207	6.3260	7.6950
1816–1825	9.8120	8.5179	14.2595	10.1203	5.2460	9.5745
1821–1830	5.5763	3.2823	8.2855	4.1798	4.4730	7.2039
1826–1835	3.8570	1.9860	4.7726	3.3436	4.5650	5.5165
1831–1840	3.8959	1.9446	4.1904	3.4908	4.8630	5.2025
1836–1845	4.5687	1.8634	6.4149	4.2518	5.0180	6.9310
1841–1850	5.8603	3.9002	7.1017	5.7729	5.1700	6.4637
1846–1855	6.1714	3.8637	4.9219	5.5765	4.7920	3.6008
1851–1860	7.9957	8.0174	6.8983	9.3775	4.4220	3.3894
1856–1865	10.6048	12.8937	3.8460	13.4459	5.1060	-0.9952
1861–1870	9.6415	10.6081	5.4568	11.7851	6.0300	2.5570
1866–1875	9.8772	3.4746	14.2917	3.7681	6.2160	10.4934
1871–1880	11.1317	2.8760	13.5094	3.0262	5.4070	7.6892
1876–1885	9.0914	2.8889	10.5276	2.6841	4.4740	5.8650

1881–1890	5.8773	2.3212	7.1645	2.9260	3.9150	5.1824
1886–1895	5.4643	1.8481	6.7957	2.5590	3.6800	4.9951
1891–1900	5.8450	1.3998	6.6023	2.2453	3.4450	4.1955
1896–1905	4.7230	1.6341	4.1204	2.3289	3.3290	2.7378
1901–1910	3.7586	2.7680	2.5605	3.8932	3.5780	2.3906
1906–1915	3.6939	2.9531	2.1360	3.8887	3.8890	2.3361
1911–1920	2.4765	4.3113	−4.5897	8.8690	4.3340	−2.6512
1916–1925	5.1381	6.2141	−0.4826	14.5947	4.5710	−0.6181
1921–1930	7.4178	3.5337	9.4017	7.3273	4.3800	6.3982
1926–1935	6.6082	5.6277	9.4179	6.5304	4.1580	7.0285
1931–1940	6.4086	5.6476	7.8549	6.8969	3.5350	5.0895
1936–1945	4.1834	1.8289	1.3582	5.0792	2.8720	0.1476
1941–1950	2.8171	1.8346	−2.9158	6.4300	2.7160	−2.8927
1946–1955	2.0456	2.7143	−1.8459	6.9564	2.8670	−0.9175
1951–1960	1.1330	4.0697	−0.6299	5.0552	3.5750	1.7825
1956–1965	2.0576	4.0116	0.3266	4.3287	4.2730	2.5082
1961–1970	1.3768	5.8630	−1.5009	6.5552	5.5700	2.5679
1966–1975	2.2339	7.6263	−3.2924	8.6971	7.3210	1.5342
1971–1980	3.0662	8.4756	−4.6154	11.7575	8.8910	0.7873
1976–1985	10.1206	15.7116	2.9082	18.9184	10.9980	3.7714
1981–1989	14.2385	15.6025	8.7044	17.8512	11.0660	5.6950

S O U R C E : See appendix to Chapter 2.
N O T E : Returns are based on geometric means, whereas yields are arithmetic means.

TABLE 2.3

Decade Geometric Means and Standard Deviations for Commercial Paper:
Nominal and Real Returns, 1831–1989

Decade	Nominal return (%)	Standard deviation for nominal return (%)	Real return (%)	Standard deviation for real return (%)
1831–1840	11.1594	6.0358	11.4745	6.3797
1836–1845	10.3027	5.5753	12.2501	6.2905
1841–1850	8.6933	4.0029	9.9680	6.0925
1846–1855	10.1691	3.1658	8.8725	5.4446
1851–1860	8.7470	2.3638	7.6421	3.8461
1856–1865	7.9659	2.4921	1.3683	10.0173
1861–1870	7.8560	1.2612	3.7393	11.5154
1866–1875	8.2487	1.5629	12.5978	1.9187
1871–1880	6.8906	1.9935	9.1776	3.2450
1876–1885	5.5322	0.4681	6.9216	1.7211
1881–1890	5.5129	0.6761	6.7956	0.9371
1886–1895	6.2724	1.7072	7.6140	2.1903
1891–1900	6.6352	1.7371	7.3981	2.4730
1896–1905	5.9792	1.0016	5.3694	1.3399
1901–1910	6.1548	1.0711	4.9290	2.0224
1906–1915	6.0847	1.1522	4.4909	2.1757
1911–1920	5.6166	1.0093	−1.6661	7.3430
1916–1925	5.5006	1.3257	−0.1396	10.0175
1921–1930	5.1873	1.1630	7.1300	5.0453
1926–1935	3.4511	1.6835	6.1775	5.3611
1931–1940	1.3765	0.9622	2.7545	5.8203
1936–1945	0.7157	0.1254	−2.0154	3.7219
1941–1950	0.9341	0.3465	−4.6939	5.3238
1946–1955	1.6624	0.5727	−2.2146	5.8526
1951–1960	2.8860	0.9181	1.0926	1.8109
1956–1965	3.6539	0.5885	1.8958	0.8633
1961–1970	5.2271	1.8945	2.2402	0.7715
1966–1975	7.0854	1.8079	1.2968	1.5302
1971–1980	7.8716	2.4554	−0.1682	1.4978
1976–1985	10.5352	3.6119	3.2957	4.4561
1981–1989	10.8344	3.1812	5.4653	2.8833

SOURCE: See appendix to Chapter 2.

This episode of diverging real rates and real returns illustrates why the latter may give a better indication than the former of the incentives to save. Declining interest rates clearly provide an increased incentive for borrowers to borrow for purposes of real investment. But declining interest rates also would seem to imply a lower reward for saving. Therefore, the conjunction of higher savings rates with declining interest rates in any historical period is usually explained by positing outward shifts in economy-wide savings functions and then searching for possible explanations of such shifts. Our argument here about *returns* to saving is that declining interest

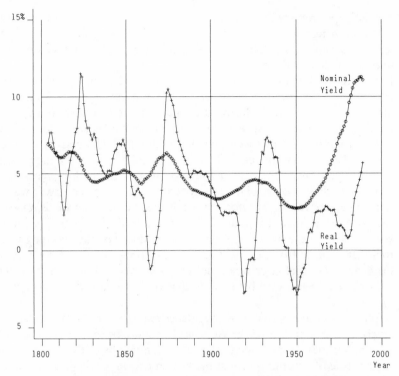

Fig. 2.2. High-grade bond yields, nominal and real, 1795–1989 (ten-year moving averages). See appendix for sources. Since the data charted are ten-year moving averages, the initial date of the charted series is 1805. The real series is formed by dividing the corresponding average annual price-level change into the nominal series, that is, $(1 + r)/(1 + p)$, where r is the annual nominal return and p is the annual CPI change; subtract 1 to obtain the real return in decimal form.

rates may actually raise such returns. In that case, it is not necessary to posit shifts in savings functions to explain increased savings rates. Savings rates will increase along the savings function in response to higher returns. We would not deny the possible relevance of shifts in the savings function as well. Rather, we are adding another explanation for increased savings in response to higher returns to the older explanation that the development of financial intermediaries raised returns to savers by making financial markets more efficient.

Our data on commercial paper returns, which do not begin until the 1830's, give us two bits of information about the antebellum financial system. The first is that short-term nominal and real interest rates were quite high relative to long-term rates and returns. (Unlike bond returns, commercial paper returns and interest rates correspond fairly closely because of the short-term nature of commercial paper.) The second is that short-term rates were already trending down, as they would, with interruptions, until the middle of the twentieth century.

Students of the history of interest rates have noted that U.S. short-term rates such as the commercial paper rate were normally above long-term rates such as bond yields during the nineteenth and early twentieth centuries.[9] The customary explanation is that a central bank and an organized short-term money market were slow to develop in the United States. This is an explanation for the relatively high short-term rates in the nineteenth century. We would add an amendment dealing with why long-term rates were relatively low compared to short-term rates in that century. It was at the long end of the market that returns diverged most from yields. One of the great attractions of holding bonds in a period of secularly declining bond yields was the high return on bonds produced by the declining yield trend. It is likely that this induced savers to prefer bonds to short-term loans, meaning that large quantities of bonds were absorbed even when their current yields were below rates that could be earned on short-term loans.

What does the financial market evidence tell us about the larger issue of antebellum economic growth? We must, of course, be cautious in assessing the implications of the evidence given the limitations of the data and the smaller role of organized capital markets in overall antebellum economic life than later. Nonetheless, some tentative conclusions are warranted. The financial watershed that is evident around 1815 is consistent with other evidence that the pace of economic development quickened around that time. Dramatic increases in nominal and real stock and bond returns become evident then and persist thereafter for decades. These increases in financial returns are consistent with the sharp decline in nominal bond yields that began around 1815 (see Figure 2.2). Our financial market evidence, of course, only identifies a change in long-term trends in yields and returns. Further detailed study of capital-market developments in the years after 1815 will be necessary before the change is fully understood.

Until the 1830's, when railroad stocks first appeared in the markets, our stock data are largely for banks in northeastern cities. Compared to later stock market data, this sample is limited in size and scope of coverage. It is likely, however, that the banks were well positioned to reflect the pulse of the northeastern industrial and commercial economy. Hence, the sustained rise in the returns to owning bank stocks that occurred after 1815 is likely a good indication of what was happening in that economy. The rise of nominal and real stock returns that occurred around 1815 might well be consistent with a "takeoff," appropriately defined, in the northeastern economy of that era. But it is not inconsistent with a gradual acceleration of aggregate growth since, although the northeastern economy likely embodied the leading industrial, commercial, and financial edges of the entire U.S. economy, it was only one component of that economy.

The Rise of the Nineteenth-Century Savings Rate

Studies primarily by Gallman, but also by Kuznets and others, have established that U.S. savings and investment rates (as a percentage of total income) increased greatly between the 1830's and the 1890's. Gross rates roughly tripled (rising from 9 to 28 percent) and net rates roughly doubled (from 9 to 20 percent) over these six decades.[10] Because the capital intensiveness of production (capital-output ratios) rose generally across economic sectors, and because real interest rates appeared to fall, Davis and Gallman argued that outward shifts in savings functions (increased savings at every level of interest rates, given income) were the primary reason for the rise in savings and investment as a proportion of income. A number of factors that may have led to rising savings proportions—falling relative prices of capital goods, demographic changes, changes in income distribution, and improvements in financial intermediation—have been discussed in the literature.[11]

Davis and Gallman emphasized the role of improved financial intermediation. Over the course of the nineteenth century there was remarkable growth in the number, types, and total assets of intermediaries, with the last datum increasing much more than total production and income. These intermediaries improved the efficiency of finance, reducing costs to borrowers while increasing the return to savers. Given some interest elasticity of investment or savings functions, or both, this improvement in the efficiency of financial markets would increase the levels of saving and investment, and therefore the savings rate, at any level of total income. If the savings function itself shifted outward, the rise in the savings and investment rates would be so much the greater. The fall of real interest rates, which Davis and Gallman argue was substantial between 1840 and 1900, is taken as evidence that both the increase in financial efficiency and the shift in savings behavior occurred over these decades.

But did real interest rates fall in the nineteenth century? Our high-grade bond interest-rate series for the whole of the century leads us to question whether there was anything like the steep decline posited by Davis and Gallman and others. Nominal rates definitely fell; they averaged over 6 percent during the first two decades of the century and less than 4 percent during its last two decades. When we adjust for changes in the price level, however, the decline is barely evident (see Figure 2.2). The overlapping-decade averages indicate (see Table 2.2) that inflation-adjusted bond yields were little different in the years from 1876 to 1900 than they had been from 1796 to 1815 and from 1831 to 1860. Between these periods of roughly similar real rates there were two periods of higher rates, 1816–30 and 1866–80. Nineteenth-century real bond rates are better characterized as fluctuating in long cycles about a horizontal trend than as exhibiting a declining trend.

Interest rates, whether nominal or real, are rather imperfect measures of the returns realized by savers, a point inadequately appreciated in the literature of economic history. In the present context the point is important because savings behavior likely is more influenced by expected real returns to saving than by whatever nominal or real rates prevail in the market at any given time. Real returns to bond investment, we have argued, can be quite different from real interest rates on bonds, because returns embody changes in principal values as well as interest yields. In the decade of the 1870's, a decade of falling prices leading to resumption of gold payments at pre-Civil War parity, nominal bond interest rates in our series averaged 5.64 percent, and real rates (ex post) averaged 8.64 percent. Average nominal returns to bondholders in that decade, however, were 10.41 percent, and real returns were 13.20 percent.[12]

Much of the long-term investment financed in the capital markets of the nineteenth century took the form of bonds. Our real returns series indicates that bondholders reaped average returns on high-grade bonds of 6 to 8 percent in the 1880's and 1890's. These real returns at the end of the century were greater than or similar to real bond returns in most earlier decades. They were, however, substantially less than real bond returns in two earlier periods, 1816–30 and 1866–85, in which real returns reached double-digit levels. Bond investors fared well throughout the nineteenth century, and extremely well from 1816 to 1830 and from 1866 to 1885.[13]

Our data also indicate that these two periods of high real bond returns were periods of comparatively high stock returns. The first period, we think, marked the initial upsurge of modern economic growth in the United States. The post–Civil War period, 1866–85, was also one of rapid growth by most indications; in addition, it was the period when the savings rate increased to a much higher level than that which had prevailed before the Civil War. In the search for the explanation of high and rising savings rates over the course of the nineteenth century, it appears from our evidence that more attention must be given to how very well indeed savers who held bonds and stocks were rewarded for foregoing current consumption.

Nineteenth and Twentieth Centuries: Comparisons and Contrasts

On the basis of his own and others' studies of long-term U.S. economic growth, Gallman extracted a number of basic stylized facts that brought out similarities and differences between the U.S. economy's performance in the nineteenth and the twentieth centuries.[14] First, aggregate real growth was considerably greater in the nineteenth than in the twentieth century, approximately 4 percent per year compared to roughly 3.1 percent. Second, in a "sources of growth" framework, the growth of factor inputs accounted for a larger proportion of aggregate growth in the nineteenth century, with the proportion attributed to the advance of total factor productivity being correspondingly less. That is, growth of the labor force, the land supply, and the capital stock (which, unlike labor and land, grew considerably faster than output) accounted for more than half of total real output growth in the nineteenth century, but only about 20 percent of growth in the twentieth century. Hence, the contribution of total factor productivity rose from less than 50 percent in the nineteenth to about 80 percent in the twentieth century. Third, because population growth slowed in the twentieth century, the growth of real output per person turned out to be roughly the same (approximately 1.5 percent per year) in the two centuries, a persistent and fascinating similarity across a long period of time. Gallman's conclusions were based on comparisons of the periods 1840–1900 and 1900–1960, but there is little reason to think that they would change much if 1810–40 and 1960–90 data were to extend the base of evidence to 180 years.

Our long series of interest rates and returns to stocks and bonds in the U.S. financial economy also allow comparisons of the two centuries. In addition, we present and discuss measures of the variability of returns over time as rough indications of the risk involved in financial investment during various periods.

Table 2.4 summarizes our returns and risk (standard deviation) measures for stocks, bonds, and commercial paper for two centuries of U.S. history, along with subperiods for the pre–Civil War years, the period 1860–1900, the nineteenth century, and the twentieth century. The table also gives the Consumer Price Index (CPI) rates of price-level change for each period. Figure 2.3, which is similar to Figure 2.1, presents in the form of ten-year moving averages our risk measures (graphed at the terminal year of each ten-year period) for stocks, bonds, and commercial paper. (Figure 2.3, like Figure 2.1, allows the reader to focus on shorter-term movements, which we will not discuss here.) For the complete period, which includes more than 190 years of stock and bond data and 160 years

TABLE 2.4

Geometric Means and Standard Deviations for Nominal and Real Returns on Common Stocks, Bonds, and Commercial Paper, and for Purchasing Power (CPI) Changes, Various Time Periods, 1790–1989

	Nominal return (%)	Standard deviation for nominal return (%)	Real return (%)	Standard deviation for real return (%)
Complete period, 1790–1989				
Stocks	8.3936	17.8904	6.9710	18.0827
Bonds	5.9389	7.0466	4.7006	9.7351
Paper	6.2723	3.6281	4.5178	6.6236
CPI	1.3299	5.4125	—	—
Prior to 1861				
Stocks	6.6278	13.3118	6.6900	14.0684
Bonds	6.1749	6.2108	6.8446	8.7869
Paper	9.5273	4.5935	9.6835	5.8485
CPI	−0.0667	4.6789	—	—
1860–1900				
Stocks	9.2261	16.2900	9.1964	13.8654
Bonds	8.0742	5.9905	8.0350	6.9469
Paper	6.6784	1.7166	6.6397	6.3477
CPI	0.0363	5.9195	—	—
Prior to 1901				
Stocks	7.6294	14.4968	7.6896	14.0139
Bonds	6.9038	6.1944	7.3357	8.1371
Paper	7.9144	3.4939	8.0030	6.2759
CPI	−0.0559	5.1566	—	—
1901–1989				
Stocks	9.3544	21.5875	6.0815	22.3982
Bonds	4.8117	7.8326	1.6748	10.5656
Paper	4.9983	3.2477	1.8558	5.5827
CPI	3.0853	5.2162	—	—

SOURCE: See appendix to Chapter 2.
NOTE: The stock returns originate in 1790. Bond returns begin in 1796. Commercial paper returns begin in 1831.

of commercial paper data, the real returns and risk follow the rank ordering predicted by finance theory: stocks highest, followed by long-term bonds, followed by short-term commercial paper. This rank ordering of returns and risk prevailed in the 1860–1900 and 1901–1989 subperiods as well.

During the pre–Civil War era, however, the rank ordering of real returns is different from the expected theoretical and actual historical pattern after 1860. Prior to 1861, bonds returned more than stocks, even though the risk (volatility of returns) was lower. Moreover, real commercial paper returns before 1861 actually exceeded both stock and bond returns, al-

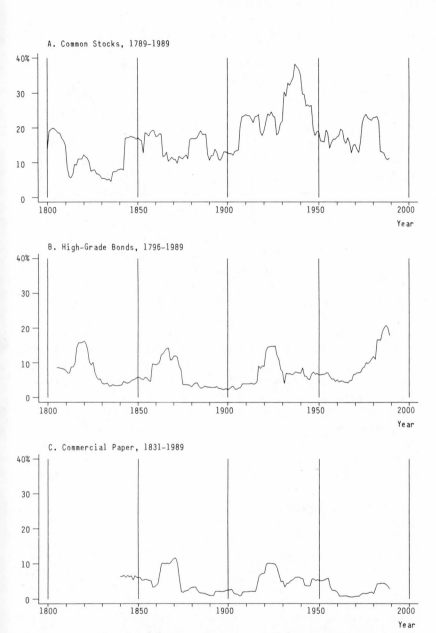

Fig. 2.3. Risk measures: standard deviation of real returns of common stocks, bonds, and commercial paper, 1789–1989 (ten-year moving averages). See appendix for sources. See notes to Fig. 2.1. The data charted are the standard deviations of annual returns for the ten-year period up to and including the year plotted in each of the panels.

though—again—the volatility was lower than that of either stocks or bonds.[15]

These results suggest that there may have been some imperfection or segmentation in the nineteenth-century capital markets, at least before the Civil War. Given the different levels of risk, investors were more adequately compensated by bonds and commercial paper than by stocks. Too much should not be made of this, however; for most of the nineteenth century, stock ownership and trading was relatively small in comparison with bond trading and short-term loan volume. The stock market did not really become a major national financial market until late in the century. Therefore, most financial market investors were in bonds, and in short-term loans such as commercial paper, rather than in stocks.

Comparison of the nineteenth- and twentieth-century returns and risks leads to some interesting results. Real returns were uniformly higher for stocks, bonds, and commercial paper from 1860 to 1900 than they have been since. In the cases of stocks and bonds, risk, as measured by standard deviations of real returns, was lower before 1901 than after, although commercial paper returns have been slightly less volatile in this century. Since the mid-1970's, volatility of bond returns has been at its highest level in our two-century series.

It is obvious that holders of stocks and bonds were better rewarded in the last century than in the present one. Real returns were higher and the variability of those returns was lower. It is well to remember, of course, that the proportion of U.S. capital formation financed through organized capital markets was lower in the last century, even though it was increasing. Nonetheless, we think that organized market conditions then may well have reflected economy-wide conditions for financing capital formation. If that is a valid thought, should we be surprised that our nineteenth-century ancestors were led to save and invest a higher proportion of their incomes than has been characteristic of the twentieth century?

Our data also indicate why common-stock investment has become of greater relative importance in this century. Unlike bonds and commercial paper, nominal returns on stock responded to inflation and actually rose in the twentieth century from nineteenth-century levels. Real stock returns have been slightly lower in the twentieth century than in the nineteenth, but relatively speaking, a financial investor in this century has been much better off in stocks than in bonds or short-term loans. Real returns on stocks from 1901 through 1989 were above 6 percent per year, whereas in bonds and commercial paper they were less than 2 percent.

From a financial investor's point of view, one of the main differences between the two centuries is inflation. Over the two centuries, the price level rose at a rate of roughly 1.3 percent per year. But across the whole of the nineteenth century there was no inflation; our data indicate that the price level declined at a barely perceptible rate of less than 0.1 percent per year. In this century, by contrast, inflation exceeded 3 percent per year. Interestingly, the variability of inflation in our data was about the same in the two centuries. This means that a person in the nineteenth century had about as much reason to expect that the inflation rate in his or her lifetime would be zero percent as a twentieth-century person has to expect it to be 3 percent. Hence, it seems that intercentury differences in long-term real financial results cannot be explained by differences in the *variability* of inflation. Compared to the nineteenth century, the stock market in the twentieth century appeared to make a much better adjustment to the fundamental difference in inflation *rates* between the two centuries than did the bond and commercial paper markets, in which the decline of real returns was precipitous. Was this a result of the equity market being relatively free in the twentieth century, whereas the debt markets, long and short, were much more subject to governmental rigging and regulation?

It is perhaps no surprise that twentieth-century real financial returns are lower than nineteenth-century returns. The ravages of inflation not entirely anticipated or the accumulation of capital leading to lower marginal productivity are among the considerations that could lead to such a result. It is more surprising, we think, that the volatility of twentieth-century stock and bond returns apparently has been greater than it was in the last century. Presumably financial markets were thinner and less developed then, so we might expect volatility of returns to have been greater. But it was not.[16] Since variability of the inflation rate was about the same in the two centuries, it cannot provide an explanation of the greater volatility of returns in this century. Another explanation is needed.

Conclusion

Long-term series of interest rates, bond yields, and bond and stock returns are valuable in their own right as indications of financial trends. But they can also help to clarify and possibly to resolve some larger issues of economic history. When did modern economic growth begin in the United States? Ever since Robert Gallman demonstrated that growth had proceeded at modern rates from 1840, when GNP could first be measured, economic historians have wondered whether it began then, as Rostow thought, or earlier, either as a sudden quickening of the pace or as a gradual acceleration. Bond and stock returns, both nominal and real, indicate a quickening of the pace of economic growth around the year 1815. Such returns pertained to only one part of the U.S. economy of that time, the industrializing northeast, which was possibly a small but rapidly growing part of the whole economy. Thus, it is possible that overall growth accelerated slowly as the small but rapidly developing component became a larger and larger part of the whole.

Similarly, economic historians have sought an explanation for the notable rise of U.S. savings rates, which Gallman first documented as occurring across the Civil War era. A number of hypotheses have been advanced. Possibly the simplest hypothesis of all has been relatively neglected. Nominal and real returns to stock and bond investment were nearly the same throughout the period 1860–1900, and they were sustained for these decades at the highest levels seen in any period of comparable length in U.S. history. This was the so-called era of the robber barons. If the financial returns we calculated for this era are accurate, it might be said that the robber barons did not have to steal. They could then amass more wealth than in other eras of U.S. history merely by saving and investing in stocks and bonds. Although nominal and real interest rates declined in this era, nominal and real returns to bond investments remained at high levels throughout the 40-year period, as did stock returns, with the exception of the decade or so from the mid-1880's to the mid-1890's. We suggest that the savings rate rose to record levels at least in part because the returns Americans received from their savings and investments were also high by earlier and later standards.

Comparing the twentieth century with the nineteenth, we find that investors in equities did relatively well in both. They were somewhat better compensated in the nineteenth century, both absolutely in real terms and in relation to risk, but the differences were not great in the two centuries. In contrast, investors in debt fared much worse in the twentieth century than in the nineteenth. They received returns that were much lower, even though their risk was as high or higher. The rate of inflation was greater in the twentieth century than in the nineteenth, but its variability was about the same in the two centuries. The twentieth-century equity market coped with higher levels of inflation much better than did the debt markets. In this sense, the old adages that stocks are a hedge against inflation, and that inflation, to the extent it is unanticipated, is especially harmful to creditors, appear to hold as long-run empirical propositions.

Appendix

Almost all of the asset return data used in this paper are based upon monthly prices, with monthly reinvestment of dividends or interest accrued. Monthly data are not always available, however. For instance, in the calculation of real returns, monthly data for the CPI are unavailable prior to 1913, monthly stock data are unavailable prior to 1802, monthly bond data are unavailable from 1820 through 1856, and commercial paper data are unavailable prior to 1831.

Since we are reporting annual holding-period returns, we have attempted, insofar as possible, to use the end-of-December values for the calculation of returns. The annual CPI data are interpolated in order to represent December values, and the annual cumulative asset returns are calculated on an end-of-month, December-to-December basis, properly deflated by division by the matching inflation rate to achieve the estimate of real returns. All real-return averages are based on geometric means and the related standard deviations.

The basic series used in this paper will be briefly described, and where appropriate, alternative series will be discussed. Most of the earlier data (prior to 1926) are our estimates and currently are not documented.

Consumer Price Index

The December values are essentially those described in a related article, improved and extended from 1871 back to 1840.[17] The data prior to 1840 are from David and Solar, extending back to 1774.[18] The quality of the data appears to be good back to 1840, but less reliable prior to that date. We have estimated, from other sources, an implicit GNP deflator and a Wholesale Price Index (WPI), and we find that the very early CPI data correspond well with the WPI, although both series deviate from the implicit deflator, showing less inflation.

Common Stock Returns

There are several sources of common stock returns. For the period 1926 to the present, we use the Center for Research in Securities Prices (CRSP) data originally constructed by Fisher and Lorie.[19] Our research indicates that these monthly data are superior to the more often used data of Ibbotson and Sinquefield and the updates by Ibbotson Associates because of their broader coverage.[20] For the period 1871 through 1925, we use the Cowles monthly data as documented by Wilson and Jones in a revised form, based upon our further research.[21] For the period 1857–71, we use the Macaulay monthly data for rail stocks (1938) in a revised form that eliminates autocorrelation of monthly returns and downward-biased estimates of volatility of monthly returns.[22] An alternative series for the 1857–1925 period is available from Schwert, who uses the same basic raw data but revises the monthly average data using a different statistical procedure.[23]

Cowles's original data from 1917 are based upon the median of the high and the low of the Standard Statistics Company weekly value-weighted index of the "500" stocks. Wilson and Jones, in an unpublished paper, have retrieved those original data, and have estimated end-of-month prices using the technique of a companion series based upon the *New York Times* daily data and the Dow Jones daily data. Using the companion series, they have made estimates of the end-of-month prices from Cowles's "average" monthly data back to 1884. They use a statistical technique for the period 1857–84 that adjusts for the positive autocorrelation and downward-biased variance of averaged data. Schwert uses a different filtering estimate for the complete period 1857–1925. Further, the treatment of dividend yields versus dividend amounts is more carefully treated by Wilson and Jones.[24]

For the period prior to 1857, the available published stock-return data are not of very high quality, and there are basically three series from which to choose. Not all of the estimates for these early years originate in the same year, and they are based on somewhat different sources and treatment of the original data, along with some different assumptions regarding the amount of returns due to dividends.

Ibbotson and Brinson present annual total returns from common stocks from 1789 forward.[25] Their data prior to 1871 are based upon the Cleveland Trust Company internal data from January 1789 to June 1831, and the Clement-Burgess data until July 1871. The coverage is poorly documented, the estimated annual returns seem rather high, and during the overlap period with the following series from 1802 to 1856, their annual volatility seems fairly high as well. We do not know whether these returns are based on end-of-month data or annual average data. The quality of the data is suspect, and we know little of the composition of the securities included in their indexes.

Schwert presents monthly stock-return data from 1802.[26] He uses the bank stock-price data from Smith and Cole plus their additional rail stock-price data until 1862, where he splices into the Macaulay rail stock data.[27] His estimated dividend yields are based on the pattern of dividend returns from 1871.

We use the same basic sources of stock-price data as Schwert, but we splice the bank data from 1802 into the available rail data beginning in 1834 on an equally weighted basis of stocks represented from banks and rails until 1843, splicing into Macaulay in 1857. We base our dividend estimates upon available data in Martin, using his estimated dividend amounts for rails from 1834 and calculating dividend yields from dividend amounts.[28] We also use the technique of calculating dividend amounts from the original data and calculating the yields from estimated amounts. We feel that our data, overall, are superior to Schwert's. For the period 1802–71, our estimated mean returns and volatility fall between the high values of Ibbotson and Brinson and the low of Schwert.

Our final series runs from 1790 through 1989. We use the Ibbotson and Brinson data from 1790 through 1801, splice into the Wilson and Jones data from 1802 through 1925, and use the CRSP data from 1926 through 1989. Like the CPI data, the quality of stock-return estimates prior to 1850 is lower than for the later period. The liquidity of stocks was restricted by the lack of a central marketplace and by time delays in communications between the markets in Boston, New York, and Philadelphia.

Bond Returns

Monthly prices of the U.S. Treasury 3-percent stock (a coupon bond) are available from Smith and Cole for the period 1795–1820.[29] Returns have been calculated from those prices for this period on the basis of monthly compounding of returns.

For the period 1820–56, monthly interest rates for comparable assets are not readily available. For this period, we have pieced together the best available annual interest rates from Homer and Sylla, and calculated annual returns.[30] The assumptions for the calculations were for a 4-percent coupon bond, with semi-annual payments, compounded annually. The rates are annual "average" values, seemingly the mean of the high and low for the year. The returns for this period are inferior to the previous and following data, both in terms of estimating the annual returns and the volatility (standard deviation) of the returns. Over relatively short time periods, the average return will not be unduly influenced, although the volatility will be underestimated.

For the period 1857–1919, Macaulay's interest rates for railroad bonds were used to calculate returns on the assumption that the rate represents a 4-percent coupon and twenty-year maturity.[31] For each month, a purchase and sale price were calculated, and the return was calculated as the percentage change in price plus the coupon yield for the month.

From 1919 to the present, Federal Reserve sources were used to obtain the interest rates for Moody's Aaa corporate bonds through the remainder of the period.[32] Returns were calculated on the basis of the same 4-percent coupon, twenty-year maturity assumption.

For the period 1926 to the present, these returns are similar to the monthly returns provided by Ibbotson Associates, who utilize a similar technique for calculating returns but use the Standard and Poor's corporate interest rate as their base.[33]

Corporate bonds were used, although it would have been desirable to use U.S. bonds instead. There were rather long periods in the 1800's and the early 1900's, however, when almost no U.S. debt instruments were in the hands of the public or actively traded on bond markets.

Commercial Paper Returns

Interest rates on commercial paper were used for the complete period. U.S. Treasury bills, a current benchmark for short rates, were not issued until 1929, and initially in small quantities. Macaulay provides the monthly commercial paper rates from Boston, based on the Bigelow and Martin data, from 1831 through 1856.[34] Macaulay's data were then used from 1857 through 1919, when Federal Reserve sources were spliced into the series. The series is described more fully in two related papers.[35] It was assumed that the commercial paper had a five-month maturity, and the monthly returns were calculated on the one-month holding period assumption.

Annual Interest Rates

An annual long-term interest-rate series (bond yields) was constructed from several sources. The rates from 1857 to the present were based on the December value of the Aaa and railroad bonds described above. For the earlier period, we relied on the rates published by Homer and Sylla, which in general are the mean of the high and low rates for each year on the particular asset used.[36] U.S. government bond yields were used when available; otherwise, we used New England municipal bond yields.

CHAPTER THREE

U.S. Migration, 1850-59

Donald Schaefer

THE POSITIVE contributions of nineteenth-century immigration to the United States are well known. Immigrants augmented the labor force, which in turn added to the growth of the nation's output. Robert Gallman, in his recently revised estimates of the sources of growth for the Net National Product of the United States, found that the growth of the labor force over the period 1840 to 1900 contributed 1.88 percent of the 3.98 percent average annual growth rate of NNP, or 47.2 percent of the total.[1] Less obvious were immigration's contributions to growth by indirectly augmenting the capital stock.[2]

At the same time, immigration's effects on the economy and society have been a continuing source of controversy. The controversy pertains to distributional issues. It has been argued that high levels of international immigration could lead to higher unemployment and lower real wages for native-born workers; immigrants may be a net drain on government social-services programs, which might raise the taxes of or lower the services available to native-born workers.[3] Even today, organizations such as the Federation for American Immigration Reform lobby for reduced immigration into the United States.[4]

In the nineteenth and early twentieth centuries, the concerns were even more poignant. International immigration was thought to have a potentially depressing effect upon real wages in eastern cities where immigrants landed. This labor-market pressure was mitigated by the frontier, with its abundant resources, which acted as a safety valve, enticing some individuals and families who were predominantly native-born, to move west (that is, to become interregional migrants), thereby preventing the decline of the real wage from reaching the point where worker rebellion was likely.[5]

Questions remain about this story, in particular questions about the accuracy of the international and interregional migration statistics that lie behind it. This topic has been explored most recently by McClelland and

I would like to thank Thomas Weiss, Richard Steckel, and Stanley Engerman for providing comments on various drafts of this paper.

Zeckhauser, who made important improvements to the underlying statistical base.[6] This paper extends that earlier work in two major ways. First, I have used a different and more detailed source of information on international immigration, which allows me to portray more accurately migration to and within the United States, especially for the period 1856–59. This source also provides more detailed information about the regional characteristics of international immigration. Second, I estimate the interregional migration behavior of the international immigrants in a very different fashion than did McClelland and Zeckhauser. Not surprisingly, my empirical results differ widely from theirs.

In this paper, I estimate international immigration to the various regions of the United States and derive interregional migration within the country. Both of these are undertaken for a single decade, the 1850's. I have confined the scope to nonblack immigration. For international migration, this means that all migrants (Caucasians and Asians alike) are included; for interregional migration, slaves and free blacks are excluded.

Method

Net interregional immigration into a region is estimated by the forward census method, which calculates net interregional immigration as

$$(1) \qquad R_i = P_{60,i} - I_i - (P_{50,i-1})S_i$$

where R_i is the net interregional migration for age group i, $P_{60,i}$ is the region's 1860 population in age group i (say ages 10 to 20), I_i is the number of international immigrants remaining in the region at the end of the decade, $P_{50,i-1}$ is the region's 1850 population in age group $i - 1$ (say up to 10), and S_i is the decennial survival rate.[7] The number of international immigrants remaining in the region is in turn a function of the decennial survival rate:

$$(2) \qquad I_i = A_i S_i^{0.1(1860-t)},$$

where A_i is the number of arriving international immigrants in age group i, and t is the year of arrival.

The method requires that enumeration be consistent between the two censuses and that survival rates, by age and sex, be uniform for regions, ethnic groups, and over the decade. This method also imposes a certain order on the computational process. First, the international immigration flow by time of entry, age, sex, and region of entry must be established. At the same time, the U.S. population at the beginning and end of the decade, broken down by age, sex, and region, must be determined. These two sets of information are then used to determine the decennial and annual survival rates by age and sex. Finally, the interregional migration flows by age and sex can be estimated. The remainder of the paper follows in that order. Many of the more detailed aspects of estimation are reserved for the appendix to this chapter.

International Immigration

International passenger arrivals were a topic of great interest to the United States Congress during the nineteenth century. From 1820 until 1874 the secretary of state was required by law to report to the Congress each session the number of passengers arriving at the various coastal ports of entry.[8] These reports, preserved as House and Senate Executive Documents in the Congressional serial set, are the basis of the international immigration series developed here.[9] Surprisingly, these reports seem to have been ignored in previous studies and in the preparation of the official international immigration series.[10]

Reported passenger arrivals are not the same as international immigration to the United States for a number of reasons. The former includes passengers born in the United States and those not intending to reside in the United States. On the other hand, certain customs houses did not report international arrivals every year, and overland customs houses did not report at all.[11] The series constructed here is based upon the passenger arrivals data but is modified to represent more closely international immigration.

Table 3.1 contains the revised series for international immigration and, for comparison, the extant official series. Two differences stand out. The official series is higher in 1850 because it includes the fourth quarter of 1849 in its yearly total. The revised series is higher in 1852 because it includes estimates for customs houses that did not report. The somewhat lower numbers in the revised series for 1854 through 1859 are mostly due to the exclusion of passengers who did not intend to reside in the United States.[12] Despite these differences, the two series show the same basic time pattern of international immigration, namely a high plateau from 1850 through 1854 followed by sharp declines in 1855 and 1858.

The secretary of state's reports on passenger arrivals allow us to estimate the regional debarkation points of international immigrants as well. These are shown in Table 3.2. The dominant region was clearly the Middle Atlantic, which received nearly 80 percent of the total. The New South (10 percent) and New England (6 percent) were the other regions with important shares. The distributions by sex were very similar to the overall regional distributions, with the exception of the West, where nearly 5 per-

TABLE 3.1

International Immigration, 1850–59

Year	Revised series	Official series
1850	280,278	369,980[a]
1851	380,612	379,466
1852	389,492	371,603
1853	369,469	368,645
1854	422,854	427,833
1855	193,965	200,877
1856	194,880	200,436
1857	244,159	251,306
1858	118,070	123,126
1859	116,654	121,282
Total	2,710,433	2,814,554

S O U R C E : The revised figures are described in the text and in the appendix to Chapter 3. The official series is U.S. Bureau of the Census, *Historical Statistics of the United States, Colonial Times to 1970*, vol. 1 (Washington, D.C., 1975), ser. C89, p. 106.
[a] Data cover the period October 1, 1849, through December 31, 1850.

TABLE 3.2

Regional Distribution of Immigrants, 1850–59

	Total immigrants	Male immigrants	Female immigrants
United States (N)	1,575,485	1,134,948	2,710,433
United States	100.00%	100.00%	100.00%
New England	6.27	5.71	7.06
Middle Atlantic	79.46	77.96	81.54
Old South	0.31	0.33	0.27
New South	10.08	10.33	9.74
Frontier	0.56	0.55	0.59
Northwest	0.17	0.16	0.20
West	3.14	4.97	0.61

S O U R C E : Secretary of State, "Passengers Arrivals to the United States," various years.
N O T E : New England includes Maine, New Hampshire, Vermont, Massachusetts, Rhode Island, and Connecticut; Middle Atlantic includes New York, New Jersey, Pennsylvania, Delaware, Maryland, and the District of Columbia; Old South includes Virginia, North Carolina, South Carolina, and Georgia; New South includes Florida, Alabama, Tennessee, Mississippi, and Louisiana; Frontier includes Texas and A rkansas; Northwest includes Kentucky, Ohio, Indiana, Illinois, Michigan, Wisconsin, Minnesota, Iowa, and Missouri; and West includes California, Oregon, Kansas, and the territories of Colorado, Dakota, Nebraska, Nevada, New Mexico, Utah, and Washington. Percentages may not add to 100% due to rounding.

cent of the male international immigrants entered the country but only 0.6 percent of the females. This difference in the West is almost entirely explained by the Chinese immigrants, who were predominantly young men.

To translate these figures into the relative numbers of males and females arriving in each region, it is necessary to know something about the size of the immigrant stream by sex. The immigrants were, not surprisingly, mostly male. Overall during this period, 58 percent of the migrants were male, with the share varying from 52 to 63 percent by region, except for the West, where 92 percent of the immigrants were male (and Chinese). These data are relatively precise, since the reports enumerate the arrivals by sex and by country of origin (the country to which they "belong") and by country in which they intended to reside.[13]

The regional breakdown in Table 3.2 differs from that of McClelland and Zeckhauser, but some broad comparisons can be drawn. The two distributions are roughly similar. For example, my combined Frontier and West region approximates McClelland and Zeckhauser's Far West, and the percentage of immigrants going to each is roughly similar (3.7 percent versus 3.2 percent). Also, the New South regions are similar in definition, and the percentage of immigrants going to each is also very close (10.1 percent here versus 10.9 percent in McClelland and Zeckhauser). On the other hand, their estimates show more immigration to New England than do mine, and they give less weight to the Middle Atlantic and the Old South.[14]

It is clear that the arrivals in the Middle Atlantic (chiefly New York City but also Philadelphia and Baltimore), the New South (almost entirely New Orleans), and New England (dominated by Boston) were of major importance. The Middle Atlantic and New England figures are not surprising. These ports are the nearest to Europe and thus are logical points of entry. But why New Orleans—especially in light of the Europeans' apparent aversion to the South? One answer might be that fares to New Orleans were relatively cheap, since passengers were in a sense "back haul" for cotton being shipped to Europe. But surely the same rationale would apply to Charleston, Savannah, Mobile, and Galveston. Yet the sum of immigrants entering those ports was dwarfed by the number going to New Orleans. A more satisfying hypothesis is that New Orleans was an entrepôt for immigrants. The city's proximity to the Mississippi River made this a convenient way to travel to the Northwest.[15]

It is difficult to obtain a precise age distribution for the immigrants, not because passengers' ages were unknown—although this was sometimes the case—but rather because ages were reported for *all* arriving passengers, including U.S. residents and those not planning to reside in the United States.[16] For certain years and certain regions, the age difference between arriving passengers and immigrants could have been large. It thus seems unreasonable to expect that an age distribution calculated from the reports on passenger arrivals will exactly mirror the distribution for immigrants.

Table 3.3 contains age distributions for passengers arriving at the major ports of entry both by region and for the United States as a whole for the

TABLE 3.3

Immigrant Age Distribution, 1854–55

	Age under 5	Age 5 to 10	Age 10 to 15	Age 15 to 20	Age 20 to 25	Age 25 to 30	Age 30 to 35	Age 35 to 40	Age over 40	Age unknown	Sample size
Male											
New England	5.26%	5.84%	6.79%	14.90%	20.69%	15.58%	10.77%	6.83%	11.81%	1.52%	25,270
Middle Atlantic	7.72	6.39	5.54	15.80	18.96	17.89	9.93	7.61	10.16	0.00	300,024
Old South	2.10	2.41	3.11	10.87	11.88	30.05	12.58	16.61	9.63	0.78	1,288
New South	5.75	9.49	6.62	13.42	17.02	15.37	11.40	6.79	14.08	0.07	43,317
Frontier	10.45	10.73	8.25	11.28	12.59	13.58	10.49	6.67	15.89	0.07	2,908
West	0.06	0.23	0.56	11.83	25.79	29.65	18.19	9.31	4.37	0.01	17,877
U.S.[a]	7.00	6.40	5.50	15.20	19.10	18.00	10.50	7.60	10.5	0.10	390,684
U.S.[b]	6.70	6.60	6.30	13.00	20.10	17.60	11.40	7.10	11.10	—[c]	—
Female											
New England	7.38%	7.78%	9.57%	21.11%	20.29%	11.98%	6.72%	4.77%	9.44%	0.96%	19,653
Middle Atlantic	11.43	9.22	7.53	19.46	17.92	12.89	6.45	5.57	9.53	0.00	190,062
Old South	5.78	4.78	4.78	23.31	27.89	15.94	5.98	3.78	7.57	0.20	502
New South	7.48	13.66	8.23	13.54	17.00	11.69	8.80	5.92	13.58	0.10	28,297
Frontier	14.01	13.10	9.55	10.24	12.06	11.28	8.01	6.87	14.88	0.00	2,198
West	0.64	2.57	6.18	26.40	32.10	19.26	8.35	2.57	1.85	0.08	1,246
U.S.[a]	10.60	9.60	7.80	18.90	18.00	12.70	6.80	5.50	10.00	0.10	249,958
U.S.[b]	9.30	9.10	8.30	16.40	21.10	12.50	8.10	5.00	10.30	—[c]	—

SOURCE: See text for regional and for U.S. 1854–55. For U.S. 1850–55 see McClelland and Zeckhauser, *Demographic Dimensions*, p. 94.

NOTE: The regional distributions are based on the largest port of entry in the region: Boston, New York, Charleston, New Orleans, Galveston, and San Francisco. There were no reports from the Northwest in 1854 or 1855.

[a] From the sum of the regional immigration figures, 1854–55.

[b] Figures for 1850–55. McClelland and Zeckhauser, *Demographic Dimensions*, p. 94.

[c] Included in the Over 40 category.

combined years 1854–55. The McClelland and Zeckhauser national age distribution of immigrants for 1850–55 is presented for comparison. The two national distributions are quite similar, especially for males. The regional distributions, on the other hand, show some marked differences. The West (San Francisco) was clearly quite different from the other regions with its lack of the very young or old and, as I noted above, its lack of females in the international immigrant stream. Once again it was the Chinese migration that dominated international immigration to the West. The Old South (Charleston) was an intermediate case, with a dearth of children among the immigrants. The conclusion I draw from these results is that the use of a U.S. age distribution is likely to distort a regional analysis of migration flows. Thus the McClelland and Zeckhauser figures are likely to be somewhat distorted by their use of a single aggregated age distribution for immigrants.

Decennial Survival Rates

There are no direct measures of the survival rates of migrants, or of native-born individuals for that matter, so I have estimated them by age and sex using census forward survivor ratios. The rates are assumed to be the same for native and foreign born, and uniform across regions.[17] The calculated rates are shown in Table 3.4. For the sake of comparison, McClelland and Zeckhauser's figures are also presented. The two sets of estimates are fairly close, as might be expected, since the studies used almost identical estimates for the population of the United States in 1850 and 1860.[18] Small differences in the survival rates cause substantial variation in the interregional migration estimates. Nonetheless, these differences by themselves are not sufficient to produce different interregional migration patterns.

TABLE 3.4

Decennial Survival Rates over the 1850's

	Revised figures		McClelland and Zeckhauser	
Age at end of decade	Male	Female	Male	Female
10 to 20	0.9673	0.9974	0.9717	1.0047
20 to 30	0.9180	0.9168	0.9087	0.9209
30 to 40	0.7767	0.7996	0.7660	0.8009
40 to 50	0.7939	0.8378	0.7999	0.8527
Over 50	0.7194	0.7382	0.7020	0.7271

S O U R C E : See text, and McClelland and Zeckhauser, *Demographic Dimensions*, p. 143.

Interregional Migration

The way is now clear to estimate interregional migration. I have produced two versions. The first, which I call the naïve estimate, assumes that all international immigrants remained within the region of their port of entry throughout the decade. This is the assumption used in earlier studies.[19] I argue below that this naïve estimate is very difficult to reconcile with demographic and historical realities, so I have produced a second version, in which I attempt to determine the regional destinations of international immigrants soon after arrival.

The naïve estimates of interregional migration, R_i, were derived for each region by sex and age group according to equation (1). The results, shown in Table 3.5, reveal some well-known patterns. The Frontier, the West, and the Northwest each had positive net in-migration, whereas the Old South, the Middle Atlantic, and New England had net out-migration. The net out-migration from the New South, however—nearly 308,000 over the decade, second only to the Middle Atlantic—is so surprising that it is unbelievable.

The incredible large net outflow from the New South indicates the unreliability of the naïve estimates. There are three grounds for rejecting the

TABLE 3.5

Interregional Migration: The Naïve Approach

(*measured in thousands*)

Age in 1860	New England	Middle Atlantic	Old South	New South	Frontier	Northwest	West
Male							
10 to 20	− 3.2	− 154.9	− 31.5	− 47.6	35.4	174.6	27.4
20 to 30	− 16.5	− 280.6	− 34.0	− 41.7	37.3	228.3	107.1
30 to 40	− 12.3	− 233.2	− 4.4	− 32.0	23.1	227.2	31.5
40 to 50	1.9	− 102.5	1.9	− 25.1	11.3	111.3	1.1
Over 50	− 7.5	− 63.7	− 11.9	− 16.4	11.7	82.5	5.3
Female							
10 to 20	− 1.8	− 148.8	− 28.4	− 41.9	34.0	163.6	23.2
20 to 30	8.0	− 168.0	− 28.0	− 42.7	24.1	173.3	33.5
30 to 40	− 10.6	− 129.6	− 12.5	− 29.1	14.8	148.0	19.1
40 to 50	− 2.1	− 65.2	− 4.0	− 17.9	7.9	73.8	7.5
Over 50	− 2.1	− 40.2	− 15.4	− 13.2	8.7	57.2	4.9
All ages							
Male	− 37.6	− 834.9	− 79.8	− 162.7	118.8	823.8	172.4
Female	− 8.7	− 551.8	− 88.3	− 144.9	89.4	615.9	88.2
Total	− 46.2	− 1386.7	− 168.1	− 307.6	208.3	1439.7	260.5

SOURCE: See text.
NOTE: Detail may not add to total due to rounding.

New South results in particular, and thus indirectly the naïve estimates as a whole. First, in a microeconomic study of internal migration for the United States over this same period, Richard Steckel is unable to find any evidence of an outflow of this magnitude.[20] Second, there are numerous state and local histories and histories of transportation that suggest that international travelers were approaching the Northwest from the New South, thus contradicting the assumption that international immigrants stayed in the region of their arrival until after the next decennial census.[21] Finally, the underlying assumption that international immigrants stayed in their region of arrival throughout the decade is not tenable demographically for the New South. My estimates of international immigration to the New South and survival rates indicate that approximately 245,000 international immigrants should have survived to the end of the decade, when they would have been enumerated in the decennial census. The 1860 census, however, enumerated only around 127,000 foreign born in the region, and noted as well that the decennial increase of foreign born in the region was only 39,000.[22] Even if every one of the 88,000 foreign-born residents enumerated in the 1850 census had died or moved out of the region during the decade—an unlikely event—the naïve estimate still implies that 245,000 foreign born should have been enumerated in 1860, when the official enumeration was only 127,000. The underlying assumption of the naïve estimate is clearly incorrect.

Table 3.6 contains the census counts of the foreign born and my estimates of surviving international immigrants for those regions that were subject to net out-migration (as shown in Table 3.5). The result for the Middle Atlantic region is similar to that for the New South, namely, the number of foreign born enumerated in 1860 is smaller than the estimated number of surviving international immigrants. This was not true for the other two regions with net out-migration, New England and the Old South. There, the increase in the foreign born was somewhat greater than the estimated number of surviving immigrants. Those regions may very well have been net importers of international immigrants.

The obvious explanation for the discrepancy between the census figures and the number of potential foreign-born residents in the Middle Atlantic and the New South regions is that these regions both were simply ports of entry for immigrants with other intended destinations. Both regions must have received a large number of persons who were on their way to the Northwest. In addition, it is likely that the Middle Atlantic served as a port of entry into the Old South (especially Virginia) and lower New England, whereas the New South served likewise for the Frontier and the West.

The weight of evidence, then, suggests that the naïve figures are not

TABLE 3.6

Foreign-Born and International Immigration for Selected Regions

(measured in thousands)

Region	Stock of foreign-born immigrants			Estimated immigrant survivors
	1850	1860	Increase	
New England	299.4	469.3	170.0	151.9
Middle Atlantic	1068.5	1651.1	582.6	1940.9
Old South	39.5	60.0	20.5	7.2
New South	87.5	126.5	39.0	244.6

SOURCE: Stock of foreign-born immigrants is from the *1860 Census of the United States*, 1:xxix. The estimation of immigrant survivors is described in the Appendix to Chapter 3.
NOTE: The selected regions are those which had negative net interregional immigration in Table 3.5. Details may not add due to rounding.

correct and that more believable estimates of the migration patterns of international arrivals are needed. I have produced these revised estimates by allowing for the possibility that international immigrants traveled beyond the region of their arrival as a part of their international immigration. In doing so I have dealt with three issues: how many immigrants continued on to another region, when they did so, and the region to which they moved. The details are contained in the appendix below. Suffice it to say that the available evidence is sparse, and numerous assumptions have been made in revising the interregional migration figures. Yet this approach seems preferable to retaining the assumption of the naïve estimate that international immigrants remained in their region of arrival when we know that this assumption cannot be correct.

The new interregional migration figures are shown in Table 3.7. They reveal an overall pattern for the decade much different than that in Table 3.5. There is much lower out-migration from the Middle Atlantic and the New South and less migration to the Frontier and the Northwest. The out-migrations from the Old South and New England show an increase, whereas the West is unaffected.

From a substantive viewpoint, the revised figures tell a very different story from that of the naïve estimates. First, there was less interregional migration than previously described. Much of what appeared to be interregional migration in the naïve estimates is nothing more than international immigration to a region different from that of the port of entry. Second, the mix of migrants was different. The Northwest was settled by fewer residents of the United States than was implied by the naïve estimates; rather, larger numbers of Europeans moved directly to the region. This brings into question the role of the western part of the United States as a "safety valve" for those looking to escape the large number of inter-

TABLE 3.7

Interregional Migration: Revised Estimates

(measured in thousands)

Age in 1860	New England	Middle Atlantic	Old South	New South	Frontier	Northwest	West
Male							
10 to 20	−5.4	−84.6	−32.9	−28.4	33.0	91.0	27.4
20 to 30	−20.8	−137.7	−36.8	−12.1	33.6	66.7	107.1
30 to 40	−16.3	−100.2	−7.0	−2.8	19.5	75.3	31.5
40 to 50	—ª	−39.4	0.6	−8.9	9.2	37.3	1.1
Over 50	−8.3	−37.2	−12.4	−7.5	10.6	49.5	5.3
Female							
10 to 20	−4.0	−73.6	−29.9	−24.2	31.7	76.6	23.2
20 to 30	4.4	−49.2	−30.4	−22.2	21.5	42.4	33.5
30 to 40	−13.0	−52.0	−14.0	−12.5	12.7	59.7	19.1
40 to 50	−3.3	−27.8	−4.8	−8.0	6.7	29.6	7.5
Over 50	−2.7	−21.1	−15.8	−7.3	8.0	34.0	4.9
All ages							
Male	−50.6	−399.0	−88.5	−59.7	105.8	319.7	172.4
Female	−18.5	−223.6	−94.9	−74.2	80.5	242.3	88.2
Total	−69.2	−622.6	−183.4	−133.8	186.3	562.0	260.5

SOURCE: See text.
NOTE: Detail may not add to total due to rounding.
ª Less than 0.05.

national immigrants flowing into and remaining in the East. International immigrants did flow into the Middle Atlantic, and many of them did stay there, but the evidence suggests that many quickly moved on to the less-settled areas of the country. Perhaps the United States agricultural frontier could equally well be characterized as a "safety valve" for Europeans.

The revised estimates are subject to a good deal of uncertainty, but I believe they pass the more appropriate or practical test of improving on the previous estimates. In the difficult world of economic history, with its enormous data gaps, ideal time series are hard to come by, and the statistical dark corners are illuminated gradually. Just as the estimates of McClelland and Zeckhauser advanced our understanding of migration when they were first constructed, so do these new figures. In particular, the revised estimates resolve the puzzling picture of the South-to-North migration evident in the McClelland and Zeckhauser figures.[23] One hopes these figures will soon be superseded by yet better ones.

Conclusion

The present migration estimates differ from those of McClelland and Zeckhauser in two ways: they make fuller use of available data sources, and they allow for the possibility that international immigrants traveled to places distant from their port of arrival into the United States. These differences yield results that enhance our knowledge of interregional movement in the 1850's. The new estimates provide a substantially different view of the role of immigrants in regional growth than do those of McClelland and Zeckhauser. The growth of the Northwest apparently was aided, to an extent not previously reported, by the addition of immigrant labor and capital.

Areas for further research include the examination of the immigration statistics for earlier decades in the nineteenth century and a quantitative analysis of the role immigrants played in the development of the regional economies. The first of these might include a reevaluation of immigration into the United States during the 1820's through the 1840's, a task made difficult by the relative lack and probable lower quality of information on the immigrants (especially compared to the post-1854 period), and the paucity of information on the foreign born in the published censuses of the United States. As to the second of these, Robert Gallman has suggested that immigrants were different from native-born Americans in their tastes, productive ideas, and political and social attitudes, and these differences could have had an effect upon economic growth narrowly defined.[24] Certainly, this is a topic worthy of further research.

Appendix: Estimation Procedures

International Immigration

The Act of March 2, 1819, and later the Act of March 3, 1855, required customs officials to keep a count of persons entering the United States from abroad and the secretary of state to submit these data to the Congress each session. This continued until 1874, when the responsibility for reporting on migration was transferred from the secretary of state to the Bureau of Statistics of the Treasury Department. The reports of the secretary of state were published annually as executive documents to Congress and are the basis for the international immigration estimates in this paper.

The reports to Congress included the quarterly returns of each customs house. Each return included a listing of the occupations of each arrival classified by sex, an age-sex tabulation, a listing by sex of "the country to which they belong," and for 1854–59, a listing by sex of "the country in which they mean to reside." The report also lists by sex the number who died on the voyage.

The reports of arrivals from the Atlantic Ocean and the Gulf of Mexico seem to be relatively complete. The returns for the Pacific (specifically San Francisco) are missing for three years in the decade. The arrivals from Canada across the Great Lakes to Detroit, Michigan, and Oswego, New York, are only partially enumerated, with only two years collected for the former and five years for the latter.

International immigration by sex is estimated as the number of persons arriving who intended to reside in the United States minus the number of persons born in the United States. The assumption is that all arriving persons who were born in the United States intended to reside there as well. The use of this measure minimizes the problem of second passages. Foreigners making repeated temporary trips to the United States are not counted because they are enumerated as not intending to reside in the United States. Similarly, return travelers "belonging to" the United States are not counted.

There were a number of minor flaws in the data. From time to time, small customs houses were listed as not having reported (as opposed to reporting no arrivals). At other times, the country to which the arrival belonged or intended to reside was missing or otherwise unusable. No attempt was made to correct these minor flaws.

Three larger problems were corrected. First, for one year (1852), the returns for Galveston showed only males when for all other years males made up approximately 60 percent of the arrivals. The returns for this year were adjusted using the average male/female ratio for 1851 and 1853. Second, there were no returns from San Francisco for 1851, 1852, and 1853. There are available returns for Chinese immigration to San Francisco for the years 1852 and 1853.[25] These, in conjunction with the ratio of Chinese to total immigration (0.90) and the male/female ratio for 1854, allowed me to estimate the number of arrivals by sex in 1852 and 1853. Using an estimate of the net increase in the number of Chinese in San Francisco from 1848 through 1852 and information on the gross and net Chinese immigration to San Francisco during the period 1852–59, I estimated the number of Chinese arriving in 1850 as approximately 5,000 and used the 1854 ratios to estimate the total number of arrivals in 1851. Obviously, this number is subject to a good deal of uncertainty, but the overall estimates are probably improved by its inclusion. Third, since the returns prior to 1854 did not include information on the arrivals' country of intended residence, the estimates of immigration to the United States are subject to an upward bias. I enumerated the 1854 arrival data (the first for which country of intended residence is available) two ways: first using the information on intended residence to achieve the desired measure, and then without regard to intended residence. For the United States as a whole, the effect of omitting information on intended residence was to raise the estimated immigration by 1 percent. For specific regions and genders, the effect was more substantial. In New England, omitting country of residence raised the number of male arrivals by 23 percent and female arrivals by 9 percent. In the Old South, the number of male arrivals was inflated by 10 percent. These results are not surprising given the coastal trade with Canada and the South's commercial ties with Europe. I corrected the estimates for these three groups for 1850–53.

The reports of the secretary of state were also the basis of the age-sex distributions for the international immigrants estimated using the procedures outlined above. In some regions, the estimates are quite reliable (the Frontier and the West), whereas in others they are subject to a good deal of uncertainty. This uncertainty arises from the fact that the age-sex tables presented in the reports refer to all arrivals, whereas the immigration figures refer only to foreign born who intend to reside in the United States. Take, for example, the Boston enumeration for the fourth quarter of 1859. Of the 2,908 arrivals, 2,037 intended to reside in the United States, and 605 of these "belonged to" the United States. Thus it is estimated that only 1,432 of the 2,908 arrivals were immigrants. It is quite possible that non-immigrants were different from immigrants with respect to age and sex, with the former perhaps more heavily weighted toward adult males than the latter. In some regions this is not a problem, since all arrivals were foreign born and all intended to reside in the United States.

U.S. Population: 1850 and 1860

The United States population estimates are taken from the published 1850 and 1860 censuses. The data seem reasonably accurate, but there are a few problems. First, the returns for San Francisco, Santa Clara, and Contra Costa counties in California are missing for 1850. No correction was made for this omission. Second, there are a number of territories that were enumerated in 1860 but not enumerated in 1850. I corrected for these omissions in essentially the same fashion as McClelland and Zeckhauser did.[26]

Survival Rates

Calculating the survival rates of immigrants to the end of the decade required a number of distinct steps. First, for the international immigrants it was necessary to determine an age distribution for arrivals each year. This was done using the regional age distributions shown in Table 3.3 above. These distributions are doubtless subject to error. Second, assuming a constant decennial survival rate by age and sex, the probability of surviving to the end of the decade varied according to the year of arrival. For each age group and each year of arrival, the appropriate survival rate to the end of the decade ($X_{i,t}$) was estimated. These were of the form

$$(2) \qquad X_{i,t} = S_i^{0.1(1860 - t)},$$

where S_i is the decennial survival rate for age group i and t is the year of arrival. Third, the different age/date of arrival cells (containing a number of immigrants with a certain survival rate to the end of the decade) were gathered into the age categories 10 to 20, 20 to 30, 30 to 40, 40 to 50, and 50 and up, where the ages are measured at the end of the decade. As a part of the gathering process, it was necessary to prorate the underlying data to fit the above age categories. The fourth step in this process was to assign an arbitrary decennial survival rate to each age group. These were set equal to 1. Then the following equation was solved for the decennial survival rate S_i:

(A1) $P_{60,i} = (P_{50,i-1})S_i + I_i$,

where $P_{60,i}$ is the U.S. population size for age group i in 1860, $P_{50,i-1}$ is the population size for the age group ten years younger in 1850, I_i is the number of immigrants surviving in 1860 who fall in age group i, and S_i is the decennial survival rate for age group i. This equation gives new values for S_i, which are used to recalculate the surviving number of immigrants (I_i). Then S_i is recalculated, and the process continues until there is no change in the survival rate. This iterative process is followed for each age category for both males and females.

Interregional Migration

Interregional migration for each region is first estimated according to the naïve model:

(1) $R_i = P_{60,i} - I_i - (P_{50,i-1})Si$,

where R_i is the net interregional migration into the region by age group i. The naïve model assumes that all international immigrants arriving in the region remained there until the 1860 census was taken.

The demographic data from the published 1850 and 1860 United States censuses are not consistent with this model for the Middle Atlantic and New South regions. The number of international immigrants remaining in these regions vastly exceeds the decade's increase in the number of foreign born in these regions, even taking into account mortality among the foreign born. Thus the naïve model must be modified to take into account movement of international immigrants out of the Middle Atlantic and New South regions. In addition, the regional destination of these international immigrants must be specified. The migration of newly arrived immigrants from the Middle Atlantic and New South is estimated from

(A2) $P_{60,i} = (P_{50,i-1})S_i + aI_i + R_i$,

where a is a positive number less than one representing the proportion of international immigrants remaining in the region until the next census and is calculated as

$$(A3) \qquad a = b\frac{\Delta FB}{I_i} + (1-b)\frac{FB_{60}}{I_i},$$

where $0 \le b \le 1$, ΔFB is the increase in foreign born from 1850 to 1860, and FB_{60} is the number of foreign born in 1860. In other words, a is roughly speaking the weighted proportion of the number of international immigrants remaining in the region of their arrival if all of the existing foreign born remained or if all the existing foreign born disappeared (through death or migration) from the region.

The weighting factor, b, is subject to a good deal of uncertainty. Barring the existence of any outside information, the Principle of Insufficient Reason suggests that b should be set to 0.5. This is in fact the value used for the Middle Atlantic region. For the New South, some outside information can be brought to bear. It is assumed below that international immigrants went from the New South ports of entry to the Northwest and Frontier regions. These regions had in 1860 a foreign-born population that was more heavily weighted toward the Germans than the Irish, these being the largest sources of international immigrants. The New South foreign-born population in 1860, on the other hand, was more heavily weighted toward the Irish. An examination of the passenger arrival records for New Orleans indicated that from 1850 through 1852 immigration was more Irish than German, but from 1853 through 1859 the situation was reversed, with more Germans than Irish arriving. Thus it seemed reasonable to set b to a lower value than 0.5. The value chosen for this paper is 0.25. Once again, the values for b are subject to a good deal of uncertainty. Unlike the assumption for I_i of the naïve estimation model, however, these assumptions are demographically possible. Moreover, as argued in the text, they are in accord with the historical record.

The above calculations are made under the assumption that all international immigrants who moved from their arrival region were continuing their international migration and should not be counted as interregional migrants. *When* an international immigrant moved to a different region in the United States is of some importance. Suppose an international immigrant arrived in the United States immediately after the census enumeration in 1850 and migrated immediately before the 1860 census enumeration. The assumption made here is that such an immigrant would not be an interregional migrant.[27] The above example is not very likely, since immigrants entered the United States throughout the decade, but certainly there are documented cases of indirect migration to a final destination. In some instances, the time elapsed between emigration and arrival at the final destination exceeded three years.[28]

The destinations for the international immigrants passing through the New South were the Frontier and the Northwest. They are assumed to have gone to these regions in proportion to the relative immigration to the two regions as estimated by the naïve model. Thus the majority are assumed to have traveled up the Mississippi River to the Northwest. For the Middle Atlantic, it is assumed that the immigrants went to the Northwest, the Old South, and New England. Since the Old South and New England were subject to net out-migration according to the naïve model, the allocation scheme used for the New South could not be used here. Instead it is assumed that 2 percent of the international immigrants leaving the Middle Atlantic went to the Old South. This is equivalent to about 20 percent of the passengers arriving at Baltimore during the decade. The rationale is that Baltimore was a more reasonable port of entry for Virginia and certain parts of North Carolina than was Charleston, the major Old South port of entry. In addition, this number of immigrants to the Old South approximates the shortfall of international immigrants relative to the increase in foreign born in this region. An additional 3 percent of the international immigrants migrating from the Middle Atlantic are assumed to have traveled to New England. This number approximates the difference between the increase in foreign born in New England and the number of international immigrants. The remaining 95 percent of the international immigrants leaving the Middle Atlantic are assumed to have gone to the Northwest.

CHAPTER FOUR

Economic History and Economic Development: An American Perspective

Barry Poulson

THE GREAT ISSUES of economic growth and development returned to the center stage of economics in the years following the Second World War. In Europe, postwar reconstruction and modernization brought a surprisingly rapid recovery from wartime disruption. America and other developed countries experienced a resurgence of economic growth, following two decades dominated by depression and war. The developing nations, particularly the newly independent ones, attempted to launch the high and sustained rates of growth that had been achieved by the developed nations. An imperative for development also came from the newly created international agencies: the United Nations, the World Bank, and the International Monetary Fund.

In the post–World War Two period, a new literature emerged that Albert Hirschman referred to as "development economics" to distinguish it from both neoclassical and radical economics.[1] Development economists attempted to model the growth process to incorporate the unique structure of the developing countries. Two issues dominated the early structuralist approach to modeling growth: the dualistic nature of the economy, and the balance between sectors in the process of economic development. Later, the central issue shifted to the distribution of income and wealth and welfare in the process of economic development. The empirical foundation for this new development economics was launched by Hollis Chenery and his colleagues at the World Bank. These writers explored the patterns of economic growth and development in the developing countries, analogous to the empirical research on the historical patterns of growth in the developed countries.

Economic historians, too, played a crucial role in this resurgence of interest, most importantly by providing the empirical content necessary to

I wish to thank Donald Schaefer, Thomas Weiss, and other contributors to this volume for their comments on drafts of this chapter. I also wish to thank Cynthia Taft Morris for her careful review of the chapter.

analyze the growth process and design policy. A rich body of empirical work was constructed covering the long-term historical patterns of change in each developed country, and cross-sectional studies compared the developed and developing countries. This school of research on the historical patterns was launched by Simon Kuznets and a group of scholars influenced by his work.

At issue in this research was the relevance of the developed countries' experience to that of the newly developing ones. The initial debate was launched in *The Stages of Economic Growth,* where W. W. Rostow argued that all countries, including the developing ones, followed similar patterns and structural changes in the process of modern economic growth.[2] That view was challenged early on by Simon Kuznets and other economic historians.[3]

This essay endeavors to show that the historical experience of economic growth in the developed countries, including the United States, is relevant to that of the developing countries. This is not to deny the major differences and unique aspects of American development, but it is argued that in the eighteenth and nineteenth centuries, the United States had to cope with many of the issues confronting developing countries today. That experience can help us to understand some of the problems the developing countries have experienced in the twentieth century. This essay will focus on just three of those issues: the pace and pattern of economic growth, the sources of growth, and structural change.

The Pace and Pattern of Economic Growth

Simon Kuznets defined modern economic growth as high and sustained rates of growth of population, income, and income per capita. Kuznets, along with a group of British and continental economic historians, identified the beginnings of growth in England in the late eighteenth century, and in other European countries and their offshoots overseas in the nineteenth century, and contrasted these modern rates of growth with the slower pace that had occurred in the world up to that time.[4] For countries attempting to launch modern economic growth in the twentieth century, it is this early period in the historical experience of growth that is most relevant. How was modern economic growth initiated in the developed countries? What can developing countries learn from that historical experience?

In the early postwar years, the consensus among many economists was that modern growth was initiated in a sharp and discontinuous acceleration followed by high and sustained rates of growth of income and income per capita. Empirical support for this view came first from research on the developed countries, with the work of Rostow being among the most influential. Rostow maintained that modern economic growth was initiated in a series of stages, the most crucial being the takeoff. In that stage, a country experienced a sharp and discontinuous acceleration in the rate of growth of income and income per capita, and rapid industrialization in which a few manufacturing industries played a leading role, pulling the rest of the economy onto a higher growth path. Rostow identified the takeoff in America in the 1840's and 1850's with the rapid growth of the iron and cotton textile industries and with high rates of capital formation in American railroads.[5] This takeoff perspective was pervasive in the development literature of the immediate postwar years. It was implicit in neoclassical growth models, as well as in the dual economy models introduced by Lewis and by Fei and Ranis.[6]

In the postwar years, a number of countries experienced what many development economists described as a growth miracle, a sharp acceleration in growth that seemed to confirm the takeoff hypothesis. The 1979 Organization for Economic Cooperation and Development Report identified ten countries as NICs (Newly Industrializing Countries), including the Asian countries Taiwan, South Korea, Hong Kong, and Singapore, as well as Brazil, Mexico, Greece, Portugal, Spain, and Yugoslavia. Another group of developing countries was expected to join the NICs in the decade of the 1980's.[7]

If the NICs viewed the transition to modern economic growth as a discontinuous takeoff followed by high and sustained rates of growth of income per capita, they were in for a rude awakening. Since 1979, the only countries to sustain high rates of growth have been the Asian NICs. The others have experienced retardation of economic growth over the last decade, and some have fallen out of the group of rapid developers completely.[8] Countries identified as potential NICs in the 1980's have fallen far short of the growth rates projected.

The growth experience of most developing countries throughout the 1980's has been one of retardation. The problem does not appear to have been simply a cyclical fluctuation. The World Bank forecasts continued stagnation, with future growth rates for the developing countries, other than the Asian NICs, far below those of the industrialized countries. Most developing countries have come to the sobering realization that they are not likely to experience a takeoff; some that thought they had are now coping with the realities of retardation in economic growth.

Even for the Asian NICs that have sustained growth throughout the postwar years, recent empirical work casts doubt on the takeoff hypothesis. The origins of growth in these countries can be traced back to the prewar period. In Taiwan and South Korea, for example, significant progress was made prior to and during the Second World War, when they were under Japanese occupation.[9] Those early investments in agriculture and agricultural processing as well as in light industries laid the groundwork for industrialization and economic growth in the postwar period. The precedent for increased investment in education and human capital also dates back to the earlier period. Viewed from this longer perspective, the transition to modern economic growth was not sharp and discontinuous, but rather covered a long period marked by episodes of economic growth and retardation. If the transition to modern growth in developing countries is marked by fits and starts that cover a long period of time, then its explanation must be more complex than that implied by the takeoff hypothesis.

Over longer periods of time, the pace and pattern of growth in developing countries has been clearly influenced by instability in the international economy. Some international shocks have had positive impacts; in Mexico and Brazil, for example, the Second World War stimulated domestic manufactures by limiting trade with the belligerent countries. Rapid advance in productivity and output for manufactures during the war laid the groundwork for postwar industrialization and economic development in many Latin American countries. Other international shocks, however, such as those in oil prices and in financial markets, as well as the worldwide recession of the 1980's, have had negative effects on economic growth in the developing countries. The explanation for the success or failure of countries in sustaining economic growth in the postwar period has depended to a considerable extent on the response made to these external shocks. These differences are especially apparent in stabilization policies and structural adjustments since the onset of the debt crises in 1982.

None of this should have been surprising. The history of the advanced countries makes clear that the transition to modern economic growth is a long, drawn-out process marked by volatility in rates of growth. The origins of that growth cannot be identified in the few structural changes implied by the takeoff hypothesis. Economic historians were among the first to express serious doubts about the idea of a takeoff into self-sustained growth, and some of the strongest criticism came from those engaged in research into the empirical foundations of early American growth.

One of the most important contributions that economic historians made was the construction of empirical evidence on early American economic growth.[10] Robert Gallman estimated national income back to 1839, and found very high rates of growth over the period 1839 to 1859, with output and output per capita increasing at average annual rates of 5 percent and 1.8 percent respectively. These rates are comparable to those for the period after 1860, and to the rates of growth estimated by Kuznets for other developed countries at an incipient phase of modern economic growth. Although this evidence was consistent with Rostow's hypothesis about the American takeoff, Gallman was skeptical. For one thing, little was known about the rate of growth in the years before the alleged takeoff. The economy's performance in that earlier period has been difficult to gauge because of the paucity of data; one economic historian referred to it as an empirical dark age.

More recently, Gallman and Engerman provided a very careful survey of the empirical work on that early period and concluded:

No full consensus has yet been established. Nonetheless, it is clear that the period (1807–1837) was one of economic growth and structural change, during which industrial production was beginning to shift from home and shop to factory. Real output expanded rapidly and most students of the period would agree that per capita product—properly defined to include home production—was also increasing, if at a rate which came to seem low by the standards of subsequent experience. Agreement becomes more difficult when the question of the relative rates of growth of per capita product in the decades before and after 1837 (1807–1837; 1837–1860) is raised. Some scholars would argue that acceleration was in evidence before the Civil War; others, only after it. But neither group would hold that acceleration was sudden; both see it as a fairly gradual process.[11]

In contrast to a takeoff, economic historians have stressed long swings or fluctuations in economic growth with a periodicity longer than the business cycle.[12] Kuznets found evidence of long swings in his work on national income, and Gallman and Engerman suggest that long swings are evident in the early nineteenth century as well:

Simplifying somewhat, we may say that the economic history of the years 1793–1860 divides into three major expansions and perhaps two and a quarter major contractions. . . . These were not business cycle movements, but they may have been Kuznets cycles (or long swings). Kuznets cycles are identified by changes in rates of growth and run between 15 and 25 years, from peak to peak or trough to trough. This seems to be a good way of looking at things.[13]

Other studies have also provided empirical support for the view that American economic growth in the nineteenth century was characterized by long swings.[14] The implication is that we must be very cautious in interpreting periods of rapid economic growth as a discontinuous takeoff. The economic growth of the NICs may also be subject to long swings.

Nor should we expect a country to sustain a smooth and constant trend rate of economic growth. As Kuznets suggested, in America the trend rate of growth of income and income per capita was steadily declining from the late nineteenth through the early twentieth centuries.[15] Gallman's work extending back to the first half of the nineteenth century also revealed evidence of retardation in the rate of growth of capital formation, as well as income and income per capita, from the late nineteenth through the early twentieth centuries.[16]

The empirical evidence, then, reveals both volatility and retardation in the pace and pattern of economic growth in America, as well as in other advanced countries, in the nineteenth century. It should not be surprising to find similar evidence of volatility and retardation in the pace and pattern of growth in developing countries in the twentieth century. Thus the post-war acceleration in the rate of growth observed in some developing countries may have been the upswing of a long swing, and the more recent retardation may reflect its downswing. A climacteric or retardation phase in the growth trend in developing countries may also become evident. The Asian NICs are likely to experience retardation as they attempt to sustain their high rates of economic growth into the twenty-first century. If the pace and pattern of economic growth in the developing countries exhibits volatility and retardation, this has important implications for policy, and this possibility cannot be ruled out on the basis of the limited evidence available so far.

The Sources of Modern Economic Growth

The simultaneous evolution of growth theory and empirical research on economic growth converged in the literature of growth accounting in the postwar period. Initially this work was conducted within the context of neoclassical growth models with rather restrictive assumptions. Subsequent research relaxed those simplifying assumptions, but the initial findings based on the simpler growth models proved to be very robust. This research in growth accounting has been criticized on a number of grounds, but as long as it is interpreted as providing insight into the sources of growth and not as causal explanations, it helps us to sort out some important issues.

One of the first puzzles posed early on by Simon Kuznets was whether differences in the rate of economic growth in developed and developing countries could be explained by differences in rates of capital formation, as implied by the simple Harrod-Domar growth model.[17] Subsequent work, utilizing a Cobb-Douglas production function, distinguished between that portion of economic growth accounted for by capital and other factor inputs, and that due to residual sources of productivity change. Cobb-Douglas production functions fitted to U.S. data for the postwar period revealed that the residual measure accounted for most of the growth in income and virtually all of the growth in income per capita.[18]

Our first glimpse into growth accounting for the nineteenth century was provided by Robert Gallman. He found that growth of factor inputs accounted for a larger share of growth in total output in the nineteenth century than in the twentieth, but that productivity advance was the major source of growth in output per capita in both centuries: [19]

Productivity change accounted for almost six-tenths of the growth of per capita NNP in the 19th century. This is lower than the figure for the 20th century (almost eight-tenths), but is by no means low.[20]

The important question raised by Gallman's analysis is how the United States was able to achieve high rates of productivity advance, and why productivity accounted for the major share of economic growth, not only in the twentieth century, but during the transition to modern economic growth in the nineteenth century as well.

Capital formation has been one of the keys. According to the evidence assembled by Davis and Gallman, even in the first half of the nineteenth century the rate of capital formation was already high, and it increased over the century.[21] In the decades before the Civil War, gross capital formation accounted for more than 10 percent and net capital formation more than 5 percent of gross national product. Those figures more than doubled over the course of the century. The rate of growth of capital formation exceeded the rate of growth of other factor inputs and the rate of productivity advance. The capital stock also increased faster than output, resulting in a capital/output ratio that increased from 2.8 to 3.4 between 1840 and 1900.[22]

This evidence seemed to support the importance placed on capital formation in early growth models, but Davis and Gallman emphasized caution. The high rate of capital formation and the high capital/output ratios in the early nineteenth century suggested that some of the acceleration in capital formation must have preceded as well as accompanied the transition to modern economic growth. Further, the increase in the rate of growth of capital formation was not smooth; rather, it exhibited periods of acceleration and retardation consistent with the long swing hypothesis. Finally, the increase in the rate of growth of capital formation occurred over most of the nineteenth century; it was not concentrated in a few decades at mid-century, as implied by the takeoff.[23]

The explanation for the rise in the capital/output ratio and for acceleration in the rate of capital formation in the nineteenth century remains in doubt. Davis and Gallman maintained that the general rise in the capital/output ratios across all sectors of the economy implies that shifts in the investment function in response to changes in aggregate demand were relatively less important than shifts in the savings function. The investment function could have shifted due to technological change or to changes in the price of capital relative to other factor inputs. Davis and Gallman concluded that the latter was probably more important because the capital/output ratios rose across all sectors. They found that the relative price of capital fell because technical advance reduced the cost of material inputs, such as iron and steel and machine tools, that went into the capital goods industry output; and falling interest rates lowered the cost of capital.

They found that the savings function shifted in the nineteenth century for several reasons. Increased rates of household savings were associated with increased commercialization of economic activity, requiring higher rates of savings to meet greater intertemporal variations in the household income stream. Davis and Gallman concluded that demographic change had a positive effect on savings rates. Rapid population growth increased the share of those economically active with higher savings rates; and decreases in mortality and increases in life expectancy increased demands for savings to finance retirement.

The emergence of modern financial institutions increased the incentives to save and invest, and improved the efficiency of capital markets.[24] Over the course of the nineteenth century, governmental institutions more clearly defined and protected property rights and provided easier access for modern capital-market institutions in competitive markets. The result was a relatively free flow of both domestic and foreign savings into productive investment and capital formation. Throughout the nineteenth century, the U.S. was a net debtor nation, attracting a significant flow of foreign investment into infrastructure, such as canals and railroads. The resulting expansion of productive capacity enabled the country to shift from being a net debtor to become the world's largest creditor nation after World War I.[25]

Growth accounting for the developing countries has revealed that productivity has advanced at a slower pace, and increases in the factor inputs have accounted for a larger share of the growth in output per capita, than has been true in the advanced nations. The pace of productivity advance in many developing countries today is slower than it was in the U.S. in the nineteenth as well as in the twentieth century. It has also been found that the rate of growth of capital formation has accelerated rapidly, and in many of the developing countries currently exceeds that of the more advanced nations. The increase in the rate of capital formation in these developing countries in the twentieth century is quite comparable to the acceleration found by Gallman and Davis for the U.S. in the nineteenth century. This evidence suggests that increases in factor inputs in general, and capital formation in particular, play a more important role in the transition to modern economic growth in developing countries today than occurred in the American transition to modern economic growth.

Many development economists have been surprised by the high rates of domestic savings and investment in the developing countries. The acceleration in capital formation in many of them has been financed primarily from increased private domestic savings, and much was generated by the traditional and agricultural sectors.[26] Farmers and producers in the traditional sectors who did not have access to modern capital-market institutions financed capital formation from their own family's or their neighbors' resources. A major source of that capital formation has been family labor applied to projects such as land clearing and improvements, and construction from readily available inputs. For poor households with limited access to modern financial institutions, the accumulation of land, tools, and construction from their own labor constitute a more important form of savings than financial assets. Only at a later stage in the growth process have modern capital-market institutions evolved to perform more efficiently the functions of financial intermediation.[27]

The evidence for the developing countries suggests a complex relationship between the demographic transition and rates of savings.[28] Neoclassical and dual-economy growth models both suggest that rapid population growth has a negative effect on the rate of savings and investment, yet empirical studies of savings and investment in the developing countries yield little evidence of this negative relationship. In poor countries, children are often viewed as an asset, contributing to the family's income and wealth over their lifetime. In primitive capital markets, where parents rely upon children to provide for them in old age, the children may be viewed as a form of savings. Similarly, expenditures for the education and health of children may be viewed as a form of investment rather than of consumption. What is clear is that family size and savings decisions are made jointly by the household, and these decisions are less likely to be influenced by each other than by other factors, such as the level of income per capita.

Capital fundamentalism, a view prevalent in the development literature of the post–World War II years, greatly influenced policies in many developing countries. In this view, an inadequate rate of domestic savings and investment was the major constraint to economic growth in the developing countries. This argument was expanded in the two-gap models introduced by Chenery and others, in which the rate of growth is constrained either by the gap between domestic savings and required investment, or by the foreign exchange gap, that is, the foreign exchange required to purchase imported capital goods, and the supply of foreign exchange generated by exports. It was a simple step from this view of capital fundamentalism to dirigiste policies: governments would have to mobilize savings and investment; and foreign aid and capital flows would have to be channeled to the host governments in developing countries.

There is little evidence from either the developed or the developing countries to support capital fundamentalism and its dirigiste policy implications.[29] In retrospect, many of the failures of developing countries in the postwar years can be attributed to policy planners who were influenced by capital fundamentalism to view savings and capital formation as exogenous to modern economic growth. Governments in many developing countries have pursued policies of financial repression (e.g., controlling interest rates, limiting entry into capital markets, and regulating financial markets). In most of these countries, the government has emerged as a net borrower rather than a net saver, crowding out private savings and investment. More recently, many of these developing countries, having learned the hard way, have shifted to policies of financial liberalization.

Nor is it clear that foreign capital flows are a necessary condition for increased rates of savings and investment. Although foreign capital has often played a significant role in the transition to modern economic growth, the evidence for both developed and developing countries is that higher rates of capital formation have been financed primarily from increased rates of domestic savings and investment. Indeed, what distinguishes the more successful of the developing countries is not their reliance upon foreign capital, but rather their success in generating higher rates of private domestic savings and investment. Even for the most successful NICs, such as Korea, most of the acceleration in capital formation was financed from private domestic savings rather than from foreign savings; and Korea quickly shifted from a net debtor to a net creditor nation. Foreign aid and capital flows channeled through governments are increasingly viewed as barriers to capital formation and modern economic growth in the developing countries.[30]

Structural Change

Our understanding of structural transformation owes much to the work of Simon Kuznets, whose broad new view encompassed demographic, technological, and economic changes as well as the institutional and ideological framework within which these changes occurred.[31] The centerpiece of this transformation has been changes in industrial structure.[32] Declines in the agricultural shares of output and inputs and the expansion of the industrial and service sectors have accompanied the process of modern economic growth in all of the developed countries.

Kuznets's time series and cross-sectional analysis of the developed countries in the late nineteenth and twentieth centuries revealed that structural transformation was accompanied by the convergence of productivity among the different sectors of the economy. The agricultural sector, with the lowest level of productivity, experienced the highest rate of productivity advance; the service sector, with the highest level of productivity, experienced the lowest rate of productivity advance. As a result, productivity in both sectors tended to converge toward that of industry.

Robert Gallman extended this analysis for the U.S. back to the early nineteenth century.[33] His studies of the early transition to economic growth in the United States and of long-term changes in agricultural productivity raised questions about the precise pattern and rate of structural change. The data problems for this early period are formidable, especially the estimates of the industrial structure of the labor force. Given the fact that around 80 percent of the labor force was engaged in agriculture at the beginning of the nineteenth century, much of the analysis of structural change hinges on estimates of productivity change in that sector.

In his early work on agricultural productivity, Gallman utilized the Lebergott labor-force series, but he expressed reservations regarding the trends in its structure.[34] In subsequent work, Gallman argued that Lebergott's series underestimated the rate of growth of the agricultural labor force in the first half of the nineteenth century. Gallman concluded that labor productivity in American agriculture advanced relatively slowly in the first half of the nineteenth century and accelerated in the second half, but he did not attempt to date the acceleration. Other research has tended to support this view of a slower rate of agricultural transformation, and more clearly identifies the period of acceleration in productivity advance after 1840.[35]

The slower pace of productivity advance in American agriculture in the early nineteenth century did not prevent that sector from experiencing rapid growth in output. The rate of growth of agricultural output prior to 1840 was, in fact, higher than that after 1840, but this was due primarily to the growth of factor inputs. The rate of growth of agricultural labor as well as land and capital was higher prior to 1840 than after. Agricultural output was advancing more rapidly than population, and the sector absorbed a rapidly growing labor force.

Gallman found, on the other hand, that the nonagricultural sector advanced at a rapid pace after 1840.[36] The structural transformation is clear in that period, with the industrial sector experiencing rapid growth in productivity and output, and absorbing a rapidly growing share of the labor force. My own work suggests that in the decades prior to 1840, structural change was slower; industrial output and labor force advanced more rapidly than their agricultural counterparts, but not at the rapid pace evident after 1840. Productivity change in both the industrial and agricultural sectors advanced more slowly in the pre-1840 period.[37]

Evidence of a relatively slower pace of structural transformation in the early nineteenth century should not obscure the important changes that did occur. Both agriculture and industry were able to absorb a rapidly growing labor force and capital stock with modest increases in the productivity of these inputs. This growth set the stage for a more rapid structural transformation after 1840. The earlier period, then, produced the crucial structural change in the transition to modern economic growth.[38]

Development economists have established a rich theoretical and empirical literature on structural change, but little of this work has focused on the initial transition to modern economic growth.[39] This literature reveals some important differences between the structural transformation in the developing countries and that which occurred in the United States and Europe in the early transition to modern economic growth. In the advanced countries during the initial transition, both the agricultural and the industrial sectors were able to absorb a rapidly growing labor force and capital stock with modest improvement in productivity. Developing countries in the postwar period have often failed to do this, and have experienced declining productivity of labor in the primary sectors and underutilization of labor and other inputs in both the primary and the industrial sectors. In many of these countries, the decline in agriculture's share of employment has lagged the decline in its share of output.[40] As a result, labor productivity in agriculture has declined, absolutely as well as relative to the industrial sector.[41]

These differences in the patterns of structural change underscore the importance of the agricultural sector during the initial transition to modern economic growth. As Chenery and Syrquin suggest, part of the difference is due to the relative abundance of land and resources in large countries such as the United States; but in many developing countries, much is due to dirigiste policies, which have either neglected the agricultural sector or, worse, benefited the urban-industrial sector at the expense of agriculture.[42] Government policies in many developing countries introduced disincentives for improvements in productivity, and in some cases decreased output and employment in the agricultural sector.[43]

Rapid industrialization achieved at the expense of the agricultural sector has ill served the developing countries. Balanced growth of the primary and nonprimary sectors of the economy appears to be a prerequisite to modern economic growth. Only after this process is well underway will a significant transfer of resources from agriculture to the more productive nonagricultural industries occur. At a mature phase of the process, agricultural productivity can advance more rapidly and converge toward that of the nonagricultural sectors, as Kuznets suggested. This pattern, however, is not likely to occur in a country just initiating modern economic growth.

Recently, some of the developing countries have begun to address the problem of improving productivity and expanding output and employment in their agricultural and traditional sectors. The key to the structural transformation in the early transition, as evidenced by the experience of the United States and other developed nations, seems to be the ability of these sectors to absorb more resources, especially labor, without a deterioration in productivity or standard of living. This may be achieved in part through technical advance, but much will depend upon the efficient utilization of the factor inputs, and in particular a more intensive use of labor.

Conclusion

What is the relevance of economic history for economic development? The work of economic historians makes clear that important lessons can be learned from the American experience of the nineteenth century. These inferences are made, recognizing the important differences between the institutional structures of the developed and the developing countries, and within the set of developing countries.

The first lesson is that the transition to modern economic growth is likely to be quite volatile. The growth process is likely to be characterized by fits and starts of more- and less-rapid economic growth, and by periods of secular retardation. These episodes may have a periodicity comparable to the long swings in American economic growth. This insight was overlooked or ignored by many developing countries in the post–World War II period, who envisioned instead that their economies would experience a takeoff into high and sustained rates of economic growth. For some developing countries, such as Mexico, this misperception led to unrealistically ambitious development policies that could not be sustained during the retardation of the 1980's. Even for the NICs that have managed to sustain growth, the historical evidence suggests that their growth may be subject to retardation as they approach the twenty-first century.

The second lesson is that the transition will be accompanied by higher rates of growth of both labor and capital inputs. An important problem, then, is a country's ability to absorb these increased inputs without encountering diminishing returns. The agricultural and traditional sectors play key roles in the transition because they account for the predominant share of these inputs. Many developing countries ignored historical precedents and for much of the post–World War II period channeled resources into the industrial sector, often at the expense of the agricultural and traditional sectors. Those resources were often mobilized through foreign borrowing and foreign aid by the government. As a result, output and productivity in the agricultural and traditional sectors fell, and those sectors were less able to absorb the rapidly growing labor force. In many cases, this resulted in rising unemployment and underutilization of the factor inputs in all sectors.

Only recently have developing countries learned the important lesson— that the transition requires a balanced growth among sectors—and revised their development policies accordingly. With balanced economic growth, the agricultural sector can play a key role, as it did in the American transition: expanding output, absorbing a rapidly growing labor force, and mobilizing higher rates of savings, investment, and capital formation. We should not expect the agricultural sector to experience rapid productivity advance, nor the industrial sector to absorb much of the labor force during the initial transition. Those structural changes are evident only at a later stage in the development process, long after the transition stage.

The final lesson from the American experience is the importance of the institutional framework for economic growth and development. Balanced economic growth requires government policies and institutions that do not exploit agriculture and traditional sectors, but rather create incentives for productive activity there as well as in other sectors. The failures of government policies in some developing countries, such as Mexico, are only now being addressed through revitalization of the agricultural and traditional sectors, and rationalization and privatization of the industrial sector.

American institutions in the nineteenth century established a capitalist system that defined and enforced private-property rights and set limits on the power of government to interfere with those private-property rights. Those institutional arrangements were conducive to productive activity as opposed to rent-seeking activity, and ultimately to rapid economic growth and development.[44] In contrast, dirigiste policies and institutions have dominated much of the developing world in the post–World War II period. There is a growing recognition that these dirigiste policies and institutions have created an environment in which there is much incentive for rent-seeking rather than productive activity. Much of the failure of developing countries to achieve sustained economic growth and development in the post–World War II period can be traced to these institutional arrangements and to the failures of public policy. The search for constitutional democracy and the recent dismantling of costly experiments in socialist economic planning in many developing countries is motivated by this perception.[45] It is the common set of human aspirations, as Kuznets reminded us, that enables us to explore the phenomenon of modern economic growth and development among all countries.

PART TWO

Institutions in Economic History

CHAPTER FIVE

❧ Institutional Change in American Economic History

Douglass North

WHAT SHAPES THE long-run growth of economies? In this essay I argue that it is the way institutions evolve that shapes long-run economic performance, and I illustrate my argument by examining nineteenth-century U.S. economic performance.[1] In subsequent sections I explore the underlying institutional characteristics of a growing economy, the nature of institutions and the relationship between them and economic performance, and the nature of institutional change; I sketch the institutional evolution of the American economy in the nineteenth century; and finally I analyze that development in the light of the framework developed in the first three sections.

Adaptive Efficiency

In order to explore the nature of long-run economic change, it is necessary to think of the issue of economic efficiency in somewhat different terms than those customarily used in standard economic theory, which examines allocation at an instant in time. The key to sustained economic growth is adaptive rather than allocative efficiency. Adaptive efficiency is concerned with the ability of a society to acquire knowledge and learning, to induce innovation, to undertake risk and creative activity of all sorts, and to resolve problems and bottlenecks of the society through time. The society that permits the maximum generation of trials is the one that has the best likelihood of solving problems through time, as Hayek has persuasively argued.[2] Adaptive efficiency, therefore, consists of encouraging the development of decentralized decision-making processes that will allow societies to explore many alternative ways to solve problems. It is equally essential to learn from failures so that change consists of the generation of organizational trials and the elimination of organizational failures.

I would like to thank Brad Hansen for research assistance, and Elisabeth Case for editing this essay.

There is nothing simple about this process, since organizational failure may be not only probabilistic, but also systematic, due to preferences with respect to ideologies that may give people, on the basis of imperfect knowledge, preferences for solutions that are not oriented to such efficiency.

Institutions define the incentive structure of a society. Different institutional rules determine what kinds of economic activity will be profitable and viable and also shape the adaptive efficiency of firms and other organizations. The institutions affect performance as a result of rules that regulate entry, governance structures, and the flexibility of organizations. In particular, rules that encourage the development and utilization of tacit knowledge, and therefore creative entrepreneurial talent, will be important. Competition, decentralized decision-making, and well-specified property rights as well as bankruptcy law are crucial. It is essential to have rules that eliminate not only failed economic organizations but unsuccessful political ones as well. The structure of rules, therefore, must be one that not only rewards successes but also vetoes the survival of maladapted parts of the organizational structure.

The criteria for realizing allocative efficiency are seldom if ever specified in terms of the institutional framework, but they implicitly include secure property rights and enforcement of contracts. The more perplexing issue is just how the rules would be balanced between the security of existing organizations and the encouragement of innovation and displacement—in effect, the creative destruction in Schumpeter's vision. It is not obvious that the ideal rules for current allocation are also ideal for encouraging the conditions for adaptive efficiency in a world of positive transaction costs.

Whether or not adaptive and allocative efficiency are compatible, the political economy of institutional evolution can and will result in a persistent tension between the security of existing organizations and innovation. It is in the interest of existing firms, trade unions, farm groups, and so on to try to devise political and economic rules that protect their own current well-being. The resultant sclerosis has been the theme of Mancur Olson's *The Rise and Decline of Nations,* but because that study is devoid of political institutions it cannot explain just how this sclerosis comes about.[3] It is essential to understand the nature of institutions, how they affect performance, and how they change in order to explore meaningfully the dynamics of economic change and, specifically, to account for structural changes in the American economy.

The Nature of Institutions

Institutions are the constraints that people impose upon themselves to structure human interaction. They consist of formal rules, informal constraints, and their enforcement characteristics. Together they provide the rules of the game of human interaction. They directly influence the cost of transacting and producing by their effect on the security and enforceability of contracts, which will in turn influence the technology employed. The costliness of defining and enforcing agreements reflects the effectiveness of the institutions. The ability at low cost to measure what is being exchanged and to enforce agreements across time and space requires complex institutional structures; conversely, the inability at low cost to measure and enforce agreements has been a consequence of institutions that have made it costly to transact. The evolution of more complex institutions that make possible cooperative exchange relations extending over long periods of time, amongst individuals without personal knowledge of each other, is the essential underpinning of the specialization and division of labor that was the basis of Adam Smith's *The Wealth of Nations*. The combination of formal rules, informal constraints, and enforcement characteristics of institutions defines the humanly devised constraints and, together with the traditional constraints of standard theory, the choice set. To understand the choices available in an exchange, one must take into account all these dimensions.

Institutional Change

A full understanding of institutional change requires knowledge of the stability characteristics of the institutions, the sources of change, the agents of change, and the direction of change.

A basic function of institutions is to provide stability and continuity to exchange relationships. A necessary condition for the low transactions costs that underlie high-income societies is channels of exchange, both political and economic, which make possible credible agreements. This condition is accomplished by the complexity of the set of constraints that constitute institutions. These include first formal constraints: rules nested in a hierarchy, each level more costly to change than the previous one. In the United States, the hierarchy moves from individual contracts to statute and common law to constitutional rules. Political rules are nested in a hierarchy even at the level of specific bills before Congress. Both the structure of committees and agenda control assure that the status quo is favored over change.

Second are informal constraints, which are even more important anchors of stability. They are extensions, elaborations, and qualifications of rules that "solve" numerous exchange problems not completely covered by formal rules, and they have a tenacious ability to survive. They allow people to go about the everyday process of making exchanges without needing to think out the terms of exchange exactly at each point and in each instance. Routines, customs, traditions, and culture are words we use to denote the persistence of informal constraints. The complex interaction of rules and informal constraints, together with how they are enforced, shapes our daily living and directs us in the mundane activities that dominate our lives. It is important to stress that these stability features in no way guarantee that the institutions are efficient (here defined simply as a set of constraints that will result in economic growth). Stability is a necessary condition for complex human interaction, but it is not a sufficient condition for efficiency.

One major source of institutional change has been fundamental changes in relative prices,[4] but another has been changes in preferences. I know of no way to explain the demise of slavery in the nineteenth century in an interest-group model. The growing abhorrence on the part of civilized human beings of one person owning another not only spawned the antislavery movements but also, through the institutional mechanism of voting, resulted in slavery's elimination. It is not that interest groups did not use the abolitionist movement to further their interests. They did. But the success of the interest groups required the ideological support of the voter.[5] The voter paid only the price of going to the polls to express his conviction, and the slave owner had no feasible way to bribe or pay off voters to prevent them from expressing their beliefs. Institutions make ideas matter.

The agent of change is the entrepreneur—political or economic. So far, I have left organizations and their entrepreneurs out of this analysis, and the definition of institutions has focused on the rules of the game rather than the players. Organizations are firms, trade unions, cooperatives (economic), legislative bodies, political parties, regulatory agencies (political), churches, athletic clubs (social). It is essential to distinguish between the constraints people impose on their interaction and the activities they and their organizations engage in within those constraints. The distinction is analogous to that in a competitive sport between analyzing the rules on the one hand and analyzing the structure and strategy of the team and players on the other. It is the entrepreneurs engaged in purposive activity to achieve objectives who make the choices that ultimately result in altering institutions. Organizations and learning alter outcomes, but how?

More than half a century ago, Ronald Coase argued that transaction costs are the basis for the existence of the firm.[6] That is, if information and enforcement were costless, it would be hard to envision a significant role for organization. What is it about transaction costs that leads to organization? The answers have ranged from the firm being a form of exploitation,[7] to a response to asset specificity,[8] to a response to measurement costs.⁹ Whatever the merits of these alternatives (and they are not altogether mutually exclusive), they all focus on the trees, not the forest. Organizations are a response to the institutional structure of societies, and consequently may alter that institutional structure.

The institutional constraints together with the traditional constraints of economic theory define the potential wealth-maximizing opportunities of entrepreneurs (political or economic). If the constraints result in the highest payoffs in the economy being criminal activity, or in a firm's sabotaging or burning down a competitor, or in a union's engaging in slowdowns and makework, then we can expect that organizations will be shaped to maximize at those margins. On the other hand, if the payoffs come from activities that enhance productivity, then we expect that economic growth will result. In either case, the entrepreneur and his or her organization will invest in acquiring knowledge, coordination, and "learning-by-doing" skills in order to enhance the profitable potential. As the organization evolves to capture the potential returns, it will gradually alter the institutional constraints. It will do so either indirectly, via the interaction between maximizing behavior and its effect on gradually eroding or modifying informal constraints, or directly, via investing in altering the formal rules. The relative rate of return on investing within the formal constraints or devoting resources to altering the constraints will reflect the structure of the polity, the payoffs to altering the rules, and the costs of political investment.

But it is not just the efforts of organizations to alter the rules that shape institutional change and hence long-run economic performance. It is also the kinds of skills and knowledge in which organizations induce the society to invest. Investment in formal education, new technologies, and pure science have been a derived demand resulting from the perceived payoff to such investment. Equally, the failure to invest in knowledge throughout history or in current Third World societies has resulted from the perception among political and economic entrepreneurs that there was not a high payoff to them from such investment. In the case of some Third World countries, educational investment has been misdirected toward higher education (where the social rate of return is low) rather than primary education (where it is high), reflecting misperception of the relevant returns. Investment in knowledge and skills with high social rates of return will continually widen the opportunity set and is an essential ingredient in adaptive efficiency.

Institutional change, then, is an incremental process in which the short-run profitable opportunities cumulatively create the long-run path of change. The long-run consequences are often unintended for two reasons. First, the entrepreneurs are seldom interested in the larger (external to them) consequences, but the direction of their investment influences the extent to which there is investment that adds to or disseminates the stock of knowledge, encourages or discourages factor mobility, and so on. Second, there is frequently a significant difference between intended outcomes and actual outcomes. Outcomes frequently diverge from intentions because of the limited capabilities of the individuals and the complexity of the problems to be solved.

The U.S. Economy in the Nineteenth Century

I expand on this analysis of institutional change by reframing a familiar story: the growth of the American economy in the nineteenth century. The basic institutional framework that had been carried over from England not only encouraged decentralized and local political autonomy but also provided low-cost economic transacting through fee-simple ownership of land (with some early exceptions in proprietary colonies) and secure property rights. The postrevolutionary enactments of the Northwest Ordinance and the Constitution codified, elaborated, and modified colonial institutions in the light of contemporary issues (and the bargaining strength of the players). They also created an institutional environment (including, for example, norms of behavior rewarding hard work) that broadly induced the development of economic and political organizations (Congress, local political bodies, family farms, merchant houses, and shipping firms) whose maximizing activities promoted increased productivity and economic growth, both directly and indirectly by an induced demand for education. Moreover, as these organizations evolved to take advantage of these opportunities, they not only became more efficient, but also gradually altered the institutional framework.[10] Not only was the political and judicial framework altered (the Marshall Court decisions, the Fourteenth Amendment) and the structure of property rights modified (Munn vs. Illinois) by the end of the century, but so too were many norms of behavior and other informal constraints (reflected, for example, in changing attitudes toward slavery and blacks, and the role of women in society and temperance). The changes were certainly not unidirectional toward increased productivity or improved human welfare (however defined). The profitable opportunities sometimes came from tariff creation, the exploitation of slaves, or the formation of a trust. Sometimes, indeed frequently, the results were unanticipated by the political or economic entrepreneurs. Exogenous forces, such as changes in political or economic conditions in the rest of the world, induced changes in the American economy by altering relative political or economic prices faced by domestic political and economic entrepreneurs and their organizations, hence leading them to actions that altered the institutional framework.

We can be more precise about the details of this process by focusing on one particular aspect of this history: the Northwest Ordinance and subsequent land policy. The ordinance was enacted by the Continental Congress in 1787 at the very time that the Constitutional Convention was being held in Philadelphia. It was the third act to deal with a whole range of issues concerned with the governance and settlement of the vast area of land to the west, and it provided a framework by which the territories would be integrated into the new nation.

The ordinance is brief. It provided for rules of inheritance and fee-simple ownership of land, set up the basic structure of territorial governments, and provided for the mechanisms by which territories gradually became self-governing. Additionally, it provided for when a territory could be admitted as a state. Then there was a series of Articles of Compact, in effect a bill of rights for the territories. There were additional provisions about good faith to the Indians, free navigation on the Mississippi and St. Lawrence rivers, public debt, land disposal, the number of states that could be divided up within the Northwest Territory, and finally a provision prohibiting slavery in the territories (although the return of runaway slaves was specified).

The provisions of the act can be traced directly to the English and Colonial background; many of them, including much of the bill of rights, were explicit provisions of colonial charters.[11] The impetus for the act was relative price changes stemming from the financial crisis of the new nation and states as they emerged from the revolution, combined with the necessity of developing policies to administer the vast territories that had been acquired as a result of the peace treaty following independence. The controversies that shaped specific provisions of the ordinance arose from their implications for the current and future distribution of political power and (not unrelated) the slavery issue.[12]

The agents of change (and their organizations) were the Reverend Manasseh Cutler (and the Ohio and Scioto Companies), who asked Congress to provide a settled plan of self-government for the proposed settlers of the huge blocks of land Congress had granted to those companies (thereby inducing Congress to establish the committee that wrote the ordinance); and Nathan Dane and Rufus King, representatives from Massachusetts and members of that committee, who wrote many of the act's provisions, specifically the one barring slavery in the Northwest Territory.[13]

The downstream consequences of the act were continually being shaped by the relative price changes that reflected the rising implicit rents to be derived from the increasing value of land together with the government's sale prices and weak enforcement policies. The consequent rapid settlement in turn altered the political balance of power. Territories became states with different interests and therefore with agendas that reshaped later public-land policies. Claims clubs emerged to thwart competitive bidding; squatters finally got a general preemption act; the minimum of units for sale was reduced, and eventually the Homestead Act was passed.

Some of the consequences may have been unanticipated. The prohibition of slavery in the new territories, for example, induced a large proportion of settlers to come from New England; they brought with them attitudes that were distinctly different from those of settlers from other regions and from those of immigrants. They were more literate, a lower proportion were tenants, and they possessed greater real-estate wealth.[14] Their attitudes played a major role in early investment in public education and in other public policies that were in distinct contrast to those which evolved in territories south of the Ohio, where slavery was permitted.

Institutional and Cliometric Economic History

Both the institutional story and the traditional economic history of the cliometrician use neoclassical price theory and the quantitative techniques of cliometrics. There is a difference between the two, however; the former abandons a crucial assumption of neoclassical theory and incorporates an important feature of institutions. Abandoned is instrumental rationality and incorporated is the increasing returns characteristic of institutions that produces path dependence.

By instrumental rationality, we mean that the actors have correct theories by which to interpret the world around them, or if they have initially incorrect theories, the information feedback that they receive will lead them to correct their theories. Herbert Simon has accurately summarized the implications of such an assumption as follows:

If we accept values as given and constant, if we postulate an objective description of the world as it really is, and if we assume that the decisionmaker's computational powers are unlimited, then two important consequences follow. First we do not need to distinguish between the real world and the decisionmaker's perception of it: He or she perceives the world as it really is. Second, we can predict the choices that will be made by a rational decisionmaker entirely from our knowledge of the real world and without a knowledge of the decisionmaker's perceptions or modes of calculation (we do, of course, have to know his or her utility function).[15]

On the other hand, if we assume that both the knowledge and the computational ability of the decision maker are severely limited, then we must model the actor's perception of the world, which in turn will shape the choices he or she makes. We are as interested in how the actors come to perceive the world as we are in the actual circumstances surrounding the actor.

In contrast to the rational person in neoclassical economics who always reaches the decision that is objectively, or substantively, best in terms of the given utility function, the rational person of procedural rationality goes about making his or her decisions in a way that is reasonable in the light of the available knowledge and means of computation.

The implications of procedural rationality as opposed to instrumental rationality are far-reaching for our understanding of economics and economic history. Institutions are unnecessary in a world of instrumental rationality; ideas and ideologies do not matter; and efficient markets—both economic and political—characterize economies. Procedural rationality, on the other hand, maintains that the actors have incomplete information and limited mental capacity by which to process that information, and consequently develop regularized patterns of behavior to structure exchange. There is no implication that the consequent institutions are efficient. In such a world, ideas and ideologies play a major role in choices, and transaction costs result in imperfect markets.

What does it mean to say that institutions are characterized by increasing returns? Institutions have large initial set-up costs (such as creation, de novo, of the U.S. Constitution), and there are significant learning effects for organizations that arise in consequence of the opportunity set provided by the institutional framework. The political and economic organizations have come into existence because of the opportunities created by the institutional (and other economic) constraints. Thus learning, coordination, and adaptive expectations effects will produce increasing returns as organizations evolve within this institutional framework. The result is a set of reinforcing mechanisms, such as network externalities, that bias incremental costs and benefits in favor of those choices that are broadly consistent with the institutional framework, and against those which would run counter to the institutional framework.

When I put the procedural rationality postulate together with the increasing returns characteristic of institutions, I get a different economic history, one that appears more closely to fit the historical record than the noninstitutional instrumental rationality approach. I shall illustrate just how different this economic history is by going back over the sketch in the previous section.

The English heritage of institutions and ideas together shaped the colonial economy. The institutional framework provided the opportunities that produced organizations—plantations, merchants, shipping firms, family farms—that resulted in a thriving colonial economy. The heritage was not just economic but political as well—town meetings and self-government, colonial assemblies. The colonists perceived and interpreted the issues that they confronted in terms of the intellectual currents—Hobbes and Locke, for example—of the times. An understanding of both the institutional heritage and the intellectual heritage is essential to make the events of 1763 to 1789 into an integrated story of political and economic organizations driven by their subjective perceptions of the issues (such as the perceived burden of the Navigation Acts) to produce the institutional framework of the newly independent nation. The institutional path and the perceptions of the actors make sense of the story and account for the radical contrast with other contemporaneous revolutions and subsequent development—the Latin American experience, for example.

The nineteenth-century American economy provided a hospitable environment for economic growth. Just what it was that made the environment hospitable has certainly occupied the attention of scholars examining the consequences of the Constitution, the evolution of the law, the role of the frontier, the contribution of immigrants, and so forth. In fact, it was the adaptively efficient characteristics of the institutional matrix (both the formal rules and the informal constraints embodied in attitudes and values) that produced an economic and political environment that rewarded productive activity, encouraged investment in knowledge and education, and provided the decentralized decision-making that maximized trials and alternative choices. It was the federal system of government that not only produced the Madisonian polity, but also produced a decentralized and competitive economic structure.

Economic historians have also paid a good deal of attention to the costs entailed in that growth. Part of the cost was the price paid for adaptive efficiency. The system wiped out losers, and there were a lot of them—farmers who went bust on the frontier, shipping firms that failed as the U.S. lost its comparative advantage in shipping, laborers who suffered unemployment and declining wages from immigrant competition in the 1850's. Another part of the cost, however, was a consequence of institutions that exploited individuals and groups—Indians, slaves, and not infrequently immigrants, workers, and farmers to the benefit of those with superior bargaining power. Both the sources of growth and the costs of that growth are common derivatives of the institutional framework.

The political framework resulted in the losers having access, albeit imperfect, to remedies for their perceived sources of misfortune. Perceived sources consisted of immediate grievances filtered through ongoing intellectual currents and ideologies of the actors. The farmer could frequently observe price discrimination by the railroad or the grain elevator, but the Populist party platform reflected overall ideological views, including the perceived burden of the gold standard, widespread monopoly, and the pernicious consequence of bankers. We cannot make sense out of the protest movements and policy prescriptions of the period without an understanding of these intellectual currents.

Nor can we make sense out of the direction of change in the polity and economy that resulted from these movements without an understanding of them. Whatever the real underlying sources of the farmers' plight that produced discontent in the late nineteenth century, it was their perceptions that mattered in changing the political and economic institutional framework.

But it was not just the farmers' perceptions that mattered. It was also the evolving subjective models of the actors of other organizations who were able to influence outcomes as a consequence of the institutional matrix. Whether the Supreme Court understood the implication of Munn versus Illinois and the many other court decisions that were gradually altering the legal framework depended on the degree to which the information feedback on the consequences of existing laws was accurate and hence gave them true models. True or false, the models upon which they acted were incrementally altering the judicial framework.

The brief story of the Northwest Ordinance illustrates the increasing-returns feature of the institutional matrix. The ordinance (together with the 1784 and 1785 enactments) created the fundamental pattern of land distribution and political expansion of the American society that persisted throughout the nineteenth century. The organizations it inspired took advantage of the opportunities created by the provisions of the law to shape U.S. territorial development. It was the network externalities arising from the economic and political features of the law that defined the opportunities. Over time, the organizations incrementally altered the institutional framework as their perceived interests dictated, but the fundamental direction of the path was not altered.[16]

A history that takes into account the subjective perceptions that influence the choices and the increasing-returns feature of the institutional framework tells a far richer story than we have had before. Institutional analysis can make American economic history truly historical and explicable, fleshing out the quantitative data that delineate the contours of the country's economic past and making sense of some that have defied analysis in the noninstitutional framework of cliometrics. To cite but one example, capital formation in the nineteenth century is a story of successive improvements in financial mediation by organizations taking advantage of the opportunities created by the basic institutional framework of secure property rights and effective legal framework.[17] The structural transformation of the economy in the nineteenth century detailed in the GNP statistics is a classic illustration of adaptive efficiency, as Poulson makes clear in his contrast between U.S. performance and that of Third World countries.[18]

CHAPTER SIX

✿ Seasonality in Nineteenth-Century Labor Markets

Stanley Engerman and Claudia Goldin

The nature of the problem of off-season slack time surely varied from region to region and time to time, reflecting differences in institutions, crop mixes, crop routines, degrees of mechanization, and the development of village and town life. The differing nature of the labor force interactions between agriculture and the other sectors in these settings is a subject clearly worthy of intensive study. While it has not been neglected, the lessons it has to teach about the process of American economic growth—and economic growth generally—have not yet been fully learned. The learning promises to be rewarding.
— Robert Gallman, "The Agricultural Sector and the Pace of Economic Growth"

MORE THAN HALF the working population of mid-nineteenth-century America was employed in one of three seasonally sensitive sectors— agriculture, construction, or fishing. The work of many others, on canals and lakes and in water-powered factories, was also hampered in winter months by the weather.[1] The many technological advances that enabled individuals to break through environmental restraints should have raised income per worker-year appreciably. Because more than half of the labor force (67.5 percent in 1850) was seasonally and involuntarily idle for about four months each year, a technological change enabling year-round employment for all workers would have increased national income by 30 percent.[2] At the average annual rate experienced from 1840 to 1900, this would amount to 16.5 years of growth. Because the work of the rest of the labor force may also have been constrained by weather, the impact of surmounting seasonality may have been much larger.

One of the several concerns of Robert Gallman's work is the effect of ignoring seasonality on various economic magnitudes. The agricultural labor force, for example, will be overstated, and its productivity in agri-

We thank Robert A. Margo, Winifred Rothenberg, and Thomas Weiss for sharing their data with us, and William Parker, Winifred Rothenberg, Don Schaefer, Thomas Weiss, and Jeffrey Williamson for comments. Sanjaya Panth ably collected data sets for the project, and his research assistance was funded by the PARSS program at the University of Pennsylvania.

culture understated, if seasonality is overlooked. Some labor attributed to the agricultural sector may produce output in another sector, or may just be idle during part of the year. Thus the measured ratio of output per worker in agriculture to that in all other sectors may be understated.[3]

Many of the technological and organizational changes that eventually reduced seasonality for the economy as a whole involved the expansion of the manufacturing sector and thus the rise of indoor work.[4] Some of these changes derived from the use of new sources of power, replacing the undependable flow of water and wind.[5] But the impact of seasonality, as Robert Gallman notes in the epigraph to this chapter, may have been diminished simply by an enhanced mobility of laborers across industries, sectors, and locations, permitting them to work at two or more employments in a year. Such mobility depends on transport costs and the flexibility of the alternative hiring sector, which in turn hinges on factors such as skill specificity, and storage and inventory costs of goods.

Many isolated examples have been found of the seasonal meshing of the agricultural and manufacturing sectors in the nineteenth and twentieth centuries.[6] One is provided by the pork-packing and hog-slaughtering houses that dotted the Ohio and Illinois countryside in the 1850's.[7] These gave winter employment to farmhands, whose search for off-season employment would otherwise have taken them farther afield. Since the seasonal industries of packing and slaughtering operated, for reasons of climate, only during the off-season in agriculture, the example provides a clear case of the interaction between sectors to which Robert Gallman refers. An extensive literature also exists on by-employments among workers in the late eighteenth and early nineteenth centuries.[8] Some have even attributed the drive for industrialization to the existence of seasonality in agriculture. Carville Earle and Ronald Hoffman, for example, have explored the hypothesis that industrialization was stimulated by the incentive to utilize seasonally unemployed or underemployed laborers.[9] How important, then, was seasonality, and how common was the meshing of the seasons in total employment patterns?

The proportion of the labor force seasonally unemployed or underemployed must have been more extensive in the nineteenth century than it was later, but there are no estimates of its magnitude.[10] And although seasonality may be less extensive as the economy is more advanced, the seasonally affected worker in the modern economy may be unemployed for longer stretches. A worker who engages in specific investments in a firm, industry, or geographic area is less likely to leave, even for a temporary position, and it is believed that such investments increased over time.

Seasonality is known to affect the wages, as well as the quantities, of labor. Lifetime or even annual wages, however, should be more similar among identically skilled individuals, independent of occupation. Outdoor construction workers, for example, might be expected to earn a package of wages, working conditions, and leisure valued the same as the fulltime earnings of their indoor counterparts. A premium may be paid to harvest and seasonal workers to transport them from the town to the field, and to entice those already working in agriculture to increase their hours of work per day. This premium, however, could decline over time with a decrease in the seasonality of labor demand and an increase in the supply of seasonal laborers. The extent of the premium to seasonal labor and its change over time may reveal much about interactions between the sectors and changes in seasonality.

Only limited evidence on seasonality and unemployment exists for the nineteenth century. We provide various estimates of seasonality and unemployment, and explore three possible means by which seasonality was surmounted in the nineteenth century. One is the expansion of sectors, such as manufacturing, that were less seasonal than agriculture and construction. The movement of workers from agriculture to industry would increase per capita output simply by the greater employment of workers over the year. A second means would be the reduction of seasonality: within the agricultural sector, through the use of machinery and the substitution of livestock for grains; and in the manufacturing sector, through the use of power sources that were not dependent on water and air flow.

Finally, even if no labor moved permanently from farm to factory, a transient group of workers, migrating back and forth during the year, could have eliminated much of the seasonal component to employment.[11] A market for hired farm labor would enable farm owners and their older sons to utilize their own time better over the seasons and possibly even to increase acreage worked per farmer. Thus a third means of reducing seasonality is through the mobility of workers across sectors and the meshing of seasonal employment demands across sectors.[12] As farming regions became more densely settled and transport costs declined, hired hands may have been better able to migrate from farm to factory and town.

Seasonality and Agriculture

The size of the seasonal labor force and its trend over time can be gauged by examining the number of hired hands in the labor force and its change across the nineteenth century. The data assembled in Table 6.1 show the number of male farm laborers per 1,000 farmers, farms, and male persons for nine midwestern states. Although the most recent estimates of the farm labor force have been used, various data problems remain.[13] The earliest date for which farm laborers were identified in the census is 1860,

TABLE 6.1

Male Farm Laborers per 1,000 Farmers, Farms, and Male Population: Midwestern States, 1860 to 1900

| | Farm laborers at least 16 years old | | | | Farm laborers at least 10 years old | | | |
	1860	1870	1880	1890	1870	1880	1890	Nonfamily[a] 1900
Illinois								
FL/F	384.3	483.6	437.8	450.8	557.1	537.6	537.6	408.1
FL/farms	411.9	571.1	478.3	557.3	657.8	587.3	664.6	384.7
FL/P	110.6	148.0	123.0	102.8	170.5	151.0	122.6	60.7
Indiana								
FL/F	276.0	403.3	443.6	408.8	462.4	564.8	497.9	293.3
FL/farms	332.2	453.8	478.6	480.4	520.4	609.3	585.0	269.6
FL/P	110.1	146.7	147.6	130.0	168.2	188.0	158.3	68.5
Iowa								
FL/F	300.6	419.9	346.8	344.4	500.6	417.5	414.6	295.3
FL/farms	435.6	502.8	394.6	415.9	599.5	475.0	500.3	282.0
FL/P	99.5	160.0	139.6	130.4	190.7	168.1	133.8	83.5
Kansas								
FL/F	231.6	380.2	294.1	287.4	429.6	372.3	372.2	242.5
FL/farms	346.8	502.8	312.0	342.9	568.1	395.0	444.2	227.7
FL/P	99.5	151.7	132.8	120.1	171.4	168.2	131.4	77.5
Michigan								
FL/F	397.0	487.1	381.5	369.6	533.9	424.5	393.9	256.9
FL/farms	563.8	598.8	412.2	402.0	656.3	458.7	453.1	238.9
FL/P	143.6	152.2	111.8	93.7	166.8	124.3	91.7	56.9
Minnesota								
FL/F	n.a.	328.6	315.3	373.1	364.4	352.3	428.6	265.5
FL/farms	n.a.	385.4	327.9	427.5	427.4	366.4	491.0	252.1
FL/P	n.a.	125.6	115.2	110.2	139.3	128.7	109.6	64.0
Nebraska								
FL/F	99.4	314.7	233.1	248.8	346.7	276.1	311.3	233.8
FL/farms	142.0	435.2	251.0	289.7	479.4	297.3	362.5	218.2
FL/P	35.6	117.0	102.6	89.7	128.8	121.6	96.5	72.1

Ohio								
FL/F	352.8	806.0[b]	435.4	409.3	944.6[b]	502.8	467.5	275.7
FL/farms	438.3	830.8[b]	458.9	462.8	973.7[b]	529.9	528.7	247.1
FL/P	119.3	201.6[b]	110.8	93.7	236.3[b]	128.0	92.2	47.0
Wisconsin								
FL/F	327.5	413.9	355.9	346.4	461.9	404.7	399.7	236.1
FL/farms	443.8	433.7	364.3	394.3	484.0	414.3	455.1	219.7
FL/P	130.0	139.3	115.0	102.5	155.4	130.7	101.3	53.7
Total (9 states)								
FL/F	336.7	499.8	383.2	319.0	574.7	457.8	437.9	—
FL/farms	420.9	570.9	412.0	374.7	656.3	492.3	514.4	—
FL/P	119.9	160.0	123.0	92.4	184.0	146.9	126.8	—

S O U R C E S : 1860 population and occupations: U.S. Census Office, *Eighth Census of the United States, 1860, Population of the United States in 1860* (Washington, D.C., 1864). 1860 farms: U.S. Census Office, *Ninth Census of the United States, 1870, vol. 3, The Statistics of the Wealth and Industry of the United States* (Washington, D.C., 1872). 1870 population: U.S. Census Office, *Ninth Census of the United States, 1870, vol. 2, The Vital Statistics of the United States* (Washington, D.C., 1872). 1870 occupations: *Ninth Census of the United States, 1870, vol. 1, The Statistics of the Population of the United States* (Washington, D.C., 1872). 1870 farms: U.S. Census Office, *Ninth Census of the United States, 1870, vol. 3, The Statistics of the Wealth and Industry of the United States* (Washington, D.C., 1872). 1880 population and occupations: U.S. Census Office, *Tenth Census of the United States, 1880, Statistics of the Population of the United States* (Washington, D.C., 1883). 1880 farms: U.S. Census Office, *Tenth Census of the United States, 1880, Report on the Productions of Agriculture* (Washington, D.C., 1883). 1890 population and occupations: U.S. Census Office, *Eleventh Census of the United States, 1890, Report on the Population of the United States* (Washington, D.C., 1897). 1890 farms: U.S. Census Office, *Eleventh Census of the United States, 1890, Report on the Statistics of Agriculture in the United States* (Washington, D.C., 1895). 1900 population and occupations: U.S. Census Office, *Twelfth Census of the United States, 1900, vol. 2, Population* (Washington, D.C., 1902). 1890 farms: U.S. Census Office, *Twelfth Census of the United States, 1900, Census*

of Agriculture, 1900, pt. 1 (Washington, D.C., 1902), and personal communication from Thomas Weiss.

N O T E : FL = farm laborers, F = farmers, and P = male population. In all years except 1860, only male farm (agricultural) laborers (FL) are included. In 1860, female farm laborers are included by necessity. The 1860 and 1890 farm laborer data make use of Thomas Weiss's data that correct for workers between 10 and 15 years old and for various errors in the 16-to-24-year-old group for 1890. None of the farm laborer figures corrects the estimates for agricultural workers possibly included in the "laborers not elsewhere classified" category. Such a correction will raise the levels but will not alter the trends in the ratios given. Farmers (F) include males and females. Population figures are for males only and in all years refer to those at least 15 years old.

*The 1900 census was the first to enumerate farm workers as family members and as a group. The nonfamily figures for 1900 are sufficiently lower than those for 1890 that some family farm members were likely to have been enumerated as agricultural laborers in the years preceding 1900. The farm laborer ratios for the total given in 1900 exceed those for any other years and are thus too high.

*Thomas Weiss has cautioned us that these numbers are vastly overstated but that he is unable to make revisions.

but in the four census years from 1860 through 1890, sons of farmers were occasionally included in the farm laborer category. In many cases, their inclusion was justified because wages were paid to sons on the family farm or on neighboring ones.[14] According to census instructions, paid laborers, but not unpaid family farm workers, were to be included in the farm laborer category. The suspicion that the rule was not consistently followed led the census in 1900 to enumerate farm laborers separately by family and nonfamily status. For that year only, therefore, nonfamily farm workers are listed in Table 6.1. Hence, the 1900 nonfamily figure understates the number of paid farm workers in comparison with the figures of the previous census years. Changing age groupings also complicate the presentation of the data, and two sets of columns are given for most of the dates: one for farm laborers older than 15 years and another for farm laborers older than 9 years of age. The levels for the two obviously differ, but the trends are virtually identical.

Each of the censuses was taken at about the same time in the agricultural cycle, and none was taken at the peak harvest period of the fall. The census of 1870 began its count in June, that of 1880 was scheduled to be taken on or about June 1, and instructions for 1890 ask for the figures as of June 1. These censuses, therefore, probably capture the majority of annual and seasonal farm laborers, but they omit those who worked on farms only during the late summer or fall, the harvest period.[15]

The market for farm laborers in the Midwest appears to have thickened considerably from sometime before the data begin in 1860 to the early 1870's. In all but one of eight midwestern states, the number of farm laborers per farm increased between 1860 and 1870; the regional average rose from 0.42 laborers per farm to 0.57 per farm.[16] Nebraska and Kansas, the least densely populated states, experienced the greatest increases: from 0.14 per farm to 0.44 in Nebraska, and from 0.35 per farm to 0.50 in Kansas. With the exception of Indiana, the number of farm laborers per farm declined, between 1870 and 1880; it then rose between 1880 and 1890, but still sometimes failed to reach the level experienced in 1860. The increasing use of farm machinery throughout the period must have enabled many farmers to reduce their labor requirements.[17] The absence of information on the number of workers at harvest time, however, makes it impossible to measure the complete effect.[18]

Farm laborers enumerated in the census may have been hired on annual or seasonal contracts or on a daily basis. There are, at present, only a handful of surveys that contain information revealing the proportion of workers hired on annual, seasonal, and daily bases. Such data are contained, for example, in a survey conducted by the state of Missouri in 1880.[19] The 187 Missouri farmers enumerated in this survey reported that they hired twice as many hands in summer as in winter. Thus, if all winter hands were also hired for the summer months, the farmers let half their summer field hands go before the winter. The inference is that half the farmhands (189/369) employed in the summer were on annual contract. A separate but related finding is that, on a farm-level basis, slightly more than half of all farms (52 percent) hired more laborers in summer than in winter, 20 percent hired the same number, and 28 percent hired no farm laborers in any season.

But the Missouri data present a much different picture from that shown in Table 6.1. There were 369 summer laborers on 187 farms, or almost 2 laborers per farm. That is, there were over four times as many summer farm laborers per farm than we have estimated for the nine midwestern states in 1880, and four times the number shown by the 1880 federal census data for Missouri.[20] Part of the difference may be accounted for by the understatement in the census of all farm workers hired over the year. That is, the Missouri survey counted all hired hands regardless of month, whereas the census enumerated only those present at the time of the census.

National surveys for a later period, 1909, show that on a nationwide basis only 29 percent of all farm laborers hired by the month were employed throughout the year in agriculture.[21] The percentage varied somewhat by region. For the North Atlantic and South Atlantic states, the figure was 34 percent; for the North Central, it was 24 percent; for the South Central, it was 29 percent; and for the West, it was 22 percent. In Missouri, for example, only 24 percent of all monthly farm laborers were employed throughout the year, about half the figure found in the 1880 Missouri survey. One possible explanation for the discrepancy—and the one we are willing to accept—is that half the farm laborers in the 1880 Missouri survey who were employed during the winter were not hired for all the winter months, and thus were not really hired for the entire year. Another possibility is that annual contracts as a proportion of all farm labor contracts declined from 1880 to 1909 as migratory labor became more plentiful.

Indirect evidence on seasonality can be gleaned from the premium paid to harvest and seasonal labor, as opposed to ordinary daily and off-seasonal labor, to attract laborers for a portion of the year. This bonus could reflect transport costs or a differential offered to compensate workers for the heightened probability of off-season unemployment.

Data on the premiums for harvest labor in the late nineteenth century are contained in George Holmes's compendium of wages paid to farm labor.[22] Two types of seasonal data are given. The most complete are for daily wages paid to harvest and nonharvest labor with and without board.

Observations from nineteen years across four regions are available for the period 1866 to 1909. The ratios for the figures without board are given in Table 6.2.[23] Less complete are the data for monthly wages paid to seasonal and annual labor, for which only four years of observations are available (see Table 6.3). The Holmes data give the monthly wage for annual contracts and for seasonal laborers. The harvest premium for daily wages is the ratio of daily wages at harvest time to those not at harvest time. To construct a premium for seasonal laborers comparable with that for the harvest, we must compute an implicit off-season payment to farm laborers. The seasonal premium is then given by the ratio of the seasonal rate to the implicit off-season rate. We compute the implicit off-seasonal rate by assuming that the monthly payment for an annual contract is a weighted average of the seasonal monthly payment and the implicit monthly payment during the off-season. The weight is the proportion of the year that constituted the season. Holmes's compendium offers only scant evidence on the number of months that constituted a season in each of the regions (see Table 6.3 note), so we have assumed a period of six months. A shorter season would increase the ratio and a longer one would decrease it.

In both cases, the premium to seasonal or harvest labor was considerable by 1880, but declined substantially by the end of the century.[24] The annual data, given in Tables 6.2 and 6.3 and graphed in the two portions of Figure 6.1, show the harvest premium rising in all regions from the end of the Civil War to the 1880's. During the period of increase, it was typically lowest in the North Atlantic states and highest in the South Atlantic and North Central states. The premium then dropped considerably during the 1880's. In the North Central states it fell by a half, plummeting from just above 70 percent in 1880 to around 35 percent at the turn of this century. It decreased less in the North Atlantic region, which had the lowest premium at mid-century. Yet even in that region, it fell from about 50 percent in 1880 to 30 percent twenty years later.

Although the harvest and seasonal wage ratios display similar trends over time, the trends may have different causes. The harvest premium is a ratio of daily wages, and daily laborers were themselves working only in the season for which data are recorded. Both wages, therefore, already include compensatory payments for the risk of unemployment. The harvest premium was presumably a further compensation for the transportation cost of bringing additional laborers into the fields, as well as an amount to entice existing laborers to work more hours per day or more days per week. The decline in both premiums, therefore, could be due to a combination of lowered transport costs, a decreased probability of unemployment among migratory laborers, and a decreased demand for harvest labor.[25] The fact that from the 1870's to 1890 the daily wage premium

TABLE 6.2

Harvest Wage Premiums, Daily Wages without Board, for Outdoor Labor
by Region, 1820 to 1909

	New England			
1820–29	1.21			
1830–39	1.30			
1840–49	1.35			

	North Atlantic	South Atlantic	North Central	South Central
1866	1.38	1.65	1.47	1.52
1869	1.48	1.68	1.59	1.49
1874–75	1.46	1.63	1.63	1.53
1877–79	1.46	1.70	1.71	1.53
1879–80	1.46	1.75	1.70	1.56
1880–81	1.51	1.69	1.74	1.54
1881–82	1.43	1.69	1.66	1.58
1884–85	1.50	1.66	1.59	1.45
1887–88	1.42	1.50	1.47	1.37
1889–90	1.40	1.50	1.42	1.49
1891–92	1.41	1.52	1.44	1.37
1893	1.35	1.56	1.37	1.40
1894	1.35	1.58	1.35	1.40
1895	1.32	1.57	1.34	1.48
1898	1.30	1.52	1.32	1.43
1899	1.31	1.50	1.33	1.42
1902	1.32	1.50	1.38	1.41
1906	1.34	1.32	1.36	1.31
1909	1.22	1.34	1.36	1.31

S O U R C E S: George Holmes, *Wages of Farm Labor*, U.S. Department of Agriculture, Bureau of Statistics Bulletin 99 (Washington, D.C., 1912). New England data were provided by W. Rothenberg; see, for example, Winifred Rothenberg, "The Emergence of Farm Labor Markets and the Transformation of the Rural Economy: Massachusetts, 1750–1855," *Journal of Economic History* 48 (Sept. 1988): 537–66.

N O T E: This table shows the ratio of daily harvest wages to daily nonharvest wages. The harvest period is defined as July and August, and average daily wages are computed independent of task, for comparability with the data from Holmes for 1866 to 1909. Rothenberg computes a harvest wage for only the tasks of haying, reaping, and mowing in July and August and a nonharvest wage for tasks other than haying, reaping, and mowing in the months from September to June. See Winifred Rothenberg, "Structural Change in the Farm Labor Force: Contract Labor in Massachusetts Agriculture, 1750–1865," in C. Goldin and H. Rockoff, eds., *Strategic Factors in Nineteenth-Century American Economic History* (Chicago, 1992).

decreased more than did the seasonal wage premium (without board) suggests the degree to which either transportation costs declined or peak harvest demand was attenuated. The decrease in the seasonal wage premium alone indicates a decline in the probability of unemployment in the off-season.[26]

Seasonal wage premiums at the national level are not available for the first half of the nineteenth century, but they do exist for New England.[27] We also report in Table 6.2 the ratio of daily wages paid in New England

TABLE 6.3

Seasonal Wage Premiums, Monthly Wages with and without Board, for Outdoor Labor by Region, *1866 to 1909*

	North Atlantic		South Atlantic		North Central		South Central	
	With board	Without board	With board	Without board	With board	Without board	With board	Without board
1866	1.68	1.33	1.65	1.39	1.58	1.35	1.88	1.54
1869	1.65	1.38	1.87	1.45	1.69	1.42	1.86	1.39
1874–75	1.49	1.42	1.66	1.31	1.49	1.33	1.59	1.39
1909	1.45	1.32	1.37	1.25	1.34	1.23	1.39	1.24

SOURCE: George Holmes, *Wages of Farm Labor*, U.S. Department of Agriculture, Bureau of Statistics Bulletin 99 (Washington, D.C., 1912).

NOTE: The implicit monthly nonseasonal wage assumes the season is six months long: $M_a = 0.5 M_s + 0.5 M_{ns}$, where M_a is the average monthly wage on an annual contract, M_s is the average monthly wage for seasonal labor, and M_{ns} is the implicit average monthly wage during the off-season. If the season is longer than six months, as it probably was in the South, the premium will be somewhat exaggerated. Holmes, *Wages of Farm Labor*, cites evidence from a Kansas survey in 1893 that the average time during which farm laborers, who were hired by the month, were employed over the year was 6.76 months.

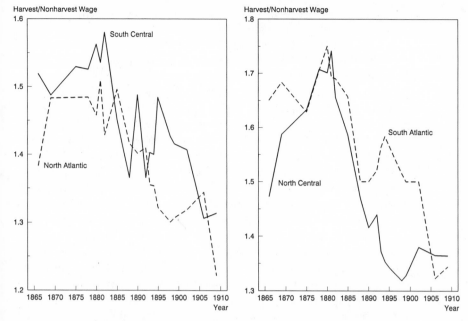

Fig. 6.1. Harvest premiums for daily wages (without board) of farm workers. Data from Table 6.2.

during July and August, which we take to be the most labor-intensive months, to those paid in the other ten months.[28] The increase in the harvest premium discernible in the Holmes data for the North Atlantic from 1866 to the early 1880's (38 percent to 51 percent) can now be extended further back in time. Harvest premiums rose beginning in the 1820's, if not earlier, and they increased in the twenty-year period between 1820–29 and 1840–49, rising from 21 percent to 35 percent.[29]

Monthly contracts were rare before the 1820's. Instead, laborers were hired by the day. In Rothenberg's data, which were culled from farmers' account books, most agricultural laborers between the late 1700's and 1820 were hired by the day. Beginning in the 1820's, however, laborers were more frequently given contracts and were paid by the month. But even during the period 1830 to 1835, the account books used by Rothenberg record 212 daily laborers and only 42 monthly laborers.[30] It is not possible to compute a seasonal premium for the monthly hires strictly comparable to that given by Holmes (Table 6.3), because Holmes did not define the term "season." If the season is taken to be only the months of June, July, and August, the implied seasonal premiums in the Rothenberg data for 1800 to 1856 are approximately equal to those in the Holmes data.[31]

Because the season was probably longer, the seasonal premium for the monthly data appears also to have risen over time.

Why the harvest premium increased from early in the nineteenth century until the 1880's is not exactly clear, but the antebellum rise may be related to the transition from daily payments to monthly contracts for laborers. Prior to the rise of monthly contracts, day-laborer wages may have been part of other contractual obligations, and thus the daily wage may not have been subject to variability over the season. According to Paul Clemens and Lucy Simler, whose evidence pertains to the Delaware Valley, not New England, the majority of hired agricultural laborers prior to around 1820 lived on their employers' grounds, like the "cottagers" who were their counterparts in England.[32] The American cottagers were often families who were contractually obligated to work a certain number of days annually for their landlords. During the rest of the year, they were free to work their own plots or to engage in cottage industry. The daily payments to these laborers, recorded in farmers' account books, did not, therefore, involve the movement of individuals for brief periods of time. Because these daily payments were contractually set along with the number of days per year, the payment recorded for a day in August may have been no higher than for one in January. But when farming became a more year-round activity, with the introduction of livestock, hay, and corn, there was less demand for cottagers. Further, as the factory system spread and many of the goods made by the cottagers became cheaper, and as their alternative wage thus became higher, the supply of cottagers was reduced. Monthly payments, and seasonal and annual contracts, began to take the place of the cottager's annual-contract and daily-wage accounting.[33] Seasonality in the demand for labor, therefore, began to be reflected in the wages paid to labor over the year.

Although the evolution of markets in hired labor in the Delaware Valley accords with the data on the premium paid to harvest laborers, researchers have not found similar factors in New England. According to Rothenberg, day laborers, even in late eighteenth-century New England, were not cottagers, but instead traveled on a daily basis from town to farm.[34] Why, exactly, the harvest premium rose in New England from the early 1800's to the 1850's is therefore not clear.

One might expect harvest and seasonal premiums to be reflected as well in the wages paid to nonfarm laborers, especially in areas close to farming communities. During the harvest period, when wages were considerably higher in agriculture, manufacturing enterprises and other employers of unskilled labor may have been forced to increase wage payments. Alternatively, they could have scheduled vacations around the harvest period. City, town, and industrial wages need not have increased as much as those on farms, because part of the harvest premium is the cost of transporting labor to the farm. The evidence concerning seasonality in nonfarm wages is slender. To compete with the construction sector in the pre-1870 period, the McCormick Company increased wages in the spring and reduced them in the fall, and the iron furnaces around Philadelphia that hired woodcutters in the winter also displayed seasonality in their wages.[35] A large sample of wages paid by the military, however, yields mixed results concerning seasonality in the antebellum period. From 1821 to 1856, for example, the military paid a 5 percent premium in the spring and summer and a 15 percent premium in the fall for civilian labor in the Midwest.[36] But similar wages paid by the military in other regions display no seasonal pattern during this period.

Seasonality and Manufacturing

The 1900 census of manufactures was the first at the national level to collect information on employment by month.[37] The data are given by state and industry, and within these by sex, but not by state and industry together. Figure 6.2 shows manufacturing employment indexes for males and females by the nine census regions.[38] The index is the ratio of monthly employment to that in the peak month, generally spring or early fall. We have not adjusted the data for increased employment across the year, and thus the growth from January to December imparts a tilt to the profiles, but this tilt should not greatly affect the seasonal component.

In almost all cases, manufacturing employment for males dips by about 10 percent during the summer, although only in the East South Central and the South Atlantic regions does it reach its nadir during those months. In the West North Central, the West South Central, and the Pacific states, the summer dip is only 5 percent of peak employment. In most regions, the trough, not surprisingly, is lower in the winter than in the summer and drops by about 15 to 20 percent of its peak employment. A double-peaked distribution of employment over the year, therefore, characterizes seasonal employment patterns among all of the regions, with peaks occurring in April and October.

Seasonal employment was more pronounced for female manufacturing workers than for males. As Figure 6.2 indicates, in almost all regions— with the exception of the Pacific—the employment trough for women during the summer is greater than that for men, and the double-peaked pattern is even more pronounced. Around 15 to 20 percent of peak labor was released over the May to July period. But an equal, or often lower, percentage was released in the December to February period. In the Pacific states, however, seasonality in manufacturing employment was due to

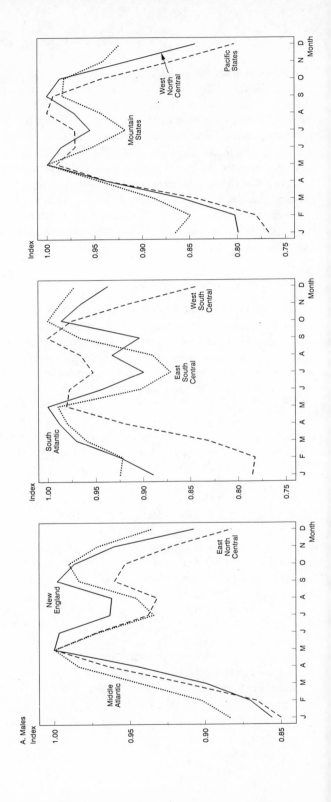

A. Males

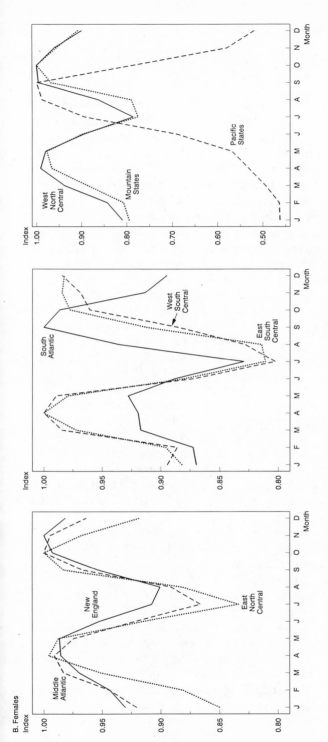

Fig. 6.2. Seasonality in male and female manufacturing employment by region, 1900. Index = monthly employment/peak employment. Data from U.S. Bureau of the Census, *Twelfth Census of the United States, 1900. Manufactures*, part 1: *United States by Industries* (Washington, D.C., 1902).

fruit, vegetable, and fish canning, and its intensive demands in the late summer and fall give the monthly employment distribution its unique shape.

The regional patterns may disguise varying industrial seasonality. Figure 6.3, therefore, disaggregates by industry at the national level. Taken together, these eleven industry groups account for almost 80 percent of all male operatives and craft workers in 1900 (the percentage of the total, by industry, is given in the graph). All industries except food have a bimodal shape, with peaks in the spring and fall, and troughs in the summer and winter. Clay (clay, glass, and stone products) is the only industry having a bimodal shape with considerably lower employment in the winter than the summer. As in the regional graphs, the ratio of trough to peak employment over the year is about 80 to 90 percent. Thus the average percentage of workers laid off sometime during the year is around 15 percent. Some of the seasonality is due to the annual closings of certain firms during August; for example, many textile mills had an annual August "vacation."[39] But, again using the example of textiles, while there are two months of employment at 85 percent of peak, there are another four months with employment at or below 90 percent of peak.

The seasonal patterns displayed in both the regional and industrial graphs might reflect the movement of labor from industry to agriculture during the summer months, although we doubt the movement was substantial for females despite their more pronounced seasonal pattern of employment. With the exception of the food category, the lowest months for employment are either in the winter months or in July and August. Most industries had surprisingly higher employment levels in the winter than in the summer. The vehicles category, for which the employment was dominated by the repair and construction of steam-car railroads, had the most prolonged seasonal trough, extending from July to the beginning of winter. The industry operated at 90 percent of peak employment during the fall harvest period, but was at almost peak employment during the spring. Steam-car railroad shops, furthermore, were located throughout the country, often near farming communities.

In many industries, particularly in the vehicles category, the seasonal pattern of employment leaves open the possibility that labor migrated over the year between industry and agriculture. Further, the patterns displayed here for 1900 may be considerably more muted than they are earlier in the nineteenth century. Seasonality in manufacturing employment, then, suggests some dovetailing of employment in agriculture and industry. Industry, it would appear, responded to labor scarcity in the summer by reducing its employment. But there is reason to believe that the troughs in industrial employment were exogenously produced by, for example, a re-

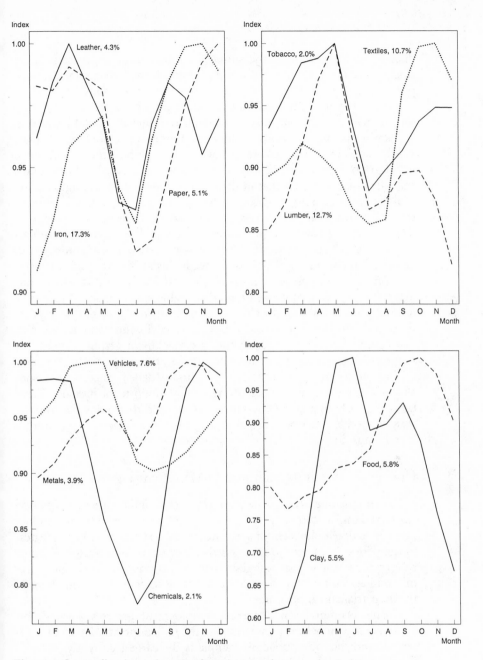

Fig. 6.3. Seasonality in male manufacturing employment by industry, 1900. Index = monthly employment/peak employment. Data from U.S. Bureau of the Census, *Twelfth Census*. Percentages are the proportion of all male production workers in the industry. Small industrial groups have been omitted and thus the percentages do not add up to 100.

duction of inputs during the summer months. Further, there is some reason to doubt that industrial laborers found substantial employment opportunities in agriculture during the trough periods in industry.

Peak employment in much of agriculture did not always occur during the summer months but, instead, often arose during the fall harvesting and spring planting periods.[40] There are important regional exceptions. Wheat farms in North Dakota and Minnesota doubled their labor usage in August over that in April and May, although their April and May usage was, in turn, four times that in the winter months. In Washington state, peak labor usage among wheat farmers was in July, and in Wisconsin it was in August, with high levels prevailing over much of the year due to dairying. But in Iowa, the peaks were in July and in September through October. In Texas cotton areas, peak labor usage was in September; in Georgia, on cotton, corn, and oat farms, it was in May through June and in September through November. In New York state, in diversified farming, the peak was October, with no discernible variation across the other months. Among all hired help in agriculture, employment was highest from April to November, and peaks occurred in June and July and in October.[41] The regional manufacturing employment graphs (Figure 6.2) suggest that dovetailing may have occurred in the North Central portion of the country, but not in the South. Thus, evidence concerning seasonality of employment in manufacturing weakly supports the hypothesis that labor regularly migrated between the sectors and that industrial employment responded to labor scarcity during the peak periods in agriculture by relinquishing workers.

Unemployment in Agriculture and Manufacturing

Data on the number of farm laborers per farm and the premium paid to seasonal farm laborers suggest that the economic loss from the unemployment or underemployment of agricultural laborers may have been greatest in the period from 1870 to 1890. Further, the seasonal character of industrial employment in 1900 suggests that the decrease in the seasonal premium in agriculture may have come about by some increased meshing of the industrial and agricultural sectors.

The most comprehensive data on unemployment, in terms of geographical and occupational scope, are found in the U.S. population census manuscripts, and the 1900 public use sample is the earliest currently available for the entire United States. The 1900 population census was the first to ask about months of idleness in all forms of gainful employment during the year. Although the 1880 census had requested months of unemployment from one's usual occupation, the results appeared too sparse to census officials and were never tabulated. The unemployment question for 1890 attempted to combine nonemployment in the current occupation and in all occupations, but the results seem to be a confusing mixture of the two. The 1900 data, therefore, provide the earliest reliable data at the national level. No available surveys of agricultural unemployment cover the 1870's and 1880's, and most others were taken in the 1890's during a major economic depression.

The census year 1900 (May 1899 to May 1900) is generally thought to have been a prosperous one.[42] Unemployment measures for that year, then, should reflect primarily frictional and seasonal unemployment, rather than that due to a downturn in the business cycle. Another data set, for Michigan farm workers in 1894, will demonstrate what happened to unemployment during a severe economic downturn. Because the Michigan data distinguish between involuntary and voluntary unemployment, they are also useful in adjusting the 1900 census data, which do not.

Two unemployment statistics are given in Table 6.4 for male farm and nonfarm workers (16 to 70 years old) in four regions. The first measure is the percentage of workers who reported they were unemployed during the census year. The second gives months unemployed, conditional on experiencing any unemployment.

Almost 40 percent of all nonfamily farm laborers experienced some unemployment during the census year, although the figure varies by region from a low of 32 percent for the Northeast to a high of 40 percent for the West. The percentage of family farm laborers experiencing any unemployment is generally less than that for nonfamily farm laborers, with the exception of the West. The percentage of farmers registering unemployment is a fraction of that for laborers, but is highest in the South.[43] Months unemployed conditional on some unemployment is within the three- to four-month range.[44] Of those who experienced any unemployment, 54 percent were unemployed for between three and four months in the Midwest (not shown in Table 6.4); that statistic is 44 percent for the South and 52 percent for the Northeast.

In the nonfarm sector, laborers and those in the building trades experienced the greatest unemployment. Between about 40 and 50 percent of these groups, depending on region, reported experiencing some unemployment during the census year. The length of unemployment, conditional on being unemployed, tended to be between three and four months, similar to that in the farm sector. Among nonfarm laborers, 42 percent were in the three- to four-month range; among building tradesmen, the figure was 45 percent; and among manufacturing workers, it was 38 percent. Manufacturing workers experienced a peak at two to three months (45 percent).

TABLE 6.4

Unemployment Measures by Region and Occupation for Farm and Nonfarm Workers, 1900

(males, 16 to 70 years old)

Farm workers

Region	Nonfamily farm laborers			Family farm laborers			Farmers		
	Observations (N)	Unemployed (%)	Months unemployed[a]	Observations (N)	Unemployed (%)	Months unemployed[a]	Observations (N)	Unemployed (%)	Months unemployed[a]
Northeast	258	32.2	4.47	113	18.6	3.35	527	4.0	4.29
Midwest	574	38.0	3.73	461	22.1	4.05	1,904	3.0	4.48
South	765	38.4	3.62	650	36.8	3.35	2,331	11.5	3.62
West	136	40.4	4.15	53	41.5	3.18	184	4.3	3.00

Nonfarm workers

Region	Laborers			Manufacturing workers			Building trades			Professionals		
	Observations (N)	Unemployed (%)	Months unemployed[a]	Observations (N)	Unemployed (%)	Months unemployed[a]	Observations (N)	Unemployed (%)	Months unemployed[a]	Observations (N)	Unemployed (%)	Months unemployed[a]
Northeast	845	43.6	4.18	2,226	22.4	3.96	563	41.5	4.25	272	13.2	4.64
Midwest	981	52.4	4.11	11,390	21.7	3.85	492	54.7	4.46	298	19.8	4.32
South	680	47.1	3.72	645	22.5	4.24	233	45.5	4.11	160	21.3	4.79
West	279	40.1	4.15	252	24.2	4.23	72	37.5	5.04	62	11.3	6.29

SOURCE: 1900 Public Use Microdata Sample.
NOTES: The seven occupational groups do not exhaust the national labor force. Omitted are trade and transportation, service, and mining. The occupational groups use the 1900 occupational codes; manufacturing includes operatives, craft workers, and supervisory personnel, but not laborers. The Northeast includes New England and the Middle Atlantic; the Midwest includes the East North Central and West North Central; the South includes the South Atlantic, East South Central, and West South Central; and the West includes Mountain and Pacific.
[a] Months unemployed for those unemployed.

These data suggest that even as late as 1900, seasonality in the employment of farm laborers, laborers in general, and those in the building trades was substantial. Between 40 and 50 percent of male workers in these groups experienced some unemployment during the year, and the mean length of unemployment over the year was about four months. Even when the sample is restricted to those experiencing fewer than nine months of unemployment, the conditional mean for nonfamily farm laborers is 3.4 months, and it is similarly invariant to the exclusion of the young or the old in the sample. For example, it is 3.8 months for the total sample, 3.75 months for those older than 19 years, and 3.7 months for those younger than 50 years. Taking out both tails of the age distribution lowers the conditional mean to 3.6 months, a change of less than a week.

The 1900 Public Use Microdata Sample indicates that in the Midwest, for example, 40 percent of all nonfamily farm workers experienced some unemployment over the year. Because at least 25 percent of all farm workers in the Midwest were hired on annual contract (from Holmes's data; see note 21), more than one-half of all farm workers not on annual contract were probably unemployed for long stretches in 1900. Of course, this also means that half of those not on annual contract did find employment during the off-season or, alternatively, did not report unemployment to census enumerators.

One direct test of the notion that integrated labor markets reduced seasonality in agriculture by meshing the seasons of farm and nonfarm work is found in Table 6.5. The correlates of the probability of unemployment, estimated as a logit, are given for nonfamily farm laborers and nonfarm laborers, including those working in manufacturing and the building trades. In both estimations, individual characteristics are included, as are variables to account for the urbanization of the laborer's county (in the case of farm laborers) and city size (in the case of nonfarm laborers).

Farm laborers employed in a county containing or adjacent to a large city (having more than 50,000 persons) and whose county of residence contained a city of at least 10,000 persons experienced about an 11 percent decrease in the probability of experiencing unemployment. Because the mean unemployment rate was about 40 percent for rural nonfamily farm laborers, the move from a rural county to one near a large city (or containing a medium-sized or large city) decreased the probability of unemployment by 28 percent. The move from a rural county to one either adjacent to a large city or containing a medium-sized one decreased the probability of unemployment by 7 percentage points, or by 17 percent. Nonagricultural workers experienced a decreased probability of being unemployed of 19 percentage points when located in a large city as opposed to a rural area, reducing the probability of unemployment by 44 percent compared

TABLE 6.5

Correlates of the Unemployment Probability Among Farm and Nonfarm Workers, 1900

	Farm laborers (nonfamily)	$\frac{\partial P}{\partial x}$	Nonfarm laborers and workers[a]	$\frac{\partial P}{\partial x}$
Mean of dependent variable	0.375	—	0.341	—
Constant	−0.807	—	1.02	—
	(1.64)		(4.25)	
Age	0.0120	—	−0.0572	—
	(0.53)		(5.23)	
Age squared × 10⁻²	−0.0105	—	0.0798	—
	(0.37)		(6.09)	
Literate (is able to write)	−0.163	—	−0.584	—
	(1.17)		(7.18)	
Never married	0.478	—	0.117	—
	(3.78)		(1.88)	
White	0.0208	—	0.098	—
	(0.14)		(1.05)	
Residence				
County contains city ≥ 10,000 and is near city ≥ 50,000	−0.453 (2.44)	−0.109	—	—
County near city ≥ 50,000, but does not contain city ≥ 10,000	−0.280 (1.63)	−0.067	—	—
County contains city ≥ 10,000, but is not near city ≥ 50,000	−0.279 (1.60)	−0.067	—	—
In large city (≥25,000)	—	—	−0.774	−0.190
			(9.88)	
In small city (10,000–25,000)	—	—	−0.627	−0.154
			(9.85)	
In town (1,000–10,000)	—	—	−0.316	−0.078
			(5.09)	
Observations (N)	1,733	—	8,607	—

S O U R C E: 1900 Public Use Microdata Sample.

N O T E: Dependent variable = 1 if a worker experienced unemployment during the census year, 1899–1900.

Equations estimated by maximum likelihood logit. $\partial P/\partial x = \beta \cdot (1 - P) \cdot P$, where the mean unemployment rate in rural areas, $P = 0.404$ in the farm case and 0.434 in the nonfarm case. Absolute values of t-statistics are in parentheses. Regional dummies were also included. The omitted variable for farm laborers is living in a county not containing a city and not near a city; more than 70 percent of farm laborers lived in such counties. The omitted variable for nonfarm laborers and workers is living in a rural area; 27 percent of the included workers lived in such areas. The dummy variables for location are exhaustive and nonoverlapping.

[a] Nonagricultural workers include those in manufacturing and the building trades. Laborers are all laborers except those in agriculture.

with that for rural workers. Rural areas increased the probability of being unemployed by 15 percentage points over small cities and by 8 percentage points over towns.[45] But because only 27 percent of nonfarm laborers and workers in manufacturing and the building trades resided in rural areas, the economy-wide effects were small.

Proximity to urban areas reduced unemployment for farm workers and nonfarm workers alike, and the impact was substantial. But 70 percent of farm laborers were not in counties containing or adjacent to cities, and 40 percent of these workers were unemployed for some portion of the year in 1900. Although urban workers in the building and manufacturing sectors were at a considerably greater risk of unemployment in rural areas, only 27 percent of them resided outside cities and towns. Thus, the meshing of employment over the season was possible only for laborers living in counties that contained cities or in those adjacent to urbanized counties. Migration over the season was particularly difficult for laborers who lived in rural America, even as late as 1900.

If the unemployment measures for the farm sector in 1900 suggest a large seasonal element, those for 1894, in Table 6.6, suggest a large cyclical component. Michigan, the state for which the data apply, did not have an unusually high rate of unemployment in 1900.[46] In fact, Michigan probably had among the lowest rates of seasonal employment in the Midwest.[47] According to Schob, many agricultural laborers in Michigan typically found year-round supplementary employment in the timber and meat-packing industries.[48] Yet the data in Table 6.6, from an extraordinary study of farm laborers, indicate that almost three-quarters had experienced some lack of employment during 1894.

TABLE 6.6

Unemployment Among Michigan Farm Laborers, 1894

	Percentage with unemployment	Observations (N)
Entire sample	74.7%	1,000
If cause is listed	73.0	965
If married	73.8	447
If cause is lack of work or bad weather[a]	51.6	965
If married	54.4	330
If cause is sickness or indisposition	11.6	965
If paid by month	69.2	770
If paid by the month and no problem in winter	56.3	504
If paid by the month and housing is provided	55.4	195

S O U R C E : Sample from Michigan Bureau of Labor and Industrial Statistics, *Twelfth Annual Report*, year ending February 1, 1895 (Lansing, 1895).
[a] Also includes other causes, together with lack of work or bad weather.

The Michigan unemployment data, unlike those in the census, give the cause of work absence. Of the 75 percent who reported days they did not work, 29 percent experienced some form of voluntary unemployment (for example, vacation), 60 percent experienced only involuntary unemployment (for example, lack of work), and 11 percent listed a combination of the two. Voluntary and involuntary unemployment are inferred from the cause of lost days reported in the survey. Causes other than "lack of work" or "bad weather" are assumed to be voluntary and include vacation, recreation, moving, at school, at home, and sickness. Combinations of voluntary and involuntary are assigned to the involuntary category. Although sickness and the lack of work that results are probably involuntary, there are several reasons for considering illness separate from other forms of involuntary unemployment. The most important reason is to isolate unemployment induced by economic circumstances. Further, unemployment today does not usually include time lost to illness because sickness benefits are often provided by employers. Various causes categorized under the voluntary heading might be due to involuntary factors, however. A young man whose search for work proves fruitless might decide to attend school, for example. But it is more likely that such an individual would have assigned at least some of his idle days to "lack of work" and be included in the involuntary category.

Using this categorization, 52 percent of all farm laborers experienced some form of involuntary unemployment. Even with the adjustment, the figure for involuntary unemployment in Michigan is higher than that in the 1900 census, which was around 40 percent and which presumably also included lost time due to voluntary reasons. Government officials who compiled the Michigan survey understood that 1894 was a particularly depressed year and that the figure for lost time exceeded that in usual years. "The average time worked (about 9½ months) will compare most favorably with any other class of labor. The principal cause for loss of time being lack of work, caused by the farmers curtailing their expenses during the depression of farm industries."[49]

Distributions of months unemployed for the Michigan and 1900 census (Midwest) data are given in Table 6.7. The census data are more tightly distributed around three to four months of unemployment than are those for Michigan farm workers, and this is true for the total column as well as for unemployment due only to involuntary reasons. The depression in 1894, therefore, caused a bulge in the short-term idleness of Michigan's agricultural workers. Note, as well, the left-skewness to the distribution of weeks not employed due to sickness, which causes the total distribution to be flatter.

Cause of unemployment was not given in the 1900 census, and although

TABLE 6.7

Distribution of Months Unemployed Among Farm Laborers Experiencing Unemployment,
Michigan (1894) and the Midwest (1900)

Months unemployed[a]	Michigan total unemployment[b] (%)	Michigan involuntary unemployment[c] (%)	Michigan sickness[d] (%)	Midwest total unemployment (%)
Less than 1	2.7	0.2	8.0	n.a.
1	15.7	10.8	25.0	4.1
2	18.8	17.7	24.1	17.9
3	18.4	17.4	21.5	33.9
4	19.6	25.2	5.4	20.2
5	9.5	11.3	4.5	6.4
6	10.6	13.4	4.5	12.8
7	1.1	0.9	1.8	0.9
8	1.3	1.4	1.8	1.4
9	1.7	1.4	2.7	0.5
10	0.4	0.0	0.9	1.0
11	0.1	0.0	0.0	0.0
12	0.0	0.0	0.0	1.0
Mean months unemployed	3.36	3.66	2.66	3.73
Observations (N)	747	425	112	574

S O U R C E S: Sample from Michigan Bureau of Labor and Industrial Statistics, *Twelfth Annual Report*, year ending February 1, 1895 (Lansing, 1895); and 1900 Public Use Microdata Sample.

[a] Unemployment in the Michigan data is expressed precisely in months and days. We have grouped unemployment to be centered on the month for consistency with the 1900 census, in which unemployment is given only in months. Thus, less than 1 month is taken to be less than 2 weeks; 1 month is assumed to be 2 weeks to less than 6.2 weeks; 2 months is 6.2 weeks to less than 10.4 weeks; and so on.

[b] Includes all workers in the Michigan sample who reported months worked.

[c] Includes only workers who reported that the cause of unemployment was "lack of work" or "bad weather."

[d] Includes only workers who reported that the cause of unemployment was "sickness" or "indisposition."

the marshals were instructed to ask months not employed, there is no direct evidence that voluntary causes (for example, sickness or leisure) were included. Yet it may be misleading to use the total figures on idleness in the 1900 census to indicate unemployment that was seasonally or cyclically induced. Intermingled with involuntary unemployment may be that which was voluntary, and the Michigan data can be used to infer residual unemployment that was not voluntary. Because some of the causes grouped in the voluntary category could have been induced by depressed economic conditions in 1894, we net out only unemployment due to illness. Just under 12 percent of Michigan's farm workers lost time to illness only. If the same proportion of farm workers would have been ill in the absence of an economic downturn, and this does seem reasonable, 26.4 percent would have been unemployed in the Midwest in 1900 for reasons other than illness.[50] The unadjusted figure from the 1900 census is 38 percent. Once again, if we use the data in Holmes on annual contracts, this implies that two-thirds of all farm laborers not on annual contract found work year-round, or alternatively did not report unemployment to the census enumerators.[51]

An additional manner of revising the 1900 census estimates based on the Michigan data is to adjust the distribution of months unemployed by subtracting months lost due to illness. The procedure accepts the estimate, made above, for the percentage of all farm laborers whose unemployment is involuntary (69.5 percent = 26.4/38). An additional set of assumptions must be made for this calculation because the census data are in integer numbers (not fractions) of months, whereas the Michigan data are in days and months. We assume that individuals responding to the census marshals rounded weeks lost into months, and that individuals who experienced less than two weeks of unemployment gave a zero for months unemployed. We assume, therefore, that those who experienced two weeks to just under six weeks of unemployment put down one month, those who experienced six weeks to just under ten weeks put down two months, and so on. These assumptions produce the months and weeks mapping given in Table 6.7.

The procedure results in an even tighter distribution around three to four months of unemployment. Almost two-thirds (66 percent) of non-family farm workers in the Midwest experiencing any unemployment were unemployed for three to four months (as opposed to 54 percent in the total figures unadjusted for illness), and 90 percent were idle for three to six months (as opposed to 73 percent in the unadjusted total figures). We infer from the large percentage who were unemployed for three to four months that the vast majority of the 25 percent of farm workers who were involuntarily unemployed were idle during the winter months.

Conclusions

Across the nineteenth century, seasonal restrictions on work time were reduced in three ways. Labor redistributed itself across sectors, moving from agriculture and other outdoor work to manufacturing, services, and other indoor work. Second, seasonality was decreased within each sector. Livestock and various grains served to smooth the agricultural work load over the year, and machinery reduced peak-load demands on the farm population. The use of steam power reduced industry's dependence on the flow of water and wind.

A third factor in reducing aggregate seasonality is that labor migrated between the two sectors, possibly reducing seasonal constraints in both. This meshing of the two sectors may have been exogenously determined. Pork packing in the nineteenth century, for example, could only be done in the winter and thus, coincidentally, dovetailed well with the agricultural season. Indeed, the peak labor demands of many manufacturing activities naturally mesh with those in agriculture. After the agricultural harvest, commodity-based manufacturing activities begin and proceed for as long as the crop lasts. Thus employment in sugar refining, cottonseed-oil manufacturing, and canning and preserving should have meshed well with the labor demands for their respective agricultural commodities. But meshing could also have been a response to peak agricultural demands for labor and thus could have been endogenous in origin. That is, manufacturing activities that were not inherently seasonal could have released labor at times of greater labor scarcity, as reflected in the seasonal or harvest price of labor in agriculture.

The evidence on the first factor—sectoral shifts—is the clearest, and thus the least interesting. Further, its significance depends heavily on the second factor, the extent of seasonality within each sector and its change over time. We presented evidence—on agricultural laborers per farm and the premium paid to seasonal help—indicating that seasonality in agriculture lessened in the 1880's. Although we have little direct evidence on the manufacturing sector, we showed that even as late as 1900, manufacturing employment displayed distinct seasonal patterns. Among the major industries, employment decreased in the summer and winter, and in most industries the trough was between 5 percent and 15 percent of peak labor usage.

The question arises, therefore, whether the summer trough fueled the labor needs of agriculture. In certain farming areas it may have, but some peak agricultural labor demands occurred in September and October, in addition to those in July and August. The precise reasons for decreased manufacturing employment in the summer are not entirely clear. Some labor, to be sure, "went fishing," some may have migrated to work on the farm, and some was simply unemployed.

Evidence on unemployment indicates that laborers and workers in the building trades were subject to a 45 percent probability of unemployment across the year, and that much unemployment was seasonal in nature. About 22 percent of manufacturing workers experienced some unemployment over the year, although this figure, and that for laborers and building tradesmen, probably includes sickness, vacation, and other downtime not subject to the control of employers.

In agriculture, we find that, after deducting for the "voluntary" component of nonemployment, about 25 percent of all nonfamily farm workers in 1900 were unemployed sometime during the year, and that most of these workers experienced three to four months of unemployment. Whether many of the 75 percent who did not report unemployment during the year were involved in a meshing of the sectors through migration depends on the proportion of farm laborers who found yearly employment in agriculture. Reliable sources indicate that about 25 to 35 percent of all farm laborers were hired on annual contract, although some additional fraction may have found yearly employment in the agricultural sector on monthly, seasonal, and daily bases. Thus, there is considerable leeway for one to argue that labor did migrate and that the sectors dovetailed in a significant manner. Additional support for this view is found in the logit regressions indicating that agricultural laborers living in counties containing or near large cities experienced a far lower probability of unemployment than did those laborers far removed from urban areas. The significance of this finding must be tempered by the fact that 70 percent of agricultural laborers lived in rural areas.

Seasonality, once an important component of the nation's unemployment, faded slowly as America industrialized and as technology circumvented the vagaries of climate. After weighing all the evidence, we believe it was not substantially reduced by a movement of laborers across sectors having seasons that meshed. Rather, seasonality gradually disappeared with the mechanization of agriculture, the decline of farming, and the industrialization of America. The reduction of seasonal unemployment was a product of various features of economic development but provided, at the same time, an added fillip to economic growth.

CHAPTER SEVEN

Risk Sharing, Crew Quality, Labor Shares, and Wages in the Nineteenth-Century American Whaling Industry

Lance E. Davis, Robert Gallman, and Teresa D. Hutchins

MANY AMERICANS have read *Moby Dick* and could identify "Call me Ishmael" as its opening sentence. Few have read Elmo Hohman's "Wages, Risk, and Profits in the Whaling Industry" and remember his opening words: "The method of wage payment in the whaling industry was a singular one."[1] It is to the spirit of Hohman rather than of Melville, however, that this paper is dedicated.

As Hohman has pointed out, a whaleman, whether captain or greenhand, was

not paid by the day, week, or month, nor was he allowed a certain sum for every barrel of oil or for every pound of bone captured. Instead, his earnings consisted of a specified fractional share, known as a lay, of the total net proceeds of a voyage. . . . The earnings of a whaleman thus constituted a reward not only for the performance of labor under peculiarly trying conditions, but also for the assumption of personal, business, and physical risks. For the size of his lay, representing his wages, depended directly upon the business risks centering about price fluctuations, as well as upon the physical risks of storm, fire, stranding, and poor luck on the whaling grounds.[2]

The effect of risks on the earnings of whalemen is illustrated by the experience of the captains who directed the vessels that sailed from New Bedford between New Year's Day 1840 and the end of 1858. If we consider

Funding for the research underlying this paper came from the National Bureau of Economic Research (programs on Productivity and Industrial Change in the World Economy, and the Development of the American Economy), the National Science Foundation, the Division of the Humanities and Social Sciences, California Institute of Technology, and the Kenan Foundation. We thank Karin Gleiter for research assistance and advice, and Lou Cain, Sherwin Rosen, and Stanley Lebergott, who read an earlier version of this paper and provided helpful suggestions.

only the more than 1,200 successful voyages in this period (those from which the vessel returned with some product), their captains' monthly earnings averaged $95.54, but ranged from a low of $1.20 to a high of $621.39. If the 146 unsuccessful voyages were also considered (voyages that brought nothing home or that ended in some maritime disaster), both the average and minimum values would be appreciably lower.

Hohman wrote more than fifty years ago. Although he examined the records of a large number of whaling voyages, it is not clear which voyages these were, or how he analyzed the data he found. He merely reports: "The detailed figures serving as a warrant for these statements were secured through an analysis of hundreds of individual accounts found in the collection of scores of original manuscript whaling account-books now in the New Bedford Public Library."[3]

In part this study parallels Hohman's, but it expands his work in some new directions, modifies some of his findings, and directly disputes others. At its core is an examination of 36,640 labor contracts drawn between ships' agents and the whalemen who signed on to 1,258 voyages that left from New Bedford between January 1, 1840 and December 30, 1858, and between January 1 and December 30, 1866.

The 1,258 voyages represent three-quarters of those which, according to Alexander Starbuck, departed New Bedford during the years in question.[4] The labor data have been linked with information on the voyages themselves—information drawn chiefly from Starbuck, Hegarty, and Dias—and the links permit the labor contracts to be examined in light of the vessels and equipment used, the grounds hunted, and the results of the hunt.[5] These records have been supplemented by account books of whaling voyages and agents' letter books that are on deposit at the Baker Library of Harvard University.

In the nineteenth century, sperm whales were hunted for sperm oil and spermaceti—the former used for high-quality lighting and to lubricate fast-moving machinery, the latter for very high-quality candles. Baleen whales (the rights, humpbacks, grays, and bowheads) were valued for both their oil and their bone. Whale oil was a less expensive (and lower quality) illuminant than sperm oil. It was also used as a lubricant for heavy machinery. Whalebone (or baleen) was made into corset stays, buggy whips, window shades, and other products that demanded both strength and flexibility.

Although at one time or another during the nineteenth century, British, Australian, and Norwegian vessels constituted a not-insignificant share of the world's whaling fleet, the American component was the largest by far; between 1820 and 1880, it accounted for more than 75 percent of all whaling vessels.[6] Of the coastal cities that served as home for the American fleet (there were 22 such cities in 1850), New Bedford was the most important. Between 1840 and 1860, its vessels accounted for just less than half of all American whaling tonnage and for an equal fraction of the nation's total catch.

The fleets of some American ports specialized in sperm whales or in baleen whales or focused their search in some particular geographic area. The vessels that sailed from New Bedford were much more catholic. They accounted for almost 60 percent of all sperm oil and more than 40 percent of all whale oil returned by the American fleet, and they hunted throughout the world. New Bedford ships' logs list visits to 55 separate hunting grounds, including such exotic and geographically disparate places as Patagonia, Delago Bay, the Okhotsk Sea, Desolation Island, and Altaho. (For purposes of this study, the 55 locations have been aggregated into four areas: the Atlantic, Pacific, Indian, and Western Arctic.)

In the 1840's and 1850's, the New Bedford component, like the entire American fleet, was heavily weighted toward ships; but it contained a substantial and growing proportion of barks and a few brigs, sloops, and schooners as well. (Of the 1,258 voyages, 854 were made by ships, 393 by barks, and only 11 by brigs, sloops, and schooners combined.) Both ships and barks were three-masted. The former were square-rigged; the latter, square-rigged on the fore and main masts, and fore-and-aft-rigged on the mizzen. Ships were usually, but not always, larger than barks (the average tonnage of the ships was 354, and of the barks, 277). Although on average barks employed fewer workers, they used about one-sixth more labor per ton than ships.[7]

The 29 men who manned a typical ship and the 26 who constituted a bark's crew were organized very similarly. What differences there were appear to have reflected the size of the vessel, the date of sailing, the projected length of the voyage, and the vessel's destination, rather than any difference in rigging. Each vessel had (1) a captain and some number of mates—always one, usually three, but sometimes as many as five; (2) a set of skilled professional mariners—between two and six boatsteerers, sometimes a shipkeeper, and occasionally a navigator or a head-a-boat; (3) a number of artisans—almost always a cooper and a carpenter, often a blacksmith, and occasionally a boat builder, a painter, a sail maker, a mechanic, a machinist, a caulker, a coppersmith, and, on rare occasions, a surgeon or a doctor; (4) some service personnel—almost no vessel sailed without a cook and a steward, and these two were sometimes supplemented by a second cook or steward, a steerage steward, or a steerage master; (5) a number of seamen—some skilled, some semi-skilled, some "greenhands"; and (6) often a boy or two. Table 7.1 provides a fairly accurate picture of the occupational structure of the crew of a typical vessel.

TABLE 7.1

Average Number of Crewmen in Occupational
Categories: New Bedford Whaling Voyages,
1840–58 and 1866

Occupation	Average number per voyage
Officers	
Captain	1.0
Mate	3.2
Skilled maritime	
Boatsteerer	3.5
Miscellaneous skilled	0.2
maritime	
Artisans	
Cooper	0.9
Carpenter	0.8
Blacksmith	0.5
Miscellaneous artisans	0.1
Service personnel	
Cook	1.0
Steward	1.0
Miscellaneous service	0.0[a]
Seamen	
Skilled seaman	2.2
Semi-skilled seaman	2.5
Unskilled seaman	10.2
Boys	0.6
Total	27.7

SOURCE: See text.
[a] Less than 0.05.

It does not, however, capture the changes in the structure that occurred over the 26 years in question.

The Whaleman's Lay

As Hohman pointed out, each member of the crew from the captain to the cabin boy received a predetermined fraction of his vessel's net catch. Even in this day of sophisticated businessmen-actors and their high-powered lawyers, the experience of the motion picture and television industries has shown that there is many a slip between gross and net. That is, it is easy to cheat on expenses, and preferable for the entertainer to draw a contract that depends upon a percentage of the final income in gross rather than net terms. But as a reading of *Variety* or the *Los Angeles Times* makes apparent, famous actors, including those who employ high-priced legal talent, still sign net contracts.

In nineteenth-century New Bedford, the whalemen, if not the agents and captains, were no more sophisticated, and the lay was calculated on the "net" value of the catch.[8] In the whaling case, the difference between gross and net was a standard set of charges incurred *during* the voyage. The nature (but not the amount) of these charges was specified in advance, and the labor contract was written to guarantee that the whaleman (along with the agent and owner) bore his share. The charges always included payments for pilotage, gauging, wharfing, cooperage, watching, cleaning, loading, and unloading. Toward mid-century, when the industry's organizational structure became more complex, the list was expanded to include commissions and insurance on oil and bone shipped home during the course of the voyage.

The whaleman's contract, however, does not appear to have presented the problems that have plagued the entertainment industry. The expenditures were all made by the captain, and the value of his lay depended on the size of the net. Moreover, his behavior was monitored on the spot by the other ship's officers, whose income also depended inversely on the size of the charges, and at a distance by the agent, who had the same incentive.

Crew members were usually paid in cash or in a bill of exchange that could be converted to cash, but the agent could, if he chose, give them their share in kind. A crewman was entitled to a full share if he returned on the ship on which he sailed, and a prorated share (based on the catch to date) if he died or was discharged for illness or other good cause. Until the 1860's, however, he was not legally entitled to any remuneration if he deserted before the voyage was completed.

It is difficult to determine the effect of the agent's right to pay in kind. Hohman suggests two reasons for the apparently frequent use of such payments when a crewman was discharged for "good reason" during the voyage. First, since there was often a lack of current information about the price of whale products, agreement about the correct level of remuneration was difficult to achieve. Second, in cases where the payment was substantial, the captain often wished to preserve his limited cash reserves. The accounts of the ship *Canton,* for example, show that over the course of eight mid-century years, a number of whalemen were paid off during a voyage with oil, in amounts that ranged from 74 to 393 gallons.[9]

At the end of the voyage, however, payment in kind was usually invoked only if there was a dispute between crewmen and the agent over the value of the catch. Although such payment is rarely mentioned either in contemporary accounts or in the whaling literature, a letter from the agent and ship owner Charles Morgan to his Boston lawyer suggests that it may have been a more common practice than a reading of the standard literature would lead one to believe.

The universal custom is for the owner to make up the voyage at a certain price after which it is optional with them to take it, or deliver the crew as they may elect & it is always the right of the crew to demand their oil but they cannot demand money if the owner is unwilling to pay it. The *Condor's* cargo has in part remained on the wharf & in store since its arrival & I have never yet settled with all concerned. I have this day been delivering to the Capt and one boatsteerer their parts or share of the oil and coffee as we never could agree upon a price & I have after several weeks delay declined purchasing much of the oil of another crew arrived since the *Condor* & many of them have taken away their oil & some have yet left it on the wharf. . . .

P.S. You will understand that voyages are always made up at a certain price whether the crew intends to purchase their shares or not. They [the agents] often decline purchasing & on the other hand the crew often declines selling.[10]

Whatever the importance of the right to pay in kind, all the evidence indicates that the rules governing the earnings of men who failed to complete a voyage became steadily more important as the duration of voyages lengthened—first as the fleet moved to more distant grounds, and then as the captains and agents found that they could keep their vessels at sea for much longer periods if they used Pacific cities (Honolulu, Lahaina, and Panama, to cite three) as transshipment points. As voyages lengthened, desertion became more of a problem. Between 1840–41 and 1857–58, average voyage length increased from 34 to 45 months. In the Atlantic the length of an average voyage rose from 22 to 36 months, in the Indian Ocean the increase was from 29 to 40 months, and in the Pacific it went from 38 to 47 months. Among the 1,258 voyages, there were 6 that lasted more than 5 years, and 2 vessels did not return until 69 months after leaving New Bedford.[11]

The evidence indicates that there was a high and increasing level of labor turnover in a typical crew. The *George Howland*, for example, a New Bedford ship that normally carried a crew of 28 to 30 men, sailed six times between 1840 and 1866. Over the six voyages, the number of whalemen who died, were discharged, or deserted ranged from 12 to 24, averaging 63 percent of the original crew.[12]

As Hohman pointed out, the form of the labor contract was idiosyncratic. Each crewman negotiated a lay—the fraction of the net proceeds realized from the sale of the catch that he would receive at the end of the voyage.[13] The flavor of those negotiations is captured in a letter from Charles Morgan to his captain, Thomas A. Norton, discussing the staffing of the ship *Hector*. After spelling out the range of lays that he was "accustomed to give in a four boat ship" (third mate 1/70 to 1/75, boatsteerers 1/90 to 1/95, seamen 1/125 to 1/130, ordinary seaman 1/135 to 1/150, greenhands 1/150 to 1/180, boys green 1/185 to 1/200, and boys not green 1/150 to 1/175), he continues, "Mr. Mayhew [a third mate] had 1/65 last voyage but that was higher than I have before given. I think 1/70 a fair lay for Mr. Wimfrenn but would give 1/67 rather than not have him. . . ." [14]

The traditional dividing line between good and so-so wages was 1/100. According to Hohman, the officers, the cooper, and the boatsteerers received so-called "short lays"—lays less than 1/100. Although this conclusion is, in general, correct, there is a record of one boatsteerer on the *Sappho* who, on an 1866 voyage, received only 1/150, and there were a number whose lays fell between 1/125 and 1/140. Moreover, there are numerous examples of less-skilled workers—shipkeepers, cooks, stewards, and even 19 seamen (to say nothing of 10 ordinary seamen)—who received lays "shorter" than the magic 100.

The "outliers" fall into two quite different categories. Most seem to stem from the perceived *ex ante* competence of the individual whaleman—that is, from the agent's and the whaleman's recognition that there were substantial differences between the potential productivity of whalemen, differences that existed even among seamen applying for the same job. In the case of the "underpaid" boatsteerers, each of the seven who received lays longer than 120 was a crewman on a vessel whose agent had signed his peers at wages in the usual range. The three other boatsteerers on the *Sappho,* for example, received lays of 1/75, 1/75, and 1/100, respectively. The "well-paid" seamen on vessels hunting in the Indian, Pacific, and Arctic grounds were often characterized as "able" or "extra-skilled," and their not-so-designated shipmates received lays more closely in line with tradition. In the case of stewards, such intravessel comparisons are difficult, since a vessel seldom had more than one. It is true, however, that the stewards on vessels hunting the three distant grounds who received abnormally short lays tended to have signed on vessels that were larger (in tonnage) and more heavily crewed than the average vessel of the same rig working those oceans. It seems likely that the larger vessels demanded stewards with higher skills, and that the potentially highly skilled applicants were rewarded.

Skill differences do not, however, explain a second group of outliers. Small vessels making relatively short cruises in the Atlantic tended to pay all their hands more (that is, to give shorter lays) than those same crewmen would have received had they signed on larger vessels for longer voyages to the more distant grounds. The voyages by the nineteen vessels, some of whose cooks, stewards, and skilled and semi-skilled seamen received "short" (less than 100) lays (one ship, eight barks, and ten brigs, sloops, and schooners), accounted for only 4 percent of the voyages by ships and 12 percent of the voyages by barks but 77 percent of the voyages by smaller vessels that hunted the Atlantic. Moreover, in each case the vessel was, on average, smaller and at sea for a shorter period of time than its peers hunting the same ground. Overall, whereas there is a significant positive relationship between the total labor share and vessel size for vessels hunting in the three distant grounds, the relationship is negative and significant for those operating in the Atlantic.[15]

Hohman says, "The able and ordinary seamen, stewards, cooks, and blacksmiths were entitled to shares which varied from 1/100 to 1/160; the green hands and boys had to be content with 'long lays' which fluctuated from 1/160 to 1/200; and instances of fractions as small as 1/250 to 1/350, were not unknown."[16] Again Hohman's conclusions are generally, but not exactly, correct. The cases of the well-paid stewards, cooks, and seamen have already been noted, but there were many ordinary seamen and blacksmiths, to say nothing of carpenters, whose earnings fell into the "long lay" range. In addition, there are contracts for boys that called for payments as low as 1/3,500, one that worked out to be 1/8,500, several boys who signed on for "clothes," and one boy who received no lay whatever (he signed on for "board").

In terms of the trend in the lays, Hohman argues that, with the exception of the shares of captains and first and second mates, the lays became longer as time passed. "His wage bargain entitled him [the whaleman], as time went on, to a smaller fractional share of the voyages for which he shipped. . . . "[17] This degradation he attributes to three factors: (1)"the gradually deteriorating character and efficiency of the crews," (2) the increasing "temptation to exploit . . . inferior crews," and (3) the substitution of capital for labor.[18] To a limited extent, these generalizations are correct. If the average lays for the first four years of the study period are compared to those of the last four, it is clear that the relative position of most skilled occupations improved, whereas the unskilled saw a deterioration in their fractional shares (see Table 7.2). Starting at the top of the income hierarchy, the data show a continuous improvement (that is, shortening) of officers' lays from 1840 to at least 1857. Between 1840–43 and 1855–58, captains' lays improved by 17 percent, first mates' by 24 percent, second mates' by 22 percent, third mates' by 19 percent, and fourth mates' by 12 percent.[19] In the case of skilled workers, the picture is less clear. On the one hand, for coopers, shipkeepers, and boatsteerers, comparison of the years 1840–43 with 1855–58 show slight (8, 4, and 1 percent) improvements; a similar exercise suggests no significant change in a steward's share. On the other hand, comparisons for cooks, carpenters, blacksmiths, and miscellaneous artisans indicate a deterioration (lengthening) of 3, 14, 17, and 14 percent, respectively. For seamen, Hohman is unambiguously correct. The lays of skilled seamen deteriorated by 15 percent and those of semi-skilled and unskilled seamen by 9 percent.

TABLE 7.2

Average Lays by Occupation, All Years, All Grounds: New Bedford Whaling Voyages,
1840–58 and 1866

Occupation	Average lay[a]	Improvement in lay, 1840–43 to 1855–58	Percentage of value of catch	Relative share[b]
Officers				
Captain	15.2	+17.3	6.58	1,219
First mate	23.2	+24.1	4.31	799
Second mate	38.4	+21.7	2.60	483
Third mate	53.9	+19.2	1.86	344
Fourth mate	72.3	+11.8	1.38	256
Skilled Maritime				
Boatsteerer	87.4	+1.1	1.14	212
Shipkeeper	115.4	+3.6	0.87	161
Miscellaneous skilled maritime	109.4	−22.8	0.91	169
Artisans				
Cooper	57.2	+8.1	1.75	324
Carpenter	163.9	−13.8	0.61	113
Blacksmith	171.3	−16.7	0.58	108
Miscellaneous artisan	171.2	−14.4	0.58	108
Service personnel				
Cook	140.3	−3.4	0.71	132
Steward	135.9	0.0	0.74	136
Seamen				
Skilled seaman	150.9	−14.7	0.66	123
Semi-skilled seaman	166.8	−8.7	0.60	111
Unskilled seaman	185.3	−8.7	0.54	100
Boy	415.1	−33.5	0.24	45

S O U R C E S : See text.
[a] Denominator of the lay ratio; e.g., captain's lay = 1/15·2. The numerators are always 1.
[b] Unskilled seaman's lay equals 100.

The position of skilled whalers improved relative to that of unskilled whalers, but even in the absence of that change, the earnings disparity was striking. If the standard is unskilled seamen, captains did very well, first mates quite well, and the other officers not badly (captains earned more than 12 times, first mates almost 8 times, and the second, third, and fourth mates from 2 1/2 to 5 times as much as a typical greenhand did).[20] Among the skilled maritime professionals, boatsteerers earned about twice as much and the "others" about two-thirds again as much as an unskilled crewman. Artisans (coopers aside) did not fare so well. Coopers earned more than three times as much as an unskilled hand (about as much as a third mate), but a carpenter's margin was a bare 13 percent, and blacksmiths and the other skilled workers received only slightly more than half that differential. Cooks and stewards did somewhat better; they earned about a third more than their shipmates who had never been to sea.[21] Finally, a skilled seaman could claim a premium of about 25 percent over a greenhand, but his semi-skilled confrere was entitled to only about half that bounty.

Given the materials with which he worked, Hohman was unable to distinguish ground-to-ground differences in lays. In fact, there were significant and systematic differentials that did not erode over time and were responsible for a significant portion of the lengthening that Hohman observed. Table 7.3 captures their general outline. Across all occupations, the more distant the ground, the smaller the fractional value of the lay, although the least-skilled occupations display the greatest interground differences. Lays were most generous in the Atlantic, about 7 percent less in the Indian Ocean, and about 12 percent below the Atlantic baseline in the Pacific and Arctic grounds. But the differences were not uniform across occupations. In comparison to Atlantic whalemen, boatsteerers' lays were almost 30 percent less when they sailed to the Pacific or Arctic, seamen's about 20 percent less, officers', carpenters', and service personnel's 10 percent less. Moreover, the differentials persisted throughout the period, de-

TABLE 7.3

Relative Lays by Ground: New Bedford Whaling Voyages, 1849–58 and 1866

	Ground			
Occupation	Atlantic[a]	Indian	Pacific	Arctic
Officers				
Captain	100	102	106	107
First mate	100	107	113	112
Second mate	100	111	116	118
Third mate	100	102	105	105
Skilled maritime				
Boatsteerer	100	115	127	130
Artisans				
Cooper	100	94	95	97
Carpenter	100	107	112	111
Service personnel				
Cook	100	107	111	114
Steward	100	107	110	113
Seamen				
Skilled seaman	100	109	116	119
Semi-skilled seaman	100	107	112	115
Unskilled seaman	100	112	120	122
Simple average,				
all occupations	100	107	112	113

SOURCES: See text.

NOTE: Lays are the denominators of the lay ratio. The numerators are always 1. Thus a long lay (large denominator) means a small fractional share of output.

[a]The base (100) is the Atlantic. Since the table is based on the denominators of lay ratios, a figure in excess of 100 means a smaller lay fraction than the Atlantic.

spite the longer voyages to the western grounds and the greater loss rates experienced by barks in the Pacific and by all vessels in the Arctic. The explanation of these persistent interground differentials is far from obvious, but an attempt is made to provide one below. Here, we are interested in the effects of the observed differentials on the trends in lays that were captured in Hohman's analysis. Because of those differentials, a part of the apparent deterioration in the average seaman's lay can be traced to the redistribution of the fleet from the short-lay Atlantic and Indian grounds to the long-lay Pacific and Arctic ones. Between 1840 and 1843, 10 percent of the labor contracts were for voyages to the Atlantic, and an additional 29 percent were for voyages to the Indian Ocean. By 1855–58, however, the Atlantic's share had declined to 5 percent and the Indian's to 10 percent of the total. Thus, between 1840 and 1858, about one-fifth of the observed change in the average lay of a skilled seaman can be attributed to geographic redistribution. In view of that redistribution, the improvement in officers' lays is truly remarkable.

The Wages of Whalemen

The lay was only a means to an end: the real wage. The whaleman was interested in the dollars that his lay commanded, or more importantly, what he could buy with those dollars. Any attempt to estimate the wage, however, raises two sets of problems, neither trivial. First, although the main component of a whaleman's compensation package came from the sale of his share of the catch, the value of the lay was not usually identical to his total income. There were both charges and supplements. There are also significant issues raised by questions of the timing of the payment and of income in kind. Second, even if adjustments can be made to compensate for these aspects of the wage bargain, there remain questions about the appropriate definition of the wage.

In terms of charges, aside from the repayment of cash and clothing advanced before and during the voyage and a small charge for the "doctor's box," a crewman's wages, as previously noted, were routinely docked for his share of certain expenses incurred by the vessel during the voyage. In the decades before mid-century, the standard charges were small. Hohman notwithstanding, they did not significantly affect the final settlement. For example, on nine voyages made by four vessels between 1827 and 1850, these standard charges reduced the average crewman's final payment by less than 0.6 percent.[22]

By the 1850's, however, the industry's structure had become more complex. Destinations were farther from New Bedford, and the time spent reaching and returning from those more distant grounds was costly. In an attempt to overcome their vessels' capacity constraints and to use their capital more efficiently, agents began to order their captains to transship a part of the catch through ports like Lahaina and, if the vessel was not full when it began the homeward trek, to attempt to purchase or to agree to transport enough cargo to fill the hold on the return voyage. Transshipments involved commissions and freight charges, and the crew was required to bear its share (crewmen were, however, credited with the interest earned on the income generated by the sale of the transshipped products from the date of their sale to the time of the vessel's return). Similarly, the oil and bone purchased to top off the cargo was not costless, but it produced a net gain for both owner and crew. Because of these institutional changes, by the 1850's the charges against gross revenues had increased. On four voyages returning after 1850, for example, the average crewman's earnings were reduced by about 3 percent.[23]

Later, during the Civil War, the threat of Confederate raiders drove insurance and freight charges to new heights. On a voyage of the *George Howland* that departed New Bedford in 1862 and returned four years later, the charges totaled $28,316 (including $13,263 for freight, $9,143 for insurance, and $5,032 in commissions), or more than 15 percent of gross revenues. It should perhaps be noted that, from the point of view of both the agent and the crew, this wartime voyage was still a financial success. Despite the record charges, the monthly net revenue (in constant dollars) was 50 percent higher than the average earned on the ship's previous seven voyages and almost 10 percent greater than on the most successful of the seven.[24] Not all vessels that put to sea during the war were faced by such heavy charges. On the bark *Callao*'s 1,093-day voyage from September 1862 to August 1865, for example, after adjustments for the interest accrued on transhipped products, the net charges amounted to only about 1.6 percent of revenues.

After the war, charges appear to have settled back into the range that had characterized the 1850's. They rose significantly above that level only when a misadventure near the end of a voyage forced the owners to pay freight charges on cargo that would otherwise have been brought back by the vessel itself.[25]

In partial offset to these charges, some whalemen earned supplements to their contracted lays. Captains usually received some fraction of the profits from the sales of clothing and tobacco from the slop chest, and sometimes a share of the slush, and they often carried on subsidiary commercial enterprises on their own account.[26] Similarly, as mentioned above, the cook was normally entitled to some fraction of the slush fund. In addition, although there are questions as to the importance of the practice, seamen did, from time to time, receive not-insubstantial bonuses for particularly good performances in sighting and catching whales.[27] On the 1834 voyage of the *George Howland,* for example, four seamen received cash bonuses ranging from $30 to $50—sums equal to between 7.5 and 12.5 percent of their lay income.[28] Also, a crew member might be the recipient of some of the traditional charges that provided the wedge between gross and net value. A seamen might well add $25 to $100 to his earnings by helping load the vessel before it set out to sea, by helping unload or clean it when it returned to port, or by foregoing shore leave on some exotic South Sea island to remain aboard ship as a watchman.

Finally, although it is impossible to assess the importance of the practice, the evidence indicates that lays were sometimes renegotiated during a voyage. In 1860, the agent Matthew Howland wrote to Valentine Lewis, one of his captains, who had reported that his crew were asking to have their lays increased. Howland told Lewis to resist, if he could, but to accede if necessary, "because we are satisfied that a good crew is cheaper at high lays than a miserable crew is for nothing."[29] On the *George Howland*'s eighth voyage (1862–66), seven crewmen (the third mate, the cooper, the steward, three boatsteerers, and a seaman) received increased lays ranging in value from $140.39 to $1,936.90 and totaling $5,557.98.[30]

Two other characteristics of the wage bargain tempered the amount of risk transferred from owner to seaman. First, although the custom had no direct effect on the final payment, the seaman received room (or at least a bunk or a place to hang his hammock) and board (such as it was). An analysis of the cost of outfitting a vessel indicates that, in 1880 dollars, the value of a seaman's food probably ranged between $3.90 and $6.70 a month.[31]

Second, with the exception of the captain and sometimes a mate or two, crewmen normally received advances before their vessels left port. Usually the advance was equal to between a quarter and a third of their projected earnings. The funds were used, and were usually sufficient, to support wives and families for the duration of the voyage, although they occasionally were supplemented by further advances, if the voyage proved unusually long or if an emergency arose. Crewmen were charged interest on advances (usually 6 percent per year), but, most importantly, advances were almost never repaid if the ship sank or returned clean (that is, without oil or bone). Moreover, if, at the end of a successful voyage, a seaman's account was still in deficit, the agent had little recourse other than to try to convince the whaleman to sign on for another of his—the agent's— voyages. Since the seaman could sign with another agent and have a clean slate, such attempts were seldom successful.

Over eight voyages of the *George Howland* (1834–66), five of the *Milton* (1869–85), and two of the *Callao* (1871–77), advances were taken by 413 of the 459 newly signed crewmen. The advances ranged (in 1880 dollars) from $1,003.25 ($1,043.38 nominal) received by the second mate of the *George Howland* in 1862 to $1.32 ($1.45 nominal) taken by Joseph Howland—a Howland family member sailing as an able seaman—of the same ship in 1838. The average was $121.66. Over these fifteen voyages, the advances amounted to just less than 10 percent of net revenues (gross returns less charges), or about 30 percent of the crew's share. Moreover, on the three voyages that yielded their owners less than $700 a month, the advances averaged 25 percent of the *total revenue*. Finally, although the evidence is very sketchy, it appears that in the postbellum period, individual advances were somewhat smaller ($115 as opposed to $127), but, as a fraction of net revenues, the proportion was probably higher.[32]

Advances were a cause of some concern among agents and, to a lesser extent, among seamen as well. Although agents were prepared to accept the losses associated with truly disastrous voyages, they were less prepared to accept those resulting from desertion. In September 1834, Charles Morgan warned one of his captains, Cornelius Howland, Jr., "The crew are generally indebted to the Owners about $110 to $120 each you will therefore be especially careful of them till you get Oil enough to secure that and over it."[33] Two months later in a letter to another captain he was even more explicit: "I think you have a good crew, but they mostly all are in debt to the Ship from $70 to $100—So please take care they dont run away before you get some Sperm Oil."[34]

Clearly, on the outbound voyage, crewmen had a strong incentive to desert; the evidence indicates that some whalemen managed to run even before their vessels left New Bedford. On the return voyage, however, the incentive shifted. It was then that the captain, and perhaps the agent, found it in his interest to convince a crewman that he should make an early departure. In November 1836, eleven months after the *Condor* left New Bedford and three months before she was scheduled to return, Morgan wrote his captain, George H. Dexter, "The carpenter too has come and tells a queer story of his being left purposely of the whole crew being without bread nine days and some other things equally probable. I did not pay much attention to him."[35]

That captains and agents tended to ease the path to desertion when a seaman's account stood in surplus was certainly the view of Navy Lt. Charles Wilkes, who commanded an expedition to the Pacific in the late 1830's and early 1840's. "Many Americans are found on the different islands, who have been turned ashore from whale-ships, or left because they have broken their liberty a single time, near the end of a voyage. Such treatment leaves too much ground not to believe that they are purposely left, in order to increase the profits of the ship-master or owners."[36] For example, in the course of the *Montreal*'s third voyage (1857–62), the vessel left five crewmen, and the evidence strongly indicates that it was the ship that deserted the crew, not the crew who deserted the ship.[37] In a similar vein, the historian A.B.C. Whipple charges that obstreperous men were often marooned on uninhabited islands and left to die. He describes in some detail the problems that U.S. consuls faced in adjudicating between captain and men: did the men desert or were they marooned? In one instance, however, Whipple describes a case where the consul was faced with an obvious case of encouraged desertion. On a four-year voyage in the early 1830's, Captain Brown of the Warren, Rhode Island, ship *Magnet* wrote this message to the consul at Callao, Peru, concerning crewmen whom the consul was to return to the ship: "I should be happy if you will have the goodness to git the men down as soon as convenient. . . . I have no one I can trust out of my ship or I would send someone up."[38] It is interesting to note that Brown remained the captain on the next voyage of the *Magnet*. Clearly the agent, Joseph Smith, Jr. (his father had been the agent for the previous voyage), was not displeased with the captain's contribution to his crew's desertion.

Although it may be impossible to discover precisely who won and who lost in this game, Hohman concludes that, on average, it was probably the whalemen who won and the agents and owners who lost.[39] Some support for his view can be found in the eight successive voyages of the *George Howland* between December 1834 and April 1886. In 1880 dollars, average advances over the eight voyages ranged from $77 to $157 (the mean was $112). Over the same voyages, the average income that accrued to the agents and owners from the crewmen who had run or were discharged for cause (i.e., their share less their advance) ranged from a loss of $3,732 to a gain of $7,966; the average was $747—a figure that amounts to just less than one-fourth of the total amount advanced. That result, however, depends entirely on the seventh voyage (October 1857 to July 1861). For the other seven the average *loss* to the agents and owners was $284, or about 8 percent of the money loaned. The exceptional voyage began during the depression of 1857, and it was marked by an average advance of only $77—well below the typical $112, and $21 less than that for any of the seven other voyages.

Since there is no systematic evidence on supplements, charges, advances, or renegotiations, the hypothetical lay payment (the lay times the value of the catch) will be taken as an approximation to, and thus as an index of, the earnings of the mid-nineteenth-century whaleman. That figure will, however, be adjusted by an estimate of the value of board in certain wage comparisons. Even if one is willing to accept these estimates, questions still remain about an appropriate definition of *the* wage. Voyages were not

TABLE 7.4

Monthly Earnings, by Occupation, All Grounds, Own Vessel: New Bedford Whaling Voyages, *1840–58 and 1866*

(current dollars)

Year	Captain	First mate	Second mate	Third mate	Boatsteerer	Cooper	Carpenter	Cook	Steward	Skilled seaman	Semi-skilled seaman	Unskilled seaman
1840	92.51	54.89	33.05	24.71	17.61	26.77	10.41	10.86	11.29	10.84	9.55	8.90
1841	71.38	45.45	29.18	21.12	14.35	22.52	7.95	8.88	9.25	8.52	8.11	6.90
1842	78.15	51.00	30.98	23.14	16.20	23.75	7.86	9.64	9.69	9.57	8.43	7.60
1843	81.55	50.54	30.98	21.87	15.05	22.56	8.80	9.17	9.74	9.04	8.34	7.71
1844	70.00	42.94	27.71	18.70	13.32	18.90	7.12	7.91	8.24	7.69	7.30	6.25
1845	66.95	42.77	26.09	20.13	12.70	21.08	7.02	7.72	7.69	7.72	5.84	6.27
1846	83.81	53.37	32.81	24.79	15.90	23.60	8.00	9.78	9.90	9.81	8.45	7.57
1847	83.08	50.58	31.88	23.70	15.72	24.14	7.86	9.49	9.90	8.76	8.08	7.51
1848	110.10	69.84	44.91	29.62	19.70	33.00	11.28	12.44	12.39	12.60	10.13	9.50
1849	104.72	68.48	41.71	28.30	19.81	30.11	11.51	12.26	12.04	11.35	10.46	9.08
1850	109.02	73.74	44.35	29.09	18.78	32.94	10.07	11.50	11.54	11.59	9.24	8.76
1851	116.66	79.40	45.82	32.42	19.64	32.79	10.50	11.90	12.62	10.85	9.41	9.20
1852	107.66	73.56	42.00	31.87	18.60	28.82	9.53	11.02	13.72	11.46	8.58	8.44
1853	123.53	85.29	48.49	35.74	21.45	34.51	12.49	13.01	14.30	10.77	10.72	9.80
1854	111.26	77.70	45.21	32.51	19.83	29.94	10.36	11.45	12.71	12.76	8.71	8.76
1855	100.51	68.52	40.08	28.79	16.34	26.37	8.92	9.34	11.19	9.33	8.54	7.37
1856	106.98	72.19	41.16	29.52	16.82	28.09	8.41	9.88	10.77	9.67	7.87	7.33
1857	93.04	65.06	38.65	26.21	14.25	22.08	7.40	9.03	9.59	7.52	7.28	6.58
1858	104.35	69.73	41.77	27.30	16.87	27.07	9.00	9.82	10.40	8.63	9.58	7.41
1866	137.55	87.95	57.30	37.14	22.22	31.39	11.17	12.34	16.15	12.17	10.62	9.73
Averages												
All years	97.64	64.15	38.71	27.33	17.26	27.02	9.28	10.37	11.16	10.03	8.76	8.03
1840–58	95.54	62.90	37.37	26.82	17.00	26.79	9.18	10.27	10.89	9.92	8.66	7.94

SOURCES: See text.
NOTE: The estimate assumes the crewman returned on the vessel on which he sailed.

short. They ranged in length from a 3-month venture into the Atlantic by the *Petrel* in 1866 to the 69 months spent in the Pacific by the *George* in 1847 and the *Courier* in 1850. Contracts were signed before a voyage began, and payment was not due until the vessel had returned to New Bedford. Moreover, a substantial portion of the original crew did not return with the vessel on which they sailed. How then should the wage be calculated? The answer is that the measure should depend on the question to be asked. Table 7.4 provides one such schedule. It reflects the earnings that the whaleman would have received from his lay had he returned on the vessel on which he departed. It is probably the best available *ex post* measure. Although it includes neither the charges against nor the supplements to the whaleman's lay, it does represent the bulk of his earnings.

The Relative Wages of Whalemen

The absolute level of wages was certainly a major concern of whalemen and remains of concern to social historians interested in questions of welfare, but it was relative wages that dictated career choices and governed the flow of men into the industry. It is, therefore, the latter measure that is of greater concern to economic historians analyzing the efficiency of nineteenth-century labor markets. The wage ashore furnishes one standard against which to measure whalemen's earnings, but it is the merchant marine that, at least at first glance, appears to provide the more relevant comparisons. The maritime data are spotty, but the work of Stanley Lebergott provides bases for comparisons of six of the twelve major whalemen's occupations.[40]

During the 1840's and 1850's, the officers who manned the whaling fleet were well rewarded, if their alternative was service in the merchant marine. Over comparable years, whaling captains received, on average, $91.55 a month, while their counterparts in the merchant service earned only $29.54 (see Table 7.5). Although the contrast is less marked for second and third mates, whalers still earned more than twice as much as merchantmen. A part of the whaling premium almost certainly reflected the uncertainty of rewards. For merchant captains, the range of salaries was from $20 to $35 per month; the lucky whaling captains who returned with some catch earned salaries that ranged between $1.20 and $621. For first mates, the mercantile range was $45 ($15 to $60), in contrast to $394 for whalers, and for second mates the ranges were $36 and $231, respectively.[41]

In whaling, officers were required not only to assume larger risks, but also to bear heavier responsibilities. Since they often hunted in uncharted waters, it was necessary that they possess greater maritime skills than typical officers in the merchant fleet. In addition, the whaling captain had to understand the whale's habits and migration patterns and to be prepared

TABLE 7.5

Comparative Monthly Wages: Merchantmen and Whalers, 1840–58 and 1866

(current dollars)

Year	Captains			First mates			Second mates			Cooks			Skilled seamen			Semi-skilled seamen		
	MM	W	W/MM	MM	W	W/MM	MM	W	W/MM	MM	W	W/MM	MM	W	W/MM	MM	W	W/MM
1840	30.00	92.50	3.08	26.00	54.90	2.11	19.33	33.00	1.71	13.75	10.90	0.79	14.00	10.80	0.77	—	—	—
1841	30.00	71.40	2.38	21.33	45.50	2.13	—	30.00	7.50	9.80	8.90	0.91	14.00	8.52	0.61	—	—	—
1842	30.00	78.16	2.61	21.00	51.00	2.43	4.00	—	—	10.00	9.60	0.96	13.00	9.57	0.74	—	—	—
1843	30.00	81.60	2.72	18.67	50.50	2.71	—	—	—	8.33	9.20	1.10	13.00	10.11	0.78	—	—	—
1844	27.50	70.00	2.55	18.67	42.90	2.30	—	—	—	8.43	7.90	0.94	14.00	7.70	0.55	—	—	—
1845	26.67	67.00	2.51	19.25	42.80	2.22	—	—	—	11.17	7.60	0.68	14.00	7.70	0.55	—	—	—
1846	28.00	83.80	2.99	20.33	53.40	2.63	19.00	32.80	1.73	12.36	9.80	0.79	14.00	9.80	0.70	8.60	8.50	0.99
1847	25.00	83.10	3.32	31.00	50.60	1.63	21.00	31.90	1.52	20.00	9.50	0.48	14.00	8.80	0.63	—	—	—
1848	30.00	110.10	3.67	22.00	69.80	3.17	20.00	44.90	2.25	12.17	12.40	1.02	15.00	12.60	0.84	10.25	10.10	0.98
1849	—	—	—	30.00	68.50	2.28	—	—	—	15.00	12.30	0.82	15.00	11.40	0.76	—	—	—
1850	27.33	109.00	3.99	17.50	73.70	4.21	—	—	—	13.00	11.50	0.88	13.00	11.60	0.89	—	—	—
1851	—	—	—	32.00	79.40	2.48	20.00	45.80	2.29	16.50	11.90	0.72	15.00	10.90	0.73	9.63	9.40	0.98
1852	—	—	—	28.00	73.60	2.63	20.00	42.00	2.10	17.25	11.00	0.64	15.00	11.50	0.77	9.53	8.60	0.90
1853	35.00	142.60	4.07	25.67	100.00	3.90	20.00	56.20	2.81	15.00	15.00	1.00	15.00	18.10	1.21	12.28	10.70	0.87
1854	35.00	109.40	3.13	46.25	76.40	1.65	33.33	44.50	1.34	27.00	11.20	0.41	15.00	12.50	0.83	9.78	8.50	0.87
1855	—	—	—	—	—	—	37.50	40.00	1.07	26.00	9.30	0.36	15.00	9.30	0.62	8.49	8.50	1.00
1856	—	—	—	—	—	—	—	—	—	—	—	—	—	9.67	—	—	—	—
1857	—	—	—	50.00	69.70	1.39	35.00	39.00	1.11	25.00	9.10	0.36	15.00	7.58	0.51	—	—	—
1858	—	—	—	—	—	—	—	—	—	—	—	—	—	8.00	—	—	—	—
1866	—	—	—	55.00	88.80	1.61	36.00	57.80	1.61	29.33	12.50	0.43	27.00	12.20	0.45	13.03	10.30	0.79
Average	29.54	91.55	3.09	28.39	64.21	2.44	23.76	41.49	2.25	16.12	10.53	0.74	15.00	10.42	0.72	10.20	9.33	0.92

SOURCES: See text. Merchantmen from Stanley Lebergott, Manpower in Economic Growth: The American Record since 1800 (New York, 1964), A-21, A-21A, A-22A, and A-22B.

NOTES: Whalers are New Bedford "own vessel," all grounds; "own vessel" means that the estimate rests on the assumption that the seaman returns on the vessel on which he sailed. MM = merchant marine. W = whaleman.

to command one of the Nantucket (or New Bedford) sleighs (as the small whaleboats were sometimes called). Although it was the captain who had the final word, the other officers were also required to possess skills beyond those asked of a mate in the sister service. On August 8, 1834, for example, Charles W. Morgan, the agent, wrote one of his captains, "I have also been thinking about Officers, who are however plenty—There is Mr. Plaskitt who was 3rd Mate on the *Russell*—if you went on a sperm whale voyage I don't think you could get a better man. I don't know how he would answer for right whaling."[42]

It is clear from reading their letters that agents believed the choice of the captain (and probably the first and second mates as well) was immensely important to the success of a voyage. Evidence that they were not mistaken can be found in a systematic quantitative analysis of the records of the voyages.[43] A comprehensive multiple regression model fit to the data on individual voyages—the dependent variable is a Caves, Christensen, Diewert superlative productivity index, and the independent variables are designed to capture decision, technological, and environmental factors that theory or contemporary accounts suggest might have been important determinants of productivity—shows that productivity was positively associated (large coefficient, and usually a reasonable significance level) with the captain's share of output.[44] In addition, the large lays accruing to captains and other officers certainly add support to the imputation of high productivity to them.

If the greater risk and the increased knowledge and skill requirements led to the relatively high wages earned by officers, what explains the wages of cooks and seamen? Wages in whaling were not higher than those in the merchant service, and it is likely that they were, in fact, lower. Over comparable periods, the ratio of earnings in whaling to earnings in the merchant marine ranged from 0.7 for cooks and skilled seamen to 0.9 for semi-skilled seamen. In only 9 of the 44 occupation years over which there are comparable data was the ratio equal to or in excess of 1.0.

Moreover, these relatively low wages were coupled with variances as high as those among the much more highly paid officers. Whereas the ranges in the merchant marine fell between 1 to 3 and 1 to 6 ($10 to $30 for skilled seamen, $5 to $20 for semi-skilled seamen, and $7 to $40 for cooks), the ranges for the comparable whalers were many times as wide. For cooks, monthly wages ranged from $0.53 to $60.00 (1 to 113), for semi-skilled seamen from $0.27 to $41.00 (1 to 153), and for skilled seamen from $0.29 to $71.00 (1 to 246).

It is generally recognized that merchant seamen "professed great contempt for 'spouters' and 'blubber-hunters'; and a real whaleman never thought of shifting his allegiance." Each industry drew from its own pool of labor, and only when both industries were working to capacity was there "competition for those hands who were willing to ship in either service."[45] Also, neither whaling nor merchant marine agents were forced to confine their search to the domestic labor market; they were able to draw from an international labor pool. Stanley Lebergott, citing contemporary sources, concludes that by the 1840's, officers and mates aside, the vast majority of seamen on American vessels were foreigners.[46]

The flavor of the typical whaling crew (and the question of the appropriate yardstick against which to measure their wages) is neatly captured in Charles Nordhoff's account of the 36-man crew of his whaler.

The captain, two mates, and three of the boatsteerers were Americans. The third mate, and one of the boatsteerers were Portuguese, natives of Fayal, as were also four of our crew. . . . The rest of the crew I find enumerated in my log as follows: two lawyer's clerks, one professional gambler, one runaway from his father's counting house in New York (this was also an amateur gambler), one New York "butcher-boy"—his name was *Mose*—six factory hands, from some small New England towns, one Boston school boy, one canal boat man, six farm boys—from various parts of New England, and western New York,—the four Portuguese before mentioned, who were whalemen, and the writer hereof, who wrote himself *seaman.*"[47]

Nordhoff described a time late in the period when the whaling industry had shrunk substantially. In the 1840's and 1850's, when the industry was at its peak, the proportion of foreigners in a typical crew would probably have been even larger.

The comparison of the wages of whalemen (but not officers) with those of merchant seamen produces results that, if they do not confirm the view that there were two separate labor markets, imply behavior outside the normal bounds of economists' assumptions. If, however, the positions in whaling and in the merchant service were really comparable, and if both industries had access to the same workers, the whalemen's willingness to accept both lower average and much more variable returns would suggest either that they were drawn from a *truly* unique pool of labor—people who believed that a small probability of a big win was a goal worth sacrificing for—or that they were paying their apprenticeship dues on the way to remunerative positions as boatsteerers or officers. More likely, the two groups were being hired for different jobs: merchant seamen as seamen, whalers as oarsmen. It is also possible that they were doing the same job, but the whalemen were just not very good at it. In fact, the evidence indicates that there is an element of truth in each of the four explanations, but at this stage it is not possible to assign a weight to each.

The merchant marine may have represented the closest maritime alternative for a whaleman, but it appears that it was shore-based opportunities, more than anything else, that forced captains and agents to look to foreign ports for their crews. Tables 7.6 and 7.7 show the trends in relative whaling-to-onshore wage rates for nine professional and skilled classes of whalemen and for the three classes of seamen. The comparisons of officers, artisans, and service personnel are based on the wages of skilled civilians employed by the Department of the Army between 1840 and 1856 as reported by Robert Margo and Georgia Villaflor. For unskilled workers, the choice for onshore laborers is larger: the wages of Margo and Villaflor's unskilled civilian employees in the Northeast, Robert Layer's New England textile workers, and Edith Abbott's unskilled factory workers and "all urban unskilled" have been used here.[48] A comparison of the years 1840 to 1843 with 1853 to 1856 in Table 7.6 indicates that the relative position of all officers vis-à-vis shore-based artisans improved by 15 percent or more. Captains and first and second mates earned more than the skilled Department of the Army civilians; their real wages increased as well, although they eroded somewhat between 1857 and 1866. For the other skilled whalemen, the story is less favorable. Although their relative position did not deteriorate (in fact, it may have improved somewhat), carpenters, cooks, and stewards all earned less than half, boatsteerers only three-fifths, and even coopers less than nine-tenths as much as Margo and Villaflor's artisans, and their real wages fell as well.

The situation of seamen was no better (see Table 7.7). Although their wages did not deteriorate relative to those of unskilled civilian employees in the Northeast, they were only about 60 percent of the level of the wages of workers ashore. If the basis of comparison is shifted either to Edith Abbott's estimates of unskilled factory workers or to her figures for all urban unskilled, the relative position of the whalemen improves, but even able seamen received significantly less than shore-based workers. Over time, there appears to have been a not-insubstantial degradation in the relative positions of all three classes of whalemen. The whaling seamen did, however, earn about as much as Massachusetts textile workers, who were chiefly female employees.[49]

It is unfortunate that the estimates of whaling earnings cannot be extended backward into the 1820's and 1830's. The secondary literature indicates that in those early decades, the work force was largely native-born American (i.e., seamen whose fathers had been born on this side of the Atlantic—including a not-insubstantial number of blacks), and the majority were trained seamen.[50] Although a precise answer depends on the wage series and the price deflator chosen, it appears that between 1840–43 and 1855–58 the real wages of unskilled workers in the United States may have risen by 20 percent or may have fallen by as much as 5 percent. No

TABLE 7.6

Relative Earnings: Whaling Officers, Artisans, and Service Personnel to Skilled Civilians Hired by the Army, 1840–56

Year	Captain	First mate	Second mate	Third mate	Boatsteerer	Cooper	Carpenter	Cook	Steward
1840	265	164	106	84	65	89	46	47	48
1841	207	137	94	73	55	76	37	40	41
1842	244	165	106	84	63	85	39	44	44
1843	238	153	99	74	55	76	38	39	41
1844	231	148	101	73	56	74	37	40	41
1845	186	124	81	65	46	68	31	33	33
1846	239	157	102	80	56	77	35	40	40
1847	235	149	100	79	58	80	37	41	42
1848	324	211	142	99	71	108	47	51	51
1849	307	206	132	94	71	99	48	50	49
1850	316	219	138	96	67	106	43	47	47
1851	342	238	144	106	70	107	45	49	51
1852	307	215	130	103	67	94	42	46	54
1853	339	239	143	110	73	107	49	50	54
1854	289	207	128	97	66	91	43	46	49
1855	251	177	111	85	56	79	39	40	44
1856	237	165	101	76	50	73	33	36	38
Average	268	181	115	87	61	88	41	43	45
Ratio of relative earnings, 1840–43 to 1853–56	0.85	0.79	0.84	0.85	0.97	0.93	0.98	0.99	0.94

SOURCES: See text.
NOTE: Whaling wages include allowance for board and cover all whaling grounds.

matter which price index is chosen, the real wages of all "enlisted" whale-men appear to have declined by more than the most pessimistic of the onshore estimates. Officers, on the other hand, clearly gained.[51] It is difficult to see how, given the wage differentials, the whaling industry could have continued to recruit trained Americans for enlisted jobs over the two antebellum decades. The most probable explanation is that it did not. Instead, the agents appear to have turned more and more to unskilled Americans and to both skilled and unskilled foreign workers. It appears that even black sailors—whose onshore opportunities must have been severely constrained—deserted the whaling fleet. Although her data are somewhat difficult to interpret, Martha Putney's survey of whaling crew lists seems to indicate that there were, on average, 2.8 black Americans on each New Bedford vessel sailing between 1803 and 1840, but only 1.5 in the years 1841–43 and 1846–60.[52]

Other interpretations are possible. For example, the industry might have represented such an unusual opportunity for risk-lovers that wages shrank as increased numbers of gamblers competed for the limited number of jobs. After all, the presence of both professional and amateur gamblers among Nordhoff's shipmates might indicate something about the degree of risk aversion shared by at least the American component of that crew, and Hohman does argue that "the device of the lay with its tantalizing possibility of a lucky voyage, served to obscure the average earnings."[53]

The data on wages indicate that, within the industry, the labor market worked quite well. Clues to the efficiency of the market internal to the industry may be gleaned from an analysis of the labor contracts of more than 10,000 greenhands who departed New Bedford over the twenty years 1840–58 and 1866. Contracts of greenhands were chosen because perceived quality differences were probably smaller among them than among seamen of greater experience. For neophyte whalemen, the real monthly wage averaged $8.34 in 1860 dollars, but there were interground differentials. Whereas lays in the Atlantic ground averaged 1/158 (0.00633), those in the Indian 1/179 (0.00559), those in the Pacific 1/189 (0.00530), and those in the Arctic 1/197 (0.00509), differences in productivity meant that the ordering of wages received was quite different. Greenhands who signed on for the Atlantic ground earned, on average, only $7.84 a month. Thanks to the banner catches by the *Cornelia*, the *Mary Ann*, and the *Tropic Bird* in 1853, that figure is more than the $7.44 average for the Indian Ocean, but it is below the $8.49 earned in the Pacific, and only five-sixths of the $9.30 reward for service in the Arctic.[54]

As an aid to understanding the workings of the whaling labor market, an attempt was made to model the wage bargain. Each agent and potential crewman was assumed to be aware of (1) the ground to which the voyage

TABLE 7.7

Relative Earnings: Skilled, Semi-skilled, and Unskilled Whaling Seamen to Various Workers Ashore, 1840–58 and 1866

	Skilled seamen to:				Semi-skilled seamen to:				Unskilled seamen to:			
	Unskilled Northeast	Massachusetts textile	Unskilled factory	All urban unskilled	Unskilled Northeast	Massachusetts textile	Unskilled factory	All urban unskilled	Unskilled Northeast	Massachusetts textile	Unskilled factory	All urban unskilled
1840	98	120	110	74	91	112	102	69	87	107	98	66
1841	66	100	93	64	64	97	90	62	58	89	83	57
1842	66	102	87	70	61	94	81	65	57	88	76	61
1843	57	102	87	72	54	97	83	68	51	92	79	65
1844	51	87	79	61	49	84	77	59	45	77	70	54
1845	51	85	83	60	44	73	71	52	46	75	73	54
1846	58	98	78	65	53	89	71	60	50	83	67	56
1847	69	95	89	66	66	91	84	63	63	87	81	60
1848	79	113	104	82	68	98	90	71	65	94	87	68
1849	67	108	91	73	63	102	86	70	58	93	79	64
1850	66	106	86	75	57	91	74	65	55	88	71	63
1851	66	103	87	73	60	94	80	67	60	92	79	66
1852	64	112	93	77	54	94	78	65	53	93	77	64

1853	63	109	89	72	63	109	88	72	60	103	84	68
1854	71	125	103	79	57	100	82	63	57	100	83	63
1855	59	107	87	69	56	102	83	65	52	95	77	61
1856	56	105	80	67	50	94	72	60	48	90	69	58
1857	—	96	72	61	—	95	71	60	—	91	68	57
1858	—	103	73	59	—	110	78	63	—	95	67	54
1866	—	88	71	59	—	82	66	55	—	79	64	53
Averages												
1840–56	64	104	90	71	59	95	82	64	56	91	78	62
All years	—	103	87	69	—	95	80	64	—	91	77	61
Ratio of rela-												
tive earnings												
1840–43 to 1853–56	0.88	0.95	1.05	0.97	0.84	0.98	1.09	1.01	1.02	0.97	1.07	1.00
1840–43 to 1855–58	1.03	—	1.21	1.10	—	1.00	1.17	1.07	—	1.02	1.19	1.09

SOURCES: See text.
NOTE: Whaling wages include allowance for board and cover all whaling grounds.

was to be primarily directed (external evidence indicates that the choice of ground was one of the agent's first decisions, and his labor recruitment decisions were made in light of that choice; moreover, the labor contract frequently spelled out the projected destination of the voyage); (2) the average catch and length of voyage of all vessels returning to New Bedford from the designated ground during the previous year (that information was readily available in the *Whalemen's Shipping List and Merchants' Transcript,* a local newspaper); and (3) the average probability of a vessel's returning safely from that ground over the previous five years (again, information well documented in the local press). The model rests on the assumption that, although it was the lay that was the focus of the negotiation between agent and prospective crewman, it was the expected real wage (or real cost) that was at the heart of the bargain.

Table 7.8 reports the results of two alternative specifications of the model. The dependent variable in Model 1 is the real value of the average catch of vessels that had returned from the designated ground in the previous year, multiplied by the lay negotiated by a greenhand in the present year—it is, in short, a proxy for the expected real wage rate.[55] The dependent variable in Model 2 is the expected real wage rate variable of Model 1 multiplied by the average probability (calculated over the previous five years) that a vessel setting out for the designated ground would actually return safely to New Bedford.[56]

There are seven independent variables. Four are suggested by theory or by contemporary accounts; three are included to test the completeness of the model. In the first set, in addition to the "common wage ashore" (included to get at the competitive pressures emanating from other labor markets), are variables designed to capture financial risk, time at sea, and the risk of spending more time at sea than expected.[57] In the second set are the three ground dummies—the Pacific was chosen as the base, and it is the implicit fourth ground. If the model captures the essence of the wage bargain, the coefficients on the ground dummies should be close to zero.

The results are mixed. The adjusted R^2s are very good, given the element of luck in the industry, and the F values are both very high and significant. Moreover, if attention is focused on the first set of variables, the model appears to have captured the principal elements of the wage negotiation that both theory and the qualitative literature suggest should have dominated the bargain. But the ground coefficients indicate that, even after the effects of the first set of variables have been factored out, there still remain substantial differences between expected earnings in the Atlantic and Indian grounds on the one hand, and in the Pacific and Arctic on the other.

Theory suggests that workers usually prefer lesser to greater financial

TABLE 7.8

Determinants of Expected Real Monthly Wage Rate in New Bedford Whaling, Greenhands, 1840–58 and 1866

	Model 1 Dependent variable unad- justed for physical risk	Model 2 Dependent variable adjusted for physical risk
Observations	10,723	10,390
F	1434.0	1447.2
Adjusted r^2	0.483	0.494
Dependent mean	$7.95	$7.33
Intercept	+ 10.237*	+ 11.038*
Real common wage rate ashore	+ 0.0847*	+ 0.0538*
Financial risk	+ 0.00247*	+ 0.00230*
(Voyage length)^2	− 0.00348*	− 0.00383*
"Time at sea" risk	− 0.00433	− 0.0471*
Hunting ground		
Atlantic	− 5.747*	− 5.860*
Indian	− 1.867*	− 2.111*
Arctic	+ 0.811*	+ 0.00876

SOURCES: See text.
* Significant at the 0.0001 level.

risk, and this conjecture is borne out by the analysis. The coefficient on "financial risk"—measured by the variance of the returns—is positive, large, and very significant. Even in the less compelling case (Model 2), it appears that a greenhand required a bonus of 35 percent to compensate him for signing in the year following the maximum variance as compared with the one following the minimum.

The variable "time at sea" is intended to be an index of the expected duration of the voyage. It is measured by the average duration of the voy-ages—by hunting ground—of vessels returning to New Bedford in the previous year. The industry's historians point out that the desertion rate rose as the length of the voyage increased, and infer that whalemen pre-ferred short voyages. It is likely, however, that the observed association reflects not a preference for short voyages, but a perfectly reasonable pref-erence for successful ones. Exceptionally long voyages tended to be unsuc-cessful. Strong-minded captains, unwilling to return with empty cargo space, would remain at sea, despite the grumblings of the crew. Leaving these cases aside, however, many men must have preferred the security of employment offered by longer voyages—a three-year voyage rather than one planned to end in two years, for example. If men with these prefer-ences dominated the market, one could expect the sign on the coefficient of the variable "time at sea" to be negative, as it is: men required a pre-mium for a short voyage.

On the other hand, the sign on the variable "risk of spending more time at sea than anticipated"—a measure of the variance of the "time at sea" variable—might very well be positive, since the variable is intended to pick up anticipations of chances of success. In fact, the sign is negative, and the coefficient is highly significant—results very difficult to rationalize.

With this exception, the first set of variables seems to capture the essence of the negotiation and indicate that the market was working fairly efficiently. The ground dummies are less successful. If the model were correct and complete, one could expect the coefficients on the dummies to be insignificantly different from zero, but this is not the case. On the positive side, in Model 1, recruitment for voyages to the Arctic ground required a premium of about 10 percent, a reasonable result in view of the dangers encountered in the Arctic. Adjustment for physical risk reduces that premium to less than 0.1 percent.[58]

Problems arise, however, in the cases of both the Atlantic and the Indian grounds. After adjusting for "physical," "financial," and "at sea" risk and for the length of the voyage, a prospective hand appears to have been willing to sacrifice $2.11 a month to serve in the Indian and an incredible $5.86 a month to serve in the Atlantic rather than the Pacific. The differences may reflect very strong tastes and biases; it is more likely that the model is simply incomplete, and the dummies are picking up the effects of the missing variables. After all, apart from the variable representing the "common wage ashore," the model does not account for the behavior of those people and institutions on the other side of the market from the seamen. Despite this shortcoming, the model provides quite helpful hints about the nature of the market.

Deterioration in Productivity and Crew Quality

Although the exact connections remain somewhat speculative, the years from 1840 through 1858 were characterized by a decline in vessel productivity on the one hand, and a gradually increasing proportion of unskilled workers and of illiterates among crews on the other (see Table 7.9). Between 1840–43 and 1856–58, for example, the average productivity index declined by more than a third, illiteracy rose by nearly 30 percent, and the proportion of unskilled seamen in the crew rose by more than a quarter. In the early 1840's, less than one-fifth of the crew was illiterate, and nine out of every twenty whalemen had some maritime experience. On the eve of the Civil War, however, more than a quarter of the crew could not sign their names, and almost three-fourths had never been to sea.

As Table 7.9 indicates, between 1840 and 1858 both measures of crew quality (literacy and the proportion of seamen who were *at least* semi-

TABLE 7.9

Productivity and Crew, New Bedford Whaling Voyages, All Grounds, 1840–58 and 1866

	(1) Productivity index	(2) Total crew who are illiterate (%)	(3) Total crew who are unskilled (%)	(4) Seamen who are unskilled (%)	Relatives on the base 1840			
					Column (1)	Column (2)	Column (3)	Column (4)
1840	0.976	21.1	29.2	52.8	1.000	1.000	1.000	1.000
1841	0.914	19.2	30.8	56.5	0.936	0.910	1.055	1.070
1842	1.101	20.1	32.4	60.7	1.128	0.953	1.110	1.150
1843	0.924	19.0	29.2	54.6	0.947	0.900	1.000	1.034
1844	0.899	22.0	33.5	63.1	0.921	1.043	1.147	1.195
1845	0.818	21.7	35.5	66.0	0.838	1.028	1.216	1.250
1846	0.874	22.6	35.4	66.1	0.895	1.071	1.212	1.252
1847	0.716	23.6	35.5	65.8	0.734	1.118	1.216	1.246
1848	0.916	25.3	34.3	65.4	0.939	1.199	1.175	1.239
1849	0.789	23.5	36.0	67.4	0.808	1.114	1.233	1.277
1850	0.864	23.3	38.7	72.5	0.885	1.104	1.325	1.373
1851	0.698	23.5	39.0	71.0	0.715	1.114	1.336	1.345
1852	0.413	22.3	39.6	72.6	0.423	1.057	1.356	1.375
1853	0.622	22.1	39.4	73.0	0.637	1.047	1.349	1.383
1854	0.639	27.5	40.6	75.1	0.655	1.303	1.390	1.422
1855	0.512	24.7	43.0	77.9	0.525	1.171	1.473	1.475
1856	0.603	26.5	42.6	77.3	0.618	1.256	1.459	1.464
1857	0.635	28.0	35.9	66.4	0.651	1.327	1.229	1.258
1858	0.416	23.8	38.1	69.2	0.426	1.128	1.305	1.311
1866	0.557	27.7	31.2	55.9	0.571	1.313	1.068	1.059
Averages								
All years	0.744	23.4	36.0	66.5	0.763	1.108	1.233	1.259
1840–43	0.979	19.9	30.4	56.2	1.003	0.941	1.041	1.063
1855–58	0.542	25.8	39.9	72.7	0.555	1.220	1.366	1.377
Percent change 1840–43 to 1855–58	−44.7	+29.7	+31.3	+29.5	−44.7	+29.7	+31.3	+29.5

SOURCES: See text.

skilled) declined, as did the index of average voyage productivity. These common changes need not bespeak causal connections. In order to pursue that topic further, a model designed to explain productivity change in general is required. The effects of changes in crew quality and the movements of other relevant independent variables can then be systematically assessed. To complete the explanation it is, of course, also necessary to consider how and why crew quality declined and how the managers of whaling voyages dealt with this development. The place to begin is with the model.

The same model used to examine the contributions of the captain to a voyage's productivity can be employed as part of the effort to deal with the problem of the changing quality of labor.[59] It has been argued in the whaling literature that because of improving opportunities ashore, the quality of labor available to the whaling industry declined as time passed. An attempt was made to capture this development by introducing indexes of real wage rates ashore as independent variables. It is assumed that increases in wages ashore, if the best whalers were bid away from the fleet, would lead to a deterioration in the quality of the whaling labor force, and thus reduce productivity.

The results of fitting the model to the voyage data (data lacking the information on occupations and lays) from the full period (1820 to 1896) are reported in the first column of Table 7.10.[60] It is obvious that the model explains the data statistically. The F statistic, the adjusted R^2, the signs and the values of the coefficients, and the significance levels are excellent. The issue of current moment has to do with the quality of labor, and the variable of interest is the index of the common wage ashore. The sign on the index is negative, the coefficient large, and the significance level high: there would appear to be some support for the "bidding away" hypothesis.

The second column reports the results of fitting almost the same model to data from the more restricted time period 1840–58 and 1866—years for which direct measures of labor quality exist. Between the specification of the model reported in the first column and that reported in the second, there is just one minor difference: the technology dummy employed in the first is irrelevant for the shorter time period. Despite this difference, the results of the two models are reassuringly similar: the relationships depicted in the equation are very stable. Indeed, the degree of stability across the four regressions is striking.

The results of fitting a third specification for the more restricted period are reported in the third column. In this instance, direct measures of labor quality are substituted for the indexes of real wage rates ashore (i.e., the common real wage ashore is dropped, and the percentages of illiterates and unskilled in the crew are added). The coefficients on the quality variables are very small indeed, and they are not significantly different from zero. There are other small changes between the results of the second and third specifications, but these are not important. The results obtained from the third model are important in one respect: the quality indexes do not appear to have been related to productivity changes.

This apparent paradox may be resolved by noting that there may very well have been two processes at work, both involving crew quality. First, the pull of onshore wages—taken together with agents' attempts to lessen labor turnover by substituting unskilled for skilled whalemen—tended to reduce the quality of workers and, therefore, productivity. Second, new techniques that permitted lower-quality seamen to function acceptably were introduced. Agents who accepted these technical changes were able to employ lower-quality seamen with some significant success. Across time, then, one might expect to find that the quality factor forced productivity down; but, in the cross section (once allowance is made for the cross-time deterioration), vessels that adopted the new technology employed lower-quality crews and were, therefore, more productive than the vessels that did not. The last specification (see the fourth column) attempts to separate these two phenomena. The results are plausible. Across time, the decline in quality (i.e., the loss of good crewmen to shore jobs) hurt productivity. In the cross section, however, vessels that employed fewer skilled workers were more productive than those that did not.

The evidence, then, suggests that the argument may be correct; but whether or not it is persuasive depends upon an analysis of the nature of the decline in labor quality and the adjustments to it that were made by agents and captains.

The rise in the proportion of illiterate and unskilled seamen in the crew of a typical vessel may also have been in part the product of agents' attempts to recruit crew members who would be less likely to desert. Contemporary sources suggest that agents, concerned with the very high rates of labor turnover, sought to employ unskilled workers who, because of their ignorance of the geography of the South Pacific or the Arctic and their lack of skills necessary to avoid capture by irate officers, would find it difficult to leave their vessels and sign on others. Nordhoff, for example, reports that, despite the almost constant demand for whaling crews, "To a sailor this avenue to a whaleship is hermetically sealed. Neither here [New York] nor in New Bedford is he at all likely to be shipped—for experience has taught the captains and owners of whaling vessels that your real tar is too uneasy a creature to be kept in good order for so long a cruise as whalemen now-a-days generally make."[61] The policy was also noted by Hohman, who reports, "The shipping-agent preferred to deal with men ignorant of the actual conditions of the industry because they were more easily imposed upon, and also because they were more dependable in observing their contracts."[62]

TABLE 7.10
Analysis of Productivity in New Bedford Whaling

Variable	Variant A	Variant B	Variant C	Variant D
Intercept	2.2*	2.4*	1.3*	2.4*
Vessel type: ships vs. all other	0.11*	0.06	0.07***	0.06
Hunting ground				
Atlantic	-0.15*	-0.40*	-0.35*	-0.39*
Indian	-0.06*	-0.12**	-0.12**	-0.13**
Arctic	0.17*	0.15***	0.09	0.13**
Time	-0.0004	0.002	-0.007	0.002
Built for whaling	-0.30	0.03	0.04	0.02
Re-rigged	0.09*	-0.19***	-0.19***	-0.19***
Whale stocks				
Baleen	0.11*	0.05	0.004	0.04
Sperm	0.05	0.25	0.50	0.23
Crowding on hunting ground	-0.004	-0.01***	-0.02**	-0.02**
Technology	0.31*			
Vessel size	0.000002*	0.000002*	0.000002*	0.000002*

	(1)	(2)	(3)	(4)
Voyage length	−0.0003*	−0.0003*	−0.0003*	−0.0003*
Vessel age	0.004*	0.006	0.007	0.004
Vessel age squared	−0.00009*	−0.0001	−0.0001	−0.00008
Last voyage	−0.08*	−0.06***	−0.05	−0.05
Real common wage ashore	−0.006*	−0.012*		−0.013*
Ratio, skilled wage to unskilled wage ashore	−0.57*	−0.27		−0.38
Illiterate (%)			0.001	0.002
Unskilled (%)			0.001	0.002**
Specialization				
In baleens	−0.095*	−0.05	−0.047	−0.05
In sperms	−0.70*	−0.71*	−0.74*	−0.74*
Captain's lay measure dummy	−0.03	0.14	−0.11	0.17
Observations (N)	2,343	991	991	991
F statistic	103.1	64.7	62.2	59.4
Adjusted R^2	0.478	0.562	0.553	0.565
Dependent mean	0.733	0.690	0.691	0.691

SOURCE: See text.

NOTE: For explanation of the variants, see text. The obervations are numbers of voyages.

* Significant at the 1% level.

** Significant at the 5% level.

*** Significant at the 10% level.

As voyage length increased, so did desertions—Herman Melville deserted twice during the heady 1840's—and, if agents' letters and the remaining account books are to be believed, labor turnover emerged as an increasingly important problem. Desertion reduced profits not only directly, through the losses associated with unrepaid advances, but also indirectly, through its effect on productivity. Since a vessel's complement usually consisted of only a few more crewmen (the shipkeepers) than the number required to provide six men for each whaleboat, an unreplaced seaman could mean the loss of an entire boat. Probably more important was the effect on productivity of the replacement of a member of one of the "closely-linked whaleboat crews, where the loss of a single cool and expert oarsman often cut down materially the captures made by a certain boat."[63]

Although technological change was not the driving force, it did act to relax certain production constraints, permitting captains and agents to adjust their work force in a way that they thought would reduce turnover. Historians of technology long argued that there was little improvement in the design of sailing ships over the course of the nineteenth century, and virtually none before 1850. More recent work has shown that they were wrong. As early as the 1830's, iron rod rigging and turnbuckles had begun to replace the traditional hemp lines, which meant that it took less skill to work aloft.[64] Between 1820 and 1845 a wide range of new equipment—capstans and windlasses, iron strapped blocks, geared steering, hold ventilators, and geared winches—came on the market.[65] Again, as in the manufacturing sector, these changes meant the work could be done by unskilled workers. Finally, after 1850, there was a near revolution aloft. Sails and rigging were almost totally redesigned. Naval architects recognized that increasing the number of sails made handling easier; therefore, conventional wisdom aside, they concluded that flat sails were more efficient than baggy ones. Ship owners responded by "subdividing the larger sails, abolishing the studding sails and other expensive 'kites,' and radically altering the sail's design—baggy sails were replaced by much flatter ones."[66] In addition, building on the improvements in the 1820's and 1830's, iron fittings became common, chains replaced rope, and mast design was greatly simplified.[67] Finally, the growth of the cotton textile industry made it possible to replace heavy burlap sails with light canvas ones. The result was again greater speed and, more importantly for whaling, the need for fewer skilled seamen.

For whaling vessels, the gain in speed was of marginal importance. There may have been some reduction in the time of outbound and inbound voyages and in the time necessary to shift from one ground to another, but speed was never of primary concern and was of almost no

importance during the period of active hunting. Similarly, there was probably little gain from the labor-saving dimensions of the technical changes.
The size of whaling crews was established chiefly by hunting demands and
always included many more men than those required to sail the vessel. In
fact, for whaling, the innovation of the new technology probably resulted
in an increase in total crew size. The changes did, however, make it possible to alter dramatically the skill profile of the crew. By greatly easing
and simplifying the tasks of setting, changing, and furling the sails, the
changes aloft made it possible for unskilled crewmen to handle most of
the above-deck work that previously had required trained hands. The technical innovations thus allowed the substitution of greenhands for able and
ordinary seamen.

The evidence, both quantitative and qualitative, conclusively demonstrates that, by any traditional definition, the quality of whaling crews
deteriorated over at least the two decades preceding the Civil War. The
qualitative sources suggest that the decline was the result of a conscious
decision by agents—a decision aimed at reducing labor turnover and thus
increasing profits. It is probably impossible to prove, however, that the
new de facto labor policies were the product of an innovative attempt to
reduce labor turnover rather than a reaction to the increasing difficulty of
recruiting native Yankee whalemen—a difficulty rooted in the rising competition for onshore labor.

It may be only coincidental, but the developing manufacturing sector
appears to have undergone a similar substitution of unskilled for skilled
labor under the aegis of new technical opportunities at about the same
time. Although it appears unlikely that labor turnover played a significant
role in that case, labor historians have recently recognized that the development of new technologies made it possible for managers to deskill their
labor force. Goldin and Sokoloff, for example, note, "The relationship
between firm size and the employment of women and children within
industries indicates that the diffusion of new large scale technologies was
associated with the substitution of women and children for men."[68]

In whaling, however, the policy was not costless to either agent or crewman. It greatly increased the twin problems of supervision and discipline,
and the direct cost of the necessary discipline was borne in the first instance by the crew. As one chronicler of the industry reports,

Examination of the crews' account books gives an insight into the changes taking
place in the kind of men who shipped aboard whalers and the measures taken by
the agents and captains to compensate for the increasingly poor quality of the
crews. Whether the decrease in quality of personnel led to the harsh measures, or
whether the methods of the captains, agents, and landsharks led to the poor quality
was a question probably debated endlessly by the owners and agents.[69]

TABLE 7.11

Average Number of Crewmen by Occupation, New Bedford Whaling Voyages, 1840–43 versus 1855–58

Year	(1) Officers	(2) Skilled maritime	(3) Artisans	(4) Service	(5) Skilled seamen	(6) Semi-skilled seamen	(7) Unskilled seamen	(8) Boys	(9) Unknown	Total
1840	4.00	3.60	1.87	1.93	3.13	3.80	8.20	0.80	0.07	27.40
1841	3.71	3.04	1.84	1.84	2.38	3.69	7.76	0.56	0.02	24.84
1842	3.69	3.00	1.91	1.91	2.74	2.55	8.55	0.52	0.14	25.02
1843	3.96	3.46	2.08	2.04	3.31	3.50	8.04	0.62	0.00	27.00
1855	4.12	3.38	2.04	1.88	1.68	1.78	12.39	0.59	0.00	27.86
1856	4.21	3.47	1.88	2.05	1.82	1.59	12.44	0.70	0.01	28.16
1857	4.26	3.68	2.19	2.01	2.39	2.76	10.38	0.56	0.00	28.24
1858	4.16	3.60	1.70	2.00	1.60	3.20	10.98	0.68	0.00	27.92
Average										
1840–43	3.80	3.19	1.93	1.93	2.83	3.28	8.13	0.58	0.06	25.73
1855–58	4.19	3.52	1.97	1.99	1.89	2.26	11.60	0.63	0.00	28.06
Change										
1840–43 to 1855–58	0.39	0.33	0.04	0.06	-0.94	-1.02	3.47	0.04	-0.05	2.32
Change (%)	+10.3	+10.3	+2.1	+3.0	-33.1	-31.2	+42.7	+7.7	-93.3	+9.0

SOURCES: See text.
NOTE: The total is the sum of the values in columns 1 through 9.

There is, however, general agreement that "the owners were content to ship such [untrained] hands . . . because capable and brutally aggressive mates could train them during their long months at sea."[70]

The stories of brutality on whaling vessels are legion, but they are neatly encapsulated in the report of the U.S. revenue cutter *Thetes* on its return from a trip to the Arctic whaling fleet in September 1906. On board were fourteen sick whalers, thirty who had been picked up shipwrecked, and two whaling captains, H. E. Bodfish of the *William Bayless* and E. W. Newth of the *Jeannette*, in irons. Both captains were charged with manslaughter in the deaths of seamen. Bodfish was, in fact, accused of kicking a seaman to death.[71]

The need for increased supervision and discipline meant that a vessel required more "capable and brutally aggressive mates," and they were not costless. Although it rid the industry of some of those skilled seamen who knew when and how to desert, the new labor policy forced the agents to hire more supervisory personnel. The result was a change in the size and composition of the crew that led to a significant increase in total direct labor costs.

Table 7.11 compares average crews in the two four-year periods, 1840–43 and 1855–58. Between those dates, despite the substitution of smaller barks for larger ships—a substitution that should have reduced crew size by 3 percent—the size of a typical crew actually increased by 2.3 men, or about 9 percent (from just less than 26 to just over 28 men). Of equal interest, however, are the changes that occurred within the crew. The increase of 2.3 men was the result of an increase of 3.5 in the number of unskilled seamen, a decrease of about 2.0 in the number of skilled and semi-skilled seamen, and an *increase* of 0.8 in the number of "professionals." Not surprisingly, the number of artisans and service personnel did not change. By the end of the period, a typical vessel carried an extra four-tenths of an officer and three-tenths of a skilled maritime professional. Those additions constitute a 10 percent increase in the number of crewmen in each of the two job categories.

Assuming that the extra officers were most likely third mates and that skilled maritime workers were paid as much as boatsteerers, the substitution of greenhands *and* skilled officers and boatsteerers for skilled and semi-skilled seamen meant that labor costs rose on average by about $24.40 a month, or about $1,050 for a typical 43-month voyage. That estimate, of course, does not reflect the fraction of the increasing wages of existing officers that can be attributed to *their* increased supervisory duties.

The effects of the change can be seen in Table 7.12. It displays, by year, the fraction of the catch that accrued to labor through lay shares (i.e., excluding charges, supplements, and the value of room and board).

TABLE 7.12
Labor's Share of the Net Value of the Catch, All Grounds: New Bedford Whaling Voyages, 1840–58 and 1866

Year	Average labor share	Maximum labor share	Minimum labor share	Relatives[a]		
				Average labor share	Maximum labor share	Minimum labor share
1840	0.309	0.340	0.281	1.000	1.000	1.000
1841	0.309	0.380	0.269	1.000	1.118	0.957
1842	0.315	0.375	0.261	1.019	1.103	0.929
1843	0.317	0.359	0.287	1.026	1.056	1.021
1844	0.317	0.388	0.265	1.026	1.141	0.943
1845	0.320	0.372	0.283	1.036	1.094	1.007
1846	0.318	0.371	0.282	1.029	1.091	1.004
1847	0.317	0.363	0.270	1.026	1.068	0.961
1848	0.317	0.352	0.263	1.026	1.035	0.936
1849	0.318	0.363	0.278	1.029	1.068	0.989
1850	0.333	0.383	0.290	1.078	1.126	1.032
1851	0.344	0.423	0.287	1.113	1.244	1.021

1852	0.344	0.386	0.299	1.113	1.135	1.064
1853	0.345	0.422	0.286	1.117	1.241	1.018
1854	0.347	0.427	0.296	1.123	1.256	1.053
1855	0.359	0.461	0.301	1.162	1.356	1.071
1856	0.362	0.433	0.309	1.172	1.274	1.100
1857	0.362	0.429	0.306	1.172	1.262	1.089
1858	0.350	0.383	0.295	1.133	1.126	1.050
1866	0.344	0.383	0.282	1.113	1.126	1.004
Maximum	0.362	0.461	0.309	1.172	1.356	1.100
Minimum	0.309	0.340	0.261	1.000	1.000	0.929
Averages						
All years	0.332	0.390	0.285	1.076	1.146	1.012
1840–43	0.313	0.364	0.275	1.011	1.069	0.977
1855–58	0.358	0.427	0.303	1.159	1.254	1.077
Percent change 1840–43 to 1855–58	14.6	17.3	10.3	14.6	17.3	10.3

S O U R C E S : See text.
*1840 = 1.000.

The view of Hohman and others before him was that on every voyage the sum of all lays was very close to 30 percent of the value of the catch, and the total was invariant over time. These figures tell a quite different story.[72] Over the two decades in question, the average labor lay share rose from about 31 percent to about 36 percent, an increase of about one-seventh.

The increase in the crew's share coincided with a shift in the geographic distribution of the fleet. The proportion of vessels hunting in the short-lay Atlantic and Indian grounds decreased and the proportion in the long-lay Pacific and Arctic grounds increased. In 1840–43, the average total lay was higher in the Atlantic and Indian grounds (0.319, as opposed to 0.310 in the Pacific). By 1855–58, despite the continuing interground differences in lays, the Atlantic-Indian and the Pacific-Arctic grounds displayed the same average figure (0.359). This apparent anomaly reflects the fact that, although the average crew size had increased in both, the increase was less than 8 percent in the Atlantic-Indian grounds in contrast to 12 percent in the Pacific-Arctic.

Changes in labor policies, whether initially innovative or merely reactive, did apparently result in higher total factor productivity for those vessels whose agents adopted them. The question remains: did the increase in productivity offset the transfer of 4.5 percent of output from owners to workers? What was the effect of the agents' "labor market innovation" on profits?

Conclusion

The system of labor payments based on contracted lays was adopted by whaling agents and owners as early as the seventeenth century. Although it bears some superficial resemblance to payment schemes in certain agricultural activities and some branches of fishing, the structure as it evolved in the whaling industry was unique. The economist Henry George greatly approved of the system of payment; it has been almost universally condemned by historians who have attempted to chronicle the development of the whaling industry.[73] Both Samuel Morison and Elmo Hohman, for example, complained about the negative impact that the institution had on the wages of seamen; Morison referred to the lay contract as "a foul system of exploitation."[74] More recent historiography has not improved the reputation of the lay. In a recent article, labor historian Gerald Williams blames the existence of "Yankee Hellships" ("legs and arms broken are considered nothing, ribs stamped in by heavy sea boots had to mend as best they could, faces smashed like rotten apples by iron belaying pins had to get well or fear worse treatment, eyes closed by a brawny mate's fist had to see") on the system of wage payment.[75]

Williams goes on to argue that, toward the end of the nineteenth century, agents and owners reaped yet another boon from the system—a boon that could not have been anticipated at the industry's peak. Because of the judicial interpretation of the lay contract, owners found themselves almost entirely exempt from the federal laws designed to improve the lives of American seamen. These laws included the Shipping Commissioner Act of 1872, which, together with its amendments, made it more difficult to shanghai sailors and guaranteed mariners a minimum level of rations, space, and medical treatment; the White Act (1898), which abolished both criminal penalties for desertion and corporal punishment; and the Seamen's Act of 1915, which provided for minimum safety standards (e.g., lifeboats).[76]

Despite its shortcomings, the system did have many interesting, and some undoubtedly useful, attributes. Owners benefited from the transfer of a portion of the risk of the voyage to the crew, although, given the regularized system of advances, the payment of room and board, and the occasional renegotiations of lays, the transfer was not complete. Moreover, even some of the critics of the lay contract (Hohman, for example) admit that at least some crew members reveled in a chance to participate in the "big lottery."

Without question, the lay contract provided an incentive system that rewarded cooperation, and it should have encouraged such behavior, an important matter. Every contemporary account of the hunt and the subsequent rendering underscores the level of cooperation required among the crewmen. Finally, the system appears to have been flexible enough to permit agents to adjust rapidly to emerging interground differences in productivity and to the reduced skill demands of the new sailing technologies.

CHAPTER EIGHT

❧ The Finance of Capital Formation in Midwestern Development, 1800-1910

William N. Parker

IN A DEVELOPING capitalist economy, capital—the produced means of production—leads a complicated and curious life. It must indeed be "financed," which means that before it is produced (or perhaps it is more accurate to say "while it is being produced"), someone must pay for it. This is in itself a natural fact, as true in a socialist economy as in a capitalist one. It results from the fact that trade and production take time, and during that time, workers must be fed, and materials and equipment must be accumulated and utilized. The unique feature of a capitalist economy is that this function—the provision of resources or of the money that will buy resources—is divided among three agencies: (1) private individuals, who may simply lend resources (e.g., land from father to son), or who may spend their own accumulated resources, whether a farmer sowing seed or a household or business firm drawing on previous savings in current use; (2) a banking system that can make loans paid out by notes or as checks on the borrowers' accounts; and (3) the state, which coins or prints moneys of its own and inserts them into the streams of exchange in the private economy, on terms set by the system of prices created there.

In the development of trade and light manufacturing in the American Midwest in the nineteenth century, the second of these three sources of finance—bank-created credit, based on private debt—was of almost exclusive importance.[1] Each region in the area, as it opened up, desperately needed something to use as money to replace the inconveniences and clumsiness of barter trade. Supplying that need could permit wealth to grow and production to increase so that a price level and the liquid means

I am indebted to the Yale Center for International and Area Studies and to the Yale Council on West European Studies for assistance as part of its studies of European financial integration under the Mellon-West European Project. Scott Redenius provided assistance with the research and footnoting. Barry Eichengreen and Martin Shubik read the manuscript and helped me to clarify the concepts, but the main biases in the paper are, of course, my own. The piece forms part of a larger essay on midwestern industrialization, which has been published in *Europe, America, and the Wider World*, vol. 2 (Cambridge, 1991).

for saving and investment spending could form. The money so created did not inflate prices; it established them, being absorbed in the balances held by individuals, stores, and small firms to conduct daily transactions, and to even out receipts and expenses over a week or a month. Charge accounts (book credit) furnished not only by merchants, but also by manufacturers who sold to jobbers on consignment, helped to bridge the gap between purchase and sale. In these circuits of credit, the role of banks was the traditional one: to "discount," that is, to buy in exchange for bank notes merchants' or manufacturers' own notes at less than their face value, turning them in effect into money that could more readily pass from hand to hand and firm to firm.

Before the National Banking Act of 1864, banks chartered by the states created the circulating medium, or rather a collection of circulating media, each set of notes generally valid at face value over a 50- to 100-mile radius, then exchanged at more distant central points at varying rates of discount against gold or one another like foreign currencies in wider trade. The time and trouble of collecting funds at a distance—and even more, the imperfect knowledge of a distant bank's portfolio—created costs and risks that the users of the system had to bear. The individual states chartered banks as stock corporations, either individually or under the so-called "free" banking acts of the 1850's, and the rules and safeguards erected were supposed to be enforced by state inspectors.[2] But in the antebellum period, where the state government itself was so often looked on as the object of private promotional schemes rather than their policeman,[3] these rules in many cases must simply have kept competitors away from the insiders who controlled their enforcement. Purely private banks—partnerships or individuals—or companies accumulating cash reserves in the course of some other business, served as a source of credit as well, and on a few occasions appear to have held deposits and issued notes.[4]

This confused tangle was only partly set straight by the National Banking Acts of 1862 and 1864.[5] That system did indeed set up a separate uniform system of banks chartered by the federal government on common terms and inspected by the office of the comptroller of the currency. The state bank notes were put out of business by a 10 percent tax and disappeared from circulation, but the state-chartered banks continued their lending activities nonetheless, dealing in the notes of the federal banks and of the federal government, and supporting a large volume of deposits drawn on by check. The role of the federal government and of specie reserves and the international capital movements to the Midwest through New York became more evident, but perhaps less important, as the nineteenth century progressed.

The financial problems of large construction projects and of heavy and expensive manufacturing plants were quite different from those of trade and light manufactures. In the latter, wages and advance payment for materials in inventory, in production, or in transit constituted the main credit needs. Such debt tended to be self-liquidating in the sense that the real capital—an inventory plus the value added by manufacture—once acquired, was turned into cash as the goods were sold, and the proceeds used in the next cycle of replenishment. In the face of the vastly growing body of such trade, the annual increment of such financial needs was nevertheless substantial. On the other hand, the large construction projects— canals, harbor improvement, and of course the railroad—could depend only to a limited degree on such small-scale sources of finance. This need was not always as large-scale and immediate as one might suppose. Even a canal or a river improvement could be effected a little at a time, and provided it led somewhere, could begin to accumulate revenues. The same was true of the railroads before 1850 and of the numerous improvements and extensions of the railroads—double tracking and spur lines—throughout the entire period. But the Midwest, lying flat between the Alleghenies and the Rockies, offered particular scope for transportation projects conceived as systems, joining points several hundred or, in the case of the transcontinentals, several thousand miles apart.[6] On a miniature scale, something of the same is true of the electric car lines that became popular in the region between 1890 and 1930, the street railways, and other municipal public works. In all such semi-public projects, the instrument for raising money was not a bank loan but a bond, and though banks might "underwrite" such issues and furnish the notes or deposits by which the amounts were transferred, they were not, as in Europe, active, but passive instruments of the development. The bases of the "security" were the expectations of the promoters, supported by the taxing power of the community in the case of public issues, and for the land grant railroads, the expected revenues from land sales and the subsequent operation.[7]

The creation of large industrial plants was similarly distanced from dependence on a commercial banking system. For small and middle-sized manufacturers, the pattern clearly must have been to grow through the reinvestment of profits, at least until the 1890's, when whole industries became ripe for "reorganization." Here (perhaps partly as a result of the Sherman Antitrust Act of 1890) the enterprise of bankers could intervene to float new issues of stock and bonds, based on expectations of profits from the consolidated firm.[8] This was notable also in the case of public utilities in the late 1920's.[9] But the earlier constructions were not carried out under such an ambitious aegis, and the banks' role was very likely to provide loans against such securities so that the development was not held up by a shortage of liquid funds.

The situation was not much different with the financing of agriculture. To one acquainted only with a sophisticated industrial and commercial system, the proportion of farm capital formation created by farm labor, and so in a sense self-financed, is truly astonishing. Beyond the Alleghenies, 15 to 20 percent of the farm labor force was used in the 1850's in clearing land alone, and the "saving" that matched such investment was simply the withdrawal of time from other farm tasks, or from "leisure."[10] The motive, after the first essential constructions and clearing, was to increase the value of the family's assets, and this way of viewing the farm, as an asset to grow in value over the years, accounts for farmers' willingness to acquire mortgage debt. The financing of land holding and land transfer created a body of debt that was no part of real capital formation but that formed the raw material for speculation and an involuted financial structure. Fortunately, agriculture did not depend on the outside economy to provide for the larger part of the mortgage loans. As late as 1920, as much as 70 percent of the farm mortgage debt was held by farmers—mostly parents who had transferred land within the family under such an arrangement, or loans derived from local rural moneylenders.[11] The "pressure" of this debt did not do much to improve efficiency on farms except to finance the landholding, which kept up farmers' hopes, and to raise land prices, even during periods of falling commodity prices. But this mode of financing removed pressures and opportunities that might have been encountered in the industrial credit system at large.

For the other part of farm credit, the medium-term livestock loans and the annual production credits for covering expenses and moving crops, dependence was on the commercial banks, as in the case of all mercantile trade. Only indirectly is this problem, the most politically explosive in American financial history, related to industrialization. It is enough here to say that the farmers could never get out from under it. In the South it was the basis of the crop lien system, and there and in the Midwest it was one of the bases of Populism. At the other end of the credit ladder stood the financing of the holding of the marketed crop, which had been harvested over a few weeks, during the entire year of consumption. By and large, farmers got paid early in the chain. Dealers could hold warehouse or elevator receipts, which they could discount at a bank, and ultimately titles to the crop could be traded in the grain pits in Chicago to serve as the basis of an immense speculation.[12] At some point, such trading served no productive purpose, but carried on a life of its own. The separation of finance from production, like the separation of sex from procreation, allowed it to become an activity carried out for its own sake. In moderation, it improved the functioning of markets, but in excess, its effects were destabilizing, disruptive, and depressive.

The Relation to Specie and the East

What has been said up to this point concerns largely the financial requirements of the several sectors of the Midwest's growing economy, and the presence of natural surpluses derived from that growth to supply the "savings" for them, under the assumption of a very simple, independent system of finance. Such a procedure has the advantage of emphasizing the indigenous quality of the growth and even of the investment, once the soils and minerals were uncovered, the techniques borrowed or invented, and the production units organized within markets, with access to labor supplies and with the prevalence of a mixture of recklessness and caution among businessmen.

But just as immigrant labor, imported equipment, and export markets made available the connection to the East and to Europe, so also the formidable system of financial arrangements organized from London by way of New York to make loans supplied an internationally valid money, and collected interest and dividends as the development paid off. If we had enough evidence on the actual size of these flows, it would be interesting to consider how development would have proceeded had these sources not been available. The midwestern banking and credit system was meshed with these sources from the very start through the use of gold for bank reserves and for settling net balances in transactions between distant places.

Before the Civil War, the western banks were restricted in the volume and type of loans by state laws, but even more by prudence, so as to maintain "convertibility" of their notes. By the Act of 1862, the national banks kept holdings of government bonds as security for their issues, but except for the wartime issue of irredeemable paper currency (the greenbacks), these were convertible or redeemable in coined gold and silver at stated ratios.[13] Irredeemable bonds issued by the Civil War government had to be exchanged at a discount. To be sure, the ultimate basis for confidence in a bank was its investments, and in a government was its taxing power. But gold acted as the symbol and pledge of financial solvency. Before 1860, bank reserves of around 15 to 30 percent against notes and deposits were universal.[14]

The international and eastern financial systems did not provide the savings for midwestern industrialization or agricultural investment, except for some mining and cattle-raising ventures at the outset, and to an appreciable degree all through the century, through the purchase of canal and railroad bonds. Those early investments were important, and the international and New York capital markets served as the channel. But steadily as the region's productive economy grew, the Midwest exhibited a growing volume of credit exchanges with the East and with England.[15] The net balance of such flows determined the availability of bank reserves. Loans came in and returns and repayment went out, but as the Midwest added a large measure of self-sufficiency in manufactures to its food-export surplus, the role of real capital imports greatly diminished.

The link with the international and national economy through specie shipments and capital flows had a complex effect of prime importance in the regional growth. First and foremost, it connected the course and level of prices to the economy of the internationally trading world. The whole price level rose and fell on the rhythms of bank credit and contraction, and on these fluctuations, sometimes analyzed as cycles of 3, 10, 20, and 40 years, producers' calculations and expectations were hinged. Whether this hastened or hindered the growth of investment, clear-sighted economic analysts may be able to say. Those who made the most out of these fluctuations were those who, like Andrew Carnegie, were able to remain independent of the capital market and expand when investment was cheap.[16] To do that required a confidence in the trend that overrode the ups and downs.

Moreover, in the Midwest's great secular growth, physical productivity did not, of course, rise proportionately in all sectors and occupations. Nor did relative prices all change with changes in relative costs and relative demand. In two striking cases, farm prices and the price of labor, the machinery seemed to outrage many contemporaries, but in retrospect the results were nonetheless unusually favorable to industrial investment. Prices of manufactures were protected to a degree by the Republican policy of a high tariff, especially when sustained behind the tariff through industrial combinations. Farm prices could not have benefited by protection; agriculture had virtually no foreign competition on the domestic front, and even in some foreign markets. Whatever effect this had on the terms of trade between the sectors was compounded by the greater inflexibility of farm supply adjustments. The matter will probably always remain unsettled, but there appeared at the time to be pressure on agriculture's share of the nation's income during the period of falling prices that dominated the 1870's and 1890's.[17] The same phenomenon has been alleged in a different guise in the market for labor where immigration should have persistently undercut the possibility of wage rises commensurate with productivity growth. On balance, the connection to world prices may have put a squeeze on farmers, which both kept food cheap and pushed some of the population off the farms; combined with free immigration, it also routed a certain portion of the productivity gains in manufacturing away from wages and into profits. But though those phenomena attracted much attention at the time, the result was not necessarily restrictive of economic expansion. The capital market with its many devices kept credit cheap to businessmen and encouraged investment. This meant that the general price level did not fall in proportion to long-term productivity gains. Through complex sets of waves, and many sharp peaks and troughs, the price level emerged from the period 1820–1910 showing little overall trend in the face of a continuously growing volume of output and transactions. Such stability meant that a portion, but not all, of the productivity gains— at least after 1900—did go to farmers and workers in the form of higher money incomes. And that, too, was necessary to create a growing purchasing power to match the growing output.

The Midwest's industrial credit system thus walked a thin line between an excessive stringency, locked to the supplies of gold and the rigid rules of the gold standard, which would have kept prices low but interest rates high, and an excessive inflationary leniency, which would have choked off mass demand through higher prices. These are matters that take the discussion into the economic rules and practices of the world economy at the time of the Midwest's growth, and into political issues—the tariff and the gold standard—that were featured in the platforms of the two contemporary political parties. The important fact for development is that the connection to world markets did not destroy the region's growth potential, even if it may not have done much to help it along. The "natural" sources of savings and investable funds in the region were ample and, given a moderate supply of money, could be turned into real investment.

An ideal credit system may be characterized, as the River Thames was described in a happy preindustrial time by a seventeenth-century poet, to be a river:

> Though deep, yet clear,
> Though gentle, yet not dull;
> Strong without rage,
> Without o'erflowing, full.[18]

Such a supply the Midwest had, and through the devices of the tariff and open immigration, its political leaders could allow relative price distortions to occur, with accompanying accumulation of profits, without carrying the game so far as to kill the goose that laid the golden eggs. In particular, with respect to heavy industrial capital—construction, machinery, the innumerable items of productive equipment, and later the prime consumer good, the automobile—the ultimate source of real capital formation did not lie, in any case, in stocks and bonds, money, credit and saving, or in finance at all. As in early agriculture, where the sector's capital was formed by the farm labor itself, early industrial fixed capital was expensive because the fashioning of tools and primitive machinery required much hand labor and skill. The eighteenth-century tools, largely handmade and hand-operated, were a precious heritage passed from father to son. Power—first foot power, then water power, then, after 1880, the gas engine and electric motor—changed all that. Tools could be made by powered tools, and when worn out could be readily replaced. These possibilities were apparent by 1820 in New England and outside of Philadelphia, and later above Cincinnati and below Cleveland. They met their supreme demonstration after 1900 as the automobile industry grew outside of Detroit.[19] The area became alive with machine shops, to produce not only the parts to be fed into the assembly lines, but also machinery to make the parts.

With the reductions in cost and improvement in quality of the heavy metals, there was a fall in the cost of machine tools.[20] The impact of cheaper and better iron and steel was then felt doubly in the machinery products—mining and railroad machinery, typewriters, presses, boats, bridges, and urban buildings. A steady and reinforced fall occurred then in the real costs of capital equipment. It was this beneficial spiral, and not simply the various ingenious inventions of financial instruments, that stood at the heart of midwestern industry's real capital formation.

Money and Federal Mercantilism

An historical approach to money and credit takes them as folk customs, developing of their own motion for the convenience and profit of their users, first for merchants, and then for all others who hold natural surpluses that they seek to exchange. Rules were evolved in the world community, standards set, an ethic of faith and trust elaborated, objectified and symbolized by gold. So powerful a current was the world's stream of money that the strongest states in Europe, beginning in the sixteenth century, were not able to stand against it. To create a money was, next to an army, the most spectacular achievement of a national state. A nation could ordain a currency unit, could coin metals with the impression of the head of the prince, and could in such units pay soldiers and collect taxes. The royal household, like any self-sufficient unit, could live within its own self-confirming structure of money and prices. Since it had a monopoly of the courts of justice, and put its armed force at their disposal for settling disputes and enforcing obligations, it could create the doctrine of legal tender and make available its police services only to such moneys as conformed. But as we have seen for the economy of the Midwest, the game was up once a region sought to go beyond the limits of its own exchanges, or in the case of the state, its own power. To enter the markets of the world, even the king of France or Spain had to trade, to adopt merchants' standards, to pay merchants' prices, and to use the merchants' metals at merchants' rates.

In the end, governments were left with the largely accounting function of naming a currency unit and defining it in terms of metal, so that prices formed around it in response to its trading value. The monetary history of the United States is a history of efforts to gain the advantages to the state of a connection with world markets, notably in the ability to borrow during wars, while retaining some degree of independence of policy. In the pre-Jacksonian period, through the First and Second Banks of the United States, the federal government was largely responsible for the spread of the uniform gold-based system of reserves and convertibility. Following the National Banking Act of 1862, the Civil War government married itself to the system, though by substituting bonds for gold as a reserve it did get some accommodation to its needs. The issue of greenbacks by the Federal Treasury under the Ohioan Salmon P. Chase was another expression of independence, almost of defiance of the money market.[21] By the same token, the agonized and early resumption of specie payments brought the system back under the influence of the precious metals supplies. So strong was this current that even the government's efforts under strong populist pressures to monetize silver in the 1890's could not swim against Gresham's law. The credit system's only defense against the dominance of gold was its ability to economize on reserves through the invention of financial intermediaries in great profusion. These did not really bypass the banking system, however, but tailored its varieties and forms of instruments—stocks, bonds, investment banks, life insurance companies, savings banks, and so on—to the demands for convenient forms that an economy of growing wealth was able to afford.

In the course of the American Midwest's growth, then, natural surpluses of labor and commodities appeared. The system of money and credit called "capitalist" was then able to place these surpluses at the disposal of those who could use them over a cycle of crops and manufactures and during the construction of public works and private plants and equipment. In turn, production could be accomplished faster and with maximum efficiency in the use of materials and labor. An intensely time-conscious production system was made possible and, once possible, became compulsory for the individual and the firm. The connection to the world money flows and the controls and rules of the federal government largely facilitated this regional achievement, though those connections were not an unmitigated help. Most crucial was the ability of what was called the region's "business interests" to dominate the mercantilist policies of the federal government, particularly to insulate a growing manufacturing segment from the European competition and to keep labor flowing through Ellis Island. The Republican party was an essential ingredient in the midwestern business culture.

PART THREE

Political Economy in
American Economic History

⚴ Toward a New Synthesis on the Role of Economic Issues in the Political Realignment of the 1850's

Robert William Fogel

ECONOMIC ISSUES have roamed in and out of explanations for the Civil War and the political crisis that preceded it. Between the two world wars and continuing through the 1950's, it was common to argue that the Civil War was the outcome of a struggle between two incompatible systems of economic organization. The war was the means used by the rising capitalist class to destroy a system—chattel slavery—that was inimical to the capitalist mode of production.[1] This "progressive" interpretation of the war was given a special twist by Phillips, Ramsdell, and their followers, who argued that the Civil War was unnecessary because its internal economic contradictions would have soon led to the self-destruction of the slave system, even in the absence of a war.[2]

Economic explanations for the political crisis of the 1850's and the Civil War were largely replaced during the 1970's by a cultural explanation for the clash. Although these cultural explanations have roots that reach back to the debates of the late 1830's, the 1840's, and the 1850's, the argument was set forth in modern form by Craven in 1942 and more powerfully by Foner in 1970.[3] As Foner put it, the two decades preceding the Civil War "witnessed the development of conflicting sectional ideologies, each viewing its own society as fundamentally well-ordered, and the other as both a negation of its most cherished values and a threat to its existence." When the Republican party came into being, it sought to mobilize its forces around the proposition that "two profoundly different and antagonistic civilizations . . . were competing for control of the political system."[4]

The debate touched off by Foner has pushed research toward a more complex and more directly political analysis of the breakup of the second

I have benefited from comments and criticisms of an earlier draft by Thomas Alexander, Jean Baker, Charles Calomiris, Stanley Engerman, Ronald Formisano, Eugene Genovese, James Grossman, Ralph Lerner, James McPherson, Robert Margo, Robert Swierenga, and Sean Wilentz.

party system and of the political realignment of the 1850's.[5] While the emerging new synthesis incorporates important elements of the view that the realignment reflected a growing cultural divide between the North and the South over the slavery issue,[6] it also incorporates important elements of the work of the ethnocultural school of political historians,[7] and of historical polymetricians.[8] In this connection, a good deal of attention has been focused on the nativist movement of the 1850's as the catalyst for the destruction of the second party system and for a political realignment along sectional lines.[9] The recognition of the pivotal role of the nativist movement has sparked a reexamination of the role of economic issues.[10] The focus of interest this time is not so much the clash between the industrial capitalists of the North and the landed aristocracy of the South, which now seems less acute than it did to the "progressive" historians. Rather, the new focus represents a return to the issues long probed by labor historians such as Commons and Ware, and more recently by Montgomery, Pessen, Feldberg, Ashworth, Wilentz, and Ross: the factors that led to increasing pressure on the living standards of nonfarm northern workers from the mid-1840's through most of the 1850's, and the political responses to these pressures.[11]

This paper is aimed at providing an overview of the role of economic issues in the political realignment of the 1850's. It attempts to integrate arguments set forth elsewhere by a number of scholars into a coherent whole. Although the view that emerges rests on a considerable amount of new research, much work remains to be undertaken before the numerous issues raised by this interpretation can be resolved. Consequently, this paper suggests not only the lines of a possible new synthesis on the role of economic issues in the political realignment of the 1850's, but also an agenda for research needed to resolve many issues that have been inadequately confronted.

The Changing Role of Economic Issues

Economic issues played an important part in the political realignment of the 1850's, but there was no one persistent issue that by itself can explain that realignment.[12] Nor were economic issues more dominant than ideological, political, social, or cultural issues. As with other issues, economic issues waxed and waned, and as they did politicians sought to exploit each in turn to advance their political objectives. Included among these politicians were a small number who were dedicated to the abolition of slavery, and who were able to exploit the breakdown of the second party system to advance their objectives. The overriding proposition in the interpretation outlined in this paper is that both economic and social issues were in flux and that competing groups of politicians were struggling to find ways of turning these often novel issues to their advantage. Within that framework, I would emphasize six different ways in which economic issues affected the political realignment of the 1850's.

First, there were the early, and initially unsuccessful, efforts by abolitionists to insert an economic dimension into the abolitionist indictment of the South. This period of early experimentation with economic issues extended from the late 1830's to the late 1840's.

Second, there was the rise of a new set of economic issues, quite different from those which originally defined the second party system, which were related to the explosive rate of urbanization and the unprecedented rate of immigration. These issues, which arose sporadically between 1820 and 1844, came to the fore between 1848 and 1855. The acute phase of political reaction reflected a triple economic crisis (declining real wages, rising unemployment, and deteriorating health and life expectations) experienced by northern nonfarm workers. Concern with unchecked immigration and the attendant crises were critical to the spontaneous breakaway of nativist workers in the North from the Whig and Democratic parties during the years 1851–55.

A third phase in the development of economic issues began when certain antislavery leaders sought to exploit the Kansas crisis in order to gain control of the nativist breakaway and push it in an antislavery direction. Not all of the antislavery leaders in the Whig, Democratic, and Free Soil parties appreciated the need to stress the economic dimension, but Henry Wilson and Joshua R. Giddings (who were originally Whigs), Galusha A. Grow and Nathaniel P. Banks (who were originally Democrats), and especially Horace Greeley, did.

The next aspect of the development of economic issues involved the effort to consolidate and extend Republican support between the end of the 1856 election and the outbreak of the crisis of 1857. During this period of economic recovery in the North, Republican leaders led by Greeley intensified the economic indictment of the South, exploiting the books by Frederick Law Olmsted and (especially) Hinton Rowan Helper, and arguing that the expansionist impulse of the South stemmed from its economic failure.

Another phase in the development of economic issues occurred after the outbreak of the crisis of 1857, which strained Republican unity. Republicans were taken off the hook, however, by the brevity of the crisis and the strong recovery, as well as by the Democratic outrage over Helper's book, which became the center of the struggle to organize the House in December 1859 and January 1860.

Finally, the attempt to promote economic issues took a new turn when

Buchanan vetoed the Homestead bill in June 1860. This was the culmina-
tion of a process that turned free land from a divisive issue in Republican
ranks into a unifying issue.

The Timing of Economic Issues

In analyzing the economic component of the political realignment of
the 1850's, it is important to keep in mind that the economic issues just
summarized were not part of some underlying general economic crisis of
capitalism. From the standpoint of economics, they are relatively distinct
issues whose coherence was mostly a product of political rhetoric. I stress
this point at the outset because not enough attention has been given to
the disjunctions in economic developments across regions and classes during the antebellum era.

Of the seven economic crises between the end of the War of 1812 and
the outbreak of the Civil War, only those of 1819–20 and 1837–38 were
similar in their regional impact. The northern recession of 1826–28 was a
depression in the South that lasted until 1831. Similarly, the brief though
sharp northern recession of 1841–43 began in the South a year earlier,
lasted two years longer, and was more severe. On the other hand, the
severe northern recession of 1857–58 coincided with one of the South's
most vigorous booms. The impact of immigrants on labor markets, so
devastating to native artisans in the North during the first half of the 1850's,
was much more confined in the South. The effect of the cholera epidemic
of 1849–50 was far more severe in the North than in the South.[13]

Figure 9.1 shows how different the pattern of railroad construction was
in the Old Northwest and in the South during the 1850's. Although the
South and the Northwest showed a similar pattern of rising annual construction between 1849 and 1853, construction dropped off sharply in the
Northwest after 1853. The rate of decline in that region was so rapid that
by 1859, the annual rate of construction was not only far below its 1853 peak,
it was even below the level that had prevailed at the beginning of the
decade. In the South, annual railroad construction fell off only in 1854 and
1855. It rose sharply in each of the remaining years of the decade. By 1859,
southern construction was not only three times greater than it had been at
the start of the 1850's, it was also well above the 1853 peak.

The disjunctions in economic experience across classes of free workers
are most visible in the North, where a spontaneous political protest movement of nativist workers arose during a period of generally strong economic growth. It is unlikely that the nativist political movement would
have come close to the northern successes it obtained in 1853–55 without
the pressures on labor markets generated by the massive immigration of

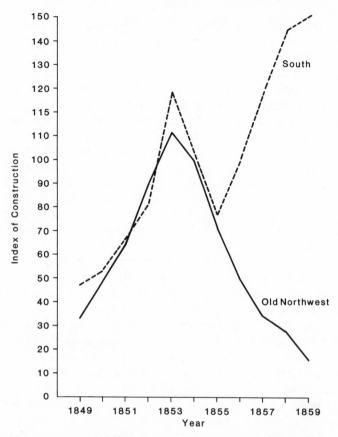

Fig. 9.1. A comparison between the railroad construction cycles in the Old Northwest and in the South during the 1850's (average of 1852 – 1854 = 100). The northern index is computed in the manner indicated in Fogel, Galantine, and Manning, *Evidence and Methods*, entry 66. The series was extended to 1859 using data for 1861 and 1862 from U.S. Bureau of the Census, *Tenth Census of the United States*, vol. 4 (Washington, D.C., 1883), table 8. That source also provided the data for the southern index.

1848–54, by the high inflation rates of those years, by the massive dumping of immigrant railroad workers onto the labor markets of the states of the Old Northwest beginning about 1853, and by the acute public-health crisis of 1849–55 (promoted by a combination of massive immigration and over-rapid urban expansion) during which cholera and other alarming diseases became endemic in the major cities of the North.

These economic issues arose quite independently of the antislavery movement and were entirely outside of the realm of economic issues origi-nally raised by the antislavery militants. It was not until the Kansas crisis that a handful of antislavery militants saw a method of developing eco-nomic issues in such a way that they would not only make deep inroads into the growing Know-Nothing constituency, but also appeal to the northern left-wing, class-oriented militants of the Democratic party, many of whom had seized on the free land issue as a panacea. Democrats of this stripe were appalled when passage of the Kansas-Nebraska bill in the spring of 1854 was coupled with the defeat of the Homestead bill as Demo-crats in the South Atlantic states reversed their position and voted against land reform as a bloc. Labor leaders who had been aloof from the antislav-ery movement suddenly began to accept the theory that there really was a "slave power" conspiracy aimed not merely at thwarting their campaign for a homestead act, but at bringing slaves into direct competition with free northern labor.[14]

Horace Greeley was far more prescient than other Whig leaders in rec-ognizing the potential for merging the free land and free soil questions by hooking them onto the Kansas issue. He was a year ahead of Thurlow Weed and William Seward, and close to two years ahead of Lincoln, in concluding that this combination of issues provided the opportunity to create a winning coalition, one based primarily on northern Whigs but with the potential of drawing in key elements of the left-labor Democrats and of luring back northern Whigs who had bolted to the Know-Nothings. Of course, Weed, as a coalition-builder, faced constraints that required him to proceed more deliberately and cautiously than an issue innovator. Greeley may have been capricious in personal and political relationships and lacking in the patience and steadiness needed to forge a broad leader-ship for the new coalition, but he was superb in charting and promoting a new ideological line.[15]

It is true that economic issues were not at the center of the Republican appeal in 1856. They certainly were not put into the 1856 platform. But nativist issues that played an important role in the Republican campaign were also omitted from the platform. There were good reasons for such reticence. Although both anti-Catholicism and nativism appealed to major sections of the Republican constituency, they were too divisive to be the basis for a coalition consensus. So the anti-Catholic and nativist appeals were left to those newspapers and organizations within the Republican coalition that wished to promote them. Given the fragility of the Repub-lican coalition, the official program had to be confined to those points which united the subgroups of the party.[16]

Thus, while all components of the coalition pushed the antislavery theme, there was an understandable rhetorical division of labor among the elements of the coalition, each element combining the central antislavery theme with those subthemes most congenial to their particular constitu-encies. In 1855 and 1856, Massachusetts Republicans such as Banks and Wilson combined antislavery with labor and nativist appeals, whereas Greeley tried to counter the nativist appeal (until 1856) and worked assidu-ously to give an economic dimension to the antislavery appeal, which he aimed especially at journeymen and farmers. These Republican strategists recognized that to counter the nativist appeal effectively, there had to be at least a rhetorical identification with the economic concerns of the Know-Nothing constituency.[17] Robert C. Winthrop gave recognition to the role of economic issues in the Republican campaign of 1856, which he de-scribed as one-third Missouri Compromise, one-third Kansas outrages, and "one-third disjointed and misapplied figures, and a great swelling of words and vanity, to prove that the South is, upon the whole, the very poorest, meanest, least productive, and most miserable part of creation."[18]

Between early 1856 and late 1857, economic issues played a role different than they had played during the period 1851–55. The economic recovery of the North between 1855 and mid-1857, the relatively steady price level, and the sharp reduction in immigration sapped the vitality of the Know-Nothing movement (which focused on economic problems in the North) and permitted Republicans to push the theme of the superiority of the northern economy over the southern economy. During this period, Greeley reinvigorated the economic indictment of slavery, seizing upon Helper's book, which he enthusiastically promoted in the *Tribune* with an initial eight-column story and follow-ups.[19]

The economic crisis of 1857–58 posed a severe threat to the Republican coalition, not only because it was almost exclusively a northern crisis, but also because the various elements of the coalition differed on policies to alleviate the crisis. The coalition was spared a split on this issue by several fortunate events: the swift, sharp recovery that began in 1858; the continu-ing drop in immigration, which eased pressures on labor markets; and the decline in food prices, which served to raise the real wages of workers in both urban and rural areas.[20] These conditions made it possible for Repub-licans in 1859 and 1860 to press the theme that the booming northern economy was infinitely superior to that of the South and that northern prosperity was endangered by an economically backward slave South that saw expansion into the North as the only solution to its otherwise hopeless economic bankruptcy. Southern leaders, made exceedingly self-confident and increasingly nationalistic by the powerful economic boom in the South that occupied most of the decade, took the northern bait. Their outrage over the northern calumny of their economic and social system turned attention away from northern economic problems (which were only temporarily alleviated), and gave credence to the claim that the North was menaced by the political and economic aggression of the South.[21]

The use of the land-reform issue also changed from 1854–55 to 1859–60. During the first period, although a divisive issue in Republican ranks, land reform contributed to the bolt of some militant labor leaders from the Democratic party. It also helped to infuse the "slave power" slogan with economic content. By 1859–60, after southern hostility to a homestead act became overwhelming, and especially after Buchanan announced his intention to veto the pending bill (a threat he carried out in June 1860), land reform became a unifying issue in Republican ranks. So the Republican platform of 1860 combined the two slogans—keeping the territories for free men and land reform—in much the same way that they had been combined by the left-labor forces in 1854.[22]

In elaborating on these economic issues I do not in any way mean to slight the emphasis that a number of scholars have placed on the political issues. I see both as extremely important and as reinforcing one another. I do not mean to argue that economic issues were more important than the political or the cultural indictments of slavery, but rather that they were an additional feature of the general indictment of slavery that was decisive in giving the coalition its margin of victory. Although much more work needs to be done in showing how these economic factors affected electoral behavior, studies of elections in Massachusetts and New York indicate that economic issues contributed significantly to the political realignment in these states.[23]

The Ethnic and Residential Distribution of Nonfarm Male Labor in the North

Although information on the ethnic composition of the labor force was collected by the 1860 census, that information was not reported in the published census volumes. Nor do the published volumes provide a distribution of workers in urban and rural areas. It is possible, however, to recover this missing information by drawing random samples of the manuscript schedules of the 1860 census. Such samples were drawn for the rural North by Bateman and Foust and for northern cities by Moen.[24] Properly weighting the Bateman-Foust and Moen samples will produce the desired distribution of workers.

Table 9.1, which was derived from such a procedure, shows how large a share of the northern market for nonagricultural jobs went to foreign-born workers.[25] The competition was heaviest in the cities, where foreign-born workers accounted for 58 percent of the artisans, 54 percent of semi-skilled workers, and 72 percent of the ordinary laborers. Overall, 54 percent of all male urban workers were foreign-born. Among female urban workers, the foreign-born share was 63 percent.[26] The competition for jobs felt

TABLE 9.1

The Distribution of the Northern Male Nonagricultural Labor Force
Between Natives and the Foreign Born, 1860

(*in thousands*)

Occupational category	Urban[a]		Rural		Total North	
	Native	Foreign born	Native	Foreign born	Native	Foreign born
Professionals and proprietors, upper	79	41	145	20	224	61
Professionals and proprietors, lower	200	114	48	12	248	126
Artisans	193	262	360	88	553	350
Semi-skilled	81	95	29	11	110	106
Ordinary laborers	89	234	397	134	486	368
Unknown	7	4	—	—	7	4
Total	649	750	979	265	1,628	1,015

S O U R C E : See note 25 for the sources and methods used in constructing this table.
N O T E : For this table, the North is defined to include New England (Maine, New Hampshire, Vermont, Massachusetts, Connecticut), the Middle Atlantic (New York, New Jersey, Pennsylvania), and the North Central (Ohio, Michigan, Indiana, Illinois, Wisconsin, Iowa, Missouri, and Minnesota, as well as the territories that subsequently became North Dakota, South Dakota, Nebraska, and Kansas).
[a] "Urban" is defined as places with populations of 2,500 or more.

by the Old Americans (third generation or greater) was even stronger than is suggested by Table 9.1, since about 23 percent of the natives had foreign-born parents and were largely Catholic or Lutheran.[27]

One of the most striking features of Table 9.1 is the large share of nonfarm male workers who lived in the rural areas: 47 percent. This finding is particularly important for political analysis, since it underlines the danger of equating nonfarm workers with urban workers. This danger is even more acute if one focuses on the behavior of native-born voters. When urban is defined as places with 2,500 or more persons (as is done in Table 9.1), slightly more than 60 percent of all the native male nonagricultural workers lived in rural areas. When urban is defined as places of 10,000 or more persons, the rural share of native nonfarm workers in the North rises to 70 percent.[28]

The last finding does not imply that nonfarm workers predominated in the rural areas. Farmers and agricultural laborers account for about 70 percent of the male rural force in the North. The rural sector of the North was so much larger than the urban sector in 1860, however, that it took nearly as many persons in nonagricultural occupations to service rural needs as to service urban needs. Indeed, there were actually more doctors, lawyers, clerics, and other upper professionals in the rural areas than in urban areas. The rural areas needed the services of many blacksmiths, carpenters, coopers, and other artisans, some of whom (such as blacksmiths) were more numerous in the rural areas than in the cities.

It should also be remembered that in 1860 many manufacturing workers lived in rural areas. Such industries as saw mills and grist mills constituted a larger share of manufacturing than they do today and were almost wholly located in rural areas. Many blast furnaces, especially those using charcoal or bituminous coal, were also located in rural areas because it paid to be located close to sources of raw materials. Power was another reason for locating factories in rural areas. In 1860, water power was often more economical than steam power, which meant that factories were often located at the fall line of rivers that were generally beyond the outskirts of cities in antebellum times.[29]

The ethnic and residential distributions of nonfarm workers are particularly important for understanding the political realignment of the 1850's. Table 9.1 indicates that in 1860 there were 1,628,000 native males in the nonfarm northern labor force, of whom about 81 percent, or 1,319,000, were of voting age. Of these, about 77 percent, or 1,019,000, were natives born of native parents. Assuming that 87.3 percent of the electorate voted in 1860,[30] and given that the total vote for the president in the seventeen states of the North was 3,443,000, the total northern electorate was 3,944,000. It follows that adult nonfarm native males of native parents accounted for about 26 percent of the northern electorate, although they represented only about a sixth of the northern labor force (which, including women and males under age 21, was about 6,319,000 persons).[31]

Information on the residential and ethnic distribution of voters is critical to many unresolved issues in the analysis of popular voting behavior during the 1850's. A case in point is the extent to which the Know-Nothings drew their support from nonfarm voters in the elections of 1853–56. The finding that, at least in Massachusetts and New York, the Know-Nothings had substantial support from nonfarm workers, many of whom were Catholic or Lutheran, suggests that class as well as ethnocultural issues played an important role in the 1850's.[32] Furthermore, if, as suggested by Table 9.1, a quarter of the voters in rural counties were nonfarm workers, it cannot be assumed that the support for the Know-Nothings in these counties in 1856 came overwhelmingly, or even mainly, from farmers. The same point applies to the explanation of the rural Republican vote in 1860.

The Changes in the Northern Electorate and the Shifting Partisan Affiliations of Old Americans

The timing and amplitude of the immigration cycle of 1841–61 (measured from trough to trough) is critical to an understanding of the political realignment of the 1850's (see Figure 9.2). It has long been known that

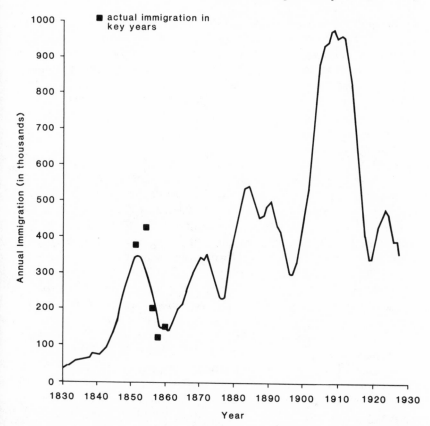

Fig. 9.2. Seven-year moving average of annual immigration, 1830–1927. Computed from the immigration data in U.S. Bureau of the Census, *Historical Statistics,* pp. 105–6.

the northern population grew rapidly between 1820 and 1860 and that a vast upsurge in immigration played a major part in that process. However, the absence of data on place of birth in the censuses before 1850 and the failure of the published censuses of 1850 and 1860 to reveal place of birth by age, sex, and occupation have made it difficult to unravel the independent contributions of immigration and natural increase to the growth of the labor force. Drawing samples from the manuscript schedules has clarified some issues. In 1860, foreigners comprised 30 percent of the urban population (37 percent in cities with 10,000 or more persons), 41 percent of the nonagricultural adult male labor force of the North, and 55 percent of that labor force in northern cities with more than 10,000 persons. Hence foreign-born competition for jobs was much greater than is implied by the published census report, which indicates that 18 percent of the northern population was foreign-born.

There was also great variation in immigrant pressure on labor markets over time, because immigrants arrived in waves. The crest of the antebellum wave was reached in 1854, after which immigration rates declined sharply. The impact of these waves on labor markets is illustrated by New York City. In 1855, more than three-quarters of that city's labor force was foreign-born, but just five years later the foreign-born share had declined to 61 percent.

So the timing of immigration and the distribution of immigrants over space are very important for understanding the economic distress suffered by native northern labor during the last two decades of the antebellum era, and of the political realignments stimulated by this distress. It is also important to differentiate between entrants into both the labor force and the electorate who were children of recent immigrants (and hence, mostly Irish or German Catholics and German Lutherans) and those who were children of native parents (largely Protestants of British descent).

The significance of these distinctions for the changing composition of the northern male labor force between 1820 and 1860 is revealed by Table 9.2.[33] Here, persons and their descendants who entered the country up to 1820 are designated "Old Americans," whereas arrivals from 1820 on, and their descendants, are designated "New Americans." Table 9.2 indicates that in the absence of migration, the rate of natural increase of the northern labor force during the antebellum era was about 2.8 percent per annum, which is a high rate of natural increase in the labor supply by current U.S. standards. The combination of exceptionally high immigra-

TABLE 9.2

The Division of the White Male Labor Force of the North into "Old Americans" and "New Americans," 1820–60

(*in thousands*)

Year	(1) Male Old Americans[a]	(2) Northern male labor force	(3) Male New Americans[a]	(4) Column 3 as a percentage of Column 2
1820	931	1,155	224	19.4
1830	1,289	1,654	365	22.1
1840	1,742	2,452	710	29.0
1850	2,247	3,641	1,394	38.3
1860	2,779	5,137	2,338	45.5

S O U R C E : See note 33 for the sources and methods used in constructing this table.

[a] "Old Americans" are persons and their descendants who entered the country up to 1820; arrivals from 1820 on, and their descendants, are designated "New Americans."

tion rates and high natural rates greatly increased the northern competition for jobs. Between 1820 and 1860, the labor supply of New Americans increased at a rate of over 6 percent per annum, which nearly doubled the number of new jobs that had to be created in the North during the antebellum era. That rate was often too high to sustain, with the consequence that labor markets frequently became glutted.

The heavy influx of immigrants between 1820 and the early 1850's also had far-reaching effects on the nature of the American electorate and on political alignments in the North. Table 9.3, which is based on a simulation model described elsewhere, presents estimates of the number of naturalized adult males and foreign-born voters at each presidential election between 1824 and 1860.[34] The key feature of this table is the explosive addition of foreign-born voters between 1852 and 1860, a lagged result of the enormous expansion of immigration between 1846 and 1854. As a consequence, the share of northern voters who were foreign-born rose from under 10 percent in 1840 to over 25 percent in 1860, with over two-thirds of the increase coming during the last eight years of the antebellum era.

Table 9.3 does not reveal the full shift in the ethnic composition of the northern electorate. It is necessary not only to distinguish between foreign-born and native voters but also to distinguish among native voters. The native voters of native parents (i.e., third-generation Americans or greater) probably voted much differently from immigrants (first generation) and their children (second generation).

What is at issue is less a matter of the speed of acculturation than of religious affiliations and ethnic origins. In the 1850's, third-generation whites and greater in the North were overwhelmingly (93 percent) descended from British and other northern European nationalities and were overwhelmingly reformed evangelical Protestants.[35] Second-generation whites in the 1850's, however, were largely of Irish and German ancestry and were mainly Catholic and Lutheran.

The implications of these demographic changes for the political realignment of the 1850's are spelled out in Table 9.4, which presents estimates of the ethnic distribution of northern voters for the Democrats in 1852 and 1860.[36] It shows that the percentage of the Democratic vote that came from second-generation voters remained constant, while the percentage coming from "Old Americans" (third generation or greater) declined precipitously. In 1852, over 62 percent of the Democratic votes came from voters who were third generation or greater. By 1860, the votes that the Democrats received from these Old Americans had dwindled to the point where they accounted for less than 40 percent of the party's support. Although it is true that the Democratic party of the North continued to draw most of its votes from natives, about one-third of these natives were descended

TABLE 9.3

An Estimate of the Number of Foreign-Born Voters and Naturalized Adult Males, 1824–60, by Year of First Presidential Election Following Naturalization

(in thousands)

	Naturalized voting males age 21 or older									
	1824	1828	1832	1836	1840	1844	1848	1852	1856	1860
First presidential election following naturalization[a]										
1820 or earlier	149	143	136	129	122	107	95	78	60	46
1824	10	10	9	8	8	7	6	5	3	3
1828	—	10	10	9	8	8	7	6	5	3
1832			15	14	13	12	11	10	9	7
1836				31	29	27	25	23	20	18
1840					64	60	56	52	48	42
1844						96	91	85	78	72
1848							111	105	98	91
1852								147	139	130
1856									316	298
1860									—	492
Total naturalized in all U.S. at each election	159	163	170	191	244	317	402	511	776	1,202
Total naturalized in North at each election[b]	137	140	147	165	210	273	346	440	669	1,036
Estimated number of naturalized males who voted in North at each election	37	82	83	99	175	223	266	342	592	904

SOURCE: See note 34 for the sources and methods used in constructing this table.
[a]The way to read the first 12 rows of each column is illustrated by the column for 1824: In 1824 there were 159,000 naturalized males age 21 or older, of whom 149,000 were naturalized before the election of 1820 and 10,000 were naturalized between the elections of 1820 and 1824.
[b]In this case, "North" includes the states (not the territories) listed in Table 9.1 plus California and Oregon.

TABLE 9.4

An Estimate of the Ethnic Composition of the Northern Democratic Vote in 1852 and 1860

	1852 voters		1860 voters	
	N (thousands)	(%)	N (thousands)	(%)
Naturalized citizens	207	17.3	620	39.1
Natives born of foreign-born parents	241	20.2	346	21.8
Natives born of native parents	748	62.5	621	39.1
Total	1,196	100.0	1,587	100.0

S O U R C E : See note 36 for the sources and methods used in constructing this table.

mainly from Irish and German stock and were more Catholic and Lutheran than reformed evangelical. The Democratic party of the North had lost the contest for the allegiance of the Old Americans.[37]

Table 9.4 does not imply that native-born, nonfarm workers were preponderantly Democrats before 1852. This is not yet an issue that can be fully resolved from the evidence at hand. As Table 9.5 indicates, however, the northern native vote in 1852 split almost equally between Democrats (989,000) and the Whigs/Free Soilers (1,071,000).[38] Regressions not yet reported suggest that in the North, the Whigs/Free Soilers did slightly better than the Democrats among farmers and slightly worse among non-farmers.[39] Hence, it appears that in 1852, northern nonfarm workers were about equally split between the Democrats and the Whigs/Free Soilers. Table 9.5 also indicates that as late as 1852, the Whigs/Free Soilers were able to control over 39 percent of the naturalized vote. Nor did the Democrats have an overwhelming share of the foreign-born vote in the North much before 1852. In the election of 1844, the Whigs/Libertyites obtained about 47 percent of the naturalized vote and the majority of the second-generation vote. Moreover, the Old Americans split their votes equally between the Democrats and the Whigs/Libertyites in that election.

Despite the rising ethnic polarization in local elections during the 1840's and the early 1850's, such polarization did not really get under way at the presidential level until after the 1852 elections. Table 9.5 shows that the defection of Old Americans from the Democrats to the Whigs/Free Soilers between 1844 and 1852 was slight. The increase in the Democratic share of the naturalized vote did not mean that the Whigs were losing their base among their traditional naturalized constituencies (the British, the pietistic Germans, and the Protestant Irish). Rather, it reflected the changing composition of the naturalized vote: Irish Catholics, German Lutherans, and German Catholics accounted for much of the increase in the naturalized

TABLE 9.5

Sources of Support Among Northern Voters in the Elections of 1844, 1852, and 1860

(*in thousands*)

	1844				1852				1860			
	Whigs/Liberty Party		Democrats		Whigs/Free Soil		Democrats		Republicans/Constitutional Union		Democrats	
	N	%	N	%	N	%	N	%	N	%	N	%
Naturalized citizens	104	46.6	119	53.4	135	39.5	207	60.5	284	31.4	620	68.6
Natives born of foreign-born parents	229	56.5	176	43.5	272	53.0	241	47.0	269	43.7	346	56.3
Natives born of native parents	672	50.0	672	50.0	799	51.6	748	48.4	1,438	69.8	621	30.2

SOURCE: See note 38 for the sources and methods used in constructing this table.

NOTE: Percentages in each election sum horizontally.

vote between 1844 and 1852 and for the vast majority between 1852 and 1860. The flight of the Old Americans from the Democrats did not begin until after 1852, when the New Americans began to eclipse the Old Americans as the main base of the Democratic party in the North.

What underlaid the partisan realignment of the 1850's, then, was a vast change, not just in the outlook, but in the personnel of the northern electorate in just eight years. Between 1852 and 1860, at least 15 percent of the eligible voters of 1852 died. Moreover, so many new voters entered the electorate during the same time span that they constituted about 43 percent of the northern electorate in 1860. About 55 percent of these new entrants were "New Americans." This change in the electorate was extraordinary. It was not only far larger than the change between, say, 1840 and 1848, but the rate at which New Americans were replacing Old Americans was so rapid that had it continued for another eight years, Old Americans would have been reduced to a minority even in their own heartland. Indeed, if over the two decades from 1848 to 1868 that rate had prevailed, Old Americans would have declined from more than two-thirds to just 47 percent of the northern electorate.

Problems in Measuring Changes in the Standard of Living

In *Without Consent or Contract*, I referred to the economic distress that afflicted native nonfarm workers in the North during the 1850's as a "hidden depression" because of the scant attention it has received from economic historians during the past three decades. My earlier work encouraged that neglect. I was one of the scholars writing in the late 1950's and early 1960's who contributed to the view that the two decades from 1840 to 1860 were a period of dramatic and broadly based economic growth and economic transformation in the North. This process, I noted, extended from 1820 to the end of the nineteenth century and "appears to have been interrupted only during the last half of the 1830's, the first half of the 1850's, the Civil War decade, the last half of the 1870's, and the last half of the 1890's."[40] My analysis depended heavily on Gallman's new (in 1960) series on commodity production and was buttressed by a variety of other time series on manufacturing output, agriculture, and commerce. The impression of rapid economic growth during the last two decades of the antebellum era was further reinforced by Easterlin's estimates of personal income per capita by region and Gallman's development of GNP per capita for the nineteenth century, extending back to 1830 in manuscript and to 1839 in published form.[41] These data confirmed the early findings that the northern economy was growing quite rapidly between 1840 and 1860, especially in the Northeast.

Additional research by numerous cliometricians between 1960 and the late 1970's seemed to confirm this basic finding.[42] The national income accounts, various indexes of real wages, and a number of other measures seemed to give the same answer. Although there were periodic business cycles, these were relatively brief phenomena, superimposed on such a strong upward secular pattern of growth in per capita income and real wages that they did not really undermine the view that the period from 1820 to 1860, especially from 1840 to 1860, was one of general prosperity and of rapid general improvement in the standard of living. We were aware that labor historians had a much dimmer view of the period, emphasizing the hardships experienced by the urban laboring classes, but their evidence was mainly anecdotal and easy to dismiss.

The first quantitative time series that cast doubt on the optimistic view of northern economic growth appeared late in 1978. That series, on the life expectations of native-born whites, peaked during Washington's administration and then began to decline, reaching a trough about the time of the Civil War that was about 15 percent below the previous high. An independent series on stature at maturity showed a similar pattern, with mean heights of native-born white males declining by over four centimeters between 1830 and the beginning of the 1890's, with most of the decline occurring during the three decades preceding the Civil War.

These results were so contrary to our expectations that we did not know what to make of them. Our first inclination was to presume that they were artifacts of the data sources (genealogies for $e°_{10}$ and military records for heights) and of the statistical procedures used in developing the time series. Several years spent probing these possibilities and a substantial expansion of the data base led us to conclude that the findings were real.[43] How are we to reconcile national income accounts that show strong economic growth between 1840 and 1860 with the data showing that life expectation and stature were declining? In pursuing this question we have started from the assumption that the national income accounts are basically correct, and that future improvements in existing estimates are unlikely to produce large changes in the basic time series. Caution is needed, however, in the inferences drawn from these time series. McCutcheon's recent analysis of the sources of growth in northern per capita income between 1840 and 1860 revealed that increases in labor productivity within the agricultural and nonagricultural sectors accounted for hardly 20 percent of northern economic growth between 1840 and 1860.[44] Of the remainder, a third was due to the decline in fertility rates and to the high rate of foreign immigration (mainly at prime working ages), both of which raised per capita income by raising labor-force participation rates. The balance was due to shifts of labor between the agricultural and nonagricultural sectors.

These complexities, which were not deeply probed previously, indicate the need for a much greater degree of disaggregation in the antebellum accounts. Even such disaggregation may not be adequate, however, since the data required for the construction of national income accounts are available only for census years. As it turns out, 1839–40, 1849–50, and 1859–60 are all at or close to the peaks of business cycles. Hence, measures confined to these years cannot reveal how severe the downturns were between the peaks. Moreover, sectoral aggregates do not reveal how different persons within the various sectors fared: farmers versus hired labor in agriculture; merchants versus clerks in commerce; factory owners versus factory hands in manufacturing; and native versus foreign workers in all of the sectors.

Measures of real wages by socioeconomic groups are an obvious approach to this problem.[45] When Engerman and Gallman assessed the available evidence on trends in U.S. economic growth between 1783 and 1860, however, they concluded that the data on nominal and real wages then available were poor measures of changes in per capita income.[46] Part of the problem was that the nominal wage data only covered limited occupational categories. Another problem was that these data only applied to a few localized labor markets at a time when the national integration of labor markets was still limited. There were similar problems related to the indexes of prices that had been used to convert nominal wages into real wages.

The series on nominal wages between 1820 and 1855 published by Margo and Villaflor overcame several of the problems that concerned Engerman and Gallman.[47] Further improvements in these series were made by Goldin and Margo.[48] The new wage data are drawn from military records of wages paid to civilians who worked as common laborers, teamsters, clerks, and in a wide array of skilled crafts. These men were recruited in local labor markets in the vicinity of 313 army installations in all regions of the nation. Examination of the data indicates that the army paid competitive wages and was too small an employer in most labor markets to affect the equilibrium wage rate.[49]

The deflated series for the Midwest show that the real wages of skilled workers (artisans plus clerks) declined by 24 percent between 1848 and 1855. The corresponding figure for the Northeast is 18 percent. The decline in the real wages of laborers between the same dates is 28 percent in the Midwest and 10 percent in the Northeast. These figures may be taken as a lower bounds on the decline in the real income of native nonagricultural labor in the North. They are a lower bounds because the Margo-Villaflor-

Goldin series, like other indexes of real wages, suffer from several short-comings when they are used as a measure of the trend in the annual real income of native nonagricultural workers.

The first problem, generic to the use of data on daily or weekly wage rates as indexes of annual income, is the implicit assumption that employment is constant from year to year. Margo and Villaflor call attention to this problem by pointing out that during the depression of 1837–43, real wages rose because prices fell more rapidly than nominal wages.[50] Such gains were limited only to those who continued to work more or less a full work year, however. The real income of workers as a whole declined sharply, despite the rise in daily rates, because of widespread unemployment and because of reductions in the number of days of work for those who were not laid off for long stretches of time. It was the massive unemployment in New York City following the crash of 1837 and its devastating effect on the working classes that so appalled the young Horace Greeley and radicalized him on labor issues.[51] An index of real daily wage rates not only fails to capture that distress, but makes one of the most severe depressions in American history look like a boon to workers.

This point has an important implication for the period 1850–55. Despite the fact that the Margo-Villaflor-Goldin index shows a substantial decline in real daily wages during these years, the actual decline in the annual income of workers was probably much larger, both because work years were reduced and because unemployment increased. If, for example, unemployment in the nonagricultural sector increased from about 3 to about 15 percent between 1853 and 1855, that factor alone would make the decline in the average annual wage of northeastern workers 67 percent greater than shown by the index of daily wage rates. Such a rise in unemployment is quite plausible, not only because of the massive immigration from the beginning of 1850 to the end of 1855, but also because of the massive layoffs of railroad construction workers and the associated decline in residential construction.[52]

Another difficulty with current real wage indexes concerns the inadequacy of the price deflators. A major problem is the neglect of or inadequate attention to the sharp rise in the cost of housing in large cities. Moreover, there were wide differences between cities in rates of change in prices of food and other consumer goods and services. Consequently, price indexes vary widely depending on the localities from which the prices are drawn and the scope of the items covered. Although the four price indexes displayed in Figure 9.3 all show a marked rise in the price level between 1848 and 1856, there are significant differences in the amplitude of rise.

The largest increase shown in Figure 9.3 is in the Berry series, which pertains to Cincinnati.[53] If the Berry index (as modified by Goldin and

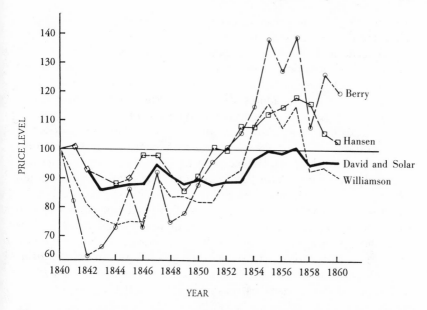

Fig. 9.3. A comparison of four indexes of the price level, 1840–60. Data from Berry, *Western Prices;* Alvin Hansen, "Factors Affecting the Trend of Real Wages," *American Economic Review* 15 (1925): 27–42; David and Solar, "Bicentenary Contribution," pp. 1–80; and Williamson, "American Prices," pp. 303–33.

Margo) is used to deflate the Margo-Villaflor series on unskilled labor in the Midwest, one obtains a fall in real wages of about 28 percent between 1848 and 1855.[54] Even without taking account of housing prices or unemployment, the midwestern decline is more than twice that of the Northeast, pointing up the error frequently made in relying on northeastern data to characterize trends in the living standards of all northern labor. When a plausible allowance is made for an increase in unemployment related to the termination of the railroad and nonrailroad construction booms, the decline in the real wages of midwestern laborers between 1848 and 1855 reaches 37 percent.[55]

Deskilling is another aspect of the decline in real wages that has yet to be incorporated in current indexes. These indexes implicitly assume that the distribution of workers across occupations remained constant over time. The labor literature stresses, however, that deskilling was common between 1848 and 1855, since employers used the excess supply of labor to reclassify native artisans to lower skilled categories and found other means of reducing wages (such as charging workers for materials and floor space) that are not incorporated in the nominal wage data.[56] If just 10 percent of artisans were reclassified to common laborers, such deskilling alone would have amounted to a 5 percent reduction in the average wage of artisans.[57] Thus, the joint effect of the price rise (excluding housing), increased unemployment, and deskilling may have reduced the wages of midwestern artisans by about 31 percent between 1848 and 1855, a decline nearly twice as large as that indicated by the movement of daily wages alone.[58]

It is also necessary to address the implicit assumption that the trend in real wages was identical for native and foreign workers. The labor literature suggests that although the level of wages was lower in given occupations for immigrants than for natives, their wages may have risen over time relative to those of natives. The closing of the wage gap appears to have occurred as immigrants broke the labor monopolies of native workers and gradually worked their way into the system.[59] If that is the case, then the real wages of native workers fell more rapidly than the current series indicate, since the current series combine the more rapid upward movement in the nominal wages of foreign workers with the more modest nominal gains for native workers. It may soon be possible to unravel this issue, since recently discovered wage records contain the names of the workers, and so provide a reasonable basis for inferring nationality.

Measuring the Cost of Urban Housing

The price of urban housing, as already indicated, is one of the most vexing of the unresolved issues facing economic historians who want to measure trends in the cost of living before the Civil War.[60] Some scholars have omitted it from their cost-of-living indexes because of the absence of suitable data. Others have sought to develop proxies in lieu of the desired data. One widely used series on consumer prices employs a weighted average of the wages of common labor and of construction materials as a proxy for rent. Still others have used the series on residential rental charges contained in the Weeks report.[61]

None of these efforts has proved successful. Newspapers, welfare agencies, and government documents report severe and unprecedented overcrowding and skyrocketing rental charges from the mid-1840's to the mid-1850's in New York, Boston, Brooklyn, Philadelphia, Buffalo, Cincinnati, Chicago, and St. Louis.[62] Yet the Hoover index shows that expenditures on rent were remarkably constant:[63]

1851	100
1852	100
1853	100
1854	102
1855	103

The problem, as Lebergott pointed out, is that the rental data came mainly from companies that provided subsidized housing for their employees.[64] The rates charged for such housing showed virtually no variation during either the inflation of 1851–56 or the even sharper inflation of the Civil War. Moreover, these firms were located mainly in small cities, such as Lawnenberg, Indiana; Oswego, New York; Canton, Steubenville, and Zanesville, Ohio; and New Cumberland, (then) Virginia. All of these cities had less than 10,000 persons in 1860; some had declining populations.[65]

Another unresolved problem relates to the assumption that the share of rent in the expenditure of workers remained constant despite rates of increase in urban rentals that may have been two or three times as rapid as the increases in other prices. It has been reported that the ratio of rents to the construction cost of housing rose tenfold between the late 1840's and the mid 1850's in cities that were the principal targets of immigrants. Such reports may be exaggerations or may refer to exceptional cases. Even if the ratio only doubled, however, the implied annual rate of increase in rental rates between 1848 and 1854 is over 12 percent.

Even if workers responded to rent gouging by cutting back on the amount of space they purchased, a proper index of costs would have to take account of the deterioration in the quality of housing that was purchased, since overcrowding greatly increased morbidity and mortality rates. Whether one used beginning- or end-period weights, such quality adjustments would show much sharper rises in rental costs than unadjusted prices. Moreover, if quality is held constant, the share of housing in consumer budgets would rise sharply between 1848 and 1854 in the major urban centers of the North.[66]

Whether it is possible to secure the data needed to measure accurately the rising cost of worker housing in northern cities between 1830 and 1855 remains to be determined. Searches are now under way for such data, but it is too soon to predict the outcome of these efforts.

Conclusion

During the two decades between 1840 and 1860, the total output of the northern economy increased by about 82 percent (an annual rate of about 3.0 percent). Although most of this growth was due to the rapid increase of the population, the real per capita income in the North also grew rapidly, averaging about 1.3 percent per annum.[67] The benefits of these increases, however, were unequally distributed in time and space, and across occupational groups. Much remains to be learned about the inequities, but it appears that labor in the nonagricultural sector was the principal loser, at least in a relative sense. Within this sector of the labor force, it appears that foreign-born labor might have scored some gains while native-born labor suffered some losses.

Because of the strong surge of the northern economy in 1859 and 1860, coupled with the sharp decline in immigration (the main source of the growth in the nonagricultural labor force), the real income of northern labor apparently recovered from its lows in the mid-1850's. This conclusion is suggested by recent work on the income accounts of the North, which indicates that labor productivity in the nonagricultural sector was virtually the same in 1860 as in 1840.[68] However, the fact that even after the strong surge of the economy during the two years preceding Lincoln's election, nonagricultural labor productivity was virtually the same as it had been two decades earlier, has two other implications. First, it tends to confirm the proposition that nonagricultural labor hardly shared in the strong overall gains in per capita income. Second, since there were rapid advances in the technology of manufacturing and transportation during this period, and rapid increases in capital formation, constant labor productivity implies that it was the exceptionally high rate of growth in the number of workers (possibly coupled with labor speedup) that prevented nonagricultural labor from sharing more fully in the growth of per capita income.[69]

Although the income accounts provide significant insights into the status of labor from one census year to another, they do not reveal the economic conditions of workers during noncensus years, particularly between 1848 and 1856, when the second party system was destroyed. The time series recently constructed by Margo, Villaflor, and Goldin provides improved information on one key measure. Their work shows that between 1848 and 1855, the decline in the real daily wages of unskilled workers in the Midwest was 28 percent, and the corresponding decline for skilled workers was 24 percent. Since the price deflator they used does not yet take account of the sharp rise in the cost of urban housing, it is likely that the inclusion of that cost will push the midwestern decline in real wages to well over 25 percent. In the Northeast, real daily wages fell by about 13 percent. Since the housing crisis was much more acute in northeastern cities than in midwestern cities, however, it appears likely that the gap in the rates of decline in real wages between the Midwest and the Northeast will narrow somewhat, although at this point it is difficult to say by how much.[70]

Indexes of real daily wages do not measure the effects of unemployment, deskilling, or labor speedup, all of which contributed to the economic distress of workers during the 1850's and made the slide in the real annual income of nonfarm workers between 1848 and 1855 steeper than the slide in the real daily wage rates of particular occupations.[71] Much work remains before these effects can be measured with precision, but the available evidence suggests that unemployment increased sharply, especially between

1853 and 1855, and hence had a significant effect on the real annual incomes of workers.

Three considerations support this inference. First, the collapse of the northern railroad construction boom alone dumped about 83,000 workers onto the nonfarm market for labor during these two years. Nonrailroad construction also reached a peak in 1853 and experienced a comparable collapse during 1854 and 1855. Since the nonrailroad construction sector was more than twice as large as the railroad construction sector, it is likely that a total of about 280,000 construction workers, about 10 percent of the nonfarm labor force in the North in 1853, had to seek employment in other sectors.[72]

Second, it is unlikely that the workers released by the collapse of the construction boom could have been absorbed by other sectors of the economy without displacing workers already employed. Although manufacturing and services did not experience as severe a collapse as construction did, the available evidence indicates that these sectors were also in recession. Berry reported heavy declines of production in the midwestern iron industry during 1854 and 1855, which resulted from "numerous and heavy failures." The output of the cotton textile industry, according to estimates developed by Davis and Stettler, peaked in 1852 and stagnated for the next three years. Although foreign-born workers were able to find jobs in textiles, it was at the expense of the native workers whom they displaced when they accepted reduced rates of compensation per piece. Figures for the traffic on New York canals and railroads, much of which originated in the Midwest or was bound for the Midwest, indicate that commerce was also in recession during 1854 and 1855.[73]

The third consideration is the heavy pressure put on northern nonfarm labor markets by the influx of foreign-born labor. Between 1850 and 1855, the number of nonfarm workers in the North increased by about 710,000, an increase of 32 percent in just five years (or an annual increase of 5.7 percent). During the upswing in the construction cycle, the construction sector (railroad plus nonrailroad) absorbed between 200,000 (in 1851) and 76,000 (in 1853) additional workers per year, most of whom were foreign-born. Since manufacturing and commerce were also expanding, the downward pressure on real wages exercised by heavy immigration was abated by the coincidence of the upswing in a long construction cycle with the expansion phase of a short trade cycle. After the collapse of the construction boom, however, the 280,000 construction workers displaced in 1854 and 1855 had to compete not only with workers displaced from manufacturing and commerce during the contraction phase of a mild trade cycle but also with about 260,000 new entrants into the northern nonagricultural labor force, most of whom were new immigrants. Displaced and new workers together accounted for about 18 percent of the northern nonagricultural labor force at the end of 1855.[74]

Since only the agricultural sector was buoyant during these years, it is doubtful that more than a small proportion of the job seekers could have found jobs without displacing other workers.[75] Indeed, those who were unemployed (mainly recent immigrants) did undercut the real wages and employment standards (mainly of natives or earlier immigrants) in their effort to alleviate their dire circumstances. So, to many of those who held jobs prior to 1853, the new wave of immigrants appeared to be responsible for their unemployment or their declining standard of living.

Relief came in 1856, when an upswing in the economy, coupled with a sharp decline in immigration, brought employment to many of the job seekers. Because the process of absorption was interrupted by the Panic of 1857, it was not until 1859 that the excess supply of nonfarm labor in the North was converted into excess demand, causing real wages to exceed the 1848 peak.[76]

It is against this background of economic distress and recovery that the political convulsions in the North during the 1850's need to be analyzed. Unemployment and declining real wages among northern nonfarm workers were not the only issues on which the politics of this period turned, but they were important issues that concerned a substantial share of the northern electorate. To understand the political realignment of the 1850's, it is important to understand the interplay of these economic issues with the ethnocultural and antislavery issues.

CHAPTER TEN

❧ Entrepreneurial Experiences in the Civil War: Evidence from Philadelphia

J. Matthew Gallman

THE DEBATE OVER the economic impact of the Civil War is familiar to most economic historians. While an earlier generation saw the conflict as triggering substantial economic growth, later scholars—responding to Thomas Cochran's provocative essay, "Did the Civil War Retard Industrialization?"[1]—usually agreed that whereas much of the northern economy prospered during the war years, the Civil War's impact on long-term economic growth was slight. The case for more substantial economic change has generally concentrated on a particular sector of the economy or on the effects of specific legislation—banking, tariffs, taxes—passed by the Republican-dominated war Congress.[2] Much of this literature has approached the Civil War as a brief episode in the long-run development of the nineteenth-century American economy. The evidence has been mined for significant, measurable "impacts."

But the war also provides an excellent opportunity to address a more general set of issues concerning the influence of government policies—in this case, military spending—on economic behavior.[3] Here the critical concern is not so much to gauge the net impact of war on economic growth as it is to consider the economic ramifications of an expanded federal role as a purchaser of goods and services. Such an analysis can contribute both to our understanding of nineteenth-century economic growth and development and to larger discussions of the impact of military spending on economic development.[4]

My purpose is to consider the effect of the Civil War on Philadelphia entrepreneurs as revealed in the credit reports assembled by R. G. Dun and Company. When the war began, Philadelphia's Schuylkill Arsenal housed all the uniforms for the nation's 16,000-man regular army. As the conflict progressed, the city's central local and manufacturing diversity assured its businesses an integral position in the developing war-contracting

I would like to thank Charles Cheape, Stephen Hughes, Thomas Weiss, Lou Galambos, and Stanley Engerman for their comments on earlier drafts.

system. These characteristics make Philadelphia particularly well-suited to this study.[5]

In 1841, New York wholesaler Lewis Tappan established the Mercantile Agency to gather credit information for sale to subscribers. Tappan collected his information from correspondents—mostly lawyers—who were well acquainted with local businesses. In 1859, R. G. Dun assumed ownership of the rapidly expanding Mercantile Agency.[6] R. G. Dun's agents typically filed semi-annual reports on local businesses. Any business that had applied for credit or appeared likely to seek loans was liable to fall under R. G. Dun's net. A complete report of a business included the names of all partners, an estimate of the establishment's net worth, any unusual activities that might affect its credit, a comment on the character of the owner, and a credit rating—usually "poor," "good," "very good," or "excellent." In practice, the entries varied tremendously. In some cases, the reporter submitted complete updates every six months; in other instances, reports came years apart.

The reports lend themselves to rudimentary quantitative analysis, but they are particularly valuable because the individual accounts often provide glimpses beneath the data. This analysis concentrates on the wartime histories of 138 Philadelphia firms that the R. G. Dun reporters described as having government contracts.[7] Their collective experiences are compared with those of a control sample of 491 firms.[8]

Several conclusions will emerge. First, Philadelphia's war contractors were a numerous and diverse lot. Thus, wartime profits were distributed over many sectors of the local economy. Second, eventual war contractors clustered in two groups: fairly large, established firms that were well situated to meet the government's needs; and new, often small, companies established specifically to fill government contracts. Many of the established firms sought war contracts following declines in their private business. Third, in most cases, established firms made only slight adjustments in their peacetime products to fill military needs. Finally, although war contracting helped some struggling companies survive, it was rarely a route to riches. Often, in fact, firms performing military work ran into trouble owing to slow government payments. Each of these findings points to the larger conclusion that the Civil War contracting system served to minimize the impact of government spending on economic growth and development.[9]

Philadelphia's War Contractors

The evolution of the Union Army's supply system is an excellent metaphor for the North's wartime experience. When the war began, state and regimental quartermasters scrambled to outfit a hastily assembled army. Soon, under the guidance of Quartermaster General Montgomery C. Meigs, a multitiered supply system emerged in which some goods were produced in government arsenals while private contractors provided a wide array of raw materials and finished products. Following the conflict's first chaotic months, Congress passed legislation requiring open bidding for all government contracts. Often those who secured contracts passed on the work to subcontractors. For the purposes of this study, "military contractors" include all firms reported as producing goods to fill contracts for some war-related government agency.[10]

The R. G. Dun records generally noted the type of war contract held by each firm. More than a quarter of these businesses (Table 10.1) supplied uniforms to the army, and an additional 16 percent furnished boots, shoes, haversacks, and canteens. The firms trading with Philadelphia's vast network of military hospitals suggest the war's diverse economic opportunities. George Snowden sold surgical instruments to the Army's Medical Department; druggists J. Wyeth and Brother supplied medicine to local hospitals; the hardware firm of W. W. Knight, Son and Company did

TABLE 10.1

Philadelphia War Contractors in R. G. Dun

Type of contract	N[a]	%	Type of contract	N	%
Clothing	31	27.4	Stockings	1	0.9
Haversacks and canteens	11	9.7	Hospital bedsteads	1	0.9
Guns/rifles	8	7.1	Ship timber	1	0.9
Boots/shoes	7	6.2	Hay and feed	1	0.9
Blankets	6	5.3	Stoves	1	0.9
Saddles	5	4.4	Potatoes	1	0.9
Tents	4	3.5	Gun locks	1	0.9
Swords/bayonets	4	3.5	Propellors	1	0.9
Cannons	3	2.7	Surgical instruments	1	0.9
Ships	3	2.7	Horses	1	0.9
Bread	2	1.8	Locomotives	1	0.9
Wagons	2	1.8	Caps	1	0.9
Saddle trees	2	1.8	Ship engines	1	0.9
Food	2	1.8	Drugs	1	0.9
Coal	1	0.9	Shot and shell	1	0.9
Brushes	1	0.9	Shipping	1	0.9
Drums	1	0.9	Harness leather	1	0.9
Mint acids	1	0.9	Artificial limbs	1	0.9
Lumber	1	0.9	Total	113	100.0

SOURCE: The R. G. Dun and Company Collection, Baker Library, Harvard University Graduate School of Business.

[a]Includes ten war contractors with assumed "type of contract" based on antebellum activities rather than a specific statement indicating the nature of the contract. These ten cases include seven clothing, two saddles, and one boots and shoes. In twenty-five other cases, the type of contract was not given and could not be determined.

"a large bus in the Mfr of Hospital Bedsteads for [the] Govt"; grocer George D. Moses fell upon hard times in 1863 but recovered by "supplying the Hospitals with Groc[eries]"; 25-year-old Charles W. F. Calvert kept his new embroidery business afloat through "the Manufr of shirts & draws for Army Hospital purposes"; lumber dealer Warren F. Ferguson shared in the wartime building boom by selling materials for the construction of "2 or 3 hospitals and the Arsenal." [11]

Others profited in more unorthodox ways. German immigrant C. M. Zimmerman sold drums to the army, and bought a farm with the proceeds. John Livesey's dry goods company failed shortly before the war, but by late 1865 he had "made considerable money by furnishing potatoes to [the] Govt" and was worth an estimated $20,000. By April 1864, Condit Pruden reportedly had sold the government 100,000 saddle trees, at a profit of between 50 and 75 cents each. And, in one of Philadelphia's oddest instances of profiting from the war, Dr. B. Frank Palmer grew wealthy by earning "the Govt contracts and patronage for supplying disabled soldiers & officers with artificial limbs." [12]

Pruden's case is also unusual in that his wartime saddle tree contract continued an antebellum relationship with the government. Coal dealers George F. Tyler and W. E. Stone, blank-book manufacturer James B. Smith and Company, and wheelwright Henry Simons also maintained established government contracts into the war years. But, as we shall see, most Philadelphia war contractors made adjustments to meet military demands. [13]

In addition to those military contractors who are the focus of this essay, the R. G. Dun records describe numerous local traders who found other ways to profit from the war. After leaving the 88th Pennsylvania Volunteers, William H. Shearman opened a hotel on Race Street catering to "officers and soldiers awaiting discharge." [14] Book dealer J. W. Bradley failed in May 1861 and then tried (unsuccessfully) to recover by "getting up a history of the war." [15] Several local tradesmen closed their shops and became sutlers, selling goods to the soldiers in the camps. [16]

Philadelphia's war contractors were, on average, larger and older than firms in the general sample. Table 10.2 compares the size of the war contractors with the general sample. Of 128 war contractors with estimated sizes, 39 percent were worth $100,000 or more. Only 11 percent of the sampled firms were this large. Conversely, 57 percent of the sampled firms and only 14 percent of the war contractors had an estimated worth under $15,000. [17] This difference in average size could indicate that larger firms were more adept at securing contracts, but the data also reflect the fact that contracting companies were often manufacturers, whereas a large share of the sampled establishments consisted of small retailers. [18]

In 104 of 138 cases, the reports reveal the approximate age of the firm. These "years of origin" are compared with the general sample in Table 10.3. Thirty percent of the contracting businesses were organized before 1851, compared to 25 percent of the firms in the general sample. Conversely, 32 percent of the companies in the general sample and only 19 percent of the war contractors began doing business in the five prewar years. Among established companies, older firms were apparently somewhat better prepared to win war contracts. Table 10.3 also indicates, however, that a disproportionate number of military contractors first opened their doors between 1861 and 1865 (29 percent as opposed to 20 percent in

TABLE 10.2

*Estimated Firm Size: War Contractors
Versus the General Sample*

Estimated worth	Contractors (*N*)	Sampled firms (*N*)
$99,999 or more	50	49
$50,000–99,999	24	32
$25,000–49,999	28	50
$15,000–24,999	8	61
Less than $15,000	18	257
Total	128	449

SOURCE: R. G. Dun and Company Collection, Baker Library, Harvard University Graduate School of Business.
NOTE: This table includes only those cases where the value of the firm could be estimated. These estimates relied on both dollar estimates of net worth and qualitative descriptions.

TABLE 10.3

*Age of Firm: War Contractors Versus
the General Sample*

Year founded	Contractors (*N*)	General sample (*N*)
Before 1851	31	89
1851–55	23	80
1856–60	20	114
1861–65	30	71
Total	104	354

SOURCE: R. G. Dun and Company Collection, Baker Library, Harvard University Graduate School of Business.
NOTE: This table includes only firms with estimated years of origin. Twenty-one firms from the general sample that were founded between 1856 and 1860 but went out of business before 1861 are excluded.

the general sample). This difference reflects the substantial decline in new firm starts during the war. In the five prewar years, 135 businesses opened in the general sample, compared to 71 between 1861 and 1865.[19]

Philadelphia's war contractors can be divided into established companies that shifted their activities to fill war contracts and firms founded to meet the military demand. The R. G. Dun reports often noted that firms had begun specifically to produce military goods. H. G. Haedrick and Company formed in 1862 to manufacture "cartridge boxes & bayonet sheaths"; J. W. Watson made tents; and J. C. Bower went into business in 1864 producing haversacks.[20] Twenty-two-year-old Adolph Hochstadter quit his father's firm and borrowed $6,000 from friends to manufacture uniforms.[21] W. F. Hansell left another establishment in 1862 and quickly "made money" selling army clothing to the government.[22] In a wartime atmosphere of economic caution, in which Philadelphia saw relatively few new business starts, war contracting presented attractive options for hopeful entrepreneurs.[23]

The combined evidence from Tables 10.2 and 10.3 shows that at least some contractors came from the ranks of Philadelphia's oldest and wealthiest firms. But Table 10.1 suggests that most types of contract were not monopolized by one or two local establishments. The records of contracts signed in Philadelphia confirm this apparent breadth of participation. For instance, the 278 contracts for equipment signed between 1862 and 1864 were filled by 101 different companies.[24] Moreover, the R. G. Dun reports indicate that some established firms that turned to war contracting did so less out of strength than out of weakness.

R. G. Dun's agents occasionally noted unusual changes in the fortunes of a business. Taken collectively, these "ebbs and flows" shed further light on the characteristics separating war contractors from other Philadelphia firms. Table 10.4 groups the agents' annual comments into three categories—those having a good year, those having a bad year, and those in serious trouble—and compares the experiences of war contractors with those of the general sample.[25] The evidence from the general sample indicates that when the Civil War broke out, business suffered through an initial year of hardship, followed by several years of recovery, and then a second decline near the end of the conflict. Beneath this pattern lay great diversity. In 1862, for instance, 14 of 342 companies (4 percent) were in serious trouble; another 13 (4 percent) experienced difficulties; but 11 other firms (3 percent) had begun expanding. The war contractors followed a similar chronology: a high percentage of firms ran into trouble in 1861, whereas roughly a fifth improved their standing in both 1862 and 1863. Although the timing of peaks and valleys is essentially the same as in the general sample, the war contractors' experiences were far more volatile. A

TABLE 10.4

Evidence of Annual Fluctuations: War Contractors Versus the General Sample

	Total[a] (N)	Good year N	Good year (%)	Bad year N	Bad year (%)	In trouble[b] N	In trouble[b] (%)
		War contractors					
1860	97	0	0	4	4	4	4
1861	112	6	5	5	4	10	9
1862	120	26	22	9	8	2	2
1863	122	23	19	0	0	7	6
1864	125	10	8	2	2	0	0
1865	110	2	2	4	4	4	4
1866	88	1	1	5	6	1	1
1867	73	0	0	1	1	4	5
1868	62	0	0	0	0	1	2
		General sample					
1860	364	0	0	4	1	8	2
1861	341	4	1	9	3	21	6
1862	342	11	3	13	4	14	4
1863	339	10	3	2	1	2	1
1864	336	8	2	10	3	9	3
1865	321	3	1	4	1	4	1
1866	293	0	0	3	1	1	0
1867	253	3	1	7	3	4	2
1868	224	1	0	3	1	4	2

SOURCE: R. G. Dun and Company Collection, Baker Library, Harvard University Graduate School of Business.

NOTE: This table records the frequency of unusual comments recorded by the R. G. Dun agents. See text and note 25. See Table 10.5 for companies that went out of business each year.

[a]Total includes all businesses definitely in existence in that year.

[b] "In trouble" means the company experienced serious trouble (e.g., suspension, etc.).

higher percentage of firms that eventually became war contractors ran into trouble in 1861 than did firms in the larger sample. And a much greater share of war contractors experienced substantial gains in the mid-war years. This suggests that war contractors turned to the government when their normal activities ran into trouble. The high percentage of war contractors enjoying good years in 1862 and 1863 demonstrates that supplying the army was a profitable occupation. But it also could indicate that many of these companies were "down" in 1861, making their later successes particularly noteworthy to the credit reporters.[26]

The reports offer a wide assortment of cases in which firms turned to government contracting out of desperation. The (aptly named) Phoenix Iron Company suspended payments during the Panic of 1857 and had barely returned to good standing when the secession crisis brought on another wave of suspension. In September 1861, while still under extension, the firm received a favorable report from R. G. Dun's agent because of "large [cannon] contracts with the Government which will help them very materially." Although Beggs and Rowland, wheelwrights, were "a little tight" in May 1861, they remained good for credit because of a government contract which, it seemed, "will ultimately place them in a gd position." On April 19, 1861—only days after the firing on Fort Sumter—an R. G. Dun agent reported that he "could not advise cr to any amt" to jeans manufacturer Bolton Winpenny because of "little if any demand" for his product; two months later the firm had reportedly "obtained a contract from [the] Government for Kerseys." By early 1865, Winpenny's firm was valued at over $100,000.[27]

Frequently, companies with economic ties to the South turned to military contracting when their normal operations fell into disarray. A survey of the R. G. Dun records on Philadelphia's wartime businesses yielded 53 firms, engaged in a wide range of enterprises, with prewar southern ties. Nearly all experienced some difficulties as the war commenced, and 30 of these either suspended or failed before 1866.[28] At least nine of the firms with southern ties turned to government contracting; nearly all of these cases fit the proposed profile: a firm seeking the military's business when familiar avenues closed. Philadelphia tailor Robert Clifton had a prosperous antebellum business with stores in Nashville and Norfolk. With the outbreak of war, Clifton's business failed, and he "settled at 50%" with his creditors. By 1864, he had earned $50,000 from government contracts and had settled his old debts. Michael Magee saw a $100,000 saddlery business fall apart when he lost his trade with New Orleans, but successful government contracts allowed him to retire a wealthy man in 1865. George Evans and William Hassall enjoyed a thriving Ladies Dressing Trimmings business before the Civil War; when the conflict cut off their southern market, they began manufacturing knapsacks and haversacks for the Union Army.[29]

The characteristics of contractors and the range of their products suggest the diversity of Philadelphia's war-contracting history. Some contractors were old, established firms, others came together simply to fill a military demand. Many clearly proceeded from strengths, whereas others turned to government production when the uncertainty and dislocation of secession brought them to the brink of failure.

Wartime Experiences

As we have seen, many companies were formed specifically to meet government demands. Of the remainder, some continued established relationships with the government, and most continued to produce their familiar products, perhaps with slight adjustments to meet the military's needs. Whereas some entrepreneurs threw their energies into war manufacturing, filling government contracts was often a minor portion of a firm's wartime activities. Dry-goods merchant Abraham Ritter sold blankets to the military to supplement his retail trade; woolen manufacturer Martin Landenberger had "good & very profitable Govt contracts," but also "made money rapidly by introducing fancy woolen articles for ladies wear"; and wealthy architect and builder John Rice picked up some extra profits in 1861 by "manufg muskets for the government."[30]

The credit reports offer ample evidence of manufacturers adjusting their operations in response to military demands. In October 1861, the report on George W. Simons and Brother, manufacturers of gold chains, thimbles, and pencils, noted that "they have altered thr machinery for the mfr of swords & are dg a large & profitable bus." The partnership of George Richardson and William Overman had been variously engaged in selling grain and manufacturing umbrellas when the war began. In March 1861, before the outbreak of hostilities, a skeptical R. G. Dun agent reported that they had leased a mill and bought $35,000 in equipment in preparation for the production of "patent rifles." By early 1863, they were "said to have made abt $200,000." In mid-1864, the agent noted that the firm owned a large factory, enjoyed good government contacts, and although "not popular . . . are perfectly good." Allen Ridgeway and Company's manufacturing concern specialized in making coffee mills before the war. In order to shift to the production of sword bayonets, they "expended considerable money on Machinery etc," which resulted in temporary financial difficulties in 1862.[31]

Such adjustments among Philadelphia's metal industries were widespread. Philip S. Justice shifted from the production of railway spring machinery to muskets and rifles; in 1861, the Fair Mount Fork Works began "altering & having machinery made for the purpose of mfg cavalry sabres" and bayonets; North, Chase and North—a leading Philadelphia iron foundry—recovered from the secession crisis by selling shot and shell to the government.[32] Similarly, many of Philadelphia's textile manufacturers shifted their factories over to war work. Carpet manufacturer James Lord, Jr. began producing blankets; cotton-duck trader John W. Everyman earned over $100,000 supplying tents to the government; necktie maker E. Oppenheimer survived the war by subcontracting work in various military goods.[33]

Most of these shifts apparently required only modest alterations, but in several cases firms underwent substantial retooling to meet the new wartime demands. Such adjustments could have had a far-reaching effect on the local economy as manufactories invested in machinery or constructed new buildings. And although the evidence is scanty, several credit reports hint at the importance of war contracting as a stimulus to technological development. Among the most noteworthy are the reports on C. Sharps and Co. In June 1861, the R. G. Dun agent noted that "he has lately invented a Rifle which is said by those who have examined it to be superior to anything of the kind in the world." Four months later, R. G. Dun reported that "we understand they have a Government contract to mfr. 500 stand of arms of his [Sharps's] new patent. This contract will not pay them any profit as they have been to a large expense in altering thr machinery."[34] Both Jesse Butterfield's blacksmith-shop-turned-arms-manufactory and the Cooper Arms Manufacturing Company also reportedly profited from wartime arms patents.[35]

Whether they simply sold their traditional wares to a new buyer or reshaped their operations to fill the military demands, Philadelphia's war contractors—like its other businesses—had to navigate a volatile wartime economy. Although they are not consistently sensitive to subtle shifts, the R. G. Dun reports contain sufficient information to offer a broad comparison of the "failure rate" of the war contractors with that of the general sample. Table 10.5 compares the failure rate of war contractors with that of the general sample using two measurements.[36] The first calculation for each group, "complete cases," includes only those firms where the report

TABLE 10.5

Final Year in Business: War Contractors Versus the General Sample

	War contractors			General sample		
	Complete cases[a]	Estimated cases[b]	All cases	Complete cases[a]	Estimated cases[b]	All cases
1861	0	0	0	15	10	25
1862	4	0	4	15	27	42
1863	3	0	3	8	12	20
1864	4	1	5	13	3	16
1865	13	0	13	28	3	31
1866	9	4	13	19	4	23
1867	9	3	12	10	8	18
1868	3	8	11	12	27	39
1869	2	3	5	5	6	11
1870 and after	51	14	65	215	12	227
Total	98	33	131	340	112	452

SOURCE: R. G. Dun and Company Collection, Baker Library, Harvard University Graduate School of Business.
NOTE: See note 33 for a discussion of methods.
[a]Cases in which an exact year of failure is given.
[b]Cases with an estimated final year.

gives an exact year of failure. The second calculation, "estimated cases," includes the final year of operation where the evidence is less exact.[37]

The long-term failure rate for the 131 war-contracting firms with known or estimated final years appears quite similar to the general sample of 452 wartime cases. Sixty-five of 131 war contractors (49.6 percent) survived until 1870, whereas 50.2 percent of the larger sample lasted through the war decade. But this apparent similarity masks a clear difference. Only 25 war contractors (19.1 percent) failed between 1861 and 1865, whereas 29.6 percent of the overall sample failed during the war years. This does not necessarily indicate that trading with the government was a wise buffer against wartime turbulence. Many war-contracting firms were formed following the disruptive secession crisis. Moreover, the war contractors that weathered the war's first winter were, on average, larger and older establishments than their counterparts in the general sample. Under normal circumstances, such characteristics provided protection against abrupt failure in crisis.[38] In fact, larger war-contracting firms fared slightly worse than those in the general sample. Only 4 of 43 sampled firms (9.3 percent) worth over $100,000 (with known or estimated final years) went out of business during the war, and one of these folded during the 1861 panic. In contrast, 7 of 38 large war contractors (18.4 percent) closed between 1861 and 1865. Similarly, "young" war-contracting firms were less likely to survive the war than similar establishments in the general sample. Ten of 29 war contractors (34.5 percent) established between 1861 and 1865 went out of business before 1866, whereas only 16 of 71 such establishments (22.5 percent) in the general sample did so. (Neither group managed as well as the businesses formed between 1856 and 1860. Despite the Panic of 1857, only 21 [15.6 percent] of these young antebellum firms failed before 1861.[39])

The case histories suggest the range of wartime experiences. Although many new firms flourished by concentrating on government contracts, others found the road more rocky. C. W. Williams and Company, gunlock manufacturers, opened their doors on September 1, 1861, to provide gun locks "for parties holding Govt contracts." The following March, R. G. Dun's agent reported that they had spent $12,000 on machinery with an additional $8,000 earmarked for future investment. These capital outlays had left them "a little short in money matters owing to the expensiveness of the machinery." Eight months later, they had sold out to a Connecticut firm.[40] In December 1861, R. G. Dun's reports listed Charles A. Edwards as owning a new concern with "a large contract for the Manufr of shoes for the Government." After seven months, the firm had "no known means," and that December it was out of business.[41] The clothing firm of Rosenberg and Bohm opened in early 1863 with an estimated worth of $40,000 and a claim that it had $500,000 in government contracts. But R. G. Dun's agent could not corroborate that assertion, and within ten months it had closed its doors.[42]

Among the established firms that turned to government work, the reports offer various cases in which war contracting left healthy companies even better off. In 1860, William G. Mintzer had a solid business producing fly nets and other items. Throughout the war he profited from the "Manufr of military goods." By 1864, his estimated worth had risen from $40–50,000 to $50–60,000. Saddler W. V. Wilstack was "well off" before the war and grew rich through "a large contract to furnish the Govt with cavalry equipment." The saddlery firm of William S. Hansell and Sons was known as "one of the best in line" in 1861; by 1864, it had "added largely to their means" through military contracts. The firm of Wilson and Childs stood among Philadelphia's leading wheelwrights before the Civil War; in 1864, R. G. Dun's reporter noted that the 30-year-old company had profited from "an excellent govt bus & made money rapidly since the war."[43]

Some firms certainly grew rich through war contracting. Emanuel Hay and his brother ran a modest woolen-and-worsted shop valued at $10–12,000 in 1859. By 1862, government work had left the seventeen-year-old partnership in "a better position than ever." In February 1865, an R. G. Dun agent estimated their worth at $100,000.[44] But despite contemporary claims, war contracting does not appear to have thrust many new names into the ranks of Philadelphia's wealthiest men. At the close of the war, local bookdealers sold a printed summary of the "Rich Men of Philadelphia" based on income-tax returns for the year ending April 20, 1865.[45] The list included 36 men who had annual incomes of over $100,000. A search of the R. G. Dun index yielded reports on 26 of these prosperous Philadelphians. The reports suggest that ten of these men did not grow appreciably more wealthy during the war, and only four clearly became rich because of the conflict. Of seven with wartime government contracts, only one, William L. Hunter, Jr.—who engaged in a wide range of war-related activities—gained great wealth thereby.[46]

Rather than helping the rich get richer, government contracts appear to have enabled struggling companies to turn their fortunes around. As we have seen, many who sought military contracts did so out of weakness, if not desperation. The credit reports indicate that this strategy often succeeded. G. Hoff ran a modest cap establishment for over a decade until the secession crisis forced him to suspend payments. Hoff eventually settled with his creditors at 50 percent and rebuilt his business selling uniform caps to the military. Clothiers Rockhill and Wilson suspended payments during the Panic of 1857 and fell upon hard times again in 1861, but by 1862, uniform contracts had left them in "better condition than they have been for some time," and in 1864 the partners were worth an estimated $75,000 apiece. Leather dealer John A. Evers lost credit judgments in 1863, but recovered by securing "a large contract for making 16 inch cavalry boots"; W. W. Knight, Son and Company's hardware establishment was valued at over $75,000 in 1861, ran into serious troubles in 1862, and recovered— under the name Knight and Son—in 1863 by selling hospital bedsteads to the government. The fancy-goods business of W. T. Fry and Company struggled when the war began, but survived by manufacturing "canteens, haversacks and fancy articles for officers in the Army." Reeves, Buck and Company, iron manufacturers, failed in 1854, 1857, and 1861, before turning to the production of rifled cannons.[47]

These cases help explain the midwar improvements described in Table 10.4. But the agents also described more war contractors as "declining" or running into "trouble" (16 percent) in 1862 and 1863 than they did their counterparts in the general sample (10 percent). The differences are not great, but if military contracting guaranteed prosperity, one would antici- pate less (rather than more) frequent trouble among war contractors. One explanation is simply that some firms did not turn to government contract- ing until the middle of the war. But the R. G. Dun reports also demon- strate that government contracting was not always a sure cure.

Sometimes government contracting proved insufficient to restore firms to their antebellum health. Tailors F. Sarmiento and Thomas McGrath ran a "gd & profitable" business in mid-1861, but over the next several years they fell behind in payments and repeatedly lost credit judgments. In June 1862, R. G. Dun's reporter noted that the partnership had "been engaged on [a] Govt contract with Henry Simons and are not supposed to have made much if any money." Three years later they remained "pretty well covered up" with debts. Sarmiento and McGrath managed to return to prosperity in the postwar years, but fellow clothier Granville Stokes was not so fortunate. In July 1863, his report read: "Has been dg a good & paying bus. [and] has had several Govt contracts for clothing by which it is supposed he made considerable money." Nevertheless, five months later Stokes lost several credit judgments and was no longer deemed safe for credit; by September 1864, he had sold out his business. Commission mer- chant Henry W. Scott's problems began during the Panic of 1857. Finally, in 1862, R. G. Dun reported that he "has given up the Commn bus and is now engaged in filling Army clothing contracts." Within a year, that effort had failed, and Scott had "rent[ed] a mill & machinery at Norristown, Pa and [was] Manufg goods for Govt contractors."[48]

It is not really surprising that some struggling firms were unable to parlay government contracts into renewed success. The recurring source of their troubles is less expected. Repeatedly the R. G. Dun records de- scribe marginal firms suffering from slow government payments. Stove manufacturer Samuel Hill seemed to have recovered from the secession crisis when he signed a government contract "amounting to some 10 to 15 [thousand] $s" in 1861. But two years later he was still losing credit judgments while awaiting a "pretty large balance due to him." Blacksmith Jesse Butterfield opened a small gun-making establishment with his son in early 1862, and they immediately turned to government work. By the middle of the year, they ran into difficulties because "their cap[ital] is sm and the Govt being rather slow in payments they are unable to meet thr bills as promptly as heretofore." Although the agent expressed confidence in the "hardworking hon[est]" pair, they lost several credit judgments the following year and were out of business by early 1865. George Richardson and William Overman made a successful transition from umbrella-making to arms manufacturing, but they had to sell out to the more wealthy American Arms Company in early 1865 because they had been "unable to collect promptly a large amt due them by the Govt."[49]

More stable companies managed to keep in business despite slow payments from the government. The clothing firm of Strauss and Goldman earned an excellent credit rating in 1860 and 1861; therefore, in 1862, the R. G. Dun agent remained confident despite reporting that they were "a little short at present not having received thr money from the Govt."[50] Bishop, Simons and Company profited handsomely by shipping goods for the military, although in early 1862 their future had appeared in doubt because of slow government payments. Neafie and Levy, a large engineering firm, secured substantial wartime profits in naval production and apparently did not miss the "large amount of back monies due them by [the] Govt" that they received in 1866. The shipbuilding firm of Hillman and Streaker fared similarly. From early in the conflict they built gun boats for the navy and maintained a strong credit rating; in mid-1866 they "received considerable back pay due from [the] Govt."[51]

The diverse experiences of Philadelphia's war contractors mirror the range of companies that sought to trade with the military. Some were quite large and well established, others relied on very modest capital. Many made only minor adjustments to meet the new wartime demand, often maintaining an established business with war contracting as a mere sideline. Other firms were organized specifically to meet military needs or invested heavily in new machinery to meet military demands. Although the credit reports suggest no single pattern, the war contractors generally had more volatile wartime histories than their counterparts in the general sample. Several factors explain this volatility. First, the sudden military demand presented opportunities for rapid success. Second, war contractors appear to have come disproportionately from firms weakened by the secession crisis. Third, though the lure of government revenues attracted many Philadelphia entrepreneurs, the reality of slow payments often proved crippling.

Postwar Experiences

Although our focus has been on wartime entrepreneurial choices, the postwar histories of war contractors shed light on the war's economic legacy. The transition from war to peace after the Civil War—like the transition after all such conflicts—sent a destabilizing shudder through the economy. Many war contractors took that shift in stride, as they had the mobilization for war. Machine manufacturer Alfred Jenks ran a firm valued at $250,000 in 1860; in 1865, having spent the war filling large contracts for rifled muskets, his company was valued between $250,000 and $300,000. For some, the shift to peace meant a return to old activities, but other war-related businesses had to change to survive. No arms manufacturers were reported as shifting to the production of ploughshares, but sword manufacturer William H. Gray turned to gas fixtures, and the Cooper Arms Manufacturing Company made a successful postwar transition to making hinges.[52]

Not all war contractors fared so well (see Table 10.5). While the wartime failure rate was low, 49 of the 119 war contractors (41.2 percent) with known or estimated final years that survived to 1865 went out of business between 1865 and 1868, as opposed to 31.8 percent (111 of 349) of the general sample.[53]

Often these postwar failures occurred shortly after contractors lost their military customers at the war's end. This was particularly true of companies established to meet military demands. Only 8 of 30 (27.6 percent) war-contracting firms founded during the war survived until 1870, compared to 40.8 percent among the general sample. W. S. Robarts went into business in 1861 to manufacture woolen army stockings. In 1865, after recording four years of prosperity, R. G. Dun's agent noted that Robarts had failed after "[losing] heavily on Army contracts lately which has irretrievably embarrassed him." J. H. Purdy and Company opened their doors in December 1864 and immediately prospered by selling corn vinegar to the Commissary Department. The following July, an R. G. Dun agent reported that they "did a good bus & made money until the war closed . . . but are not dg much now." By the following May they were out of business.[54]

Established companies that enjoyed substantial wartime contracts were also particularly susceptible to postwar declines. Cloth dealers DuHadaway and Dodson grew from a "modest" business in 1860 into a $75,000 firm in 1865 by earning "considerable money on Govt contractors." The first two postwar credit reports noted that the business had "made no money," and in April 1867 the two dealers sold out. Even Philadelphia's largest manufactories were not immune from postwar disaster. Locomotive builders Richard Norris and Son suffered discomfort in 1861. But the firm soon returned to prosperity with the aid of "an immense Govt & regular business." Nevertheless, in March 1866, an R. G. Dun agent reported that it had been closed for most of the previous year and then reopened on a smaller scale. The following year's report noted that all of Norris's shops were closed.[55]

Whereas lost credit judgments or slow payments often foretold the postwar demise of a war contractor, some firms closed their doors without reported discomfort. W. F. Hansell went into business for himself in 1862 to manufacture army clothing. The enterprise profited throughout the war and went out of business, with no reported explanation, soon afterwards. Sailmaker Charles E. Miller shifted to tent production when the Civil War began and "was supposed to have made money." In April 1865, within weeks of Lee's surrender, R. G. Dun reported Miller as out of business.[56] Certainly these postwar closings may have been accompanied by unreported financial embarrassment, but it is also possible that savvy entrepreneurs simply moved on to other things when the shooting stopped. This was clearly Joseph F. Page's story. In 1859, Page left a coal-trading partnership to go into the clothing business. By 1862, he had received "some good contracts from the Govt" and had soon "made a large amt of money" manufacturing army blouses. By mid-1864, Page's business was valued at $100,000. Two years later, after the close of the war, R. G. Dun reported that Page was "not dg any bus now, investing his surplus in Govt securities" and was "well off." The next report noted that Page was "out of bus."[57]

These postwar histories, although quite diverse, support the general impression that Philadelphia's war contractors can be divided into two camps: those who acted out of strength, often dedicating only a portion of their resources to military production; and those who either formed to fill war contracts or turned to military contractors out of desperation. Within either group the likelihood of postwar difficulties was great. But for those entrepreneurs who relied heavily on military contracts, the transition to peacetime was particularly rocky.

Conclusion

I have argued elsewhere that whereas the Civil War touched most aspects of Philadelphia's economic life, its lasting effect on the structure of the local economy was not great.[58] The entrepreneurial responses to military demands followed several patterns, each of which shaped the war's impact on Philadelphia's economic development. First, a tremendous number of Philadelphians sought to turn the diverse military requirements to their advantage. Profits could be earned by trading with the various branches of the Army and Navy, with individual regiments, or even with local military hospitals. Other tradesmen sold their wares directly to individual soldiers or their families. A second pattern of behavior indicates which entrepreneurs decided to become war contractors. More than a quarter (30 of 104) formed new companies during the war, generally to produce military goods. Such decisions presumably recognized the lure of government dollars as well as the relative lack of opportunities in the private sector. Among established businesses, there were certainly many strong firms that took advantage of military profits. But war contracting was often a haven for the weak. Companies left reeling by the secession crisis or in jeopardy after losing their southern contacts repeatedly sought refuge in supplying the military.[59] The sorts of enterprise chosen suggest a final pattern of response. Most established firms seeking contracts were able to fill a government demand with only minor adjustments, and often new companies were formed by entrepreneurs with some related experience.

How do these patterns of individual decision-making help explain the war's limited impact on the longer-term process of economic development? First, the diverse array of businesses receiving contracts (as well as the large number of companies only marginally involved in government contracting) undercut any tendency for federal spending to speed the process of economic centralization. Second, by attracting new businesses and weakened firms rather than relying on the city's strongest establishments, government contracting presumably had a balancing effect on the distribution of wealth. Finally, the preference shown by entrepreneurs to stay close to their familiar areas of endeavor—and the high rate of postwar failure among those firms established solely to meet war contracts—helps explain the minimal long-term sectoral changes within Philadelphia.[60]

Certainly much of this entrepreneurial behavior depended less on individual reactions to federal spending policies than on circumstances peculiar to the Civil War or to Philadelphia's economy. The mix of arms, equipment, and food required by a mid-nineteenth-century war did not strain the capacities of a peacetime economy as much as modern warfare does. That is, much of the material required to support an army in the field was not strikingly different from what the same individuals might consume at home. Philadelphia, with its large manufacturing output produced largely by small establishments, was particularly well suited to make the necessary adjustments. But it is also appropriate to see the Civil War as an early episode of major federal spending that had some influence on shaping behavioral patterns. Certainly the quartermaster general was in a position to limit access to war contracts, but by filling individual contracts through public bids he left room for widespread involvement. More importantly, while Philadelphia's entrepreneurs recognized the potential benefits of war contracting (R. G. Dun's credit agents clearly saw a war contract in hand as reason for enhanced public confidence), it appears that they also viewed such activities as a gamble. Businesses that turned to the government out of weakness also acted in desperation. Those which only filled the occasional contract hedged their economic bets by maintaining a private trade.

Why might the more conservative entrepreneur have steered clear of excessive government work? One explanation may lie in the limited nature of the demand. Philadelphians did not anticipate a long war, and the peacetime government had had little use for military contractors. A further reason was simply that after 1861, most sectors of the economy boomed. War contracting aided this reversal, but profits in producing for the private sector were ample for established businesses.[61] But the most telling evidence is the relationship that many contractors had with the government. Frequently the R. G. Dun agents reported businesses struggling under accumulated debts while they awaited delayed government payments. Even firms that did not fall into serious trouble must have been inconvenienced when reimbursement did not arrive until many long months after Appomattox. When considering the decision to bid for military contracts, Philadelphia's wartime entrepreneurs had to weigh such uncertainty against the anticipated gains.

CHAPTER ELEVEN

✕ The Nineteenth-Century Silver Movement and Aggregate Price Uncertainty

Colleen M. Callahan

AMONG THE FUNDAMENTAL issues in economics are the extent to which money is simply a veil over real economic activity and the extent to which it can significantly alter the pace of that activity. Over the last 35 years, much research in economic history has left to the side the issue of money in the economy and has concentrated instead on the real factors that contribute to long-run economic growth and improved living standards.[1] Individuals, however, are the driving force behind economic growth; they make decisions regarding resource allocation on the basis of relative prices, both actual and expected, which they can come to know only by comparing nominal variables. The ability of individuals to anticipate the future aggregate price level is critical for long-run decision making; it is essential information in the effort to separate true changes in relative prices from changes in the general price level.

The ease with which the future price level can be forecast often depends on the nature of the monetary regime in place. This paper investigates the effect of the monetary regime on the predictability of the aggregate price level in the United States since the late nineteenth century and develops various measures that describe the ability of a typical individual to forecast changes in the one-year-ahead price level. It also argues that, since part of the traditional gold-standard period was marked by controversy over the return to bimetallism, there was a substantial degree of uncertainty over the strength of the commitment of the United States to the gold-based monetary standard. The push by the silver movement to return to bimetallism is argued to be a primary contributor to the relatively high levels of price uncertainty found in the gold-standard years. In turn, this uncertainty may have had a bearing on real economic activity.

I would like to thank Richard Froyen, Roger Waud, an anonymous referee, and the editors of this volume for helpful comments.

Background

Price-level predictability is an unusual variable to have at the center of economic analysis, but it is nonetheless worthy of examination. Price-level stability or predictability is beneficial to an economy because it encourages specialization of production and long-term planning. A stable long-run price level also eliminates the risk that the value of financial assets will be eroded by inflation.[2] Moreover, current concerns about price stability have spawned policy suggestions. The inability of the world's current monetary arrangement to achieve price-level stability has brought forth proposals for a return to a commodity-based monetary system, such as the nineteenth-century gold standard.[3]

The focus of much previous research on monetary regimes has been a comparison of an average measure of price uncertainty computed over the gold-standard years, 1879–1914, to its average for the post–World War II period.[4] The findings run counter to the traditional view that the gold standard automatically provided low levels of price uncertainty. Aggregate price-level uncertainty was relatively higher during the gold-standard period than over the years since 1945.[5] The studies agree, even though the authors employed different methods of estimating price level uncertainty.

A reexamination of the main conclusions found in previous work confirms the unexpectedly high relative level of uncertainty before 1914. An explanation is found in an examination of the historical details of the classical gold standard and, in particular, in a questioning of whether that period in the United States is an appropriate example of a commodity money standard. I argue that the lack of confidence regarding the continuation of the gold standard was a reflection of the late nineteenth-century movement to include silver as a part of the money supply. I then test the hypothesis that the free silver movement was associated with the high level of measured price uncertainty during the classical gold-standard period.

Previous Estimates of Aggregate Price Uncertainty

Benjamin Klein and Allan Meltzer have constructed alternative estimates of the ability of a typical individual to forecast the one-period-ahead price level.[6] Their approaches differ because of the equations used to forecast the price level and because of the alternative strategies employed in estimating the variability of that forecast, which is taken as the price uncertainty measure. Klein relies on an autoregressive model of the first-difference of the price level as the forecasting equation. Meltzer employs the Multi-State Kalman Filter (MSKF) as his forecasting equation. The

MSKF is a univariate time-series model that allows for the incorporation of different types of shock to the price level.[7]

An important feature of any forecasting equation is that it can be used to make ex ante forecasts; that is, it must rely only on information that is available (if not actually, at least in principle) to the individual making the forecast.[8] Klein employed a moving regression strategy, where the sample used for estimation is constructed by adding new observations as time passes and deleting the earliest observation. Although this method has intuitive appeal, since it seems to parallel closely the behavior of a typical forecaster, the technique is subject to difficulty in its econometric interpretation, primarily because the model is based on the premise that the variance can be described by a single parameter, yet generates changing variances by moving the sample used for estimation.

The MSKF approach employed by Meltzer and by Meltzer and Robinson explicitly allows for changing variances. It also produces ex ante forecasts since the estimation technique evaluates new information one period at a time. Its primary drawback is that it requires strong prior assumptions about the parameters that cannot be adequately revised as the model is confronted with the data.

There is some difference of opinion about the relevant starting and ending dates of the classical gold standard as well as about the appropriate twentieth-century period for comparison. Klein divides his results into three periods: the 1883–1915 gold-standard period, the 1916–55 transition period, and the 1956–76 new-standard period. Meltzer identifies six monetary regimes extending from 1890 to 1980.[9] Meltzer and Robinson examine three periods for the United States: the classical period, which began in 1889 and ended in 1913; the Bretton Woods period, which extended from 1950 to 1972; and the fluctuating exchange-rate period, which included the years from 1973 to 1985.

Despite the differences in the definitions of both the classical gold-standard period and the post–World War II years, each set of estimates indicates that price uncertainty was relatively higher under the gold standard than during the most recent time period. Klein's estimates of average price uncertainty are higher for the gold-standard period than for the new-standard period, although his results indicate that the highest level of uncertainty occurred during the "transition period," which includes the years between the two world wars. Meltzer and Robinson's estimates show approximately the same level of uncertainty for the classical period and the Bretton Woods period (which excludes the period between the First and Second World Wars); the fluctuating exchange-rate period, however, had a lower level of uncertainty.

One of the difficulties in interpreting these results is the lack of comparability in period length and in the methods and data used. My estimates of price uncertainty for each of the approaches to measuring the variability of price-level forecasts allow comparison on a consistent basis.[10] The details of these methods are described in the appendix to this chapter.

In contrast to previous studies, I see the years since 1880 as being best divided into two regimes. This choice reflects the view that the monetary system of the United States changed fundamentally when the Federal Reserve was created; thus the regimes consist of years before 1914 and years since. It does seem necessary, however, to consider separately the years between the start of the First World War and the end of the Second World War, since they were times of extraordinary upheaval. The period from 1915 to 1945 does not merit special consideration when judged by the criterion of a changed monetary regime; the decision to treat those years separately is simply a practical one.

The uncertainty statistics computed for the two approaches, the moving regression (MR) and the MSKF, are reported as averages over three time periods in Table 11.1. The classical gold-standard period includes the years 1884–1914, whereas the years after the start of operations by the Federal Reserve are divided into the interwar period, 1915–45, and the postwar period, 1946–81. The data used in estimation are described in the appendix below.

The striking feature of Table 11.1 is that for both uncertainty measures, the most recent period shows the lowest average uncertainty, whereas the interwar period is characterized by the highest level. The classical gold-standard period is consistently described in Table 11.1 as one with a relatively high level of uncertainty when compared to the postwar period. This finding confirms the earlier conclusions of Klein, Meltzer, and

TABLE II.I

Mean Levels of Price Uncertainty, 1884–1981

Monetary regime	MR measure	MSKF measure
Traditional gold standard		
1884–1914	1524	1276
1884–1896	2489	1452
1897–1914	827	1150
Interwar period		
1915–1945	7366	11057
Post–World War II		
1946–1981	1076	637

SOURCE: See text.
NOTES: All measures are multiplied by 10^6. The MR measure is computed by the moving regression method; the MSKF measure is computed by the Multi-State Kalman Filter method. Each measure is of the one-period-ahead forecast error variance.

Meltzer and Robinson. It is, along with the previous findings, at odds with the traditional view of the gold standard, which predicts relatively low measured uncertainty when compared to the postwar fiat-money regime.

The challenge is how to explain this result, which is inconsistent with the traditional view and so clearly unaffected by the method used to calculate uncertainty. The hypothesis evaluated here is that a lack of confidence in the maintenance of the gold standard over the late nineteenth century in the United States explains the unexpectedly high relative level of price uncertainty during that period. The lack of confidence in turn, it is argued, stems from the free silver movement. The goal of that movement was to require the Treasury to buy all silver offered to it at a fixed price, thereby causing an expansion of the money supply and undermining the usual discipline of the gold standard.

The Silver Movement and Price Uncertainty

From 1834, when the ratio of gold to silver at the mint was changed to 1:16 from 1:15, until 1873, the United States was on a bimetallic standard that operated de facto as a gold standard. This was due to the inappropriate setting of the official prices for gold and silver: silver was undervalued at the mint; therefore, the silver dollar did not circulate as money.

In 1873, the United States officially left the bimetallic standard by refusing to coin the silver dollar. At the time, this simply reflected the reality that silver coins had not circulated as money for almost 35 years. Two years after the passage of the law that repealed silver coinage, the market price of silver began to fall, and its sale to the mint began to look attractive to producers. Of course, they were no longer allowed this privilege, so they decided to push Congress for the restoration of free coinage.[11]

Theoretically, there could have been two concerns regarding the free coinage of silver. First, if the mint price happened to be set appropriately, it could have led to an increase in both the money supply and the general price level, reversing the deflationary pressure characteristic of the late nineteenth century. Second, a bimetallic standard could have developed into a de facto silver standard if the market price of silver continued to fall. This would have come about if the Treasury had set the ratio of gold to silver prices below the lower limit necessary for gold to circulate. In particular, the mint price of silver would have been too high compared to its market price. If the market price of silver continued to drop, all gold would have eventually left circulation.

Evidence in the writing of Frank Taussig suggests that the contemporary view of the probable effects of free coinage was consistent with these theoretical arguments.[12] Taussig claimed that free coinage of silver would result in a huge and prompt flow to the Treasury and that the gold standard would quickly break down in the United States as the redemption of greenbacks and Treasury notes destroyed the gold reserve.

Of course, free coinage of silver never became law, despite the efforts of the silver movement, and bimetallism was never realized in its pure form. Instead, two partial legislative successes regarding silver coinage were achieved: the Bland-Allison Act in 1878 and the Sherman Silver Purchase Act of 1890. The Bland-Allison Act authorized the coinage of between $2 million and $4 million in silver each month by the Treasury. These purchases of silver were to be paid for either in checks drawn on the mint, payable in silver dollars, or in silver certificates.[13] The legislation represented only a partial victory for the silver movement, since it provided only for limited silver coinage and did not open the mints to all suppliers of silver.

The importance of the Bland-Allison Act lies in the direct and indirect effects on the economy of the silver coinage it authorized. A direct effect is defined as the contribution of the silver purchases to the money supply.[14] It appears that this effect alone was not large enough to have led to the abandonment of the gold standard. The total contribution of the Treasury to the monetary base totaled about $150 million over the period 1879–90, compared to a total increase in the base of over three times that amount.[15] An indirect effect refers to the impact on expectations regarding the continuation of the gold standard. In this case, expectations were affected primarily by the pressure for repeal of Bland-Allison. The demand for repeal developed out of two very different motivations. First, there was the continued push for free coinage on the part of the silver movement. Second, there was an opposition group working for repeal combined with a firm recommitment to the gold standard. It was by no means certain which group would succeed, so the coinage allowed under the Bland-Allison Act added to uncertainty over the nature of the future monetary standard, and therefore contributed to aggregate price uncertainty as well.[16]

Pressure for the repeal of Bland-Allison continued throughout the 1880's, and, considering the variety of proposals brought before Congress, there was no clear signal as to what, if anything, might replace it. A turning point in the free silver movement turned out to be the bill introduced in early March 1889 by Nevada senator William M. Stewart. His resolution demanded the purchase of $4 million of silver each month. This amount would have approximately exhausted the current monthly production of silver mines, satisfying the silver producers, and would have contributed about $6 million in additional standard silver dollars to the money supply each month.[17]

The Sherman Silver Purchase Act grew out of a bill passed by the House on June 14, 1890, which explicitly allowed for free coinage; the Senate added amendments, striking out free coinage and replacing it with a fixed purchase of silver. The specific requirement of the Sherman Silver Purchase Act was that the Treasury purchase 4.5 million ounces of silver per month at prevailing market prices. The purchases were paid for by the issuance of the Treasury notes of 1890. The notes were direct legal tender redeemable in either gold or silver, at the discretion of the Treasury. Like the Bland-Allison Act, the Sherman Silver Purchase Act had both direct and indirect effects on the economy.

The total dollar value of the monthly purchase of silver under the Sherman Silver Purchase Act varied directly with the market price of silver: the higher the market price, the more Treasury notes were issued in payment for the required 4.5 million ounces of silver. The varying market price created uncertainty as to the size of the monthly contribution to the money supply due to these purchases and represented an important difference between the requirements under the Bland-Allison Act and those under the new Sherman Silver Purchase Act. With the former act, there was a maximum monthly contribution to the money supply of $4 million. Under the Sherman Silver Act's provisions, the upper limit was determined by the market price of 4.5 million ounces of silver.[18]

The direct effect of the silver purchases made under the 1890 act was substantial, because the purchases led to a significant increase in the monetary base. The contribution amounted to $168 million over the three years 1891–93. The significant export of gold that took place over the same time period, however, meant that the monetary base rose only $54 million.[19]

In addition to augmenting the money stock, the purchases of silver made under the Sherman Silver Purchase Act affected the outflows of gold from the United States and the Treasury's stock of gold. These changes are categorized as an indirect effect of the act because they contributed to, and were a reflection of, the public's worry and distrust over the government's ability and desire to maintain the gold standard.

Two events are taken as indicators of the indirect effects of the silver movement after the passage of the Sherman Silver Purchase Act: the gold outflows from the United States and the amount of gold held in the Treasury. The Treasury's gold reserve came under serious attack for the first time in the spring of 1891. Other runs on the Treasury occurred in December 1892, spring 1893, January 1894, December 1894, January 1895 (when $45 million in gold was withdrawn), and November 1895. Beginning with the attack in 1891, the Treasury defended itself by issuing bonds in exchange for gold coin. This strategy was unsuccessful: the gold stock fell from $190 million in 1890 to $118 million in 1891. It declined further to

$114 million in 1892, to $95 million in 1893, and finally to a low of $65 million in June 1894. By June 1895, gold holdings had accumulated once again at the Treasury, reaching a level of $108 million. Gold holdings never fell below $140 million after 1897.

Gold withdrawn from the Treasury was both shipped abroad and held by the nonbank public in the United States. Friedman and Schwartz see the silver purchases as the primary cause of both the "external drain"—the flow of gold abroad—and the "internal drain"—the public's withdrawal of deposits from the banking system and increase in their holding of gold.[20]

The historical details surrounding the traditional gold standard regime in the late nineteenth century suggest the following four hypotheses regarding the pattern of aggregate price uncertainty. Uncertainty should be higher (a) on average over the period when the silver forces were active, 1879–96, than in later years; (b) immediately following passage of the Bland-Allison Act and the Sherman Silver Purchase Act, 1878–80 and 1890–92; (c) when the expectation of the complete success of free silver was high, 1888–90; and (d) immediately following the 1897 turning point in the price level.

The first hypothesis is based on the observation that if the free silver movement had been successful in gaining unlimited access to the mint for silver producers, it was possible, perhaps likely, that silver would have been overvalued at the mint and would have displaced gold in the money supply. As a result, the United States would have been on a de facto silver standard, having a fixed exchange rate with other silver-standard countries and a floating exchange rate with other gold-standard countries. It is probable that the dollar would have depreciated vis-à-vis the gold-standard countries as silver became the standard. Increased agitation for free silver was likely to have reduced confidence that the government would have been able to maintain the existing gold parity. The relevant evidence for this hypothesis is a comparison of average uncertainty levels over the years of the silver agitation, 1879–96, with the levels over the later years, 1897–1914. If the average levels for the earlier period are higher than for the later one, this would support the claim that the silver movement contributed to relatively high levels of aggregate price uncertainty.

The second hypothesis concerns what I have termed the "direct effect" of the silver purchases. Both the Bland-Allison Act and the Sherman Silver Purchase Act required the Treasury to purchase a minimum quantity of silver each month. Although the monthly contribution to the money supply was limited to between $2 million and $4 million under the Bland-Allison Act, there was no explicit limit to the dollar value of the monthly purchases made under the Sherman Silver Purchase Act.

Understanding both the actual and the potential increase in the money supply due to the silver purchases is essential to understanding the nature of the uncertainty surrounding the direct effect of silver. If the silver purchased by the Treasury to comply with the two laws had been completely hoarded by the Treasury, the purchases would have represented only a price-support program for silver and not a source of increase in the money supply. In these circumstances, the purchases would have been financed by either higher taxes or increased government borrowing. The silver acquired would then have represented an increase in Treasury cash that was exactly offset by a decline when the payment for the silver was made. There would have been no overall effect on the money supply.

The actual increase in the money supply due to silver purchases was in fact substantially different from this scenario, both because of the changing behavior of the Treasury in putting the silver money into circulation and because of the other actions undertaken by the Treasury that affected the monetary base. Over all the years of the silver purchases, 1879–93, silver and the Treasury notes of 1890 added about $500 million a year to the monetary base. During the same period, the total monetary base grew by $740 million, indicating that other influences on the monetary base did not offset the impact of silver; instead, they supplemented it.

Since the silver purchases were responsible for about 65 percent of the increase in the monetary base over the period 1879–93, it would appear that the direct effect of silver on the base was substantial and would have been viewed as an activity that made it more difficult for the government to maintain the gold standard. If the direct effect had been important in increasing price uncertainty, we should find relatively higher levels of uncertainty immediately after the passage of the Bland-Allison and Sherman Silver Purchase Acts, when the exact size of the direct effects was unknown.

The third hypothesis refers to the indirect effects of the silver movement on price uncertainty, namely, the impact of the silver movement on expectations regarding the commitment of the government to the gold standard. I argue that the silver purchases and the continued agitation for free silver may have contributed to the gold outflow over the period 1891–93, increased doubts about the gold standard, and contributed to price uncertainty. An appropriate test of the hypothesis that the radical silver legislation that was discussed in Congress resulted in increased price uncertainty is an examination of the pattern of uncertainty during the time these proposals were being considered. Large spikes, or increases, in aggregate price uncertainty after these laws were proposed between 1888 and 1890 would provide support for the hypothesis.

The final hypothesis regarding the pattern of uncertainty during the traditional gold-standard period concerns the relationship between the 1896 turning point in the price level, the behavior of aggregate price uncertainty, and the size of the forecast errors. Theoretically, the declining price level, which characterized the late nineteenth-century American economy, served as an incentive for more gold to be produced and imported to the United States. It could be argued that observers who understood the workings of a commodity-based monetary system would have been expecting an eventual increase in gold production or inflows, and would have been quickly convinced that the turnaround had been achieved once the price level began to recover even slightly.

The last hypothesis contends that the turnaround in the price level was associated with higher price uncertainty as individuals adjusted their forecasts to the new behavior of the price level, but that the increase was short-lived since individuals were expecting a recovery of prices for quite some time. In addition, since the silver issue was effectively settled both by the election of 1896, when the silver candidate William Jennings Bryan was defeated, and by the inflow of gold that began in the same year, we expect that uncertainty over the continuation of the gold standard fell after that point, reducing price uncertainty as well. The test of this hypothesis will involve the comparison of aggregate price uncertainty before and after the 1896 reversal in the price level, and then a comparison of the peak in uncertainty after 1896 to the peaks of the previous years of the silver movement.

Can the Silver Movement Account for Changes in Price Uncertainty?

The gold-standard years are separated into two parts: the period prior to 1896, when the silver movement was most active, and the period after 1896, when the movement was no longer a serious threat to the gold-based system (although Bryan did run again for president in 1900). I have calculated two uncertainty series, but I focus on the results that use the MR measure. The two measures yield somewhat different results, the disparities taking on greater importance when the year-to-year pattern of uncertainty is considered in evaluating the hypotheses about the silver movement. I focus on the MR measure because I have greater confidence in its ability to measure changes in uncertainty when they are most warranted—after large forecast errors have been observed. When the other uncertainty series was considered, there were some points of disagreement regarding the magnitude and direction of change in the uncertainty measure.

Using the criterion of minimum mean squared error (MSE) to distinguish between the MR and MSKF measures, the latter performed better over the period 1884–1914. The MSE of the forecast has two drawbacks, however, as a guide to the best series in this context.[21] First, it is an end-of-period statistic and thus of limited use in evaluating a forecasting equation before that time. Second, the MSE ignores the confidence of forecasters in their prediction.

I think it is important to take into account the confidence that individuals had in their forecast, an aspect of forecasting reflected in the uncertainty statistic. Individuals are regarded as caring not only about the predicted mean of the aggregate price level, but also about the variance of that prediction. As a more meaningful standard, I propose that the best forecast equation would be one where high ex ante uncertainty was associated with a high ex post forecast error, so that in some sense, the low level of confidence was justified.[22]

I implement this principle by asking the following question regarding the gold-standard period: in which model is it more often the case that, in a year when the uncertainty measure is above (below) the mean, the absolute value of the forecast error is also above (below) the mean? For the MR series, this symmetry occurs in 19 of 31 years. In the case of the MSKF model, the symmetry occurs in 13 of 31 years.[23] Judged by this standard, the MR series is preferred to the MSKF. Thus, even though the MR series does not provide the minimum mean square error, it shows a stronger pattern of high ex ante uncertainty accompanied by high ex post forecast errors.

The comparisons above give mixed signals on which uncertainty measure and forecasting equation is more appropriate. By the minimum MSE criterion, one should choose the MSKF measure. When some weight is given to the relationship between ex ante uncertainty and subsequent error, the MR series does far better than the MSKF series.

The evidence concerning the first hypothesis has a straightforward interpretation. As can be seen in Table 11.1, the average level of uncertainty is relatively higher over 1884–96, the period of silver agitation, than over 1897–1914, when the silver issue was no longer a strong economic or political issue. This relationship is true for both measures of uncertainty. This means that I cannot reject the hypothesis that the period of silver agitation was also one of relatively high aggregate price uncertainty.

On the basis of this evidence, I conclude that a significant part of the explanation for the surprising finding of relatively high price uncertainty over the *entire* gold-standard period can be found in the level of uncertainty over the period before 1896, when there was good reason to question the commitment of the United States to the gold standard. In fact, if the traditional gold standard were evaluated only over the years after the silver issue was resolved, conclusions about the relationship between the levels of uncertainty during the gold standard and the post–World War II fiat-money period would have to be revised. The MR uncertainty measure shows a lower average level of uncertainty from 1897 to 1914 than over the more recent subperiod; this is a reversal of the pattern in which the entire pre-1914 period is used as the basis of comparison.

Analysis of the annual peaks and troughs allows the evaluation of the impact of the direct and indirect effects of the silver movement on uncertainty. This further allows us to draw conclusions about the relationship between the price level turnaround in 1896–97 and uncertainty. The pattern of annual change generally reinforces the conclusion drawn from the evaluation of average uncertainty, that the silver agitation was associated with high price uncertainty. This result, however, ignores for the moment much of the disparity in year-to-year movements across the uncertainty series.

The direct effect of the silver movement refers to the actual contribution of the silver purchases to the monetary base. Since the period of substantial and continuous contributions took place over 1891 and 1892, we would expect to see increased levels of uncertainty over these years. Figure 11.1

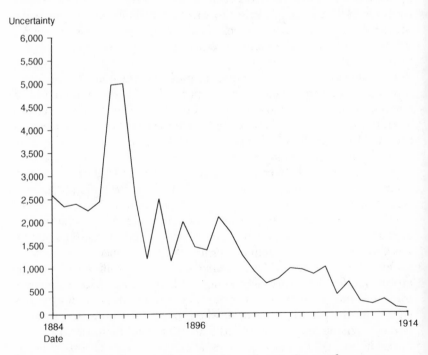

Fig. 11.1. Price uncertainty: moving regression estimates. See text for sources.

shows the annual movements in uncertainty estimated from the moving regression approach. The peak in 1893, which represents a 107 percent increase over the 1892 value of uncertainty, is consistent with the argument that the accumulated silver purchases did cause a rise in uncertainty. Although the peak is dated 1893, it is based on information through 1892. In addition, since all the MR measures of uncertainty are ex ante and thus contain no information from the year in which the forecast is made, it is appropriate to interpret the 1893 peak as reflecting the silver purchases made in 1891 and 1892. The other uncertainty series does not reflect a similarly timed increase. The MSKF series in Figure 11.2 indicates no sign of an increase in uncertainty after the silver purchases began.

The indirect effect of the silver movement on uncertainty should have been highest over the period 1888–90, when the probability of the complete success of the free silver movement was likely to have been relatively high. As Figure 11.1 indicates, the MR series was relatively low and stable until the peaks of 1889 and 1890. Uncertainty increased by 102 percent from 1888 to 1889, moved up slightly in 1890, and fell by 48 percent in 1891.[24] Both of these relatively high estimated values for uncertainty are based on

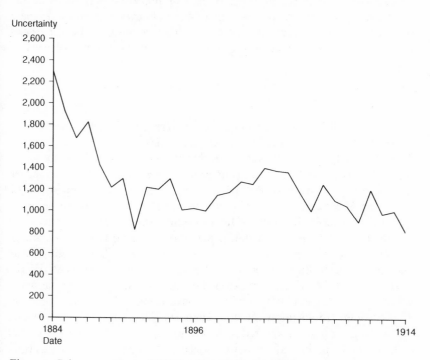

Fig. 11.2. Price uncertainty: MSKF estimates. See text for sources.

data that includes information for 1888, the year in which Senator Stewart introduced a bill calling for large silver purchases, but excludes information from 1890, when the Sherman Silver Purchase Act was passed. It is clear that if these peaks were attributable to the silver agitation, it was only via the indirect effects. No actual increase in the level of silver purchases had taken place before late 1890.

The final hypothesis refers to the path of aggregate price uncertainty after 1896. This year is a watershed both because it represents a trough for the entire pre–World War I period and because it was the year of political defeat for the free silver candidate, William Jennings Bryan. The succession of positive increases in the price level, viewed in the context of the previous pattern of deflation, can be expected to have increased aggregate price uncertainty for some time after 1896–97. At the same time, Bryan's defeat represented the end of the silver movement as a powerful political force and paved the way for the import of gold to the United States and the gold inflation that followed. This suggests that uncertainty should have returned to a relatively low level as individuals became convinced that the gold standard was in fact going to remain in place.

The MR series provides support for this proposed pattern of uncertainty. It shows an increase from 1897 to a peak in 1898, and then a decrease after 1898, as can be seen in Figure 11.1.[25] The evidence in the MR series indicates there was a relatively quick recovery of the confidence level of forecasts after 1896–97.

Summary

This paper has considered in detail the behavior of aggregate price uncertainty over the traditional gold-standard period. The most important finding is that uncertainty was relatively higher over the years of the silver agitation, 1884–96, than during the remainder of the period, when silver was no longer a major issue. The conclusion, based on a comparison of the mean uncertainty level between 1884 and 1896 and the mean between 1897 and 1914, holds for both of the uncertainty series that were estimated.

The finding provides a possible explanation for the observation made at the outset of the paper—that the gold-standard period, as a whole, was one of relatively high uncertainty when compared to the post–World War II period. The controversy over the nature of the monetary standard, which revolved around whether the monetization of silver would force the United States to abandon the gold standard, plays an important role in accounting for that unexpected relationship.

In order to gather additional evidence that might support this argument, I also examined the annual movements in uncertainty and evaluated three specific hypotheses. In each case, the MR pattern of uncertainty provided evidence that was consistent with a strong link between the silver movement and price uncertainty. Support for the direct effect of the silver legislation was found in the 1893 peak in uncertainty. The indirect effect of the silver movement on expectations was supported by the double spike in 1889 and 1890 apparent in the MR series. Finally, uncertainty seems to have risen as individuals adjusted their forecasts from the environment of deflation before 1896 to the rising price level after 1897.

Appendix

Techniques to Measure Price Uncertainty

This appendix outlines the rationale behind each of the measures of price uncertainty and provides the details about the estimation technique. The first measure of price uncertainty is a moving regression (MR) estimate similar to the one constructed by Klein. Instead of using an autoregressive model that explains the current price level only by its own lagged values as Klein does, I employ a theory of price determination derived from an aggregate demand and aggregate supply framework.[26] The model also incorporates a one-period information lag regarding the values of aggregate variables and the assumption that expectations about variables are best linear unbiased estimates of future values. This approach results in the following reduced form equation for the price level:

$$(1) \qquad p_t = \beta_0 + \beta_1 t + \beta_2 x_{t-1} + \beta_3 m_{t-1} + \beta_4 y_{t-1} + e_t,$$

where p_t represents the aggregate price level, t is a time trend, x_{t-1} is lagged nominal GNP, m_{t-1} is a measure of lagged import prices representing a supply-side shock, y_{t-1} is lagged real GNP, and e_t is a white noise disturbance term.[27]

In this formulation, an individual's prediction of the next period's aggregate price level is based only on past information except for the trend term. Given the expected signs of the parameter estimates derived from the theoretical model, the predicted price level will be higher: the higher the past level of aggregate demand, the higher the past level of import prices, and the lower the past level of real output (which, given nominal income, implies that prices were higher last period).

The uncertainty statistic in this model is defined as the variance of the forecast error for a one-period-ahead prediction of the price level based on a moving regression of the preceding fourteen observations. This sample size is small enough to allow for price-level forecasts and the uncertainty measure to be generated beginning in 1884, given that the available data series start in 1869.[28] Yet it is large enough to provide adequate observations for estimation.[29]

The uncertainty statistics derived from the MSKF depend on many parameters. In the MSKF, future observations do not influence past parameter estimates, but the estimates do depend on a single data series and on the many assumptions and constraints that are imposed on the model. The MSKF proposes that the price level is determined by the following time series model:

(2) $\qquad p_t = \theta_{1,t} + \varepsilon_t,$

(3) $\qquad \theta_{1,t} = \theta_{1,t-1} + \theta_{2,t} + \phi_t,$

(4) $\qquad \theta_{2,t} = \theta_{2,t-1} + \delta_t,$

where

(5) $\qquad \varepsilon_t \sim N(0, V_\varepsilon),$

(6) $\qquad \phi_t \sim N(0, V_\phi),$ and

(7) $\qquad \delta_t \sim N(0, V_\delta).$

Here, p_t is the observed value of the price level after logarithmic transformation, θ_1 is the "true" underlying level of p at time t, and θ_2 is the prevailing "true" underlying growth rate. The disturbances, ε_t, ϕ_t, and δ_t, are serially uncorrelated, mutually independent, normally distributed errors. The observational errors are represented by ε_t, the shocks to the level by ϕ_t, and the shocks to the growth rate by δ_t.

Since both the "true" level and the "true" growth rate are unobservable variables, the model has been designed to extract information from the observed values of p_t to determine the most likely values of both θ_1 and θ_2 at each point in time. Note that the underlying level is assumed to be a random walk with stochastic drift θ_2, whereas θ_2 itself is a random walk. The Kalman Filter principle is applied to infer the prevailing value of the underlying parameters by combining the forecast error in period t with information in the covariance matrix.

The major contribution of the multi-state approach is that it does not impose an arbitrary time-series model with a fixed set of parameters on the data. A variety of models is evaluated with the data, and the most appropriate model is given the largest weight in the forecast. The models are distinguished from each other only by the specification of the variances of θ_1 and θ_2. Forecasts of the log of the price level are computed as weighted averages of the forecasts from the individual models. As time passes, the weights of the separate forecasts are adjusted according to the success of each model over the recent past. In this way, a feedback channel from the data to the model is created.

Six different models are used here. Three of these incorporate "small" shocks, three incorporate "large" shocks.[30] Within these two basic categories is a model with a relatively large V_ε corresponding to a transitory shock, a model with a relatively large V_ϕ corresponding to a shock to the level of the series, and one with a relatively large V_δ corresponding to a shock to the rate of change of the series.

The strategy of the MSKF is to compute the probability, subsequent to observation p_{t-1}, that the process was in state i in period $t-1$. After observing p_t, there are 36 possible paths for the model: it could have been in any 1 of 6 states in the previous period, and in any 1 of 6 in the current period. The probability of state i is updated based on the forecast error associated with that state's model after p_t is known. If the forecast error is large for a particular model, the likelihood function will be small, resulting in a lower probability that the model is the correct one. In this way, all 36 possibilities are weighted by how well they perform against the data. Before the next observation is evaluated, the 36 possible states are reduced again to 6 by summing across each of the 6 past states for each present state.

The uncertainty statistic depends on the matrix of transition probabilities as well as on the forecast error variance associated with each of the 36 possible states and on the updated first moments of the probability distribution.[31] In contrast, the measures of variability used by Meltzer and Robinson are the mean absolute error of one-period-ahead forecasts and the root mean square error. They compute, for each regime, the mean absolute error for each type of shock: transitory, permanent shocks to the level, and permanent shocks to the growth rate. The measure here is based on the forecast error variance and model probabilities.

Data Used in Estimation

Income and prices. The data used to estimate the price prediction equations over the years 1884–1981 are the annual figures on U.S. nominal income, real income, and the implicit price deflator.[32]

Relative import prices. It is difficult to find an overall measure that can adequately capture the notion of an aggregate supply variable for 100 years. The U.S. experience from 1973 until 1980 makes it clear that changes in the price of imports (especially energy imports) can have important real and nominal effects on the economy. The importance of this variable for the late nineteenth century is less obvious. It is likely that more favorable supply shocks, such as immigration, may have played a larger role. Conversely, immigration is not so important for the post–World War II period. Similar arguments could be made concerning many other series that may serve as appropriate supply-side variables.

I settled on relative import prices because of evidence that estimation of the equation for the more recent period without the inclusion of the import price would represent a misspecification. The decision to extend the use of the import price variable to earlier years was based on the desire to have a single estimable model over the period 1879–1981.

In general, the import valuation required by customs is the foreign selling price (actual transactions or wholesale) plus expenses necessary before shipment to the United States. The import-price series does not reflect the final price to producers or consumers when tariffs are charged. Adjusting for this omission by including the average tariff paid in each year made no significant difference to our results.[33]

CHAPTER TWELVE

❧ The Triumph of Oligopoly

Louis Galambos

THE INDUSTRIAL STRUCTURE labeled oligopoly has long created problems for historians and economists alike. It has also been a particularly thorny issue for the Antitrust Division of the Justice Department, the Federal Trade Commission, and the courts, all of which have been forced over the years to decide what public policy toward oligopoly should be. In the recent past, some of the thorns have fallen off. But only because of a de facto abandonment of the structural side of the federal antitrust policy, not because of an improved understanding of oligopoly or a clarification of de jure policy toward this industrial structure.[1]

For historians, the problems of explanation and interpretation have actually increased in the past few decades. An earlier breed of liberal historians simply lumped oligopoly with monopoly—as did most Americans, I believe—and condemned them both as unwarranted, reprehensible concentrations of economic power and wealth.[2] The leaders of large enterprise were robber barons. Their influence on politics was as negative as their impact on America's industrial economy.

In the years since World War II, however, this progressive interpretation of history and the liberal ideology that sustained it gradually lost their hold on our understanding of the past and our analysis of the present. As that transformation took place, the ideological condemnation of the genus gave way to analysis of the different species, and the distinction between oligopoly and monopoly thus became more important. Now historians— especially business historians—needed an explanation of where oligopoly came from, how it functioned, and what its implications were for the business system, the economy, and the society as a whole. It was now essential to explain why oligopoly was so prevalent and monopoly so rare. For a time, none of these questions were answered with any authority.

Alfred Eichner, writing in 1969, attacked the first problem—the origins of oligopoly—in a case study of the Sugar Trust at the turn of the century.

I would like to thank Tom Weiss, Naomi Lamoreaux, Les Hannah and his colleagues in the Modern and Contemporary Economic History Seminar at the University of London, George Smith, and John Kenly Smith for their helpful comments on drafts of this paper.

Basing his analysis on thorough research in primary and secondary materials, Eichner concluded that public policies, not economic forces, were the primary factors accounting for the transition in this case from near-monopoly to oligopoly. The Trust lost a substantial share of the market because a combination of civil suits and federal antitrust action hampered its operations, even though the combine had won an important antitrust case, *E. C. Knight*, in 1895.[3]

Eichner's conclusion was intriguing, but it seemed for the most part to fall on deaf scholarly ears. There were few follow-up studies, no efforts to refine or test his hypotheses for the entire economy; indeed, more recent histories of U.S. enterprise in the modern era have taken an entirely different tack. In general, the focus among business historians has shifted from political economy to an analysis of the economic factors that have shaped the structure of the modern firm and industry.

Two recent studies by historians of business behavior offer excellent illustrations of the transformation that has occurred. Naomi Lamoreaux's perceptive treatment of the merger movement that began in the late nineteenth century deals with oligopoly only in passing, but it nonetheless plays an important role in her analysis of consolidation.[4] Lamoreaux portrays the merger movement of these years as a deviation from the normal "path of development" that "led to stable oligopolistic industrial structures."[5] In the years that followed 1904, competition sifted out the inefficient near-monopolies, pulling those industries back to "the alternative development path" that led in most cases to oligopoly.[6] Did oligopoly triumph because it was the most efficient structure? Lamoreaux leans towards "Yes" and concludes with "Probably." It is, she says, "impossible to say at this time, given the state of our knowledge."[7]

Not so for Alfred Chandler. His answer—developed in a series of meticulously researched and boldly analyzed books and articles—is a strong, unequivocal "Yes!"[8] In the most recent of the books, Chandler describes the three-pronged investments in large-scale production, in distribution, and in management that gave these industrial giants their "powerful competitive advantages. Their industries quickly became oligopolistic . . . ," he says, "dominated by a small number of first movers." The first movers strove for greater success "through functional and strategic effectiveness." This involved "improving their product, their processes of production, their marketing, their purchasing, and their labor relations."[9] They beat their rivals into growing markets and out of declining ones: they were quick and effective.

Chandler provides answers for almost all of our questions: oligopoly emerged because very large first movers were more efficient than smaller firms in serving national and international markets; they produced and distributed more efficiently; they used research and development to improve products and processes; they were efficient purchasers of supplies and marketers; they competed through product differentiation and advertising and through good strategic choices as to which markets to enter and which to leave. Clearly, this new style of competition was better for the economy, for society, and for business itself.[10]

On only one of the questions does Chandler's massive opus seem ambiguous, and that is our question about the origins of oligopoly. The author for the most part rejects Eichner's hypothesis: in the Chandler vision, public policy in the United States did not shape the most important aspects of the nation's industrial and business structures; entrepreneurs and managers in search of efficiency performed that task. But this gives rise to a basic paradox. The fundamental logic of the economies of scale and scope—in oil, for instance—lead us to anticipate that a first mover like Standard Oil would be almost impossible to dislodge from any significant part of the market it controlled.[11] Remember, that share was once 90 percent of the U.S. market. Bear in mind that first movers like Standard Oil were in Chandler's characterization quick as well as efficient. Nonetheless, challengers emerged. Chandler's explanation is: "They [the challengers] came most often when rapid demographic changes had altered existing markets and when technological change had created new markets and diminished old ones." But we are left to ponder why the near-monopolists, the first movers like Standard Oil, failed to perceive and respond effectively to these changes? Why then did monopoly become the exception, oligopoly the rule? That was true in oil—after all, Exxon was not an only child; she ended up with six sisters—and in most other industries. Although *Scale and Scope* does not explain why that would be true, Chandler certainly agrees with Lamoreaux that oligopoly was the normal path of development.[12]

Most economists would probably agree about the path but disagree with Chandler about where that path took the industrial economy. Frederick Scherer's comprehensive study of industrial market structures and economic performance carefully analyzes the theory and evidence on oligopoly.[13] Scherer candidly admits that in this area of theory "the most that can be hoped for is a kind of soft determinism" ("spongy" might actually be a better word).[14] And he acknowledges, too, that the empirical evidence on such a crucial issue as the impact of oligopoly on innovation is far from conclusive.[15] But throughout, Scherer is skeptical about the social consequences of high levels of concentration, concerned about the barriers to entry in oligopolistic industries, and convinced that the chief objective of the architects of the turn-of-the-century mergers was market power, not economies of scale. As he notes, "Monopoly power was such a striking result of numerous mergers around the turn of the century that one could hardly deny with a straight face that it was intended."[16] With Adam Smith, he urges public vigilance.[17] Scherer favors a firmly enforced antitrust policy: "There is much to be said for a policy that errs on the side of a hard line against mergers."[18]

Those economists who follow the lines of analysis developed by Oliver Williamson have of course developed a more Chandleresque treatment of one aspect of concentration: vertical integration in the modern firm.[19] The transactions-cost or market-failure approach to the evolution of the modern firm stresses the efficiencies achieved by combining functions in the sort of organization that is the building block of oligopoly. But transactions-cost theory does not directly confront Scherer's critique, because it posits no efficiencies stemming from the horizontal combination that makes for an oligopolistic structure.[20] Nor does it help us understand why—or if—the giant firms in an oligopoly could be characterized as quick, efficient, and innovative over the long term.

Left with these several, sometimes contradictory, sometimes partial conclusions, my suggestion is that we try a somewhat different approach to the problem of oligopoly. I would like to conceive of various institutional "forms," rather than firms, competing for survival. In this scheme, political institutions could exercise an important influence on survival. In the case of oligopoly, the political environment à la Eichner may have been an important factor shaping the institution, and we can deal with that relationship by opening our conceptual framework to noneconomic variables. We will be attempting to analyze from this perspective what advantages dominant forms had over the alternatives, both from the point of view of the individual business unit and from that of the society. We will look with particular care at the transitions, when the dominant forms changed, as a means both of analyzing the causal factors prompting the structural transformation and of understanding how the new dominant institution functioned—again, from two perspectives: that of the business unit and that of the society. We will consider the three major forms enshrined in the literature: the atomistic, highly competitive structure; monopoly (actually, near-monopoly); and oligopoly. We can begin by sketching in brief terms the situation that existed in the nineteenth century in the United States.

The Nineteenth Century

Through most of the nineteenth century, the dominant structure was clearly the atomistic, highly competitive alternative.[21] Monopoly was of course a viable alternative, as was oligopoly—especially in local and regional markets. Why was the atomistic structure so ubiquitous, then? Not because of political constraints on either monopoly or oligopoly. It was the end of the century before state and federal governments instituted anti-trust policies, and they did not become very effective until the early decades of the twentieth century.[22]

From the perspective of the firm, either monopoly or oligopoly would seem to have held the promise of higher profits in the short term, and perhaps in the long term as well. Efforts to achieve that goal through loose combinations were legion.[23] But neither monopoly nor oligopoly was common in America through most of the century. Instead, competition was intense (especially, of course, on the downturn of the business cycle), bankruptcies frequent, and sharp price fluctuations a painful fact of life in most businesses. In those industries in which firm size was growing relative to the market—Lamoreaux calls them "proto-oligopolies"—competition was particularly fierce and rivalries clearly defined.[24] But for most individual businesses, effective monopoly or oligopoly apparently cost more than they were worth in an economy experiencing rapid growth primarily (although not exclusively) through new inputs of land, labor, and capital.[25]

From the perspective of the individual business unit, the opportunities for growth and capital appreciation put a premium on the ability to remain flexible and to innovate. That could best be achieved through relatively small organizations, even though they could not achieve monopolistic power. Nor could they achieve economies of scale or scope.[26] Costs were thus high for both production and distribution, but since most firms were price takers, prices seem to have hovered close to marginal costs in the manner so comforting to most economic analysts.

For the society, this situation was clearly desirable, even though costs (and thus prices) remained relatively high. The economy was growing so rapidly and economic opportunities were so omnipresent in America that the nation could well afford to pay those relatively high prices, to wink at occasionally successful cartels, and even to accept a highly skewed distribution of income and wealth.[27]

The Transition to Monopoly

Near the end of the nineteenth century, these conditions changed dramatically, and the initial restructuring involved a trend toward monopoly. The "proto-oligopolies," as well as many atomistic industries, were transformed. The major opportunities in this newly integrated national market were apparently best realized by the large, integrated organizations that Chandler has described so well; for these centralized, professionally managed corporations, however, fixed costs were high and the old style of price competition was threatening, as Lamoreaux has carefully established.[28] The cost/benefit ratio of the monopolistic form had fallen; within a generation, the heart of America's industrial economy was transformed.

Monopolistic power and economies of scale and scope were intertwined in a manner that enables us to blend the analyses of the economists and the new business historians. That the central objective of the businessmen organizing combines was monopolistic power seems to me (with Scherer) beyond question: the four leading tobacco firms in the United States had already achieved vertical integration and significant economies of scale *before* they combined to form American Tobacco. The Supreme Court decided that monopoly power was the intention of that merger and that monopoly power was the result.[29] So it was with Standard Oil. Ralph and Muriel Hidy researched the origins of the Trust thoroughly and concluded that its primary goal was the preservation and consolidation of a position entailing monopoly power.[30] The Supreme Court agreed. No new evidence has appeared since their history was published. In light of the fact that the organization manifestly achieved monopoly and to a lesser extent monopsony, there seems no reason to deny that John D. Rockefeller came by his 90 percent control of the market and devised the Trust for the reasons advanced in the firm's own documents.[31]

But as Chandler makes clear, the story did not stop with the formation of the Trust. Standard Oil and *most* of the successful combines went on to achieve the types of economies (scale and scope) that would protect their market positions efficaciously over the long term.[32] Indeed, during the period 1897–1920, the economy effectively weeded out many of those first movers which could not do so, which could not coordinate their empires, which could not make the three-pronged investments critical to long-range success.[33]

When they did so and became seemingly permanent elements of America's industrial economy, they were still exercising market power. They lowered costs and prices, but they were able to keep prices above costs in the manner explicated by economic theory.[34] Otherwise, the companies would have been unable to invest in their expensive research and development facilities or in many of the other accoutrements of the twentieth-century corporate economy—including histories of the sort that the Hidys and others have produced.[35]

The Transition to Oligopoly

Although monopoly or near-monopoly was economically a comfortable position for the monopolist, it was offensive to many Americans. Some bought from the monopolies and thought their prices too high; others sold to them and thought their prices too low; still others objected on more general grounds to power seemingly unchecked.[36] Hence the anti-trust movement at the state and federal levels of government, and a companion movement toward state or federal regulation.[37] By the early decades of the twentieth century, these twin movements had begun to have a decisive impact on business strategic planning and on corporate behavior.

The new political setting raised the price of monopoly and, as outlined by Eichner, accelerated the trend toward oligopoly. In a small number of cases the government actually broke up combines, as it did, for instance, in the tobacco, oil, and gunpowder industries.[38] More important was the manner in which public policy influenced business decisions by posing the threat of hostile action. Let us return to the oil industry and look more closely at how this process worked. By the 1890's, Standard Oil had made all the correct investment decisions. It was in a secure market position (controlling, as we noted before, about 90 percent of the domestic market) and had mastered the economies of scale and scope. But by reducing its economic risk and uncertainty to almost zero, Standard had greatly increased its political risk and uncertainty. When the Gulf Coast oil fields opened up at the turn of the century, Standard was unable to prevent the entry of new firms, several of which became major players in the industry. Why not? Because in Texas, a state antitrust law blocked Standard's direct entry into the new southwestern fields.[39] Ten years later, Standard paid an even higher price for reaching and attempting to preserve a near-monopoly position when the Supreme Court broke up the combine.[40]

Astute business leaders recognized the political vulnerability of monopoly. Most were willing to increase their economic risks by accepting oligopoly as an alternative and thus decreasing their political uncertainty. Others bought a higher degree of certainty by accepting political controls. Theodore Vail, president of the American Telephone and Telegraph Company, struck just that sort of deal—after surrendering part of his monopoly position by divesting the Western Union Company.[41] In recent years, a substantial literature has developed over the manner in which those accommodations were achieved, their economic implications, and the way business thus came to influence the nature of the modern U.S. administrative state.[42]

Constrained by public policy, monopolists also were handicapped by their relatively sluggish performances as innovators. Some found it difficult to innovate without the spur of effective competition from other large-scale firms. Most were preoccupied with the tasks of perfecting their large, centralized, hierarchical bureaucracies; they quickly achieved economies of scale but found it far more difficult to develop within the firm institutions that would promote and sustain the process of innovation. In the steel industry, J. P. Morgan's great combine, U.S. Steel, was a substantially less aggressive innovator than Carnegie had been. Similarly, General Electric in its early years struggled as it tried to find a corporate mechanism for effectively developing new products.[43] GE's experience with the new field of x-ray technology was revealing: the company moved too slowly and "was beaten to the marketplace by the more nimble Knott company."[44] Although GE later became a very successful innovator, most of the near-monopolists were less creative.[45] Thus, the near-monopolies gave way to oligopoly in part because, as Scherer has concluded, *very* high levels of concentration are seldom accompanied by highly innovative performances.[46] Second, third, and fourth movers emerged to fill the interstices left uncovered by sluggish first movers or by first movers constrained by the threat or reality of antitrust or regulatory responses.

Only the most exceptional of the near-monopolists were able to develop the organizations and the supporting culture to sustain technological innovation. Alcoa was one of the few. By aggressively developing new products and new uses for aluminum, by building plants in anticipation of increased demand, and later by investing heavily in research and development, Alcoa was able to preserve its market share long after its basic patents had expired. After 1910, AT&T also laid the institutional and cultural foundations for Bell Labs, one of the most successful of the nation's industrial laboratories. In neither case, however, was an innovative performance ultimately a defense against the antitrust policy. Lowering their economic risks in the U.S. market to near zero, both firms left themselves vulnerable to political attack. Eventually they ran afoul of public policy and suffered fates similar to those of Standard Oil and American Tobacco.[47]

The Triumph of Oligopoly—Before the Fall

The type of oligopolistic competition that emerged as the near-monopolies surrendered market share proved to be beneficial over the long term both to the firms involved and to the society: to the firms because it prevented ossification, ensuring that managements would keep their organizations innovative and efficient over the long run; to the society because it ensured that the United States would continue to achieve productivity gains—our major source of growth in the twentieth century. This transpired because under conditions of oligopoly, firms were still able to keep prices sufficiently above marginal costs to give management substantial leeway in making investments that would ensure the long-term growth and security of the corporation. This "oligopolistic margin" has disturbed most economists, in part because it consisted of discretionary funds whose allocation could not be explained by reference to a market theory. Indeed, that was and is the case.[48]

The manner in which firms have deployed the margin can, however, be analyzed historically at the level of the firm, the industry, and the national economy. For much of the twentieth century—certainly through the 1960's—the available data on productivity increases and on the growth of the economy seem to constitute a prima facie case for concluding that on balance, the triumph of oligopoly continued to be as desirable for the society as it was for the individual firm.[49] Because the performances were industry- and firm-specific, they varied; hence the ambiguity that Scherer detects in the studies of technological innovation under conditions of oligopoly. With as much concentration as there was in the United States in these decades, however, one cannot avoid the conclusion that in a dynamic sense the oligopolistic *form* was on balance conducive to growth by way of innovation.

In order to analyze the process of innovation under conditions of oligopoly, we will need to go beyond technological change—broadening the traditional concept of innovation—and it will be useful as well to distinguish between those innovations which were "adaptive" and those which were "formative."[50] The "adaptive" innovations were incremental and frequently were associated with the processes of production and distribution. "Formative" innovations—whether in technology, in finance, or in organization—broke decisively with past experience in the manner analyzed long ago by Joseph Schumpeter.[51] Frequently, their economic impact could be seen in aggregate statistics on the performance of the national economy.

The recent literature of business history suggests that large firms in oligopolistic industries were particularly adept at adaptive innovation. Two recent studies of large firms in oligopolistic settings provide some insight into how the transition to oligopoly affected the long-term process of technological innovation. David Hounshell and John Kenly Smith's prodigious volume on R&D at Du Pont is a rich source of description on both the managerial problems of remaining innovative over the long term and the keys to success in the case of this particular firm.[52] The company and its managers had to learn and relearn how to be successful at R&D. Research management was a new skill, and successful practitioners had to "learn by doing" how to keep their operations focused and productive. One of the most important decisions top management had to make was the choice of a research manager who could handle three vital interfaces: the interaction between the industrial laboratory and the corporation; between the research and the development teams; and between the company's R&D and the larger systems of science and engineering outside the firm. These larger systems were essential sources of new ideas, of "momentum" in technical change.[53]

Prior to the 1930's, one of the most successful innovative strategies was to buy into a new product, purchasing patents and an embryo organization, and then to use Du Pont's immense resources—in capital, managers, and R&D talent—to improve the product and processes so as to achieve economies of scale and scope.[54] The Du Pont history suggests that the firm's marginal advantage during the early decades of the twentieth century was in adaptive technical innovation and that the strategy of buying in was optimal for both the company and the national economy.

Other large companies followed a similar path. At AT&T, many of the most important innovations during the early years of the industrial laboratory were adaptive, system- or network-building developments. Standardization was an important aspect of adaptive innovation, on the development side of R&D. It has been common to denigrate development efforts of this sort, comparing them unfavorably with so-called basic research. But "adaptive" or incremental innovation was extremely important to these firms and to the national economy. It seems likely that these sorts of innovations make up a substantial part—probably most—of the residue we label as productivity growth.

In the case of Du Pont, however, the company altered its strategy, with consequences that are important to the theme of this paper. Antitrust considerations in the 1930's forced Du Pont to abandon the practice of buying in. The firm began to emphasize "formative" innovations and scored an outstanding success (1935–40) with nylon.[55] So far so good. But in subsequent years, Du Pont kept trying to duplicate the nylon episode, with very little success. Bureaucratic inertia kept Du Pont on that course even though experience was strongly indicating that the organization had no marginal advantage over smaller rivals in this regard. Had the setting been atomistic, Du Pont might well have folded in the early 1930's and would certainly not have been able to sustain the investments in R&D needed to bring nylon to market. Had the setting been monopolistic rather than oligopolistic, Du Pont might have continued to run in place much longer than it did after discovering nylon.[56] Oligopoly thus provided enough of a cushion to sustain innovation and at the same time sufficient competitive pressure to jar management into adopting a new strategy that would set the firm back on a successful innovative course. Throughout this transition, Du Pont deployed its oligopolistic margin aggressively, sustaining heavy investments both in basic research and in development.

The Alcoa story—as recounted by George David Smith and by Margaret Graham and Bettye Pruitt—is an equally valuable source of data, particularly because it enables us to compare the firm's performance under conditions of monopoly and of oligopoly.[57] Both before and after the antitrust suit that led to the oligopolization of the industry, Alcoa was technologically innovative, especially in the realm of process (that is, adaptive)

developments. But the aluminum giant was—like every other business bu-
reaucracy—inclined over time to experience some ossification. Thus, after
the antitrust suit, the pressure of strategic competition under conditions
of oligopoly forced Alcoa to improve its long-term performance as an innovator.[58] Economies of scale were so important in this industry that an
atomistic, highly competitive form was beyond the realm of imagination
to all but the most dedicated devotee of antitrust. Oligopoly in this industry, as in most other high-tech sectors of the economy, was the optimal
structure over the long run.

This conclusion seems even more acceptable if we significantly broaden
our concept of innovation. Much of the literature on innovation focuses
only on technology. Although this is certainly an important aspect of the
growth of the economy and of the firm, many successful business organizations appear to have gained their competitive edge by innovating across
a very broad front. Thus, they developed new modes of finance and fiscal
controls, new styles of distribution, new personnel programs, new patterns of labor relations, new political capabilities, and new forms of organization. They devised adaptive, and from time to time formative, innovations in these areas, as well as through R&D.

As modern firms developed their staff organizations, staff services thus
began to make important contributions to the efficiency of the firm. Here,
too, as in R&D, links to the professional organizations, publications, and
creative leaders outside the firm were vital sources of new ideas. Here, too,
"momentum" could be achieved. Here, too, leadership was an essential
element of sustained innovation. One of the important aspects of leadership was the maintenance of creative boundaries between the firm and
other types of institutions. Indeed, in some cases, an innovative staff could
give an organization the competitive advantage it needed to push its way
into a market dominated by a powerful first mover.[59] Without the oligopolistic margin, firms could not have afforded these staffs; without the pressure of oligopolistic competition, they would have been less likely to make
effective use of them over the long term. This they appear to have done in
the United States during most of the twentieth century.

The Oligopolistic Margin and the Fall from Grace

As the so-called American Century—that prosperous *quarter*-century
following the end of World War II—drew to a close, however, American
business suffered a stunning fall from grace. So prosperous were the postwar decades that many corporate leaders had begun to believe the dogma
preached by the Harvard University Graduate School of Business Administration and other centers of business education.[60] In brief, they had be-

gun to believe that good managers could handle any range of business activities, however diverse. In the 1960's, the oligopolistic margin had thus been diverted by many U.S. companies into conglomerate investments instead of dividends or further investments in innovation.[61] An entire generation of CEOs was beguiled by opportunities in markets they neither understood nor, as it turned out, were able to master quickly enough to make their firms competitive.[62] The oligopolistic margin was also used to buy new layers of staff that turned out to be either superfluous or dysfunctional. They have subsequently been shed by many corporations, which report favorable results from their organizational diets.[63] In some industries, the margin was used to buy labor peace. American Century labor pacts—as well as the adversarial system of labor relations that they reflected—locked many firms into situations in which they were unable to make the most economically effective use of their margin when competition intensified.[64]

Indeed it intensified. While American attention was focused on the war in Southeast Asia between 1965 and 1975, while the U.S. government was struggling with the 1973 energy crisis, while Watergate was generating its brand of obsession with Washingtonian politics, the nation's rivals were positioning themselves for the intense global competition that would dominate the 1970's and 1980's.[65] As U.S. companies fell by the wayside in several industries, new global oligopolies began to emerge—along with serious questions whether American firms would be able to deploy the margin as effectively as their best foreign competitors.[66] Firm- and industry-specific evaluations of that performance gave way to nation-specific treatments and to considerable hand-wringing over the future.

Whatever the outcome of this competition, the form that seems most likely to emerge is that of global oligopoly. No longer will national economies be the proper units for evaluating industrial structure or performance.[67] If that is the case, it will transpire for essentially the same reasons that oligopoly triumphed in most sectors of the American economy: that is, because oligopoly was the industrial structure that ensured that firms large enough to achieve economies of scale and scope would over the long run remain innovative enough to preserve their positions of power without incurring political reprisals. The effective management of the oligopolistic margin will be the key to success, as it has been in the American economy during the past century.

Guideposts to a Dynamic Model

This slalom run between the flags of Industrial Organization Theory and the New Business History suggests, I believe, that a new paradigm, a new, dynamic model of the firm, is emerging. Framed in terms of growth over the long run, this new concept of the corporation will draw elements from both market theory and institutional history.[68] Contributions to enhanced productivity through economies of scale, scope, and system, through improvements in process and product, through innovations across a broad front (from the bottom up and the top down), will play a central role in the new paradigm, as will failure to achieve these goals. Every shift in market share involves both a successful innovator and a firm (or firms) that went to sleep at the switch. Both will figure in a dynamic model of the firm.

The links between the firm and its environment will be emphasized. Successful organizations create new social roles and new knowledge, but they also make creative use of professional expertise and knowledge outside of the firm. They maintain creative boundaries. Similarly, they accommodate to and shape their political environments. The new paradigm will perforce put the politics back into political economy.

It will also give a central role to leadership and to the key individuals who shape the development of the firm. Whether they are CEOs, research managers, vice presidents of financial services, or heads of the personnel department, individuals make the crucial decisions that keep organizations innovative or allow them to sag.[69] They shape and are in turn influenced by the corporate culture of the firm, a set of values that can either discourage innovative behavior or reward the kinds of performance that lead to successful growth over the long term. Both organizational culture and leadership will be important components in a dynamic model of the type of firm that has accounted for the triumph of oligopoly in the twentieth-century U.S. economy.[70]

Reference Matter

❧ Notes

Preface

1. The conference, "Economic Development in Historical Perspective," was held on September 22, 1990.

2. The "pioneers" included in this volume are Lance Davis, Robert Fogel, Douglass North, and William Parker.

Introduction

1. Carter Goodrich, "Economic History: One Field or Two," *Journal of Economic History* 20 (Dec. 1960): 534.

2. Early on, one of the contributors to this volume, William Parker, wrote an article titled "Economic Development in Historical Perspective," *Economic Development and Cultural Change* 10 (1961): 1–7. Other approaches to understanding growth and development emerged and have flourished, but the value of solid historical analysis is still recognized. Recently, Cynthia Morris and Irma Adelman turned to history to test propositions about development that had been generated by their cross-sectional study of contemporary economies, *Society, Politics, and Economic Development* (Baltimore, 1971). The result of their examination is *Comparative Patterns of Economic Development, 1850–1914* (Baltimore, 1988), a summary of which can be found in their "Nineteenth-Century Development Experience and Lessons for Today," *World Development* 17 (1989): 1417–32.

3. W. W. Rostow, *The Stages of Economic Growth* (Cambridge, 1960).

4. A. K. Cairncross, "In Praise of Economic History," *Economic History Review*, 2d ser., 42 (1989): 181.

1. Weiss: Economic Growth

1. There is a long history of debate by economists and economic historians on the topic, beginning with Robert Martin, *National Income in the United States, 1799–1938* (New York, 1939), and including Simon Kuznets, "Long-Term Changes in the National Income of the United States of America since 1870," in Simon Kuznets, ed., *Income and Wealth of the United States: Trends and Structure*, International Association for Research in Income and Wealth, Income and Wealth Series 2 (Baltimore, 1952): 23–241, esp. 221–41; William Parker and Franklee Whartenby, "The Growth of Output Before 1840," in William Parker, ed., *Trends in the American Economy in the Nineteenth Century* (Princeton, 1960); Douglass North, "Early National Income Estimates of the U.S.," *Economic Development and Cultural Change* 9 (1961): 387–96; and George Rogers Taylor, "American Economic

Growth Before 1840," *Journal of Economic History* 24 (Dec. 1964): 427–44. Summaries of the discussions can be found in Stuart Bruchey, *The Roots of American Economic Growth* (New York, 1965); Stanley Engerman and Robert Gallman, "U.S. Economic Growth, 1783–1860," *Research in Economic History* 8 (1983): 1–46; Diane Lindstrom, "American Economic Growth Before 1840: New Evidence and New Directions," *Journal of Economic History* 39 (Mar. 1979): 289–301; and Barry Poulson, *Value Added in Manufacturing, Mining, and Agriculture in the American Economy from 1809 to 1839* (New York, 1975).

2. See W. W. Rostow, *The Stages of Economic Growth* (Cambridge, 1960), chap. 4.

3. Ibid., p. 37. For the purpose of gauging what the investment share might be, he postulated a hypothetical increase of two percentage points in the per annum rate of growth of real output per capita (p. 41).

4. Ibid., p. 39.

5. An opinion held earlier was that modern growth was ushered in by the Civil War, or at least during the decade of that war. See, most notably, Charles Beard and Mary Beard, *The Rise of American Civilization*, vol. 2 (New York, 1933); and Louis Hacker, *The Triumph of American Capitalism* (New York, 1940).

6. Paul David, "The Growth of Real Product in the United States Before 1840: New Evidence, Controlled Conjectures," *Journal of Economic History* 27 (June 1967): 151–97.

7. In a more recent work, David has revised his estimate of growth slightly downward, from 1.22 to 1.17 percent per year for the period from 1800 to 1835. The reduction arises from a broadening of the measure of gross domestic product (Paul David, "Invention and Accumulation in America's Economic Growth," in Karl Brunner and Allan Meltzer, eds., *Carnegie-Rochester Conference Series on Public Policy*, no. 6 [Chicago, 1974], pp. 179–228).

8. David, "Growth of Real Product," p. 156.

9. Ibid., p. 195. This result rests on a comparison of the economy's performance in two subperiods, 1800 to 1835 and 1835 to 1855, marked off because the beginning and ending years of each lay in approximately the same position of the business cycle. According to David, around 1800, the mid-1830's, and mid-1850's, "the U.S. economy experienced strong pressure on existing capacity, and rising prices, generated by high levels of demand." The earlier period's growth of 1.22 percent per year was virtually equal to the 1.3 percent for the latter (p. 156). This general conclusion can be seen in David's figures reproduced in Table 1.1, although those figures reflect a slightly different dating of subperiods.

10. Ibid., p. 155. The earlier acceleration may have been the nail in the coffin of Rostow's takeoff in the 1840's, but it did raise the specter of a takeoff in the 1820's. David, however, viewed this acceleration as an upsurge in "a broader pattern of recurring variations of the per capita product growth rate" (p. 156).

11. Robert Gallman, "The Statistical Approach: Fundamental Concepts Applied to History," in George Taylor and Lucius Ellsworth, eds., *Approaches to American Economic History* (Charlottesville, Va., 1971), pp. 63–86; and Gallman, "The Agricultural Sector and the Pace of Economic Growth," in David Klingaman and Richard Vedder, eds., *Essays in Nineteenth-Century Economic History* (Athens, Ohio, 1975), pp. 35–76.

12. Gallman ("Statistical Approach," pp. 71–81) estimated that the flow of perishable consumption per capita was quite steady over the course of the nineteenth century, rising mildly from $42 in 1800 to $45 in 1840, primarily because of changes in the composition of the population. When these estimates of perishable consumption were subtracted from the per capita income figures implied by David's conjectural growth rates, the residuals were quite small, implausibly so in Gallman's view. My per capita income figures imply residuals for the earliest years that seem high enough to pass Gallman's test. Moreover, the changes in the new residuals from 1800 to 1840 imply an income elasticity of demand for nonperishables that is more consistent with other evidence for the nineteenth century than that implicit in David's income figures. See Michael Haines, "Consumer Behavior and Immigrant Assimilation," National Bureau of Economic Research, *Working Paper Series on Historical Factors in Long Run Growth*, no. 6 (Cambridge, Mass., 1989); and Jeffrey Williamson, "Consumer Behavior in the Nineteenth Century," *Explorations in Economic History* 4 (1967): 98–135.

13. The measurement of growth before 1840 also rests on the estimating assumptions underlying the Towne and Rasmussen figures on farm gross product, in particular that per capita consumption of most farm products was constant during the period. See Marvin Towne and Wayne Rasmussen, "Farm Gross Product and Gross Investment in the Nineteenth Century," in Parker, ed., *Trends in the American Economy*. Since both the David series and the Weiss series on farm productivity rest on these same farm output estimates, these assumptions are not a source of the different results, no matter how historically inappropriate they may be.

14. The basic idea was formulated by Kuznets in "Long-Term Changes." The equation is derived from the identity that output per capita (O/P) is equal to output per worker (O/LF) times the fraction of the population engaged as workers (LF/P). In turn, O/LF for the nation is equal to the weighted average of O/LF in the two sectors, agriculture and nonagriculture, where the weights are the shares of the labor force engaged in agriculture (S_a) and nonagriculture (S_n). In David's formulation, it was also assumed that output per worker in nonagriculture remained equal to a constant multiple of that in agriculture ($O/LF)_n = k(O/LF)_a$.

15. This in turn has an indirect impact on the rate of advance in nonfarm industries by virtue of the assumption that productivity change in that sector equaled that in farming. Given the absence of evidence on the growth of nonfarm output or productivity, some assumption about their behavior was required, but not necessarily this particular one. David argued that nonfarm productivity likely increased faster than farm productivity, and he made the assumption of equal rates of advance in order to bias downward the estimated rate of growth in the years before the alleged takeoff might have occurred. It is not certain that the bias works in this direction, and in the refined estimates presented below I alter this assumption.

16. There is also an indirect effect through the estimate of k, which is determined in part by the labor-force estimates in the base year of 1840.

17. For ease of exposition I refer to the "Lebergott series." Lebergott ("Labor Force") developed the estimation procedures and produced the initial estimates,

whereas David ("Growth of Real Product") revised some of the figures, especially for 1800. Lebergott now accepts David's figure for 1800. See Stanley Lebergott, *The Americans* (New York, 1984), p. 66.

18. The total labor force is the sum of the workers in five population components: free males aged 16 and over, free females aged 16 and over, free males aged 10 to 15, free females aged 10 to 15, and slaves aged 10 and over. The estimate of the number of workers in each group is the product of the population in the group and the group-specific participation rate.

The estimates are based on the concepts and coverage used by the decennial censuses of the nineteenth century. They are more precisely termed "gainful worker" counts and are known to exclude workers engaged in certain types of activity, household work in general, especially married women working as boardinghouse keepers or unpaid family-farm workers. Recent work has tried to estimate the importance of these omissions, but those efforts have been confined to the period after 1880. (See Marjorie Abel and Nancy Folbre, "A Methodology for Revising Estimates: Female Market Participation in the United States Before 1940," *Historical Methods* 23 [1990]: 167–76; Christine Bose, "Devaluing Women's Work: The Undercount of Women's Employment in 1900 and 1980," in Christine Bose, Roslyn Feldberg, and Natalie Sokoloff, eds., *Hidden Aspects of Women's Work* [New York, 1987]: 95–115; Penny Ciancanelli, "Women's Transition to Wage Labor" [Ph.D. diss., New School for Social Research, New York, 1983]; and Claudia Goldin, *The Gender Gap* [Chicago, 1990].) There are no such estimates for earlier years that would permit an adjustment of the census data to a comparable coverage over time, so I have not corrected in any year for such omissions.

19. The national totals obtained as the sum of the state estimates are within 2 percent of Lebergott's figures, or my earlier estimates, which were derived at the national level. See Stanley Lebergott, "Labor Force and Employment, 1800 to 1960," in Dorothy Brady, ed., *Output, Employment, and Productivity in the United States after 1800* (New York, 1966), table 1; Thomas Weiss, "Revised Estimates of the U.S. Workforce, 1800 to 1860," in Stanley Engerman and Robert Gallman, eds., *Long-Term Factors in American Economic Growth* (Chicago, 1986), table 1.

20. All this work proceeds on the assumption that the census counts are accurate, or at least equally reliable at the various census dates. Several researchers have shown that the census undercounted population, at least in some years and places. Among others, Ansley Coale and Melvin Zelnick, in *New Estimates of Fertility and Population in the United States* (Princeton, 1963), have argued that the enumerations in the postbellum period (actually since 1855) were low. So far, however, the evidence of underenumeration in the antebellum censuses pertains to specific places, and it is not known whether the entire census in any year, much less all years, was subject to the same degree of error. See also Richard Steckel, "Census Matching and Migration," *Historical Methods* 21 (1988): 52–60, for a summary of the case studies pertaining to the antebellum years.

21. This work is described in Thomas Weiss, "The Assessment and Revision of the Antebellum Labor Force Statistics" (manuscript, University of Kansas, 1988). There were no occupational data reported for 1800, 1810, and 1830, so we estimated these in other ways.

22. Of particular value is my assessment of the 1820 and 1840 censuses in order to determine which industries were covered, which age and sex portions of the population were included in the counts of workers, and which state counts were in need of revision (see Weiss, "Assessment and Revision").

23. The details are presented in Weiss, "Assessment and Revision," and "Estimation of the Farm/Nonfarm Distribution of Laborers" (manuscript, University of Kansas, 1987).

24. My revisions were carried out by examining the county and subdivision data in much the same manner as had been done by Richard Easterlin, "Interregional Differences in Per Capita Income, Population, and Total Income, 1940–1950," in Parker, ed., *Trends in the American Economy*, pp. 126–32, and by Lebergott, "Labor Force." My corrections and additions to the census counts of farm workers amount to 233,000 in 1820 and 164,000 in 1840. By comparison, Easterlin increased the 1840 farm count by 104,000 workers. Lebergott reduced the 1840 count by 148,000 workers and increased the 1820 figure by 401,000.

25. The 1820 census was vague about which occupations were to be counted, but it did report only on agriculture, commerce, and manufacturing. These were referred to as "the three principal walks of life" (U.S. Bureau of the Census, *Twenty Censuses: Population and Housing Questions, 1790–1980* [Washington, D.C., 1979], p. 11).

26. The absolute increase is slightly smaller in the new series than in the old.

27. Gallman was suspicious about the Lebergott series because it showed changes in the farm labor force that seemed inconsistent with the changes in the rural population. The inconsistency seemed greater in the antebellum period, when the farm share of the labor force declined by a substantially greater percentage than the rural population share. Gallman focused on the changes between 1800 and 1850, noting that "the agricultural share of the work force fell by 28 percentage points between 1800 and 1850, at a time when the share of the rural population in total population was declining by only 9 points" ("Agricultural Sector," p. 38).

28. For the entire century, the correlation coefficient for the decadal changes in the farm share and that in the rural population is much higher for my series than for the Lebergott series (0.909 vs. 0.239).

29. In constructing the conjectural estimates presented in Table 1.1 it was assumed that nonfarm productivity advanced at the same rate as farm productivity. If estimates of farm output (calculated as the product of the farm labor force and the output per worker figures shown in Table 1.3) are subtracted from the conjectural total, the residual figure yields a slower rate of nonfarm productivity growth. This results from the upward bias of the nonfarm residual due to the estimating procedure. This bias is relatively larger in the earlier years.

30. It is worth pointing out that the growth of the agricultural labor force was quite rapid throughout the antebellum period. An impressive aspect of American development during this period was the agricultural sector's capacity to absorb this labor and still show modest advances in productivity. See Poulson's essay in this volume for a discussion of this idea.

31. The weight is based on the relative sectoral output per worker figure for 1840. For that year, output per farm worker is slightly lower and output per nonfarm worker slightly higher using my labor-force estimates rather than Lebergott's.

32. The growth of per capita output in my series is aided by a more rapid rise in the participation rate.

33. This was David's concern as well. After constructing his farm labor productivity series and pointing out that virtually all of the advance took place during the 1820's and 1830's, he asked, "How reasonable a set of conjectures does this particular farm labor productivity index constitute?" ("Growth of Real Product," p. 177).

34. David, "Growth of Real Product," p. 177.

35. Gallman, "Agricultural Sector," p. 36.

36. Towne and Rasmussen, "Farm Gross Product," p. 261.

37. Ibid., table 1.

38. Martin Cooper, Glen Barton, and Albert Brodell, "Progress of Farm Mechanization," U.S. Department of Agriculture, *Miscellaneous Publication*, no. 630 (Washington, D.C., 1947), p. 6.

39. Leo Rogin, *The Introduction of Farm Machinery*, University of California Publications in Economics, 9 (Berkeley, 1931).

40. Clarence Danhof, *Change in Agriculture* (Cambridge, Mass., 1972), p. 60.

41. Towne and Rasmussen, "Farm Gross Product," p. 259. It should also be noted that the different picture of agricultural productivity growth rests entirely on the labor-force estimates, and in particular on the different adjustments that Lebergott and I made to the census counts of farm workers in 1820 and 1840. As argued earlier and elsewhere (Weiss, "Assessment and Revision"), my adjustments improve upon the earlier estimates.

42. See Stanley Engerman, "Discussion of the Conjectural Estimates," *American Economic Review* 57 (May 1967): 307–10; Gallman, "Statistical Approach"; and Engerman and Gallman, "Economic Growth."

43. At the same time, the level of output per worker in that sector is biased upward, and so influences the intersectoral shift effect on output growth.

44. For comparison with the earlier formulation, the estimating equation could be expressed as follows:

$$O/P = LF/P \left[S_a(O/LF)_a + S_n(O/LF)_n \right] + O_s/P,$$

where the sectoral output figures exclude the value of shelter and the last term adds in shelter output on a per capita basis. In practice, the equation was estimated as

$$O/P = (W_a LF_a + W_n LF_n + O_s)/P,$$

where W is output per worker in agriculture (a) or nonfarming (n). In each year from 1800 through 1830, the figure for nonfarming equals the 1840 figure extrapolated backward on an index of a weighted average estimate of output per worker in manufacturing and nonmanufacturing.

45. Kenneth Sokoloff ("Productivity Growth in Manufacturing During Early Industrialization," in Engerman and Gallman, eds., *Long-Term Factors*, table 13.6, p. 698) presented a range of rates of productivity advance for the period from 1820 to 1860. I have used his longer-term average of 2.3 percent per year for the period 1820 to 1850, based on his value-added output series, calculated with aggregated data. (See Table 1.6 for a discussion of this choice.)

The wide range of estimates Sokoloff presents suggests that there may be a wide margin of error in these numbers. For a discussion of the likelihood that the magnitude of error is larger for the nonagricultural productivity estimates than for the agricultural, see Barry Poulson, "Estimates of the Value of Manufacturing Output in the Early Nineteenth Century," *Journal of Economic History* 29 (Sept. 1969): 521–25.

46. The assumption that productivity advance in the rest of the nonfarm sector was equal to that in farming may bias upward the rate of growth before 1840 because service productivity, other than in transportation and perhaps distribution, probably did not advance that fast. In 1840, 49 percent of the service-sector labor force was engaged in personal services, in which there was probably no productivity change. See Thomas Weiss, *The Service Sector* (New York, 1975), table 17, p. 49. Evidence for the twentieth century indicates very low rates of productivity growth in personal services. See Victor Fuchs, *The Service Economy* (New York, 1968).

47. Since manufacturing output per worker was below that in the other nonfarm industries, the increase in manufacturing's share of the nonfarm labor force (from 41 percent in 1820 to 43 percent in 1840) slowed down slightly the entire sector's productivity advance. This nonfarm figure may still be biased upward because the rapid advances in manufacturing estimated by Sokoloff pertain to northeastern manufacturing, and it is unlikely that productivity in southern and midwestern industry was advancing as rapidly. If it were assumed that manufacturing productivity in those other regions grew only as rapidly as U.S. farm productivity, then the weighted nonfarm rate of productivity advance would have been around 0.75 percent per year.

48. The Towne and Rasmussen farm output series underlies the productivity calculations. I revised upward their estimate of hog and cattle production in the years from 1800 to 1830, which lowers the rate of growth of output by only 0.08 percent per year between 1800 and 1840. I also revalued the entire series in 1840 prices, which raises the rate of growth of farm output by about 0.08 percent per year between 1800 and 1840. The net effect of the two changes is to lower gross domestic output per capita by about $1.00 in the years 1800 through 1830.

49. The levels of the residuals implied by the refined output figures are not as high as in my base case, but are well above David's (see Table 1.1, bearing in mind that the residuals reported there include an unspecified amount for the rental value of shelter).

50. John McCusker and Russell Menard put the colonial rate between 0.3 and 0.6 percent per year between 1710 and 1770. See *The Economy of British America* (Chapel Hill, 1985), pp. 55–56 and 267. More recently, Morris Altman (in "The Economy of Colonial America," *Social History* 20 [1987]: 337–42) has argued that the more likely rate falls near the lower end of the range. So the refined estimate of the antebellum rate of growth of 1.06 percent per year falls comfortably between the likely colonial growth rate and the postbellum rate of 1.7 percent.

2. Sylla et al.: U.S. Financial Markets

1. On GNP, some of the key studies are Simon Kuznets, *National Product since 1869* (New York, 1946); Kuznets, *Capital in the American Economy* (Princeton,

1961); Robert Gallman, "Gross National Product in the United States, 1834–1909," in Dorothy Brady, ed., *Output, Employment, and Productivity in the United States after 1800*, Studies in Income and Wealth 30 (New York, 1966), pp. 1–76; and Lance Davis and Robert Gallman, "Capital Formation in the United States During the Nineteenth Century," in Peter Mathias and M. M. Postan, eds., *The Cambridge Economic History of Europe*, vol. 7, pt. 2 (Cambridge, 1978), pp. 1–69. For a comparison of economic growth in the nineteenth and twentieth centuries, see Robert Gallman, "The Pace and Pattern of American Economic Growth," in Lance Davis et al., eds., *American Economic Growth: An Economist's History of the United States* (New York, 1972), ch. 2. For the quantitative dimensions of pre-1840 economic growth, see Paul David, "The Growth of Real Product in the United States Before 1840," *Journal of Economic History* 27 (June 1967): 151–97; Gallman, "Pace and Pattern"; and Stanley Engerman and Robert Gallman, "U.S. Economic Growth, 1783–1860," *Research in Economic History* 8 (1983): 1–46.

2. A more complete description of the data base is given in the appendix to this chapter.

3. Barry Poulson, "Economic History and Economic Development: An American Perspective," in this volume.

4. W. W. Rostow, *The Stages of Economic Growth* (Cambridge, 1960).

5. David, "Growth of Real Product."

6. Thomas Weiss, "Economic Growth Before 1860: Revised Conjectures," in this volume.

7. Returns for any ten-year period are sensitive to values at the beginning and end years. The overlapping-decade averages presented in Tables 2.1, 2.2, and 2.3 are helpful in overcoming this deficiency and in spotting changes in trend. Figure 2.1 presents in graphical form every ten-year average of real returns for each of the nearly 200 years. The overlapping real returns of the tables thus represent one-fifth of the points graphed in Figure 2.1. It should be remembered that the return presented or portrayed for any given year is the return realized from buying an asset ten years earlier and holding it for the ten-year period including that year. In the case of commercial paper, a short-term asset, the assumption is that the funds invested were rolled over, that is, reinvested in commercial paper throughout the ten-year period.

8. The stabilizing effects of the Second Bank are set forth in historical detail by Bray Hammond, *Banks and Politics in America from the Revolution to the Civil War* (Princeton, 1957). Stanley Engerman argues on the basis of monetary statistics that these effects were evident in increased public confidence in the banking system as well as in the banking system's confidence in itself; see Engerman, "A Note on the Economic Consequences of the Bank of the United States," *Journal of Political Economy* 78 (July/Aug. 1970): 725–28.

9. See Sidney Homer and Richard Sylla, *A History of Interest Rates*, 3d ed. (New Brunswick, N.J., 1991), chs. 16–17.

10. See Gallman, "Gross National Product," and Davis and Gallman, "Capital Formation." Another recent and yet-unpublished paper that discusses the savings-rate issue is Lance Davis and Robert Gallman, "Savings, Investment, and Economic Growth: The United States in the Nineteenth Century," presented at the

Max Hartwell symposium at the University of Virginia in October 1990. This paper has helped us to clarify our own thinking in our work here.

11. See Davis and Gallman, "Capital Formation," and John James and Jonathan Skinner, "Sources of Savings in the Nineteenth Century United States," in Peter Kilby, ed., *Quantity and Quiddity: Essays in U.S. Economic History* (Middletown, Conn., 1987), pp. 255–85. In their recent paper, "Savings, Investment, and Economic Growth," Davis and Gallman give more emphasis to the role of intermediaries in increasing savings rates through movements along the savings function resulting from increased returns to savers, a point that is in accord with our argument here.

12. Our argument is that savings responds to *expected* real returns, while our data are in terms of *realized* real returns. Were expected returns similar to realized returns? Or were nineteenth-century bondholders surprised year after year by the high real returns they earned on their holdings? We think the evidence that nineteenth-century bond yields were persistently below short-term market interest rates supports the former view.

13. Our finding of high real interest rates and bond returns is confirmed in the recent research of Kenneth Snowden, "Historical Returns and Security Market Development, 1872–1925," unpublished manuscript, University of North Carolina at Greensboro, 1989. Snowden, however, appears to disagree with us on the issue of whether high bond returns were anticipated by bondholders.

14. Gallman, "Gross National Product"; Gallman, "Pace and Pattern"; and Davis and Gallman, "Capital Formation."

15. The comparison is somewhat flawed because commercial paper returns are available for a shorter period than stock and bond returns before 1861, from 1831 rather than from the 1790's. For the same reason, the apparent higher returns for commercial paper "prior to 1901" in Table 2.4 are also flawed; in the comparable period 1831–1900, the nominal returns of stocks and bonds are 8.64 and 7.15 percent, so stock returns exceeded commercial paper returns during this seventy-year period. Bond returns, however, were lower than commercial paper returns even in this comparable period.

16. We reached a similar conclusion in an earlier paper based on a somewhat shorter data set. See Jack Wilson, Richard Sylla, and Charles Jones, "Financial Market Panics and Volatility in the Long Run, 1830–1988," in Eugene White, ed., *Crashes and Panics: The Lessons from History* (Homewood, Ill., 1990), pp. 85–125.

17. Jack Wilson and Charles Jones, "A Comparison of Common Stock Returns, 1871–1925 with 1926–1985," *Journal of Business* 60 (Apr. 1987): 239–58.

18. Paul David and Peter Solar, "A Bicentenary Contribution to the History of the Cost of Living in America," *Research in Economic History* 2 (1977): 1–80.

19. Lawrence Fisher and James Lorie, "Rates of Return on Investments in Common Stocks: The Year-by-Year Record, 1926–1965," *Journal of Business* 41 (July 1968): 291–316.

20. R. G. Ibbotson and R. Sinquefield, "Stocks, Bonds, Bills, and Inflation: Year-by-Year Historical Returns, 1926–1974," *Journal of Business* 49 (Jan. 1976): 11–47; and Ibbotson Associates, *Stocks, Bonds, Bills, and Inflation 1990 Yearbook* (Chicago, 1990).

21. Alfred A. Cowles and Associates, *Common Stock Indexes*, 2d ed. (Blooming-ton, Ind., 1939); and Jack Wilson and Charles Jones, "Returns on Stocks, Bonds, and Commercial Paper: Long-Term Construction, Analysis, and Comparison," unpublished manuscript, North Carolina State University, 1988.

22. Frederick R. Macaulay, *Some Theoretical Problems Suggested by the Movements of Interest Rates, Bond Yields, and Stock Prices in the United States since 1856* (New York, 1938).

23. G. William Schwert, "Indexes of Stock Prices from 1802 to 1987," *Journal of Business* 63 (July 1990): 399–426.

24. Wilson and Jones, "Returns on Stocks."

25. R. G. Ibbotson and G. P. Brinson, *Investment Markets* (New York, 1987).

26. Schwert, "Indexes of Stock Prices."

27. Walter Smith and Arthur Cole, *Fluctuations in American Business, 1790–1860* (New York, 1962; originally published in 1935).

28. Joseph Martin, *History of the Boston Stock and Money Markets: A Century of Finance* (New York, 1969; originally published in 1898).

29. Smith and Cole, *Fluctuations*, p. 171.

30. Homer and Sylla, *History of Interest Rates*, table 58, pp. 286–87. The yields used in our calculations were those of federal government bonds, 1820–32; New England municipal bonds, 1833–42; and federal government bonds, 1843–56.

31. Macaulay, *Some Theoretical Problems*.

32. Board of Governors of the Federal Reserve System, *Banking and Monetary Statistics* (Washington, D.C., 1976); *Annual Statistical Digest* and *Federal Reserve Bulletin* were used for post-1970 data.

33. Ibbotson Associates, *Stocks, Bonds, Bills, and Inflation*.

34. Macaulay, *Some Theoretical Problems*.

35. Wilson and Jones, "Returns on Stocks," and Wilson, Sylla, and Jones, "Financial Market Panics."

36. Homer and Sylla, *History of Interest Rates*, table 38, pp. 286–87.

3. Schaefer: U.S. Migration

1. Robert Gallman, "The United States Capital Stock in the Nineteenth Cen-tury," in Stanley Engerman and Robert Gallman, eds., *Long-Term Factors in Ameri-can Economic Growth*, Studies in Income and Wealth 51 (Chicago, 1986), p. 190.

2. Robert Gallman, "Human Capital in the First 80 Years of the Republic: How Much Did America Owe the Rest of the World?" *American Economic Review* 67, no. 1 (Feb. 1977): 27–31; Larry Neal and Paul Uselding, "Immigration, a Neglected Source of American Economic Growth: 1790–1912," *Oxford Economic Papers*, 2d ser., 24, no. 1 (March 1972): 68–88.

3. There are noneconomic issues as well. The reports of the Commissioners of Immigration in the early twentieth century contain many special reports on the moral character of Asian immigrants.

4. Julian Simon, *The Economic Consequences of Immigration* (Cambridge, Mass., 1989), p. xxvi.

5. A useful analysis of the various forms of the safety-valve hypothesis is found in Ellen van Nardoff, "The American Frontier as a Safety Valve—The Life,

Death, Reincarnation, and Justification of a Theory," *Agricultural History* 36 (1962): 123–42.

6. Peter McClelland and Richard Zeckhauser, *Demographic Dimensions of the New Republic: American Interregional Migration, Vital Statistics, and Manumissions, 1800–1860* (New York, 1982).

7. For explanations of this method, see Everett Lee, Ann Ratner Miller, Carol P. Brainerd, and Richard A. Easterlin, *Population Redistribution and Economic Growth: United States, 1870–1950*, vol. 1 (Philadelphia, 1957), pp. 15–54; and McClelland and Zeckhauser, *Demographic Dimensions*, pp. 20–27, 30–32.

8. Two acts covered this requirement. The first, the act of March 2, 1819, regulating passenger ships and vessels, provided for the basic report, whereas the second, the act of March 3, 1855, regulating the carriage of passengers in steamships and other vessels, added, among other things, the requirement that the intended residence of the arriving passengers be enumerated.

9. The ten reports used here are: House Executive Document 16, 31st Cong. 2d sess.; H.E.D. 100, 32d Cong. 1st sess.; H.E.D. 45, 32d Cong. 2d sess.; H.E.D. 78, 33d Cong. 1st sess.; H.E.D. 77, 33d Cong. 2d sess.; H.E.D. 29, 34th Cong. 1st sess.; Senate Executive Document 54, 34th Cong. 3d sess.; S.E.D. 32, 35th Cong. 1st sess.; S.E.D. 92, 35th Cong. 2d sess.; H.E.D. 32, 36th Cong. 1st sess. Many of these reports are available as both House and Senate Executive Documents.

10. For example, McClelland and Zeckhauser (*Demographic Dimensions*) make use of William J. Bromwell, *History of Migration to the United States* (New York, 1856). When the Bromwell data end in 1855, McClelland and Zeckhauser assume that the "age and sex patterns of immigrants entering for the entire decade, 1850–1859, were the same as the recorded patterns for the years 1850–1855" (*Demographic Dimensions*, p. 40). The official international immigration series from U.S. Bureau of the Census, *Historical Statistics of the United States, Colonial Times to 1970*, vol. 1 (Washington, D.C., 1975), ser. C89, is based on United States Immigration Commission, "Abstract Report of the Immigration Commission," vol. 1, S. Doc. 747, 61st Cong. 3d sess., which in turn is in part based on either Bromwell or the recapitulations of the reports of the secretary of state, since, as shown in Table 3.1, when the enumeration period is changed from the year ending on September 30 to the calendar year, a fifteen-month flow is given (following Bromwell) for the transitional year. By using the secretary's reports directly, I have placed the series on a calendar-year basis for the whole decade.

11. There are reports for Oswego, New York, for 1855–59 and for Detroit, Michigan, for 1858–59. These customs houses would have enumerated passengers entering the United States from Canada on ships crossing the Great Lakes.

12. We do not know if in fact these passengers left the United States. Doubtless, some of them stayed, while others enumerated as intending to reside in the United States left the country. For example, the Chinese who immigrated to San Francisco were all enumerated as intending to reside in the United States, yet there was a steady outflow of Chinese from that port in the 1850's.

13. There is some question about the underlying quality of the reports given to the State Department by the customs houses in the early years of the century. See Farley Grubb, "The Reliability of U.S. Immigration Statistics: The Case of Phila-

delphia, 1815–1830," *International Journal of Maritime History* 2, no. 1 (June 1990): 29–54. Secretary of State W. L. Marcy made efforts to improve the reporting by customs officials in the mid-1850's and was responsible for the amendment of the Act of March 2, 1819 by the Act of March 3, 1855.

14. One other difference between the two sets of estimates is their inclusion of a separate category "overland from Canada." In my estimates there is a partial measurement of the flow of immigrants from Canada to the United States through Oswego and Detroit for the later years of the decade.

15. There were approximately 3,000 steamboat arrivals each year in New Orleans. These would be available to carry passengers upstream. See William F. Switzler, *Report on the Internal Commerce of the United States*, House of Representatives, Executive Document 6, pt. 2, 50th Cong. 1st sess., Jan. 30, 1888, p. 221. Louis Hunter (*Steamboats on the Western Rivers* [Cambridge, Mass., 1949], pp. 417–22) makes the point that steamboat travel on the western rivers (including the Mississippi) not only was a bargain but also was more comfortable than overland travel. Switzler, *Report on Internal Commerce*, p. 190, notes, "The immigrant guidebooks of [1810–1820] . . . declare the river route preferable, as being cheaper, more rapid, and more satisfactory than traveling across the country where there were few, if any, roads."

16. At some customs houses, most notably New Orleans, age distributions occasionally were not enumerated.

17. There is evidence that the foreign born and the white native born had similar survival rates in the United States during the 1870's (Lee et al., *Population Redistribution*, pp. 17, 23). Data on the uniformity of survivor rates across states for 1929–31 and 1939–41 can also be found in ibid., pp. 35–44. Deviations from the national average seem to be chiefly confined to older adults (55 years and up).

18. Details of the estimation of the U.S. population are reserved for the appendix to this chapter.

19. "One problem remains: to estimate where immigrants settled prior to the next census. Part of the difficulty was overcome by assuming that immigrants arriving by sea remained in the region of entry until the next census" (McClelland and Zeckhauser, *Demographic Dimensions*, p. 42).

20. Richard Steckel, "Growth and Development in the Antebellum South: Old Debates and New Directions," in Lou Ferleger, ed., *Agriculture and National Development: Views on the Nineteenth Century* (Ames, Iowa, 1990), pp. 177–78; Steckel, "Household Migration and Rural Settlement in the United States," *Explorations in Economic History* 26, no. 2 (1989): 193–94.

21. For example, see Mark Wyman, *Immigrants in the Valley: Irish, Germans, and Americans in the Upper Mississippi Country, 1830–1860* (Chicago, 1984), ch. 1; Oscar Winther, *The Transportation Frontier: Trans-Mississippi West, 1865–1890* (New York, 1964), ch. 6. Louis Hunter (*Steamboats*, pp. 660–62) gives some statistics of the extensive upriver travel on steamboats during the decade.

22. U.S. Bureau of the Census, *Eighth Census of the United States* (Washington, D.C., 1860), 1: xxix.

23. McClelland and Zeckhauser, *Demographic Dimensions*, p. 7. The outflow of interregional immigrants from the New South is 134,000 over the decade, down

substantially from the 308,000 estimated by the naïve technique. This is still a large outflow, but one more believable and explicable in terms of transportation networks. It should be recognized that the breakdown of the South into three regions is different from that of McClelland and Zeckhauser because I wanted to identify a frontier area. If I had combined the New South with the Frontier, there would have been no net outflow of interregional immigrants from that region, but rather a small inflow. This result is not sensitive to the choice of weights in the weighted average estimation technique. If one assumed that all the existing immigrants in the New South did not remain in the region over the decade but rather died or left the region, then the net outflow from the combined region would be approximately 1,700.

24. Gallman, "Human Capital," p. 29.

25. California State Senate Special Committee on Chinese Immigration, *Chinese Immigration: The Social, Moral and Political Effect of Chinese Immigration* (Sacramento, Calif., 1876), p. 171.

26. McClelland and Zeckhauser, *Demographic Dimensions*, pp. 89–90. One exception is in the treatment of Minnesota, where I did not add 42,203 to the 1850 population.

27. On the other hand, an international immigrant who arrived immediately before the census enumeration in 1850 and who moved from the arrival region immediately after that enumeration would be considered an interregional migrant in this paper.

28. Robert Ostergren, "Prairie Bound: Migration Patterns to a Swedish Settlement on the Dakota Frontier," in Frederick Luebke, ed., *Ethnicity on the Great Plains* (Lincoln, Neb., 1980), p. 84.

4. Poulson: Economic History

1. Albert Hirschman, *Essays in Trespassing—Economics to Politics and Beyond* (New York, 1981).

2. W. W. Rostow, *The Stages of Economic Growth* (Cambridge, 1960).

3. At the other extreme were writers in the neo-Marxist and Dependencia schools, who argued that the problems of the developing countries were unique. The historical experience of the developed countries was relevant only in explaining how colonialism and neocolonialism have established the basis for capitalist exploitation of the developing countries. See, for example, Paul Baran, *The Political Economy of Growth* (New York, 1957); Raul Prebisch, *The Economic Development of Latin America and Its Principal Problems* (Lake Success, N.Y., 1950).

4. See especially the following works by Simon Kuznets: "Long-Term Changes in the National Income of the United States of America since 1870," in Simon Kuznets, ed., *Income and Wealth of the United States: Trends and Structure*, International Association for Research in Income and Wealth, Income and Wealth Series 2 (Baltimore, 1952), pp. 23–241; *Economic Change* (New York, 1953); *Modern Economic Growth* (New Haven, Conn., 1966); *National Income: A Summary of Findings* (New York, 1975).

5. For a discussion of the literature critical of the "takeoff hypothesis" as it relates to early American economic growth, see Barry Poulson, *Economic History of the United States* (New York, 1981), pp. 185–89.

6. W. Arthur Lewis, "Economic Development with Unlimited Supplies of Labor," *The Manchester School* 22 (May 1954): 139–91; J. C. Fei and Gustav Ranis, *Development of the Labor Surplus Economy* (Homewood, Ill., 1964).

7. OECD, *The Impact of the Newly Industrializing Countries in Production and Trade in Manufactures* (Paris, 1979).

8. Some of the NICs that experienced very rapid rates of growth in the 1950's and 1960's, such as Brazil and Mexico, have yet to recover from the energy price shocks and debt crises they experienced over the last decade.

9. See, for example, H. Pack and L. E. Westphal, "Industrial Strategy and Technological Change: Theory Versus Reality," *Journal of Development Economics* 22 (1986): 87–128; Larry Westphal, Yung Rhee, and Gary Pursell, *Korean Industrial Competence: Where It Came From*, World Bank Staff Working Paper no. 469 (Washington, D.C., 1981).

10. See especially the following works: Robert Gallman, "Commodity Output, 1839–1899," *Studies in Income and Wealth* 24 (1960): 13–67, Gallman, "Gross National Product in the United States, 1834–1909," in Dorothy Brady, ed., *Output, Employment, and Productivity in the United States after 1800*, Studies in Income and Wealth 30 (New York, 1966), pp. 3–76; Paul David, "The Growth of Real Product in the United States Before 1840," *Journal of Economic History* 27 (June 1967): 151–97; Barry Poulson, "Estimates of the Value of Manufacturing Output in the United States in the Early Nineteenth Century," *Journal of Economic History* 29 (1969): 521–26; Thomas Weiss, "Economic Growth Before 1860: Revised Conjectures," this volume.

11. Stanley Engerman and Robert Gallman, "U.S. Economic Growth, 1783–1860," *Research in Economic History* 8 (1983): 17.

12. Simon Kuznets, *Capital in the American Economy* (Princeton, 1961), p. 53.

13. Engerman and Gallman, "Economic Growth," p. 9.

14. Barry Poulson, "Value Added in Manufacturing, Mining, and Agriculture in the American Economy 1809–1839," in S. Bruchey, ed., *Dissertations in American Economic History* (New York, 1975); Barry Poulson and J. Malcolm Dowling, "Background Conditions and the Spectral Analytic Test of the Long Swings Hypothesis," *Explorations in Economic History* 8 (1971): 343–53; Poulson and Dowling, "The Climacteric in U.S. Economic Growth," *Oxford Economic Papers* 25 (1972): 420–34; Poulson and Dowling, "Long Swings in Factor Flows Between Great Britain and the United States," *Papers and Proceedings of the American Statistical Association Meetings* (1974): 1–25; Poulson and Dowling, "Long Swings in the U.S. Economy, A Spectral Analysis of Nineteenth- and Twentieth-Century Data," *Southern Economic Journal* 40 (1974): 473–80.

15. Kuznets is somewhat ambiguous about the existence of retardation in the rate of growth of income per capita. He states, "If we assume that the depression of the 1930's is cancelled by the expansions that preceded and followed it, and regard the long term averages as truly representative secular levels, we find retardation in the rate of growth not only of total income, but also of product per head and per worker. If, however, we omit the depression and the war years and regard the 1946–1955 averages as secular levels, there is no clear case for retardation in the rate of growth of product per capita or per worker" (Kuznets, *Capital*, pp. 77–78).

16. In his own words, "Comparing the experiences of the two centuries, then, we find marked retardation of the rate of growth of the real magnitudes [for capital formation], just as has been previously discovered with respect to the real national product" (Robert Gallman, "The United States Capital Stock in the Nineteenth Century," in Stanley Engerman and Robert Gallman, eds., *Long-Term Factors in American Economic Growth*, Studies in Income and Wealth 51 [Chicago, 1986], p. 185). Other researchers have found evidence for a retardation or pause in the long-term trend of economic growth in both the United States and Great Britain in the late nineteenth and early twentieth centuries, but the nature of and causes for this so-called climacteric remain controversial in the economic history literature (see, for example, Poulson and Dowling, "Climacteric in U.S. Economic Growth").

17. Simon Kuznets, *Modern Economic Growth: Rate, Structure and Spread*, Studies in Comparative Economics, no. 7 (New Haven, 1966).

18. Moses Abramovitz, *Resource and Output Trends in the United States since 1870*, National Bureau of Economic Research Occasional Paper 52 (New York, 1956); R. M. Solow, "Technical Progress, Capital Formation and Economic Growth," *American Economic Review* 52 (May 1962): 76–86; Richard Nelson, "Aggregate Production Functions and Medium-Range Growth Projections," *American Economic Review* 54 (Sept. 1964): 576–606. That early work was followed by a wealth of literature exploring the sources of change in productivity and explicitly incorporating productivity change into alternative specifications of the production function. For a critical survey of this literature, see Allen Kelly and Jeffrey Williamson, "Sources of Growth Methodology in the Low-Income Countries: A Critique," *Quarterly Journal of Economics* 87 (Feb. 1973):· 138–47; Richard Nelson, "Recent Exercises in Growth Accounting: New Understanding or Dead End," *American Economic Review* 63 (1973): 462–68. Most recently, see the careful and detailed exposition of Dale Jorgenson, "Productivity and Economic Growth," in Ernst Berndt and Jack Triplett, eds., *Fifty Years of Economic Measurement* (Chicago, 1990), pp. 19–118.

19. Gallman, "U.S. Capital Stock," and "The Agricultural Sector and the Pace of Economic Growth: U.S. Experience in the Nineteenth Century," in David Klingaman and Richard Vedder, eds., *Essays in Nineteenth-Century Economic History* (Athens, Ohio, 1975), pp. 35–76. Gallman's findings are in contrast to those of Moses Abramovitz and Paul David, who argued that increases in the factor inputs accounted for most of the growth in output per capita, and that productivity was advancing at a much slower pace in the nineteenth century than in the twentieth. See Moses Abramovitz and Paul David, "Reinterpreting Economic Growth: Parables and Realities," *American Economic Review* 63 (1973): 428–39.

20. Gallman, "U.S. Capital Stock," p. 191.

21. Lance Davis and Robert Gallman, "Capital Formation in the United States During the Nineteenth Century," in Peter Mathias and M. M. Postan, eds., *The Cambridge Economic History of Europe*, vol. 7, pt. 2 (Cambridge, 1978), pp. 1–69.

22. Ibid.

23. Davis and Gallman also found that the increase in the ratios was ubiquitous across all sectors of the economy in the nineteenth century. Although industrial-

ization cannot account for acceleration in the rate of capital formation in early American economic growth, it was important in the way in which the capital stock was assembled. Ibid., "Capital Formation," pp. 14–30.

24. Davis and Gallman found that a number of other factors, such as income distribution, foreign savings, and increased incorporation, had an insignificant effect on increased savings rates in the nineteenth century. They also found that government savings were small, but the indirect effects of government in defining and enforcing property rights and establishing the legal framework for the evolution of private financial institutions were crucial. Ibid., pp. 1–69.

25. Mira Wilkins, *The History of Foreign Investment in the United States to 1914* (Cambridge, Mass., 1989), pp. 616–25.

26. Clive Bell, "Credit Markets and Interlinked Transaction," in Hollis Chenery and T. N. Srinivasan, eds., *Handbook of Development Economics* (Amsterdam, 1988), pp. 763–831.

27. William Parker, "The Finance of Capital Formation in Midwestern Development, 1800–1910," in this volume.

28. Mark Gersovitz, "Savings and Development," and Nancy Birdsall, "Economic Approaches to Population Growth," in Chenery and Srinivasan, eds., *Handbook of Development Economics,* pp. 381–425 and 478–535, respectively.

29. In many developing countries, foreign savings have been channeled by governments into projects that have had little impact on economic growth and have saddled the developing countries with a heavy foreign debt. This mismanagement of financial resources has been accompanied in many cases by mismanagement of macroeconomic policies. These policies assumed that the public sector could accelerate the rate of domestic savings and capital formation; but there is little evidence that the public sector has a higher propensity to save, or that it is more efficient in channeling savings into productive investment and capital formation than the private sector in the developing countries. The expanded role for the public sector has instead displaced private savings and investment in many of these countries.

30. Peter Bauer, *The Development Frontier: Essays in Applied Economics* (Cambridge, Mass., 1991).

31. Simon Kuznets, "Quantitative Aspects of the Economic Growth of Nations," a series of ten articles published over the period from 1956 to 1967 in the journal *Economic Development and Cultural Change*.

32. Precursors of Kuznets were Colin Clark, *The Conditions of Economic Progress* (London, 1940); and A. G. B. Fisher, "Production, Primary, Secondary, and Tertiary," *Economic Record* 15 (1939): 24–38. Clark explored the causes for this structural transformation in terms of Engels effects and productivity change, and these issues have remained at the forefront of the analysis of structural change.

33. Robert Gallman and E. Howle, "Trends in the Structure of the American Economy," in Robert Fogel and Stanley Engerman, eds., *The Reinterpretation of American Economic History* (New York, 1971), pp. 25–37; Robert E. Gallman, "Changes in Total Agricultural Factor Productivity, 1800–1840," *Agricultural History* (Jan. 1972): 191–210; Gallman, "Agricultural Sector," pp. 35–76.

34. At the time there were two labor-force series available. Stanley Lebergott's

series showed a sharp decline in the agricultural share of the labor force before 1840, whereas that of Solomon Fabricant showed a relatively stable share. Stanley Lebergott, "Labor Force and Employment, 1800 to 1960," in Dorothy Brady, ed., *Output, Employment, and Productivity in the United States after 1800* (New York, 1966), pp. 117–205; Solomon Fabricant, "The Changing Industrial Distribution of Gainful Workers: Comments on Decennial Statistics, 1820–1940," *Studies in Income and Wealth* 11 (1949): 42.

35. My work on economic growth in the early nineteenth century, based on the Fabricant labor-force series, revealed a slower pace of advance in agricultural productivity in the period prior to 1840, and acceleration in the period after 1840 (Poulson, "Value Added"). Weiss shows a lower level for the agricultural work force at the beginning of the century and a more rapid growth up to 1840 than the Lebergott series, and shows continued acceleration in productivity advance in agriculture from 1800–1820 to 1820–40, and again to 1840–60 ("Economic Growth Before 1860," tables 2 and 3).

36. Gallman and Howle, "Trends in the Structure"; and Engerman and Gallman, "Economic Growth."

37. My own work suggests an acceleration in total productivity advance for the economy as a whole from the pre-1840 period to the post-1840 period (Poulson, "Estimates," pp. 521–26, and "Value Added," pp. 138–50). Weiss ("Economic Growth Before 1860," tables 1 and 6) also concludes that the growth of productivity and of income per capita for the economy as a whole accelerated in each twenty-year period from 1820 to 1860.

38. This evidence for the United States is supported by comparable studies of structural change in Europe during the initial transition to modern economic growth. See, for example, Angus Maddison, "Economic Growth and Structural Change in the Advanced Countries," in I. Leveson and J. W. Wheeler, eds., *Western Economies in Transition* (Boulder, Colo., 1980).

39. One of the few studies of structural change during the initial transition in developing countries is Arthur Lewis, *Evolution of the International Economic Order* (Princeton, 1978).

40. See, for example, the many works of Chenery, and Chenery and Syrquin. They identify three stages in the structural transformation: primary production, industrialization, and the developed economy. In the primary stage, agricultural production is predominant, and grows more slowly than manufacturing, resulting in a relatively slow pace of economic growth for the entire economy. Hollis Chenery and Moshe Syrquin, "Typical Patterns of Transformation," in H. Chenery, M. Syrquin, and S. Robinson, eds., *Industrialization and Growth: A Comparative Study* (New York, 1987).

41. Chenery and Syrquin found that most of the labor migrating out of the agricultural sector was absorbed not in the industrial sector but in the nontradable goods sector. Although the industrial sector has advanced rapidly, it has not increased significantly as a share of the total labor force in many developing countries. Chenery and Syrquin, "Typical Patterns."

42. Chenery and Syrquin, "Typical Patterns."

43. Mexico, for example, largely neglected the agricultural sector in its push for

industrialization throughout much of the postwar period. The Ejito or communal form of land ownership has absorbed a rapidly expanding agricultural labor force, but only at the expense of declining productivity and output. The absence of property rights provides little incentive for an efficient utilization of the agricultural labor force in Mexico. For a discussion of the role of policy and institutions affecting agricultural productivity in developing countries, see Y. Hayami and V. Ruttan, *Agricultural Development: An International Perspective* (Baltimore, 1985).

44. See Douglass North, "Institutional Change in American Economic History," in this volume.

45. Cynthia Taft Morris notes correctly that the revolutionary changes occurring in the institutions of Eastern Europe and the developing countries reflect motives beyond the search for economic and political liberty. Cynthia Taft Morris and Irma Adelman, "Nineteenth-Century Development Experience and Lessons for Today," *World Development* 17 (1989): 1417–32.

5. North: Institutional Change

1. This essay summarizes and elaborates on some of the conclusions in a recent study by the author entitled *Institutions, Institutional Change and Economic Performance* (Cambridge, 1990).

2. F. A. von Hayek, *The Constitution of Liberty* (Chicago, 1960).

3. Mancur Olson, *The Rise and Decline of Nations* (New Haven, Conn., 1982).

4. Douglass North and Robert Thomas, *The Rise of the Western World: A New Economic History* (Cambridge, 1973).

5. Robert Fogel, *Without Consent or Contract* (New York, 1989).

6. Ronald Coase, "The Nature of the Firm," *Economica* 4 (1937): 386–405.

7. Stephen Marglin, "What Do Bosses Do?" *Review of Radical Political Economy* 6 (1974): 33–60.

8. Oliver Williamson, *Markets and Hierarchies: Analysis and Antitrust Implications* (New York, 1975), and *The Economic Institutions of Capitalism* (New York, 1985).

9. Yoram Barzel, "Measurement Cost and the Organization of Markets," *Journal of Law and Economics* 25 (1982): 27–48.

10. Alfred Chandler, *The Visible Hand* (Cambridge, Mass., 1977).

11. Jonathan Hughes, "The Great Land Ordinances," in David Klingaman and Richard Vedder, eds., *Essays on the Economy of the Old Northwest* (Athens, Ohio, 1987), pp. 1–18.

12. Douglass North and Andrew Rutten, "The Northwest Ordinance in Historical Perspective," in Klingaman and Vedder, *Essays*, pp. 19–36.

13. Hughes, "Great Land Ordinances."

14. Jeremy Atack and Fred Bateman, "Yankee Farming and Settlement in the Old Northwest," in Klingaman and Vedder, *Essays*, pp. 77–102.

15. Herbert Simon, "Rationality in Psychology and Economics," in Robin Hogarth and Melvin Reder, eds., *Rational Choice* (Chicago, 1986), pp. 25–40.

16. North and Rutten, "Northwest Ordinance."

17. Lance Davis and Robert Gallman, "Capital Formation in the United States During the Nineteenth Century," in Peter Mathias and M. M. Postan, eds., *The*

Cambridge Economic History Of Europe, vol. 7, pt. 2 (Cambridge, 1978); and Barry Poulson, "Economic History and Economic Development: An American Perspective," in this volume.

18. Poulson, "Economic History and Economic Development," this volume.

6. Engerman & Goldin: Nineteenth-Century Labor Markets

1. We focus here only on the direct effect of climate in influencing seasonal patterns of production, primarily in agriculture, construction, and manufacturing. Seasonality was of obvious importance in transportation, as well. Thomas Senior Berry's study of the Mississippi River steamboat rates pointed to a "wide and erratic seasonality" that ended by the 1880's after the railroads captured much of the traffic. See Berry, *Western Prices Before 1861: A Study of the Cincinnati Market* (Cambridge, Mass., 1943), pp. 47, 62–68. See also Louis Hunter, *Studies in the Economic History of the Ohio Valley* (Northampton, 1934), pp. 5–49, on transportation changes, and for a more general discussion of "seasonal aspects of economic life of the Ohio Valley before the age of big business."

2. The 67.5 percent figure uses the agricultural and total labor-force estimates in Thomas Weiss, "Economic Growth Before 1860: Revised Conjectures," in this volume, and the construction and fishing estimates are from U.S. Bureau of the Census, *Historical Statistics of the United States* (Washington, D.C., 1975), ser. D167–181. The assumption that these workers were unemployed for four months during the year is consistent with evidence for the late nineteenth century. The assumption that all other workers were not unemployed during the year imparts a downward bias to the impact of reducing seasonality. The assumed increase in the work year for those initially in seasonally sensitive sectors could be due to changes in the seasonal pattern of producing specific products, a shift in the product mix within a given sector (for example, the move from grains to livestock), or an intersectoral move to a sector with a less-seasonal pattern of work.

3. The ratio of agricultural product per laborer to that in all other sectors has been used to infer growth in per capita output for the 1800 to 1840 period, to explain growth in later years, and to analyze the efficiency of factor markets in the nineteenth century. It is, therefore, an economic magnitude of some importance. A possible indication that the ratio is downwardly biased in the mid-nineteenth century is that it is considerably lower in the United States than in England. One estimate of the ratio, considered an upper bound because it includes the value of home manufactures on the farm, is barely above 0.5. On the computation and magnitude of the ratio in the United States, see Paul David, "The Growth of Real Product in the United States Before 1840," *Journal of Economic History* 27 (June 1967): 151–97. See Weiss, "Economic Growth Before 1860," in this volume, for a more recent application of the ratio. In the nineteenth century, however, the U.S. ratio was in the middle of the thirteen countries for which data are presented in Simon Kuznets, *Economic Growth of Nations: Total Output and Production Structure* (Cambridge, Mass., 1971), pp. 290–92, 298. The extent to which these differentials in relative productivity reflect differences in seasonality remains to be determined.

4. Although in early modern Europe, and to some extent in America, in the eighteenth and early part of the nineteenth century, household manufacture, with

its labor-force mix biased by gender and by age, helped to mitigate the problems of labor seasonality. See, for example, Maxine Berg, *The Age of Manufactures: Industry, Innovation and Work in Britain, 1700–1820* (New York, 1986), and the classic work of Rolla Tryon, *Household Manufactures in the United States, 1640–1860: A Study in Industrial History* (Chicago, 1917).

5. See, for example, the discussions in Louis Hunter, *A History of Industrial Power in the United States, 1780–1930*, vol. 1, *Waterpower in the Century of the Steam Engine* (Charlottesville, Va., 1979).

6. For a discussion of urban-rural relocation for seasonal employment within the year, see David Schob, *Hired Hands and Plowboys: Farm Labor in the Midwest, 1815–60* (Urbana, Ill., 1975), pp. 89, 150, 169; Allan Bogue, *From Prairie to Corn Belt: Farming on the Illinois and Iowa Prairies in the Nineteenth Century* (Chicago, 1963), pp. 182–87; J. Sanford Rikoon, *Threshing in the Midwest, 1820–1940: A Study of Traditional Culture and Technological Change* (Bloomington, Ind., 1988), p. 51; and, for this pattern of mobility within the meat-packing industry, see Rudolf Clemen, *The American Livestock and Meat Industry* (New York, 1923), pp. 111–13. In a discussion of the "harvest labor problems in the wheat belt" in the early twentieth century, D. D. Lescohier, *Harvest Labor Problems in the Wheat Belt* (Washington, D.C., 1922), notes that "residents of the towns of the small-grain States who hire out to farmers in their own localities constitute a large fraction of the total army of harvest hands" (p. 15). See also George Holmes, *Supply of Farm Labor*, U.S. Department of Agriculture, Bureau of Statistics, Bulletin 94 (Washington, D.C., 1912), pp. 75–78, on the interaction of farm and urban labor markets.

7. On packing and slaughtering houses, see Schob, *Hired Hands*, p. 169; also Clemen, *American Livestock and Meat Industry*, pp. 110–13. Margaret Walsh (*The Rise of the Midwestern Meat Packing Industry* [Lexington, Ky., 1982], pp. 15–37) points to the impact of seasonality on the extent of entrepreneurship in the industry.

8. On the nature and extent of by-employments in the late eighteenth and the nineteenth centuries, see, in particular, Winifred Rothenberg, "The Emergence of a Capital Market in Rural Massachusetts, 1730–1838," *Journal of Economic History* 45 (Dec. 1985): 781–808; Lucy Simler, "Those Who Live by Wages: Agricultural and Industrial Workers in Rural Pennsylvania, 1750–1820," unpublished manuscript, 1988; Paul Clemens and Lucy Simler, "Rural Labor and the Farm Household in Chester County, Pennsylvania, 1750–1820," in Stephen Innes, ed., *Work and Labor in Early America* (Chapel Hill, 1988), pp. 106–43; and Alexander Keyssar, *Out of Work: The First Century of Unemployment in Massachusetts* (Cambridge, 1986), p. 12. The problem of occupational classification when there is by-employment was discussed in the census instructions in detail in both 1820 (distinguishing criteria for "principal" and "occasional, or incidental" occupations) and 1890 (distinguishing that upon "which he would ordinarily be engaged during the larger part of the year"). See Carroll Wright, *The History and Growth of the United States Census* (Washington, D.C., 1900), pp. 135, 189.

9. Carville Earle and Ronald Hoffman, "The Foundation of the Modern Economy: Agriculture and the Costs of Labor in the United States and England, 1800–60," *American Historical Review* 85 (Dec. 1980): 1055–94. See, in contrast,

H. J. Habakkuk, *American and British Technology in the Nineteenth Century: The Search for Labor Saving Inventions* (Cambridge, 1962), for a framework of industrialization that emphasizes the scarcity, not overabundance, of unskilled labor. Earle ("A Staple Interpretation of Slavery and Free Labor," *Geographical Review* 68 [Jan. 1978]: 51–65) has also argued that the seasonal patterns imposed by different crops could provide some explanation of the choices made between slave labor and free labor in the antebellum United States. For a somewhat different argument relating slavery and seasonality, see Ralph Anderson and Robert Gallman ("Slavery as Fixed Capital: Slave Labor and Southern Economic Development," *Journal of American History* 64 [June 1977]: 24–26), who point to the importance of finding off-season work for the slave labor force.

10. Labor and product markets were less integrated, the cost of transportation was higher, and the agricultural sector, in which seasonality was most pronounced, was relatively larger earlier in the nineteenth century. It has been argued, however, that over the first half of the nineteenth century, increased commercialization of agriculture and manufacturing in New York State increased the severity of seasonal pauperism. See Joan Hannon, "Poverty in the Antebellum Northeast: The View from New York State's Poor Relief Rolls," *Journal of Economic History* 44 (Dec. 1984): 1007–32. For discussions of the role seasonality played in late eighteenth- and early nineteenth-century urban social ills, see also David Schneider, *The History of Public Welfare in New York State, 1609–1866* (Chicago, 1938), pp. 258–65, and John Alexander, *Render Them Submissive: Responses to Poverty in Philadelphia, 1760–1800* (Amherst, 1980), pp. 13–16.

11. Alternatives would include adjusting to the varying longitudinal patterns of agriculture, as in the example of migrating harvest gangs for wheat in the late nineteenth century. See Fred Shannon, *The Farmer's Last Frontier: Agriculture, 1860–1897* (New York, 1945), pp. 159–61.

12. For discussions of mobility in manufacturing employment in the early nineteenth-century Northeast and the late nineteenth-century Midwest, see, for example, Jonathan Prude, *The Coming of Industrial Order: Town and Factory Life in Rural Massachusetts, 1810–1860* (Cambridge, 1983); Alan Dawley, *Class and Community: The Industrial Revolution in Lynn* (Cambridge, Mass., 1976), pp. 139–42; and Robert Ozanne, *Wages in Practice and Theory: McCormick and International Harvester, 1860–1960* (Madison, Wis., 1968).

13. The revised data come from Thomas Weiss, personal communication.

14. Gates notes that "the first source of labor was the farm family with its many children. From early youth they were trained to do the milking, haying, plowing, planting, and hauling; they knew how to handle horses, cows, and oxen; and they were reliable and careful. As they grew to maturity and were not needed on their family homestead, they hired out to successful farmers." See Paul Gates, *The Farmer's Age: Agriculture, 1815–1860* (New York, 1960): pp. 272–73.

15. Among the government reports for later periods that provide a breakdown of monthly employment in agriculture, by crop type and region, are Eldon Shaw and John Hopkins, *Trends in Employment in Agriculture, 1909–36*, WPA National Research Project, Report no. A-8 (Philadelphia, 1938), and United States Department of Agriculture, Bureau of Agricultural Economics, *Farm Wage Rates, Farm*

Employment, and Related Data (Washington, D.C., 1943). For other useful break-downs of seasonal labor requirements, see Lescohier, *Harvest Labor Problems.*

16. Note that there are no data for Minnesota in 1860.

17. For comments on the effect of agricultural technology in mitigating the excess harvest-labor demand, see, for example, John Hopkins, *Changing Technology and Employment in Agriculture*, U.S. Department of Agriculture, Bureau of Agricultural Economics (Washington, D.C., 1941), pp. 14–15, 23; Shaw and Hopkins, *Trends in Employment in Agriculture*, p. 70; and Stanley Lebergott, *Manpower in Economic Growth: The American Record since 1800* (New York, 1964), p. 246.

18. For a discussion of improvement in agricultural productivity between 1840 and 1910, suggesting the differential impact of mechanization in lowering labor requirements in harvesting and threshing in wheat and oat production, see William Parker and Judith Klein, "Productivity Growth in Grain Production in the United States, 1840–60 and 1900–10," in Dorothy Brady, ed., *Output, Employment, and Productivity in the United States after 1800*, Studies in Income and wealth, vol. 30 (New York, 1966), pp. 523–80.

19. Missouri Bureau of Labor Statistics, *Second Annual Report*, for the year ending January 1, 1881 (Jefferson City, Mo., 1881).

20. In 1880, for example, the number of farm laborers per farmer was 0.38 in Missouri and 0.38 in Michigan, 0.44 in Illinois, and so on.

21. Holmes, *Supply of Farm Labor.*

22. George Holmes, *Wages of Farm Labor*, U.S. Department of Agriculture, Bureau of Statistics, Bulletin 99 (Washington, D.C., 1912).

23. Data for the West include a changing group of states and contain too few observations for the early period.

24. The seasonal wage premium in Vermont agriculture declined at the same time. See T. M. Adams, *Prices Paid by Vermont Farmers for Goods and Services and Received by Them for Farm Products, 1790–1940; Wages of Vermont Farm Labor, 1780–1940*, Vermont Agricultural Experiment Station Bulletin no. 507 (Burlington, Vt., 1944), p. 85. Within manufacturing, a decline has been recorded for the McCormick Works after 1870 by Ozanne, *Wages in Practice and Theory*, p. 125. Hunter (*Studies in the Economic History of the Ohio Valley*, pp. 21–23) points to the role of the railroad in solving the seasonality problem regarding transportation in the Ohio River Valley.

25. Note, as well, that the differences between the "with" and "without board" cases in Table 6.3 reflect the implicit payment for board in both the numerator and the denominator. That is, if the value of earnings plus board were equal in the two contracts, the seasonal premium would have to be higher for the board-inclusive case. For example, let w^s be the seasonal monthly payment for a laborer who also receives board in-kind, let w be the off-seasonal monthly payment for a laborer who receives board in-kind, let $\hat{w}^s$ be the seasonal monthly payment without board, and let $\hat{w}$ be the off-seasonal monthly payment without board. Also let b be the implicit dollar value of board per month. In equilibrium, $\hat{w}^s = w^s + b$, and $\hat{w} = w + b$, that is, the worker who receives board gets, in dollar terms, the same amount as the worker who receives only a wage. Therefore, $(\hat{w}^s/\hat{w}) < (w^s/w)$, or the without-board ratio must be lower than the board-inclusive ratio.

26. Timothy Hatton and Jeffrey Williamson, in "Unemployment, Implicit Contracts, and Compensating Wage Differentials: Michigan in the 1890s," Harvard Institute of Economic Research Working Paper no. 1481 (May 1990), find that there was complete compensatory payment in the agricultural sector to laborers who were subject to greater unemployment, primarily because they were hired on a daily basis rather than through annual contracts.

27. See Winifred Rothenberg, "The Emergence of Farm Labor Markets and the Transformation of the Rural Economy: Massachusetts, 1750–1855," *Journal of Economic History* 48 (Sept. 1988): 537–66; and Adams, *Prices Paid by Vermont Farmers*.

28. We thank Winifred Rothenberg for making her daily and monthly wage data available to us. It should be noted that Rothenberg reports somewhat higher harvest premiums by defining the harvest wage to be both task- and month-specific. When the harvest wage is that for mowing, haying, and reaping in July and August and the nonharvest wage is that for all other tasks in the months from September to June (as in Rothenberg's work), the harvest premium is between 1.33 and 1.40 for the time period 1820 to 1859. See Winifred Rothenberg, "Structural Change in the Farm Labor Force: Contract Labor in Massachusetts Agriculture, 1750–1865," in C. Goldin and H. Rockoff, eds., *Strategic Factors in Nineteenth-Century American Economic History* (Chicago, 1992).

29. Adams's data show an increase in the premium paid for July and August labor from 1790–99 to 1820–29 (*Prices Paid by Vermont Farmers*, p. 85).

30. We are not yet certain whether these data indicate a preponderance of daily laborers or merely a greater recording of daily hires in the account books. If each day of labor were recorded separately, there would be about 23 times more daily recordings than monthly recordings.

31. The seasonal premium is computed as follows. Rothenberg's data are for individual contracts and give the monthly wage, the number of months, and the starting month. For each individual, therefore, the proportion of the contract that is "seasonal," α, can be computed. Assume that all contracts are implicitly given by $M_a = \alpha M_s + (1 - \alpha)M_{ns}$, as in the note to Table 6.3. That is, the average monthly wage (M_a) is equal to a weighted average of the seasonal monthly wage and the nonseasonal monthly wage, with the weight given by the proportion of months worked in season. We split the Rothenberg data into three groups: 1800–1819, 1820–39, and 1840–56. Within each we calculated the seasonal wage for individuals who worked only during the three highest-paying months, June, July, and August. We then solved for M_{ns} using the definition given above, and took the means by year group. The results are: 1800–1856 = 1.343; 1800–1819 = 1.268; 1820–39 = 1.454; and 1840–56 = 1.309. These numbers bracket those given by Holmes (*Wages of Farm Labor*) for the North Atlantic region in the 1860's. It is likely, however, that the season was defined by Holmes as lasting five to six months, and therefore that the seasonal premium in New England from 1800 to 1856 was considerably lower than later in the century.

32. Clemens and Simler, "Rural Labor."

33. As part of this change, there was some shift in the overall composition of the agricultural labor force. Rather than involving the full family, those hiring out for agricultural employment were more generally male, young, and unmarried, the pattern more typical for the remainder of the century.

34. Provided by Winifred Rothenberg, private communication.

35. According to Ozanne, "The agricultural implement business was seasonal. If a good year was anticipated, production of reapers was stepped up in January, rising to a peak in June and July. . . . Spring wage increases at McCormick's were selective. . . . The purpose of this spring wage increase was no doubt to lessen the competition for labor of the building construction industry, which worked only in the summer months. Fall wage cuts came when cold weather stopped building construction" (*Wages in Practice and Theory*, p. 17). The seasonal pattern of wages was only a pre-1870 characteristic of the industry (p. 125). See also Earle and Hoffman, "Foundation of the Modern Economy," and Joseph Walker, *Hopewell Village: A Social and Economic History of an Iron-Making Community* (Philadelphia, 1966), p. 230.

36. These data were generously provided by Robert Margo. See Robert Margo and Georgia Villaflor, "The Growth of Wages in Antebellum America: New Evidence," *Journal of Economic History* 47 (Dec. 1987): 873–95, for a description of the data set.

37. A discussion and analysis of seasonality in manufacturing in the early twentieth century is contained in Simon Kuznets, *Seasonal Variations in Industry and Trade* (New York, 1933). Parker Bursk (*Seasonal Variation in Employment and Manufacturing Industries* [Philadelphia, 1931]) also examines industry data from the first quarter of the twentieth century and reports that those industries whose plants averaged more than forty employees had less seasonality than did smaller firms.

38. In regard to hours worked per day at different times of the year, based on the 1880 census of manufactures, Jeremy Atack and Fred Bateman ("How Long Did People Work in 1880?" National Bureau of Economic Research Working Paper, DAE series no. 15 [Aug. 1990]) indicate that 68 percent of firms had the same number of hours worked per day in the summer as in the winter, 4 percent had more in the winter, and the remainder had more in the summer. Presumably manufacturing seasonality was influenced both by weather factors influencing production and by the alternative opportunities for agricultural employment in the countryside.

39. This may have been due to the seasonal reduction in water power. See Hunter, *History of Industrial Power*. Textile production was affected also by heat and humidity.

40. For a detailed description of the agricultural work year, see James Covert, *Seedtime and Harvest: Cereals, Flax, Cotton and Tobacco: Dates of Planting and Harvesting East of Meridians 102–104 in the United States*, U.S. Department of Agriculture, Bureau of Statistics Bulletin 85 (Washington, D.C., 1912).

41. See Benjamin Free, *Seasonal Employment in Agriculture*, Works Progress Administration (Washington, D.C., Sept. 1938), pp. 11–58, and Covert, *Seedtime and Harvest*.

42. See, for example, Robert Gallman's annual GNP estimates, underlying his decade estimates, in "Gross National Product in the United States, 1834–1909," in Brady, ed., *Output, Employment, and Productivity*, pp. 37–76, and the recent industrial production index of Jeffrey Miron and Christina Romer, "A

New Monthly Index of Industrial Production, 1884–1940," *Journal of Economic History* 50 (June 1990): 321–37.

43. One may reasonably wonder how a full-time farmer could be unemployed. Perhaps the farmers who reported unemployment had by-employments and were unemployed from these jobs. The somewhat anomalous results for family farm workers and farmers in the South are likely due to higher tenancy rates in that region.

44. The variation that exists in the conditional number of months of unemployment seems to reflect an apparent negative relationship between the percentage claiming any unemployment and the number of months unemployed. The conditional mean increases as fewer individuals experience any unemployment, suggesting the existence of some chronically unemployed persons, perhaps due to health reasons.

45. Duration of unemployment, conditional on experiencing some unemployment, varied somewhat differently with the urbanization variables. For the farm laborers, duration increased by about 0.6 of a month in counties containing large cities above that in either rural counties or those containing or adjacent to small cities. In the nonfarm sample of workers, months of unemployment once again was higher in all cities than in rural areas, but was highest for those in small cities. Thus, unemployment for farm laborers living near large cities involved longer duration, but the probability of falling into unemployment was smaller. Those already in urban areas—the nonfarm workers—had unemployment spells that were less affected by the size of the city. In fact, larger cities appear to have given laborers more options to search for employment than smaller cities did.

46. See Timothy Hatton and Jeffrey Williamson, "Wage Gaps Between Farm and City: Michigan in the 1890s," Harvard Institute for Economic Research Discussion Paper no. 1449 (Cambridge, Mass., 1989), for discussion and analysis of the Michigan farm data used here, as well as other related data sets for Michigan. See also Hatton and Williamson, "Unemployment, Implicit Contracts, and Compensating Wage Differentials."

47. The 1900 Public Use Microdata Sample is too small to explore this notion. There were 44 nonfamily farm workers in the sample, 14 of whom experienced unemployment. The conditional mean for these 14 workers is 3.21 months.

48. Schob, *Hired Hands.*

49. Michigan Bureau of Labor and Industrial Statistics, *Twelfth Annual Report*, year ending February 1, 1895 (Lansing, Mich., 1895), p. 233.

50. Assume that unemployment consists of a voluntary component (here taken to be only illness) and an involuntary component (everything else). Further, the voluntary and involuntary components, as defined here, are assumed to be uncorrelated. An economic downturn, for example, does not increase the incidence of sickness. Thus the same percentage of the population will be ill in the absence of an economic depression as will be ill when there is a downturn. We know from the Michigan data that 73 percent of farm laborers (with cause listed) were out of work in 1894 (see Table 6.6), and 11.6 percent of farm laborers were out of work due to illness. Therefore, 61.4 percent were, by assumption, involuntarily unemployed. In 1900, during far better times, 38 percent of all farm laborers were unemployed.

Therefore, 26.4 percent (38 minus 11.6) of farm laborers in 1900 were involuntarily unemployed in 1900. It should be noted that Lebergott (*Manpower*) makes similar adjustments in his use of the 1890 and 1900 census data on unemployment.

51. Holmes, *Supply of Farm Labor*.

7. Davis et al.: The American Whaling Industry

1. Elmo Hohman, *The American Whaleman: A Study of Life and Labor in the Whaling Industry* (New York, 1928), reprinted New York, 1972, especially chaps. 9 and 10, pp. 217, 222. See also Elmo Hohman, "Wages, Risks, and Profits in the Whaling Industry," *Quarterly Journal of Economics* 40 (Aug. 1926): 644–71.

2. Hohman, *American Whaleman*, pp. 217, 222.

3. Hohman, "Wages, Risks, and Profits," p. 651.

4. The 1,258 voyages include all but the nine unreadable lists among the crew lists on deposit at the New Bedford Public Library that (1) include information on the whalemen's occupations and lay, and (2) overlap the voyages included in a recent study of whaling productivity. New Bedford Public Library, *Whalemen's Shipping Papers*; L. Davis, R. Gallman, and T. Hutchins, "Productivity in American Whaling: The New Bedford Fleet in the Nineteenth Century," in David Galenson, ed., *Markets in History: Economic Studies of the Past* (Cambridge, 1989). The data underlying the labor contract are cited as Davis, Gallman, Hutchins Tape no. 2, Labor. On occasion reference is made to data on voyages—but not including labor information—covering the entire period 1816 to 1906. That data base is cited as Davis, Gallman, Hutchins Tape no. 1.

5. Alexander Starbuck, *History of the American Whale Fishery from Its Earliest Inception to the Year 1876* (Waltham, Mass., 1878); Reginald Hegarty, *Returns of Whaling Vessels Sailing from American Ports: A Continuation of Alexander Starbuck's "History of the American Whale Fishery," 1876–1928* (New Bedford, Mass., 1959); Joseph Dias, "Mss.: The New Bedford Whaling Fleet, 1790–1906," manuscript on deposit in the Manuscript Room, Baker Library, Graduate School of Business, Harvard University. For a discussion of the Dias manuscript, see "The New Bedford Whaling Fleet, 1790–1906," *Bulletin of the Business History Society* 6 (Dec. 1931): 9–14.

6. In 1846, for example, when the American whaling fleet numbered 706 vessels, there were 230 registered whalers in the rest of the world. Starbuck; Edouard A. Stackpole, *The Sea-Hunters: The New England Whalemen During Two Centuries, 1635–1835* (Philadelphia and New York, 1953), p. 473.

7. The average of the brigs, sloops, and schooners (brought together in this discussion as a single class, "other") was 112 tons, and they employed more labor per ton than did either ships or barks.

8. In regard to the sophistication of captains and agents, consider the case of Captain Thomas Scullum of the *Cape Horn Pigeon*. Scullum and his vessel were falsely incarcerated by the Russians. Scullum went to international arbitration over his alleged losses—losses that included a $49,500 charge for missing the hunting season and $7,175.63 interest. He won. A. B. C. Whipple, *Yankee Whalers in the South Seas* (Garden City, N.Y., 1954), pp. 126–29.

9. Hohman, *American Whaleman*, p. 226.

10. Charles Morgan to S. Bartlett (Boston), May 24, 1837, *Charles W. Morgan*

Letter Book, mss. 252, 1820–1865, m. 847 v. 4, Baker Library. It should be noted that the *Condor* had arrived 36 days before Morgan put pen to paper.

11. Starbuck reports that the 1844 voyage of the Fairhaven-based ship *Albion* to the Indian Ocean lasted 93 months (7 years and 9 months).

12. *Account Book of the Ship George Howland 1834–1866*, Baker Library, Business Manuscript no. 76 (microfilm). Desertion had been a problem at least as early as the middle of the eighteenth century. For an early example, see Daniel Vickers, "Nantucket Whalemen in the Deep-Sea Fishery: The Changing Anatomy of an Early American Labor Force," *Journal of Economic History* 72 (Sept. 1985): 287.

13. Although the lay was a fraction, it was often referred to as the reciprocal, i.e., a lay of 1/175 was often called "a 175."

14. Charles W. Morgan to Thomas A. Norton, November 21, 1834, *Charles W. Morgan Letter Book*.

15. In the Atlantic, the single ship making a "short" lay voyage was registered at 191 tons, compared with a ground average of 301. The average size of the eight barks was 200 tons, compared with a ground average of 225. For the three smaller classes, the ten averaged 97, compared with the ground average of 112 tons. In terms of time at sea, the same comparisons show 16 to 27 months for ships, 23 to 27 months for barks, and 12 to 13 months for the smaller vessels. A regression of labor share on size and sail year shows

$$\text{SUMLAY} = -4.62 + 0.00005 \text{ TONS} + 0.00267 \text{ SAILYEAR}$$
$$(0.0001) \quad (0.0001) \qquad\quad (0.0001)$$

for the Indian, Pacific, and Arctic grounds, but

$$\text{SUMLAY} = -3.56 - 0.00010 \text{ TONS} + 0.00210 \text{ SAILYEAR}$$
$$(0.0001) \quad (0.0354) \qquad\quad (0.0001)$$

for the Atlantic.

16. Hohman, *American Whaleman*, p. 217.

17. Ibid., p. 230.

18. Ibid., p. 233.

19. The terms "lengthening" and "shortening" are somewhat confusing. Since the lay was often referred to by its reciprocal, a change from a 150 to a 170 was called a lengthening, despite the fact that it involved a reduction of the worker's share from 0.67 to 0.56 percent. Similarly, a change from a 19 to a 16.5 was termed a shortening, despite the implied increase from 5.3 to 6.1 percent.

20. These figures almost certainly understate the actual lay shares received by captains. In 121 cases (9.6 percent of the total), the captain signed a special contract that was not reported with the normal contracts (special contracts were also signed by 22 first mates, 4 second mates, 1 third mate, 2 fourth mates, and 1 boatsteerer). When these contracts could be found, they usually involved some bonus payment over and above the lay. In this study, missing values were assigned the average value for the position in the ground in question. Substituting the maximum lay in the ground made no significant difference in the results.

21. In the case of the cook, the value of the lay was almost always less than his total income from the voyage. In addition to his lay, he was typically entitled to

between one-third and one-half of the slush, as the money received from the sale of slush (refuse grease and fat from cooking) and other ship's refuse was called. On the voyage of the *George Howland* that began on June 25, 1846, for example, Andrew Lewis, the cook, earned $357.73 from his 1/140 lay and an additional $124.00 from his one-half of the slush. Thus his effective lay was 1/104 (*Account Book of the Ship George Howland*). Captains also frequently shared in the slush.

22. The average encompasses two voyages of the *Stephania* (1828–29 and 1829–30), four voyages of the *George Howland* (1834–38, 1838–41, 1842–45, and 1846–50), two voyages of the *Midas* (1827–29 and 1829–30), and one voyage of the *William Rotch* (1830–31). See *Account Book of the Ship George Howland*, and *J.&H. Coggeshall Papers*, vol. 2, no. 252, 1809–1847, c. 676, Baker Library.

23. The average encompasses one voyage of the *Benjamin Tucker* (returned 1851) and three voyages of the *George Howland* (1850–52, 1852–57, and 1857–61). See *Account Book of the Ship George Howland* and *J.&H. Coggeshall Papers*.

24. *Account Book of the Ship George Howland*.

25. On one voyage of the bark *Callao*, and four of the ship *Milton*, such offsets against wages averaged 4.4 percent. In the case of the *Callao*—condemned in Mauritius in 1877—the charges totaled 28.6 percent; in the case of the *Milton*—"arrived Panama in distress" in 1889—they amounted to 12.9 percent. In the latter case, however, if the Panama freight charges had not been incurred, the total would have been only 5.1 percent. See *Account Books: Ship Milton and Bark Callao*, mss. 252, 1862–1889, w. 552, Baker Library.

26. On seven of the eight voyages made by the *George Howland* between 1834 and 1866—voyages on which we have information (the relevant page on the 1857–61 voyage is missing)—the captains' extra income was $600.62, $168.45, $1222.65, $0.00, $621.75, $2686.10, and $775.02, respectively, an average of $867.80 per voyage, or $20.91 per month. See *Account Book of the Ship George Howland*. The slop chest contained items such as clothes and tobacco that were sold to the crew during the course of the voyage.

27. Hohman, *American Whaleman*, p. 219.

28. *Account Book of the Ship George Howland*.

29. Howland to Valentine Lewis, July 18, 1860, *Matthew Howland, Letter Book*, mss. 252, 1858–1879, H864, Baker Library.

30. *Account Book of the Ship George Howland*.

31. These rough estimates are derived from Hohman, *American Whaleman*, p. 325, and the Warren and Pearson food price index (Bureau of the Census, *Historical Statistics of the United States, Colonial Times to 1970*, part 1, series E-54 [Washington, D.C., 1975]).

32. See *Account Books, George Howland, Milton, and Callao*.

33. Morgan to Cornelius Howland, Jr., September 24, 1834, *Letter Book: Charles W. Morgan*.

34. Morgan to Reuben Russell, November 1, 1834, *Letter Book: Charles W. Morgan*.

35. Morgan to George H. Dexter, November 21, 1836, *Letter Book: Charles W. Morgan*.

36. Charles Wilkes, *Narrative of the United States Exploring Expedition during the Years 1838, 1839, 1840, 1841, and 1842*, 5 vols. (London and Philadelphia, 1845), 5: 498.

37. Hohman, *American Whaleman*, p. 67.
38. Whipple, *Yankee Whalers*, p. 132.
39. Hohman, *American Whaleman*, p. 67.
40. Merchant marine wages are taken from Stanley Lebergott, *Manpower in Economic Growth: The American Record since 1800* (New York, 1964), app. tables A-21, A-22a, and A-22b, pp. 531–38. Lebergott's data are drawn from the manuscript collections of the Baker Library and of the Essex Institute in Salem, Mass. The records do not, however, provide a complete enumeration of the wages of all the seamen on the voyages included. Thus, for the years 1840–58 and 1866, there are records of 83 voyages, but while there are wage data for able seamen for 82 of those voyages, there are captains' wages for only 34, first mates' wages for 59, and cooks' wages for 63.
41. The fact that the highest first mate's wage is $60 while the best-paid captain received only $35 does not imply that on a given voyage the first mate earned more than the captain. The apparent anomaly can be traced to the spotty nature of the data. The voyage data that yielded the highly paid mates did not include the wages of the captains. In fact, there are no captains' wages reported for any voyage after 1854.
42. Morgan to Reuben Russell, August 27, 1834, *Letter Book: Charles W. Morgan*.
43. L. Davis, R. Gallman, and T. Hutchins, "Managerial Decisions and Productivity Change: The New Bedford Whaling Fleet in the Nineteenth Century," paper presented at the Second World Congress in Cliometrics, Santander, Spain, June 24–27, 1989.
44. Depending on the precise specification, the coefficients are 1.75, 3.17, and 3.49. The first is significant at the 5 percent level, the last two at the 1 percent level. The adjusted R^2s are 0.553, 0.563, and 0.566 respectively. For a similar model, see Table 7.10. For a more thorough discussion of the model, see below.
45. The quotation is from Hohman, *American Whaleman*, p. 239, n. 12. See Charles Enderby, *Proposal for Re-establishing the British Southern Whale Fishery, Through the Medium of a Chartered Company, and in Combination with the Colonization of the Auckland Islands—Revision and Enlargement of a Letter Written to a Mr. T. R. Preston on October 31, 1846* (London, 1847).
46. Captain Frederick Murry observed in 1838 that, exclusive of officers, seven out of every ten men aboard U.S. ships coasting to and from American ports were British, with some mixture of Swedes and Danes, and that one-third of the whalers were probably British. In 1845, Congressman Reed, the chairman of the Committee on Naval Affairs, asserted that 100,000 of the 109,000 men in the Navy and merchant marine were foreigners. Again, in 1845, *Hunts Merchant Magazine* reported that "many believed that two-thirds of our sailors were not native." Lebergott, *Manpower*, p. 26.
47. Charles Nordhoff, *Whaling and Fishing* (New York, 1895), p. 46.
48. Robert Margo and Georgia Villaflor, "The Growth of Wages in Antebellum America: New Evidence," *Journal of Economic History* 47, no. 4 (Dec. 1987): 893–95; Paul David and Peter Solar, "A Bicentenary Contribution to the History of the Cost of Living in America," *Research in Economic History* 2 (1977): 16–17. The whaling wages have been adjusted to include an allowance for room and

board. The data on unskilled labor are from Edith Abbott, "The Wages of Un-skilled Workers in the U.S., 1850–1900," *Journal of Political Economy* 13 (1905): 321–67; those for Massachusetts cotton textile-mill operatives are from Robert Layer, *The Earnings of Cotton Mill Operatives, 1825–1914,* Committee on Research in Economic History (Cambridge, Mass., 1955).

49. In the textile industry it appears that women workers did not receive sub-stantially lower wages than men.

50. Between 1803 and 1840, 2,023 blacks sailed from New Bedford on the 729 voyages surveyed by Martha Putney. She finds that at least 33 boatsteerers and mates were black, as were two whaling captains, Absolm F. Baston (from Nan-tucket) and Pardon Cook (from New Bedford). See Martha Putney, *Black Sailors: Afro-American Merchant Seamen and Whalemen Prior to the Civil War,* Contribu-tions in Afro-American and African Studies no. 103 (New York, 1987), pp. 50–51, 54–55, 125. In one case of a mixed crew, the captain and first mate were killed and the ship was brought back home by the black second mate.

51. The change in real unskilled wages (1840–43 to 1855–58) using the Warren-Pearson wholesale price index as a deflator was +1.5 percent for Margo and Villaflor's unskilled workers and −3.6 percent for Abbott's "all urban unskilled." The changes for the same two series using the Williamson-Lindert consumer price deflator were 0 percent and −3.6 percent respectively; using the implied David-Solar deflator, the changes were +22.2 percent and +11.2 percent. The skill ratios are drawn from Jeffrey Williamson and Peter Lindert, *American Inequality* (New York, 1980), p. 307.

52. Putney, *Black Sailors*, p. 125.

53. Nordhoff, *Whaling and Fishing*, pp. 46, 47, and Hohman, *American Whale-man*, p. 239, n. 12. By "obscure" the author meant "to reduce the saliency of," not "to hide."

54. These averages are the estimated earnings of a greenhand who returned on the vessel on which he sailed (own vessel). They are not comparable to the depen-dent means in the regressions reported in Table 7.9. Those figures are based on the year of sailing (own year).

55. The deflator employed was the David-Solar Index of Consumer Prices. See David and Solar, "Bicentenary Contribution," pp. 16–17. The wage is Own Year (see note 54 above).

56. A one-year lag was chosen for the average value of the catch since it repre-sents the information a potential whaleman was most likely to have and be affected by. For losses, five years were chosen, because of the wide year-to-year variability of losses at sea.

57. The financial risk variable is the standard deviation of the value of the catch of vessels returning from the designated ground in year ($t - 1$). The measure of voyage length is the average interval for vessels returning from the designated ground in ($t - 1$). The measure of "at sea" risk is the standard deviation of the latter interval.

58. A coefficient that in the first model reflects a premium of $0.81 per month declines to less than $0.01 per month in the second model.

59. For a more complete discussion, see Davis, Gallman, and Hutchins, "Pro-

ductivity in American Whaling." The index of total factor productivity is a translog multilateral index. Labor and capital inputs were measured in man-months and ton-months. Land (the stock of whales) was not entered into the index, but was used in the form of lagged independent variables in the regression analysis. See Douglas Caves, Laurits Christensen, and W. Erwin Diewert, "Multilateral Comparisons of Output, Input, and Productivity Using Superlative Index Numbers," *The Economic Journal* 92 (Mar. 1982): 73–86, for a discussion of superlative indexes.

60. These data (on 2,343 voyages) are taken from the Davis, Gallman, Hutchins Tape no. 1. For a more complete description of the data and the sources from which they were drawn, see Davis, Gallman, and Hutchins, "Productivity in American Whaling."

61. Nordhoff, *Whaling and Fishing*, p. 12.

62. Hohman, *American Whaleman*, p. 62. "The question was even injected into the original shipping of a crew in the home port; for one of the reasons for preferring green hands lay in the fact that they were less resourceful in matters relating to desertion." Ibid., p. 66.

63. Hohman, *American Whaleman*, p. 65.

64. H. I. Chapelle, *The Search for Speed under Sail* (New York, 1967), p. 279.

65. Ibid.

66. E. K. Chatterton, *Sailing Ships: The Story of Their Development from the Earliest Times to the Present Day* (London, 1909), p. 266.

67. R. C. McKay, *Some Famous Sailing Ships and Their Builder Donald McKay* (New York, 1928), pp. 213–15, and H. I. Chapelle, *The History of American Sailing Ships* (New York, 1935), p. 290.

68. Claudia Goldin and Kenneth Sokoloff, "Women, Children, and Industrialization in the Early Republic: Evidence from the Manufacturing Census," *Journal of Economic History* 42, no. 4 (Dec. 1982): 755, and pp. 741–44 for a complete discussion of the evidence. See also Goldin and Sokoloff, "The Relative Productivity Hypothesis of Industrialization," *Quarterly Journal of Economics* 99 (Aug. 1984): 461–68.

69. David Moment, "The Business of Whaling in America in the 1850s," *Business History Review* 31 (Autumn 1957): p. 274.

70. Hohman, *American Whaleman*, p. 62.

71. Gerald Williams, "Share Croppers of the Sea: The Whaler's 'Lay' and Events in the Arctic, 1905–1907," *Labor History* 29, no. 1 (Winter 1988): 32, 46, 47.

72. The 30 percent figure assumed by Hohman has a long history. The figure was first given in an article written by J. R. Williams entitled "The Whale Fishery" (*The North American Review* 38 [Jan. 1834]: 105). It was repeated by Joseph Grinnell, *Speech on the Tariff, with Statistical Tables of the Whale Fishery* (1844), p. 9. Hohman found a similar figure (30.3 percent) in his compilation of "a chance sampling of seven voyages for which suitable and accurate figures were available. . . . These voyages were scattered over the period 1805 to 1850." Hohman, "Wages, Risk, and Profits," p. 669. It should be noted that neither Hohman nor others who have argued for the 30 percent figure have included the value of room and board in their determination of the labor share. The estimates that have been made in conjunction with these studies suggest that an adjustment for board alone

would have increased individual earnings by about $3.90 per month in 1840–43 and $5.60 in 1855–58. Given the average length of voyage and value of the catch, the board adjustment should add almost 8 percent to the labor share in 1840–43 and almost 12 percent in 1855–58.

73. Henry George, *Progress and Poverty: An Inquiry into the Cause of Industrial Depression and of Want with Increase of Wealth . . . The Remedy* (New York, 1962), p. 54 (bk. 1, chap. 3).

74. Samuel Eliot Morison, *The Maritime History of Massachusetts, 1783–1860* (Boston and New York, 1921), pp. 320–21; Hohman, *American Whaleman*, p. 224.

75. Williams, "Share Croppers of the Sea," passim. The description of a "Hell-ship" is from Robert Luddock, *Round the Horn Before the Mast* (London, 1893), p. 197.

76. 18 U.S.C.A. 544 still exempts whaling seamen. It provides for protection "except in any case the seamen are by custom or agreement entitled to participate in the profits or results of a cruise or voyage." Interpreted in *Johnson v. Standard Oil of New Jersey* (D.C. Md 1940), 33 F. S. 982. Williams, "Share Croppers of the Sea," passim.

8. Parker: Midwestern Development

1. The role of banks in the region's development before 1860 is realistically discussed in Donald Adams, Jr., "The Role of Banks in the Economic Development of the Old Northwest," in D. C. Klingaman and R. K. Vedder, eds., *Essays in Nineteenth-Century Economic History* (Athens, Ohio, 1975), chap. 9, pp. 208, 246. A companion study for the postbellum period is offered in Gene Smiley, "Postbellum Banking and Financial Markets in the Old Northwest," in D. C. Klingaman and R. K. Vedder, eds., *Essays on the Economy of the Old Northwest* (Athens, Ohio, 1987), chap. 9, pp. 187–224, containing good summaries of the controversies about the national capital market in the recent literature. See also Richard Sylla, *The American Capital Market, 1846–1914* (New York, 1975). The whole period for the midwestern states has been reexamined with use of extensive quantitative data by Hugh Rockoff, "The Free Banking Era, a Reexamination," *Journal of Money, Credit, and Finance* 6 (May 1974): 141–67, and more recently in an informative article by A. J. Rolnick and W. E. Weber, "New Evidence on the Free Banking Era," *American Economic Review* 73 (Dec. 1983): 1080–91. Both studies indicate that the state-chartered and "free" systems worked with much less loss and inconvenience than earlier studies, based only on stories of "wildcat" banks and frauds, had concluded.

2. Bank balance sheets available in the works on the period uniformly show deposits to be a small percentage of total liabilities. See, for example, Fred Merritt, *The Early History of Banking in Iowa* (Iowa City, 1900), with balance sheets from different points in the checkered history of the Miners' Bank of Dubuque (pp. 21, 25–26, 27–28, 41, 50, 52, 69). Although there is great doubt that the full authorization of capital stock was ever paid in, the balance sheets show that at no time did deposits exceed 8 percent of the bank's liabilities. Charles Huntington, *A History of Banking and Currency in Ohio Before the Civil War* (Columbus, 1915), contains some aggregate data and balance sheets for antebellum Ohio (pp. 76, 81, 160, 163, 179, 204, 276–82, 289–90).

3. The Illinois bank incorporation law of 1851 was based on the New York law requiring banks to deposit with the state auditor national or state bonds as backing for their notes. A bank could be forced into liquidation if it failed to redeem its notes. The bill did not rid the state of illegal paper issues as intended; the newly incorporated banks continued to fight in the courts the unchartered institutions that issued currency. The original incorporation law was supplemented in 1853 to provide a heavy penalty for illegal note issue and, due to the cooperation of the board of brokers of New York City, proved largely effective. Notes from Georgia and other states became an important part of the circulating medium after this time, largely through the efforts of Chicago firms that had set up the banks for this purpose. The Illinois banks made concerted efforts to force these institutions into liquidation by presenting their notes for redemption. George Dowrie, *The Development of Banking in Illinois, 1817–1863* (Urbana, Ill., 1913), pp. 135–42, 146.

4. To finance their operations in the winter, Burrows and Pettyman, an Iowa flour mill and pork-packing company, issued checks payable in the spring when they could ship their goods south to market. These checks, as well as the notes of other Iowa firms, circulated as currency. Erling Erickson, *Banking in Frontier Iowa, 1836–1865* (Ames, Iowa, 1971), pp. 71–73. From May 1837 until its voluntary liquidation, the Chicago Marine and Fire Insurance Company, along with many unincorporated Illinois firms, made loans and received deposits despite the prohibitions in the corporation's charter. Its deposit certificates circulated as currency. The Wisconsin Marine and Fire Insurance Company was modeled after the Chicago company, issuing notes, called "George Smith's money," from its incorporation in 1841 until the legislature forced them out of circulation in 1852. Dowrie, *Development of Banking in Illinois*, pp. 129–31.

5. On the National Banking Act, see Davis Dewey, *Financial History of the United States*, 12th ed. (New York, 1936), pp. 326–28; Paul Studenski and Herman Kroos, *Financial History of the United States* (New York, 1963), pp. 154–55. See also Eugene White, *The Regulation and Reform of the American Banking System, 1900–1929* (Princeton, 1983).

6. The following citations from the classic survey by William Ripley, *Railroads: Finance and Organization* (London, 1915), give the flavor of the history as it appeared to the leading railroad economist-historian of the 1920's. "The first railways in the United States were built from the proceeds of subscriptions to capital stock. . . . Even as late as 1868, after new styles in railroad finance had come into vogue, the capital stock of the railways of Ohio considerably exceeded in amount the aggregate of their outstanding bonds" (p. 10). "But no sooner did construction begin to extend into undeveloped territory than a new situation arose. . . . Such enterprises, instead of being solid investments appealing to a substantial local constituency, were essentially speculative. However great might be the local interest, most of the funds, except the land, must be obtained from remote capitalists in the eastern states or in Europe" (p. 11).

After the main lines were built, a railroad's construction company would raise funds, often locally, for branch lines (p. 14). Often an extension was organized as a separate company, the form of organization conditioned on the financial strength of the parent road. The parent company frequently backed the bonds of the local road. Ripley continues, "Many independent short roads and feeders, particularly in prosperous communities like Wisconsin, have been constructed by local enterprise and credit through the activity of farmers, thus seeking an outlet to markets. The right of way costs little; the labor is contributed by the subscribers; and the first light construction is financed by local borrowing. Be the enterprise a little more ambitious or, as in the Southeast, local funds less ample, the aid of city bankers may be necessary. These bankers contribute funds, such as possibly $8,000 per mile in bond, having as equity the labor and right of way put into the property prior to the loan" (pp. 32, 33).

For the development and financing of the extensive interurban electric rail systems, see George Hilton and John Due, *The Electric Interurban Railways in America* (Stanford, 1960), chaps. 1, 6.

7. Increasingly after the 1870's, bonds were sold to banking syndicates for a commission. "Anticipated profits from speculation in land along the proposed right of way were an important inducement to the construction of railroads in the early days. . . . It is indubitable that without the profits from land sales, the construction of railroads would have been greatly delayed in the early days" (Ripley, *Railroads*, pp. 18–19, 135). See Paul Gates, *The Illinois Central Railroad and Its Colonization Work* (Cambridge, Mass., 1934), pp. 26–27 and chap. 4.

8. Smiley, "Postbellum Banking," p. 192; Vincent Carosso, *Investment Banking in America* (Cambridge, Mass., 1970), chap. 2.

9. M. L. Ramsay, *Pyramids of Power: The Story of Roosevelt, Insull and the Utility Wars* (Indianapolis, 1937), pp. 14, 47–49, chaps. 6, 7, 11.

10. Martin Primack, "Land Clearing under Nineteenth-Century Conditions: Some Preliminary Calculations," *Journal of Economic History* 22 (Dec. 1962): 492.

11. Alvin Tostlebe, *Capital in Agriculture: Its Formation and Financing since 1870* (Princeton, 1957), chart 15, p. 155. See the excellent detailed discussion of tenancy as a stage in the "ladder" to full ownership in Allan Bogue, *From Prairie to Corn Belt* (Chicago, 1963), chap. 3, and of mortgaging in chap. 9, pp. 171–81. While taking due note of the importance of eastern moneylenders and of the life insurance companies after 1860, Bogue cites studies of Illinois and Iowa in which "more than half the funds loaned on farm security came from within the state concerned." He points out that the outside funds injected new money into the region (though they later drained it out in the form of interest and principal repayments), whereas the local finance often came from a seller who was willing to receive the sale price in installments (p. 175).

12. Jeffrey Williams, *The Economic Functions of Futures Markets* (Cambridge, 1986), pp. 18–19, 58, and his Yale Ph.D. dissertation (1980) of the same title, pp. 88–100, 119–22.

13. Bruce Phelps, "A Finance Approach to Convertible Money Regimes: A New Interpretation of the Greenback Era" (Ph.D. diss., Yale University, 1985), pp. 83–84, 92, 111, 113.

14. For the period 1820–58, the reserve ratio of the banking system fluctuated between a low of 14 percent in 1856 and a high of 35 percent in 1843. Peter Temin, *The Jacksonian Economy* (New York, 1969), tables 3.3, 5.2, pp. 71, 159.

15. Harry Pierce, "Foreign Investment in American Enterprise," with comments

and discussion, in David Gilchrist and W. David Lewis, eds., *Economic Change in the Civil War Era* (Greenville, Del., 1965), pp. 41–61; Smiley, "Postbellum Banking," sec. 5.

16. Jonathan Hughes, *The Vital Few* (Boston, 1966), chap. 6; Joseph Wall, *Andrew Carnegie* (New York, 1970).

17. Douglass North, *Growth and Welfare in the American Past* (Englewood Cliffs, N.J., 1966), chap. 11, esp. pp. 145–48.

18. Sir John Denham, *Cooper's Hill* (Oxford, 1642), lines 89–92.

19. The financings for the large car-assembly enterprises—Ford, Dodge, Chevrolet, Olds, and all the rest—were shoestring operations in every instance. Just as in the southern textile mills in the 1880's, machinery and parts suppliers, dealers, small local bank loans, the personal funds of partners, and family stockholders bridged the gap until the huge profits were realized for reinvestment. See Lawrence Seltzer, *A Financial History of the Automobile Industry* (Boston, 1928). Margaret Levenstein, *Information Systems and Internal Organization: A Study of the Dow Chemical Company, 1890–1914*, Ph.D. dissertation, Yale University (Jan. 1991), tells a similar story for this large Michigan firm. In Dow's case, the "original accumulation" came from Cleveland capitalists with surplus funds from the lake trade in ore and coal.

20. To explore this hypothesis would, of course, require an extensive research into the evolution of the industrial price structure from 1870 to 1914. I have made at this time only one back-of-the-envelope calculation drawn from the series for steel rails, divided by the commodity price index as given in the U.S. Bureau of the Census, *Historical Statistics of the United States* (Washington, D.C., 1975), ser. E130, E2, E40. Though the real price of rails varied over the period, the trend was clearly downward, as an index of the real prices for the five years at each end of the series attests:

1867 =	100.0	1909 =	27.7
1868 =	97.9	1910 =	26.6
1869 =	85.5	1911 =	28.9
1870 =	77.2	1912 =	27.1
1871 =	77.0	1913 =	26.8

21. Wesley Mitchell, *A History of the Greenbacks* (Chicago, 1903); for the National Banking System as a means of war finance, see pp. 37, 44–46, 103, and 109 there. The first legal-tender act and bankers' objections to this expedient are treated in chap. 2 of Mitchell.

9. Fogel: Political Realignment of the 1850's

1. Charles Beard and Mary Beard, *The Rise of American Civilization* (New York, 1933); Louis Hacker, *The Triumph of American Capitalism* (New York, 1940); Thomas Pressly, *Americans Interpret Their Civil War* (Princeton, 1954).

2. Ulrich Phillips, *American Negro Slavery: A Survey of the Supply, Employment and Control of Negro Labor as Determined by the Plantation Regime* (Baton Rouge, [1918] 1968); and Charles Ramsdell, "The Natural Limits of Slavery Expansion," *Mississippi Valley Historical Review* 16 (1929): 151–71.

3. Avery Craven, *The Coming of the Civil War* (New York, 1942); Eric Foner, *Free Soil, Free Labor, Freemen: The Ideology of the Republican Party Before the Civil War* (New York, 1970). Eugene Genovese, in *The Political Economy of Slavery: Studies in the Economy and Society of the Slave South* (New York, 1961), also raised the two-cultures theme, but applied it to the analysis of southern society.

4. Foner, *Free Soil*, p. 9. Several readers have suggested to me that Foner's argument was more ideological than cultural. Ideology is part of culture, however, and investigating the sources of belief is a central aspect of social anthropology. From an historiographic standpoint, Foner's book is part of the tradition widely referred to as the cultural approach to political history, which includes such books as Marvin Meyers, *The Jacksonian Persuasion: Politics and Belief* (Stanford, 1960); Daniel Walker Howe, *The Political Culture of the American Whigs* (Chicago, 1979); and Jean Baker, *Affairs of Party: The Political Culture of Northern Democrats in the Mid-Nineteenth Century* (Ithaca, N.Y., 1983).

5. Cf. William Riker, *Liberalism Against Populism: A Confrontation Between the Theory of Democracy and the Theory of Social Choice* (San Francisco, 1982).

6. Foner, *Free Soil*; Aileen Kraditor, *Means and Ends in American Abolitionism: Garrison and His Critics on Strategy and Tactics, 1834–1850* (New York, 1970); Richard Sewell, *Ballots for Freedom: Antislavery Politics in the United States, 1837–1860* (New York, 1976); William Cooper, Jr., *The South and the Politics of Slavery, 1828–1856* (Baton Rouge, 1978).

7. Lee Benson, *The Concept of Jacksonian Democracy: New York as a Test Case* (New York, 1969); Ronald Formisano, *The Birth of Mass Political Parties: Michigan, 1827–1861* (Princeton, 1971); Formisano, *Transformation of Political Culture: Massachusetts Parties, 1790s–1840s* (New York, 1983); Paul Kleppner, *The Third Electoral System, 1853–1892: Parties, Voters, and Political Cultures* (Chapel Hill, 1979); Joel Silbey, *The Partisan Imperative: The Dynamics of American Politics Before the Civil War* (New York, 1985); Robert Swierenga, "Ethnoreligious Political Behavior in the Mid-Nineteenth Century: Voting, Values, Cultures," in Mark Noll, ed., *Religion and American Politics: From the Colonial Period to the 1980s* (New York, 1990).

8. Thomas Alexander, *Sectional Stress and Party Strength: A Study of Roll-Call Voting Patterns in the United States House of Representatives, 1836–1860* (Nashville, 1967); Alexander, "Harbinger of the Collapse of the Second Two-Party System: The Free Soil Party of 1848," in Lloyd Ambrosius, ed., *A Crisis of Republicanism: American Politics During the Civil War Era* (Lincoln, Neb., 1990); Joel Silbey, *The Shrine of Party: Congressional Voting Behavior, 1841–1852* (Pittsburgh, 1967); Allan Bogue, *The Earnest Men: Republicans of the Civil War Senate* (Ithaca, N.Y., 1982); Bogue, *The Congressman's Civil War* (Cambridge, 1989); Kleppner, *Third Electoral System*; J. Morgan Kousser, "The Supremacy of Equal Rights: The Struggle Against Racial Discrimination in Antebellum Massachusetts and the Foundations of the Fourteenth Amendment," *Northwestern University Law Review* 82 (1988): 941–1010.

9. Michael Holt, *Forging a Majority: The Formation of the Republican Party in Pittsburgh, 1848–1860* (New Haven, 1969); Holt, "The Antimasonic and Know Nothing Parties," in Arthur Schlesinger, ed., *History of U.S. Political Parties*, vol. 1 (New York, 1973); Holt, "The Politics of Impatience: The Origins of Know-

Nothingism," *Journal of Economic History* 60 (1973): 309–31; Holt, *The Political Crisis of the 1850s* (New York, 1978); Formisano, *Birth of Mass Political Parties*; William Gienapp, "Nativism and the Creation of a Republican Majority in the North Before the Civil War," *Journal of Economic History* 72 (1985): 529–59; Gienapp, *The Origins of the Republican Party, 1852–1856* (New York, 1987); Silbey, *The Partisan Imperative*.

10. Dale Baum, "Know-Nothingism and the Republican Majority in Massachusetts: The Political Realignment of the 1850s," *Journal of Economic History* 64 (1978): 959–86; Robert Fogel, Ralph Galantine, and Richard Manning, *Without Consent or Contract: Evidence and Methods* (New York, 1991), entry 69 (cited hereafter as Fogel, Galantine, and Manning, *Evidence and Methods*). Other recent analyses of economic issues include James Huston, *The Panic of 1857 and the Coming of the Civil War* (Baton Rouge, 1987); Huston, "Economic Change and Political Realignment in Antebellum Pennsylvania," *Pennsylvania Magazine of History and Biography* 113, 3 (1989): 347–95; Charles Calomiris and Larry Schweikart, "The Panic of 1857: Origins, Transmission, and Containment," *Journal of Economic History* 51 (1991): 807–34. The discussion of economic issues by Allan Nevins in *The Ordeal of the Union*, vol. 3, *The Emergence of Lincoln, Volume I: Douglas, Buchanan, and Party Chaos, 1857–1859* (New York, 1950), chap. 7, remains very useful, as Huston has recently emphasized.

11. John Commons, David Saposs, Helen Sumner, E. B. Mittelman, H. E. Hoagland, John Andrews, and Selig Perlman, *History of Labor in the United States*, 2 vols. (New York, 1918); Norman Ware, *The Industrial Worker, 1840–1860: The Reaction of American Industrial Society to the Advance of the Industrial Revolution* (Boston, 1924). Of the more recent historians, see David Montgomery, "The Shuttle and the Cross," *Journal of Social History* 5 (1972): 411–46; Edward Pessen, *Riches, Class, and Power Before the Civil War* (Lexington, Ky., 1973); Pessen, *Jacksonian America: Society, Personality, and Politics* (Homewood, Ill., 1978); Michael Feldberg, *The Philadelphia Riots of 1844: A Study of Ethnic Conflict*, Contributions to American History no. 43 (Westport, Conn., 1975); John Ashworth, *"Agrarians" and "Aristocrats": Party Political Ideology in the United States, 1837–1846* (Cambridge, [1983] 1987); Sean Wilentz, *Chants Democratic: New York City and the Rise of the American Working Class, 1788–1850* (New York, 1984); Wilentz, "Land, Labor, and Politics in the Age of Jackson," *Reviews in American History* (June 1986): 200–209; Steven Ross, *Workers on the Edge: Work, Leisure, and Politics in Industrializing Cincinnati, 1788–1840* (New York, 1985).

12. The argument in the remainder of this section draws on Robert Fogel, *Without Consent or Contract: The Rise and Fall of American Slavery* (New York, 1989), chaps. 9 and 10. See also Fogel, Galantine, and Manning, *Evidence and Methods*, especially the introduction and entries 15, 60, 62, 68, and 69.

13. On the timing of recessions in the North, see Fogel, *Without Consent or Contract*, chaps. 9 and 10. On the timing of the southern recessions, see ibid., pp. 92–98; Fogel, Galantine, and Manning, *Evidence and Methods*, entries 20–28, 36, 37; and Laurence Kotlikoff, "Quantitative Description of the New Orleans Slave Market, 1804 to 1862," in Robert Fogel and Stanley Engerman, eds., *Without Consent or Contract: Markets and Production: Technical Papers*, vol. 1 (New York,

1991) (hereafter cited as Fogel and Engerman, *Technical Papers*). See also Yasukichi Yasuba, *Birth Rates of the White Population in the United States, 1800–1860* (Baltimore, 1961), chap. 3.

14. Fogel, *Without Consent or Contract*, pp. 350–51, 370–71, and the sources cited there.

15. Ibid., pp. 316–19; Jeter Allen Isley, *Horace Greeley and the Republican Party, 1853–1861* (Princeton, 1947); Glyndon Van Deusen, *Thurlow Weed: Wizard of the Lobby* (Boston, 1947); Van Deusen, *Horace Greeley: Nineteenth-Century Crusader* (New York, 1964); Van Deusen, *William Henry Seward* (New York, 1967); Gienapp, *Origins of the Republican Party*, pp. 123, 251–52, 287–90.

16. Gienapp, "Nativism," pp. 529–59; Gienapp, *Origins of the Republican Party*; Robert Fogel, "Problems in Modeling Complex Dynamic Interactions: The Political Realignment of the 1850s," *Economics and Politics* 4 (1992): 215–53.

17. Fogel, *Without Consent or Contract*, pp. 347–54, 375–77, 380, 384–85; Silbey, *Partisan Imperative*, chap. 7.

18. Cited by Sewell, *Ballots for Freedom*, p. 290.

19. Robert Fogel and Stanley Engerman, *Time on the Cross: The Economics of American Negro Slavery*, 2 vols. (Boston, 1974), chap. 5; Isley, *Horace Greeley*, esp. chaps. 7 and 9; and Fogel, *Without Consent or Contract*, pp. 385–86.

20. It is worth noting that the upswing in the northern economy that began in late 1858 and continued through 1860 took place despite the continuing decline in midwestern railroad construction shown in Figure 9.1.

21. Fogel, *Without Consent or Contract*, pp. 104–7, 343–44, 347–54.

22. Roy Robbins, *Our Landed Heritage: The Public Domain, 1776–1936* (Lincoln, Neb., 1962), pp. 193–95; Fogel, *Without Consent or Contract*, pp. 316–19, 346–52, 363–65; James McPherson, *The Battle Cry of Freedom: The Civil War Era* (New York, 1988), pp. 193–95.

23. Baum, "Know-Nothingism," pp. 959–86; Fogel, Galantine, and Manning, *Evidence and Methods*, entry 69. See Formisano, *Transformation*, for a somewhat different view.

24. Fred Bateman and James Foust, "A Sample of Rural Households Selected from the 1860 Manuscript Censuses," *Agricultural History* 48 (1974): 75–93. Cf. Jeremy Atack and Fred Bateman, *To Their Own Soil: Agriculture in the Antebellum North* (Ames, Iowa, 1987); Jon Moen, "Essays on the Labor Force and Labor Force Participation Rates: The United States from 1860–1950" (Ph.D. thesis, University of Chicago, 1987).

25. For the numerous occupations included in each of the first five occupational categories, see Nathaniel Wilcox, "A Note on the Occupational Distribution of the Urban United States in 1860," in Fogel, Galantine, and Manning, *Evidence and Methods*, entry 63. See entry 64 and notes to table 65.1 in the same volume for a description of the procedures used to develop totals for the whole North from the data in the Moen and Bateman and Foust samples.

26. Wilcox, "Occupational Distribution."

27. Fogel, Galantine, and Manning, *Evidence and Methods*, entries 69, tables 69.6 and 69.39; 60, table 60.9; and 63, tables 63.11–14.

28. Computed from the data in Table 9.1; in U.S. Bureau of the Census, *His-*

torical Statistics of the United States, Colonial Times to 1970, Bicentennial ed., pts. 1 and 2 (Washington, D.C., 1975), table 1, p. 22; and in Fogel, Galantine, and Manning, *Evidence and Methods,* tables 63.11–14.

29. Grist and lumber mills, stone quarrying and coal mining, and charcoal production alone accounted for 117,689 male workers in the North in 1860. By themselves, these five industries accounted for about 9 percent of the total nonagricultural rural labor force (U.S. Census Bureau, *Census of Agriculture in 1860* (Washington, D.C., 1865), pp. 677–711.

30. Fogel, Galantine, and Manning, *Evidence and Methods,* table 69.35.

31. Thomas Weiss, "U.S. Labor Force Estimates and Economic Growth: 1800 to 1860," in Robert Gallman and John Wallis, eds., *The Standard of Living in Early Nineteenth-Century America* (Chicago, 1992), table 5. The analysis in this paragraph, combined with the information in Table 9.5, implies that about 43 percent of the natives born of native parents in the electorate of 1860 consisted of nonfarm workers.

32. Baum, "Know-Nothingism," pp. 959–86; Fogel, Galantine, and Manning, *Evidence and Methods,* entry 69; see Formisano, *Transformation,* for a somewhat different view.

33. See Fogel, Galantine, and Manning, *Evidence and Methods,* entry 60, especially tables 60.5, 60.6, and 60.9, for the sources and methods of estimation.

34. See Fogel, Galantine, and Manning, *Evidence and Methods,* entry 69, p. 560, for details on the construction of Table 9.3.

35. Robert Fogel, Stanley Engerman, James Trussell, Roderick Floud, Clayne Pope, and Larry Wimmer, "The Economics of Mortality in North America, 1650–1910: A Description of a Research Project," *Historical Methods* 11 (1978): 75–109; Edwin Gaustad, *Historical Atlas of Religion in America* (New York, 1962).

36. See Fogel, Galantine, and Manning, *Evidence and Methods,* entry 69, pp. 562–67, for details on the construction of Table 9.4.

37. About 2,059,000 Old Americans voted in the North in 1860 (see Table 9.5). If the Democratic Party had retained their 1852 share of the votes of this constituency, they would have received about 997,000 votes from Old Americans in 1860 instead of 621,000. Hence, about 38 percent of Old Americans switched away from the Democrats between the two elections.

38. The figures for the 1852 and 1860 elections are from Fogel, Galantine, and Manning, *Evidence and Methods,* tables 69.6 and 69.7. The figures for the 1844 election were derived using the sources and procedures described on pp. 558–69 in the same source. See especially pp. 562–63 and the notes to tables 69.37–40.

39. See Ralph Galantine, "The Roots of Political Realignment Between 1852 and 1860: An Econometric Examination" (Ph.D. dissertation, University of Chicago, forthcoming).

40. Robert Fogel, *Railroads and American Economic Growth: Essays in Econometric History* (Baltimore, 1964), p. 128.

41. Richard Easterlin, "Regional Income Trends, 1840–1950," in Seymour Harris, ed., *American Economic History* (New York, 1961); Robert Gallman, "Gross National Product in the United States, 1834–1909," in Dorothy Brady, ed., *Output, Employment, and Productivity in the United States after 1800,* Studies in Income and Wealth 30 (New York, 1966).

42. See, for example, Albert Fishlow, *American Railroads and the Transformation of the Antebellum Economy* (Cambridge, Mass., 1965); Paul David, "The Growth of Real Product in the United States Before 1840: New Evidence, Controlled Conjectures," *Journal of Economic History* 27 (1967): 151–97; Stanley Engerman, "The Economic Impact of the Civil War," *Explorations in Economic History*, 2d ser., 3 (Spring/Summer 1966): 176–99; Engerman, "The Effect of Slavery on the Southern Economy," *Explorations in Entrepreneurial History* 4 (1967): 71–97; Lance Davis and H. Louis Stettler III, "The New England Textile Industry, 1825–1860: Trends and Fluctuations," in Brady, ed., *Output, Employment, and Productivity*; Robert Zevin, "The Growth of Cotton Textile Production after 1815," in Robert Fogel and Stanley Engerman, eds., *The Reinterpretation of American Economic History* (New York, 1971); Lance Davis, Richard Easterlin, William Parker, Dorothy Brady, Albert Fishlow, Robert Gallman, Stanley Lebergott, Robert Lipsey, Douglass North, Nathan Rosenberg, Eugene Smolensky, and Peter Temin, *American Economic Growth: An Economist's History of the United States* (New York, 1972); David Klingaman, "Individual Wealth in Ohio in 1860," in David Klingaman and Richard Vedder, eds., *Essays in Nineteenth-Century Economic History: The Old Northwest* (Athens, Ohio, 1975); Jeffrey Williamson, "American Prices and Urban Inequality since 1820," *Journal of Economic History* 36 (1976): 303–33; Paul David and Peter Solar, "A Bicentenary Contribution to the History of the Cost of Living in America," *Research in Economic History* 2 (1977): 1–80; Robert Fogel, *Ten Lectures on the New Economic History* (Tokyo, 1977) (in Japanese).

43. The basic time series on U.S. stature and an early time series of e°_{10} based on period life tables are reported in Robert Fogel, "Nutrition and the Decline in Mortality since 1700: Some Preliminary Findings," in Stanley Engerman and Robert Gallman, eds., *Long-Term Factors in American Economic Growth* (Chicago, 1986). Several additional time series on life expectation based on an improved data set and using cohort as well as period life tables are reported in Clayne Pope, "Adult Mortality in America Before 1900: A View from Family Histories," in Claudia Goldin and Hugh Rockoff, eds., *Strategic Factors in Nineteenth-Century American Economic History* (Chicago, 1992).

44. Barbara McCutcheon, "An Exploration into the Causes of the Growth of Per Capita Income in the North, 1840–1860," in Fogel, Galantine, and Manning, *Evidence and Methods*.

45. Some of the material in the next eight paragraphs is from Fogel, Galantine, and Manning, *Evidence and Methods*, entry 67. Differences with entry 67 reflect improvements in the wage series and the price deflators that are reported in Claudia Goldin and Robert Margo, "Wages, Prices, and Labor Markets," in Goldin and Rockoff, *Strategic Factors*.

46. Stanley Engerman and Robert Gallman, "U.S. Economic Growth, 1783–1860," *Research in Economic History* 8 (1983): 1–46.

47. Robert Margo and Georgia Villaflor, "The Growth of Wages in Antebellum America: New Evidence," *Journal of Economic History* 47 (1987): 873–95.

48. Goldin and Margo, "Wages, Prices, and Labor Markets."

49. Some locations at the frontier where the army employed a relatively large proportion of the civilian labor force were excluded from the construction of the wage series.

50. Margo and Villaflor, "Growth of Wages," pp. 873–95. Cf. Robert Margo, "Wages and Prices During the Antebellum Period: A Survey and New Evidence," in Gallman and Wallis, eds., *Standard of Living*.

51. Van Deusen, *Horace Greeley*, pp. 31–32.

52. See Fogel, Galantine, and Manning, *Evidence and Methods*, entry 66, for further details on the collapse of railroad construction. On the collapse of the residential construction boom, see Manuel Gottlieb, "Building in Ohio Between 1837 and 1914," in Brady, ed., *Output, Employment, and Productivity*, pp. 243–80.

53. Thomas Senior Berry, *Western Prices Before 1861: A Study of the Cincinnati Market* (Cambridge, Mass., 1943), index A.

54. Margo and Villaflor, "Growth of Wages," pp. 873–95; Goldin and Margo, "Wages, Prices, and Labor Markets." The version of the Berry index used by Goldin and Margo differs somewhat from that shown in Figure 9.3 because of the omission of nonconsumption items. If I had used Berry index A, there would have been a 35 percent decline in real wages.

55. The collapse of the northern construction boom (both railroad and other construction) threw about 280,000 construction workers onto northern labor markets in 1854 and 1855, which was about 10 percent of the northern labor force in 1853. The sources for these estimates and the reasons why most of the displaced workers could not have been absorbed until after 1855 without displacing other workers are discussed below. In the computation in the text, I assumed that in 1853 the Midwest was close to full employment, and that between 1853 and 1855 midwestern unemployment increased from 3 to 15 percent. For reasons discussed below, I believe that the assumption that midwestern unemployment only increased by 12 percentage points between 1853 and 1855 biases the computation against my argument. See note 72 below for the sources and procedures used to estimate construction layoffs.

56. See Fogel, *Without Consent or Contract*, pp. 356–59 and the sources cited there.

57. In this calculation I assumed that the wages of deskilled artisans in the Midwest fell from the average wage of artisans to the average wage of ordinary labor, using the Margo and Villaflor ("Growth of Wages," pp. 893–94) figures for 1851–56.

58. This computation is 0.83 × 0.88 × 0.95 = 0.69, where the first left-hand number represents the price effect, the second represents the unemployment effect, and the third represents the deskilling effect.

59. Cf. Oscar Handlin, *Boston's Immigrants, 1790–1880: A Study in Acculturation* (Cambridge, Mass., 1979); Robert Ernst, *Immigrant Life in New York City, 1825–1863* (New York, 1949); Holt, *Forging a Majority*; Wilentz, *Chants Democratic*.

60. This section is from Fogel, Galantine, and Manning, *Evidence and Methods*, entry 61.

61. Jeffrey Williamson and Peter Lindert, *American Inequality: A Macroeconomic History* (New York, 1980); Ethel Hoover, "Retail Prices after 1850," in William Parker, ed., *Trends in the American Economy in the Nineteenth Century* (Princeton, 1960); Dorothy Brady, "Relative Prices in the Nineteenth Century," *Journal of Economic History* 24 (1964): 145–203; Brady, "Consumption and Style of Life," in

Davis, Easterlin, and Parker, eds., *American Economic Growth*; David and Solar, "Bicentenary Contribution"; Stanley Lebergott, *Manpower in Economic Growth: The American Record since 1800* (New York, 1964); Donald Adams, Jr., "The Standard of Living During American Industrialization: Evidence from the Brandywine Region, 1800–1860," *Journal of Economic History* 42 (1982): 903–17.

62. Handlin, *Boston's Immigrants*; Ernst, *Immigrant Life*; Ross, *Workers*; John Commons, Ulrich Phillips, Eugene Gilmore, Helen Sumner, and John Andrews, eds., *A Documentary History of American Industrial Society*, 10 vols. (Cleveland, 1910), vol. 1; Commons, Saposs, et al., *History of Labor*, vol. 1; Edith Abbott, ed., *Historical Aspects of the Immigration Problem: Selected Documents* (Chicago, 1926); John Griscom, *The Sanitary Condition of the Laboring Class of New York, with Suggestions for Its Improvement* (New York, [1845] 1970); New York State Legislature, Assembly, *Report of the Select Committee Appointed to Examine into the Condition of Tenement Houses in New York and Brooklyn*, 80th sess., vol. 3, no. 205 (Albany, 1857).

63. Hoover, "Retail Prices," p. 174.

64. Lebergott, *Manpower*, pp. 341–43.

65. U.S. Bureau of the Census, *Eighth Census of the United States: Population* (Washington, D.C., 1864).

66. Cf. Fogel, "Nutrition," pp. 502–5.

67. McCutcheon, "Exploration," table 68.1.

68. Ibid.; and U.S. Bureau of the Census, *Historical Statistics*, p. 22.

69. See Kenneth Sokoloff, "Productivity Growth in Manufacturing During Early Industrialization: Evidence from the American Northeast, 1820 to 1860," in Engerman and Gallman, *Long-Term Factors*, pp. 679–736, on the rate of growth of capital and total factor productivity.

70. Other possible upward and downward biases in the Margo-Villaflor-Goldin index are discussed in Margo, "Wages and Prices."

71. To the extent that there is deskilling, there is a change in the structure of occupations that will not be captured by changes in indexes of specific daily wages. An adjustment must be made for changes in weights across wage rates in specific occupations. The role of such changes in weights and the manner of adjusting for them are described in Fogel, Galantine, and Manning, *Evidence and Methods*, entries 40 and 68.

72. In 1850, the total value of nonfarm structures was 3.4 times that of railroad structures. The labor share of construction was approximately the same in railroads and in residential construction, so that the total layoffs in the overall construction industry were approximately 3.4 times layoffs in railroad construction. On the labor share of construction in railroads and nonrailroads, see Fogel, Galantine, and Manning, *Evidence and Methods*, entry 66. The ratio of total construction to railroad construction c. 1850 was computed from Raymond Goldsmith, "The Growth of Reproducible Wealth of the United States of America from 1805 to 1950," in Simon Kuznets, ed., *Income and Wealth of the United States: Trends and Structure*, International Association for Research in Income and Wealth, Income and Wealth Series 2 (Baltimore, 1952), table 5, pp. 317–20. Total nonfarm capital consisted of lines 11 and 15. It was assumed that of the $745 million in nonrailroad, nonresidential capital, 30 percent was in either inventories or consumer durables. See note 74 below for the method of estimating the total nonfarm labor force in 1853.

73. Berry, *Western Prices*, p. 268; Davis and Stetler, "New England Textile Industry," table 4, p. 221; William Lazonick and Thomas Brush, "The 'Horndal Effect' in Early U.S. Manufacturing," *Explorations in Economic History* 22 (1985): 53–96; New York (State) Committee on Canals, *Report of the Committee on Canals of New York State 1899–1900*, table 26, p. 181.

74. The estimates in this paragraph were developed from a simulation model similar to that described in Fogel, Galantine, and Manning, *Evidence and Methods*, entry 60, except that the model applies to the entire northern nonfarm labor force, and not just males age 20 or over. Weiss's estimates of the northern nonfarm labor force in 1860 was split into native and foreign-born using the data in ibid., entries 63 and 65. Estimates of new immigrants entering the labor force were based on the immigration series reported in U.S. Bureau of the Census, *Historical Statistics*, p. 106. It was assumed that 8 percent of these immigrants left the country or died before entering the labor force, and that 86 percent of the remainder settled in the North. Immigrants who had entered the U.S. labor force were assumed to leave it (through death or retirement) at a rate of 2.2 percent per annum. The bases for the last three assumptions are set forth in Fogel, Galantine, and Manning, *Evidence and Methods*, entries 60 and 69. The labor-force participation rate of immigrants in the North, 52 percent, was computed from ibid., entry 63, and the Bateman-Foust sample. The last two sources also yielded the estimate that about 80 percent of foreign-born workers in the North entered the nonfarm sector. Consistency requirements of the model implied that natives in the northern nonfarm labor force increased at an annual rate of 2.93 percent between 1850 and 1860. The last figure includes natural increase plus net in-migration.

75. Weiss's figures ("U.S. Labor Force Estimates," tables 5 and 13) indicate that between 1850 and 1860, the northern agricultural labor force increased at an annual rate of 2.67 percent per annum. The natural rate of increase in the agricultural labor force was about 2.2 percent (Fogel, Galantine, and Manning, *Evidence and Methods*, entry 60), which implies a net shift into northern agriculture of about 128,000 workers over the decade. Even in the unlikely event that this entire net shift took place in 1854 and 1855, and that it came exclusively from the North, it would represent only about a quarter of the job seekers. Hence, although agriculture may have aided in the absorption of the unemployed, most were eventually absorbed into the nonfarm sector.

76. The Margo-Villaflor-Goldin series extends only to 1856. For 1857–60 I used the series in Williamson, "American Prices," pp. 303–33.

10. J. M. Gallman: Entrepreneurial Experiences

1. Thomas Cochran, "Did the Civil War Retard Industrialization?" *Mississippi Valley Historical Review* 48 (Sept. 1961): 197–210. Some of the material contained in this essay appeared in J. Matthew Gallman, *Mastering Wartime: A Social History of Philadelphia During the Civil War* (New York, 1990).

2. For an excellent recent survey of the literature, see Patrick O'Brien, *The Economic Effects of the American Civil War* (London, 1988). For two other review essays, see Stanley Engerman, "The Economic Impact of the Civil War," *Explorations in Entrepreneurial History* (now *Explorations in Economic History*) 3 (Spring 1966):

176–99, and Harry Scheiber, "Economic Change in the Civil War Era: An Analysis of Recent Studies," *Civil War History* 11 (Dec. 1965): 396–411. Also see Ralph Andreano, ed., *The Economic Impact of the American Civil War* (Cambridge, Mass., 1962), and David Gilchrist and W. David Lewis, eds., *Economic Change in the Civil War Era* (Greenville, Del., 1965). Cochran's initial article and much of what followed relied on the data compiled by Robert Gallman. See Gallman, "Commodity Output 1839–1899," in *Trends in the American Economy in the Nineteenth Century*, vol. 24 of *Studies in Income and Wealth* (Princeton, 1961).

3. For an analysis of the impact of a different sort of wartime legislation, see Jeffrey Williamson, "Watersheds and Turning Points: Conjectures on the Long-Term Impact of Civil War Financing," *Journal of Economic History* 34 (Sept. 1974): 636–60.

4. On the study of nineteenth-century economic growth and its application to modern developmental economics, see Barry Poulson, "Economic History and Economic Development: An American Perspective," in this volume. The implications of military spending for modern economic development are a source of continuing discussion. See, for instance, John Nef, *War and Human Progress: An Essay on the Rise of Industrial Civilization* (Cambridge, Mass., 1950); Claudia Goldin, "War," in Glenn Porter, ed., *Encyclopedia of American Economic History*, 3 vols. (New York, 1980), 3: 935–57; Saadet Deger and Somnath Sen, "Military Expenditure Spin-off and Economic Development," *Journal of Development Economics* 13 (Aug.–Oct. 1983): 67–83; James Cypher, "Military Spending, Technical Change, and Economic Growth: A Disguised Form of Industrial Policy?" *Journal of Economic Issues* 21 (Mar. 1987): 33–59; Paul Kennedy, *The Rise and Fall of the Great Powers: Economic Change and Military Conflict from 1500 to 2000* (New York, 1987), pp. 444–46 and passim. For an analysis of the relationship between military spending and private investment in recent American history, see Michael Edelstein, "What Price Cold War? Military Expenditures and Private Investment in the United States, 1890–1980," *Cambridge Journal of Economics* (forthcoming).

5. For a discussion of Philadelphia's antebellum and wartime economy, see Gallman, *Mastering Wartime*, chaps. 10 and 11; chap. 12 there contains a broader analysis of the evidence from the R. G. Dun and Company reports.

6. Sydney Ratner, James Soltow, and Richard Sylla, *The Evolution of the American Economy* (New York, 1979), p. 230. Also see James Norris, *R. G. Dun & Co., 1841–1900: The Development of Credit-Reporting in the Nineteenth Century* (Westport, Conn., 1978). The Philadelphia branch of the Mercantile Agency opened in 1845. The records of R. G. Dun and Company are housed in the R. G. Dun and Company Collection, Baker Library, Harvard University Graduate School of Business.

7. These firms were identified by scanning the twelve folio volumes from Philadelphia with at least some cases spanning the war years. This "sample" is flawed in two ways. First, it is impossible to be sure that all such reports were identified. Second, we cannot be sure that R. G. Dun's reporters noted every war contractor.

8. This sample includes all businesses that were established after 1855 or were in operation during the war years appearing on every twentieth page of the twelve "Philadelphia" volumes. Most of the quantitative comparisons in this essay will focus on the cases that existed during the war years. For a more detailed discussion of the sampling procedure, see Gallman, *Mastering Wartime*, appendix.

9. The R. G. Dun and Company data also offer small pieces of information relevant to the discussion of the importance of military procurement for technological development. For an excellent entry into the extensive scholarship on military technology, see Merritt Roe Smith, ed., *Military Enterprise and Technological Change: Perspectives on the American Experience* (Cambridge, Mass., 1985). For an application of this approach to an individual enterprise, see Merritt Roe Smith, *Harper's Ferry Arsenal and the New Technology* (Ithaca, N.Y., 1977).

10. Though it would be interesting to compare the characteristics of contractors and subcontractors, the R. G. Dun and Company data do not consistently differentiate between the two. On the contracting system, see Russell Weigley, *Quartermaster General of the Union Army: A Biography of Montgomery C. Meigs* (New York, 1959), and Gallman, *Mastering Wartime*, pp. 283–91.

11. R. G. Dun and Company Collection, Baker Library, Harvard University Graduate School of Business (hereafter RGD), Pennsylvania vol. 131: 275, 131: 284NN, 131: 284W, 139: 231, 140: 171, 141: 84.

12. RGD 134: 557, 136: 527, 133: 183, 140: 180.

13. RGD 136: 495, 136: 509, 136: 528, 133: 183.

14. RGD 139: 51.

15. RGD 135: 204.

16. For cases of businesses turning to sutling, see RGD 138: 11, 131: 270, 136: 394, and 137: 715.

17. These figures are partly a product of the estimation procedure, which typically evaluated firms based on their 1864 worth and therefore inflated the value of prosperous war contractors.

18. Nearly half (220 of 463) of the firms in the general sample with identifiable types of enterprises were either retailers or hoteliers. Gallman, *Mastering Wartime*, p. 308.

19. Philadelphia's wartime building rates indicate a dramatic decline in retail-store building compared to the five prewar years (387 new stores between 1856 and 1860; 176 between 1861 and 1865). New factory building increased, however, from 159 between 1856 and 1860 to 259 between 1861 and 1865. The latter increase may reflect the expansion of existing establishments rather than the formation of new manufacturing enterprises. See Gallman, *Mastering Wartime*, pp. 274–76.

20. RGD 141: 21, 141: 147, 141: 238.

21. RGD 140: 157. In 1863 Hochstadter took on an equal partner, and in 1866 they added several other new names. By early 1866, the company was worth over $50,000.

22. RGD 141: 11.

23. Presumably war contracting directed some investment away from nonmilitary activities, but the overall decline in new business starts, coupled with the disproportionate number of new firms among military contractors, could indicate that entrepreneurs interested in founding businesses saw few openings in the nonmilitary arena.

24. "Abstracts of Contracts, 1862–1864," no. 2226, RG 92, National Archives, Philadelphia Branch. This phenomenon is discussed more fully in Gallman, *Mastering Wartime*, p. 291.

25. Although it is useful to compare the frequency of different sorts of qualitative comments, we should not assume that all other firms experienced "normal" years. The R. G. Dun agents did not always file annual reports on each firm. Table 10.4 only measures those occasions when agents chose to make unusual comments.

26. The data in Table 10.4 are not conclusive on these points because the reports do not always identify when a firm began doing government work. Therefore, a firm that rose before securing a contract (or without much aid from the contract) would be included in this table. The reports often attributed renewed success to war contracts, however.

27. RGD 134: 545, 134: 645, 139: 131.

28. Of course, the R. G. Dun reporters might have been more likely to mention businesses with southern ties that had run into troubles because of those connections.

29. RGD 132: 471, 137: 657, 137: 612.

30. RGD 131: 284WW, 135: 38, 135: 172.

31. RGD 132: 381, 136: 516, 136: 393.

32. RGD 135: 320C, 133: 296K, 136: 585.

33. RGD 133: 296BB, 137: 455, 141: 98.

34. RGD 137: 507.

35. RGD 140: 156, 141: 201.

36. Firms went out of business for many reasons. Although the terms "failure" and "out of business" will be used interchangeably, some of the firms listed on this table closed their doors without running into financial difficulties, and others stayed in business despite continual problems. In Table 10.5, a firm is listed as "out of business" when one of the following occurred: the business failed; the owner or owners sold out; the owner died (if there were no partners); the establishment moved out of the city; or, in a few cases, a struggling firm only survived when a new partner stepped in with a substantial amount of capital. Conversely, in the following situations, firms were not listed as "out of business": when new partners joined established businesses (even though the name may have changed); when firms relocated within the city; when establishments lost credit judgments or suspended payments but stayed in business.

37. The estimated cases for the final year occur when there is more than one year between the entry noting that the firm was out of operation and the previous entry. If the firm was healthy in one entry and reported as "out of business" in the next, the estimated final year is the midpoint between the two entries. If the next-to-last entry reported that the firm was in trouble, the "final year" was recorded as the year *after* the next-to-last entry.

38. See Gallman, *Mastering Wartime*, pp. 300–308, for a discussion of the relationship between both age and size and business failure.

39. All figures include only firms with known or estimated final dates. Note that by including all 1861 and 1865 failures, the data cover roughly three prewar months and eight postwar months.

40. RGD 140: 152.

41. RGD 140: 142.

42. RGD 141: 61.

43. RGD 131: 36, 131: 121, 132: 603, 132: 431.

44. RGD 134: 603.

45. *"The Rich Men of Philadelphia"—Income Tax of the Residents of Philadelphia and Bucks County for the Year Ending April 30, 1865* (Philadelphia, 1865).

46. See Gallman, *Mastering Wartime*, pp. 324–26. In the course of the war, the resourceful Hunter profited from the government's demand for uniforms, railroads, shipping, and coal, while also trading in Treasury notes.

47. RGD 132: 481, 132: 583, 133: 138, 131: 284W, 137: 416, 137: 554.

48. RGD 132: 623, 133: 285, 136: 380.

49. RGD 132: 456, 140: 156, 136: 516.

50. RGD 138: 15.

51. RGD 138: 15, 132: 495, 140: 165.

52. RGD 134: 626, 142: 6, 141: 201. Gray's company went out of business in 1867; the Cooper Arms Manufacturing Company survived only until 1872.

53. Note that these figures include failures in 1865, the final year of the war.

54. RGD 134: 630; 139: 81.

55. RGD 134: 630, 139: 81, 134: 644, 138: 87.

56. RGD 141: 11, 141: 13.

57. RGD 136: 325. The R. G. Dun reports include several examples of partnerships valued at $100,000 and more that closed in the years after the war with no reported difficulties.

58. See Gallman, *Mastering Wartime*, pp. 257–65.

59. In several cases, wartime sutlers had experienced similar hardships in 1861. See RGD 138: 11, 131: 270, 136: 394.

60. Although government demand determined the mix of goods produced, entrepreneurial choices helped guarantee that the individual firms' adjustments involved minimal instability.

61. And some businesses profited from the reduced competition as firms turned to government contracting. For instance, Edmund Hindle and Son's Good Intent Factory enjoyed unusual profits when their chief machine-making competitor turned to war work. RGD 135: 145.

11. Callahan: The Nineteenth-Century Silver Movement

1. One example of this is Robert Gallman's work on the pace of American economic growth during the nineteenth century. His analytical framework, like that of Simon Kuznets and others, has focused on real variables, such as growth in the capital stock and in the labor force. The role of nominal variables, such as prices and the money supply, has been taken for granted and viewed as operating only in the background.

2. A full discussion of this issue is found in the editor's introduction, Barry Eichengreen, *The Gold Standard in Theory and History* (New York, 1985).

3. Economists who have proposed returning to the gold standard include Robert Mundell, Paul Craig Roberts, and Arthur Laffer.

4. There have been numerous alternative methods used to estimate the extent of uncertainty in the United States over the latter part of the nineteenth century.

Many of these use information contained in financial asset prices. For example, Robert Barsky, "The Fisher Hypothesis and the Forecastability and Persistence of Inflation," *Journal of Monetary Economics* 19 (Jan. 1987): 3–24, and Peter Garber, "Nominal Contracts in a Bimetallic Standard," *American Economic Review* 76 (Dec. 1986): 1012–30.

5. The evidence supporting this conclusion is reported in Benjamin Klein, "Our New Monetary Standard: The Measurement and Effects of Price Uncertainty, 1880–1973," *Economic Inquiry* 13 (Dec. 1975): 461–84, and Klein, "The Measurement of Long- and Short-Term Price Uncertainty: A Moving Regression and Time Series Analysis," *Economic Inquiry* 16 (July 1978): 438–52. Additional time-series evidence is presented by Allan Meltzer, "Some Evidence on the Comparative Uncertainty Experienced under Different Monetary Regimes," in Colin Campbell and William Dougan, eds., *Alternative Monetary Regimes* (Baltimore, 1986), pp. 122–53, and by Meltzer and Saranna Robinson, "Stability under the Gold Standard in Practice," in Michael Bordo, ed., *Money, History and International Finance* (Chicago, 1989), pp. 163–95.

6. Klein, "Measurement," and Meltzer, "Some Evidence."

7. The types of disturbances are transitory shocks, permanent shocks to the price level, and permanent shocks to the rate of change of the price level.

8. This constraint rules out the classical approach to parameter estimation, which incorporates all of the data in the sample.

9. Meltzer identifies the six regimes as: 1890–1914 (gold standard, no central bank), 1915–31 (gold exchange standard with a central bank), 1931–41 (mixed system with no clear standard), 1942–51 (pegged interest rates), 1951–71 (Bretton Woods), and 1971–80 (fluctuating exchange rates). See his "Some Evidence."

10. In addition to the moving-regression method employed by Klein and the MSKF estimates used by Meltzer and by Meltzer and Robinson, the autoregressive conditional heteroscedasticity (ARCH) model was used to estimate uncertainty. The strength of the ARCH approach is that it formally hypothesizes a changing variance, but its estimates of uncertainty should not be considered the best. They are based on all the information in the sample, and therefore lack a desirable property of a forecast and an uncertainty statistic, namely, that it be ex ante. Empirically, the ARCH effect was statistically significant for the gold-standard era only when the estimation period was extended beyond 1914. Although the ARCH model is popular as a measure of changing variances, it is not appropriate for my purpose. It is worth noting that the ARCH estimates show the same pattern as reported in Table 11.1 for the moving regression (MR) and MSKF estimates and provides an indication of the robustness of those results. The original use of ARCH as a measure of inflation variability was in Robert Engle, "Autoregressive Conditional Heteroscedasticity with Estimates of the Variance of United Kingdom Inflation," *Econometrica* 50 (July 1982): 987–1007, and Engle, "Estimates of the Variance of U.S. Inflation Based upon the ARCH Model," *Journal of Money, Credit and Banking* 15 (Aug. 1983): 286–301.

11. Milton Friedman, "The Crime of 1873," *Journal of Political Economy* 98 (Dec. 1990): 1159–94.

12. Frank Taussig, *The Silver Situation in the United States*, 2d ed. (New York, 1900).

13. These certificates were usually issued in large denominations, and banks were reluctant to hold them. Banks typically paid them out quickly for customs duties owed to the Treasury. The certificates did not circulate, and the accumulation of these notes in the Treasury was referred to as "dead silver."

14. Although the public cannot be forced to hold more money than it wishes, and in that sense the money stock is demand-determined, the argument here is that changes in the supply of silver coins or silver certificates could affect the equilibrium price level and interest rate, and in turn the demand for money.

15. The Treasury had three important ways of affecting the monetary base during the nineteenth century: silver coinage, the quantity of national bank notes in circulation, and the amount of cash held by the Treasury. To a significant extent, the expansionary influence of the silver purchases on the monetary base was offset by the Treasury's other actions.

16. Another aspect of the silver purchases that affected the confidence with which the public viewed the Treasury's commitment to the gold standard was the difficulty the Treasury faced in keeping the silver coins and certificates in circulation. The accumulation of silver was replacing the Treasury's holding of gold, and this raised the possibility that the Treasury might not be able to honor its commitment to pay gold to every creditor who demanded it. For example, the gold reserve fell from $150 million in January 1884 to $116 million in May 1885, edging closer to the $100 million minimum gold reserve required by law. The Treasury eliminated the threat to the gold reserve in a few months by using the government's budget surplus to purchase silver and gold. Milton Friedman and Anna Schwartz, *A Monetary History of the United States* (Princeton, 1963), pp. 119–33.

17. The difference between the $4 million in silver purchased at the market price and silver's $6 million addition to the money supply is the seignorage (which the government accrues). This occurs because each dollar issued does not contain a full dollar's worth of silver.

18. Silver's price reached a high of $1.21 per ounce in the first two months after the act and fell in the remaining months of the act's life. The declining price meant that, although the maximum monthly note issue was about $5.5 million, that level was achieved for only a few months.

19. Friedman and Schwartz regard 1891 to 1893 as years in which Treasury actions, if maintained, were significant enough to have forced the United States off the gold standard. Consider, for example, that the contribution of the Treasury to the monetary base was $275 million over these three years—almost twice the total of the preceding eleven years.

20. There were different but related forces affecting the two types of drain. The Treasury's commitment to maintaining the gold standard prompted the external drain. Distrust of the solvency of banks, particularly those in the western United States, caused the internal drain. If the insolvency of banks was caused by the additional deflation brought about by the reduced net capital inflow, which arose out of the distrust of the gold parity, then a link existed between the internal and external drains. It can be argued that that link was the silver agitation. Additional evidence that supports this view can be found in the pattern of change in the gold outflow, which shows a sharp increase from 1890 to 1893. The outflow stopped

when the administration announced in July 1893 that it would push for repeal of the Sherman Act. Friedman and Schwartz, *Monetary History*, chap. 3.

21. The MSKF has a MSE of 0.00082, whereas the MR series has a MSE of 0.0014.

22. For example, when the ex post forecast error was large and the ex ante uncertainty was very low, individuals turned out to be wrong in having had such a sense of confidence in the forecast. It seems that the "best" circumstance would be one where a high ex post forecast error was accompanied by high ex ante uncertainty, and conversely, where a low ex post forecast error was accompanied by low ex ante uncertainty.

23. The correlation coefficient between the uncertainty measure and the absolute forecast error was also calculated. The MR measure has a substantially higher correlation (a value of 0.58) than the MSKF, which has a small and negative correlation (−0.03).

24. The pattern reflected in the MSKF series is inconsistent with the association of indirect effects with higher levels of uncertainty. It does not show any increase in uncertainty in 1889 or 1890, unlike the MR series.

25. The hypothesis regarding the behavior of uncertainty after the turnaround in the price level finds support from the MR uncertainty series but not from the MSKF series, which remains essentially flat after 1896 except for a slight upward trend after 1902.

26. The aggregate demand and aggregate supply model is a variation on a Lucas-type model derived by Richard Froyen and Roger Waud, "An Examination of Aggregate Price Uncertainty in Four Countries and Some Implications for Real Output," *International Economic Review* 28 (June 1987): 353–72.

27. In the estimation, a test for first-order autocorrelation indicated that the disturbance was not white noise. A correction was made for first-order autocorrelation in each of the moving regression estimates and the estimate of rho was taken into account in computing the variance of the forecast error. All variables except the trend term are logarithms.

28. There is an additional observation lost from the sample due to the one-period lag on the independent variables.

29. Sample-size selection is essentially arbitrary in this situation; Klein chose twelve observations in his study. The sample's size was expanded so that, with two more independent variables, the degrees of freedom are the same.

30. "Small" shocks correspond to a low assumed variance of the disturbance terms; "large" shocks correspond to a higher assumed variance of the disturbances. The higher variances were 16 times as large as the small variances. This follows Edvard Bomhoff and Clemens Kool, "Forecasts with Multi-State Kalman Filters," app. 1 in Bomhoff's *Monetary Uncertainty* (Amsterdam, 1983), pp. 229–46.

31. The overall measure of uncertainty is the uncertainty associated with next period's prediction of the price level, conditional on the use of model j, weighted by the probability that the correct model is in fact j. This measure of uncertainty was derived from a result in Bomhoff and Kool, "Forecasts."

32. Milton Friedman and Anna Schwartz, *Monetary Trends in the United States and the United Kingdom* (Chicago, 1982), pp. 122–37.

Notes to Pages 240–42

33. In developing the series on import unit values, the source used for 1861–1900 was Matthew Simon, "The United States Balance of Payments, 1861–1900," in William Parker, ed., *Trends in the American Economy in the Nineteenth Century* (Princeton, 1960), p. 652. The base year is 1860. For 1879–1921, the source was Robert Lipsey, *Price and Quantity Trends in the Foreign Trade of the United States* (Princeton, 1963), pp. 146–47. The base year is 1913. For 1919–70, the source was U.S. Department of Commerce, *Historical Statistics of the United States, Colonial Times to 1970* (Washington, D.C., 1970), series U225-248. The base year is 1967. For 1971–81, the source was U.S. Department of Commerce, *Survey of Current Business* (Washington, D.C., 1971–81).

12. Galambos: The Triumph of Oligopoly

1. On the evolution of the theory and the court decisions, see F. M. Scherer, *Industrial Market Structure and Economic Performance* (Boston, 1980), pp. 176–97, 513–21, 534–44; George Stigler, "Monopoly and Oligopoly by Merger," *American Economic Review* 40 (May 1950): 23–34; Franco Modigliani, "New Developments on the Oligopoly Front," *Journal of Political Economy* 66 (June 1958): 215–32; George Stigler, "A Theory of Oligopoly," *Journal of Political Economy* 72 (Feb. 1964): 44–61; Avinash Dixit, "Recent Developments in Oligopoly Theory," *American Economic Review* 72 (May 1982): 12–17; Robert Solow, "Neoclassical Economics in Perspective," in Warren Samuels, ed., *The Chicago School of Political Economy* (East Lansing, 1976), esp. p. 47; John McGee, *In Defense of Industrial Concentration* (New York, 1971); Dominick Armentano, *Antitrust and Monopoly: Anatomy of a Policy Failure* (New York, 1982). The *Iowa Law Review* 74 (July 1989) features an interesting "Symposium: The Sherman Act's First Century: A Historical Perspective"; see especially William Kovacic, "Failed Expectations: The Troubled Past and Uncertain Future of the Sherman Act as a Tool for Deconcentration," pp. 1105–50, and Peter Carstensen, "How to Assess the Impact of Antitrust on the American Economy: Examining History or Theorizing?" pp. 1175–1217.

2. On progressive or liberal history, see John Higham with Leonard Krieger and Felix Gilbert, *History* (Englewood Cliffs, N.J., 1965), pp. 171–232; also, Samuel Hays, "The Social Analysis of American Political History," *Political Science Quarterly* 80 (Sept. 1965): 3; more recently, Thomas Bender, "Wholes and Parts: The Need for Synthesis in American History," *Journal of American History* 73 (June 1986): 120–36; and the subsequent discourse in "A Round Table: Synthesis in American History," *Journal of American History* 74 (June 1987): 107–30. See also Brian Balogh, "Reorganizing the Organizational Synthesis: Federal-Professional Relations in Modern America," *Studies in American Political Development* 5 (Spring 1991): 119–72.

3. Alfred Eichner, *The Emergence of Oligopoly: Sugar Refining as a Case Study* (Baltimore, 1969), esp. pp. 291–331. See also Eichner's *The Megacorp and Oligopoly: Micro Foundations of Macro Dynamics* (New York, 1976).

4. Naomi Lamoreaux, *The Great Merger Movement in American Business, 1895–1904* (New York, 1985). Lamoreaux focuses on a subset of industries in which there were by the late nineteenth century a handful of evenly matched firms, all of which were large enough to affect prices. She does not study atomistic industries or those dominated by a single, very large company.

5. Ibid., pp. 189–90. Lamoreaux deals with antitrust in chapter 6 (pp. 159–86), where she credits the policy with doing more to shape business behavior—i.e., particular patterns of stabilization—than industry structure.

6. Ibid., p. 190.

7. Ibid., pp. 191–92.

8. The most important of Chandler's books are *Strategy and Structure: Chapters in the History of the American Industrial Enterprise* (Cambridge, Mass., 1962), and *The Visible Hand: The Managerial Revolution in American Business* (Cambridge, Mass., 1977). For the articles, see Thomas McCraw, ed., *The Essential Alfred Chandler: Essays Toward a Theory of Big Business* (Boston, 1988).

9. Alfred Chandler, *Scale and Scope: The Dynamics of Industrial Capitalism* (Cambridge, Mass., 1990), p. 8.

10. Ibid., pp. 34–36, on "First-Mover Advantages and Oligopolistic Competition." Chandler gives "the modern industrial enterprise . . . a central role in creating the most technologically advanced, fastest-growing industries of their day. These industries, in turn, were the pace setters of the industrial sector of their economies—the sector so critical to the growth and transformation of national economies into their modern, urban industrial form" (p. 593).

11. Ibid., pp. 96–97. *Scale and Scope* gives to political factors more of a role than did Chandler's previous works, but the author's position in this case is ambiguous. Compare pp. 34–35, for instance, where politics does not enter the analysis, with p. 89, where it does. The best test is Chandler's treatment of specific changes in industry structure, as with Standard Oil; in that case, the two causal factors are said to be changes in demand and in sources of supply (see pp. 101–4).

12. Ibid., pp. 35, 92–104, 593–605.

13. See Scherer, *Industrial Market Structure*, esp. pp. 151–266, 407–38, 459–74.

14. Ibid., p. 152.

15. Ibid., pp. 430–38.

16. Ibid., p. 129. See also Eichner, *Emergence*, p. 332: "The fundamental motivation behind the consolidation movement . . . was the desire to eliminate price competition as a significant factor in business life."

17. Scherer, *Industrial Market Structure*, pp. 459–74, 497–569.

18. Ibid., p. 546; also see p. 141.

19. See Oliver Williamson, "The Modern Corporation: Origins, Evolution, and Attributes," *Journal of Economic Literature* 19 (Dec. 1981): 1537–68; and his *Markets and Hierarchies: Analysis and Antitrust Implications: A Study in the Economics of Internal Organization* (New York, 1975).

20. See Williamson, *Markets and Hierarchies*, pp. 208–33, on dominant firms, and pp. 234–47, on oligopoly. Williamson concludes that "for the present it is sufficient to rest on the observation that, on the average, concentration does not appear to have a significant influence on innovation and that, in a systems sense, an active market in inventions favors progressiveness" (p. 188).

There are two important exceptions to my general statement about the position taken by economists. First, see those scholars who follow the lines of analysis developed by McGee and Armentano (cited in note 1 above; see also the important article by Harold Demsetz, "Industry Structure, Market Rivalry and Public Policy,"

Journal of Law and Economics 16 [Apr. 1973]: 1–70). Second, see those who are working on the theory of the core (see Lester Telser, *A Theory of Efficient Cooperation and Competition* [New York, 1987]).

21. See, for example, the following: Pearce Davis, *The Development of the American Glass Industry* (Cambridge, Mass., 1949); Glenn Porter and Harold Livesay, *Merchants and Manufacturers: Studies in the Changing Structure of Nineteenth-Century Marketing* (Baltimore, 1971); Harold Vatter, *The Drive to Industrial Maturity: The United States Economy, 1860–1914* (Westport, Conn., 1976); Thomas Cochran, *The Pabst Brewing Company: The History of an American Business* (New York, 1948); Harold Passer, *The Electrical Manufacturers, 1875–1900* (Cambridge, Mass., 1953); Harold Williamson and Arnold Daum, *The American Petroleum Industry, The Age of Illumination, 1859–1899* (Evanston, Ill., 1959); William Haynes, *American Chemical Industry: Background and Beginnings* (New York, 1954); Thomas Parke Hughes, *Elmer Sperry: Inventor and Engineer* (Baltimore, 1971); Reese Jenkins, *Images and Enterprise: Technology and the American Photographic Industry, 1839 to 1925* (Baltimore, 1975). See also Louis Galambos and Joseph Pratt, *The Rise of the Corporate Commonwealth: United States Business and Public Policy in the Twentieth Century* (New York, 1988), pp. 17–37.

22. Hans Thorelli, *The Federal Antitrust Policy: Origination of an American Tradition* (Baltimore, 1955).

23. Most of the sources cited in note 21 above mention loose combinations. See also Victor Clark, *History of Manufacturing in the United States from 1607 to 1914*, vol. 2 (Washington, D.C., 1929); Eliot Jones, *The Trust Problem in the United States* (New York, 1921); William Ripley, ed., *Trusts, Pools and Corporations* (Boston, 1916); Henry Seager and Charles Guilick, Jr., *Trust and Corporation Problems* (New York, 1929). Cartels are discussed at length in Chandler, *Visible Hand*; see also Paul MacAvoy, *The Economic Effects of Regulation: The Trunk-Line Railroad Cartels and the Interstate Commerce Commission Before 1900* (Cambridge, Mass., 1965); and Lamoreaux, *Great Merger Movement*, esp. pp. 14–16, 24–27, 69–71.

24. I am indebted to Naomi Lamoreaux for the idea of "proto-oligopolies." Clark, *History of Manufacturing*, vol. 3; Donald Adams, Jr., "Prices and Wages," in Glenn Porter, ed., *Encyclopedia of American Economic History* (New York, 1980), 1: 229–46. See the figures on business failures in U.S. Bureau of the Census, *Historical Statistics of the United States: Colonial Times to 1970* (Washington, D.C., 1975), pt. 2, pp. 912–13.

25. Robert Gallman, "The Pace and Pattern of American Economic Growth," in Lance Davis, Richard Easterlin, and William Parker, eds., *American Economic Growth: An Economist's History of the United States* (New York, 1972), pp. 15–60.

26. See, for instance, Philip Scranton, *Proprietary Capitalism: The Textile Manufacture at Philadelphia, 1800–1885* (New York, 1983); and the sources cited in note 21 above.

27. On the growth of the economy, see Moses Abramovitz and Paul David, "Reinterpreting Economic Growth," *American Economic Review* 63 (May 1973): 428–39; Simon Kuznets, *Modern Economic Growth: Rate, Structure and Spread* (New Haven, 1966); and Kuznets, "Notes on the Pattern of U.S. Economic Growth," in Edgar Edwards, ed., *The Nation's Economic Objectives* (Chicago,

1964), pp. 15–35. On the opportunities associated with that growth, see Stephen Thernstrom, *Poverty and Progress: Social Mobility in a Nineteenth-Century City* (Cambridge, Mass., 1964); Thernstrom, *The Other Bostonians: Poverty and Progress in the American Metropolis, 1800–1970* (Cambridge, Mass., 1973); Stanley Lebergott, *Manpower in Economic Growth: The American Record Since 1800* (New York, 1974). On the distribution of income, see Lee Soltow, *Men and Wealth in the United States, 1850–1870* (New Haven, 1975).

28. Chandler, *Visible Hand*; Lamoreaux, *Great Merger Movement*.

29. Malcolm Burns, "Outside Intervention in Monopolistic Price Warfare: The Case of the 'Plug War' and the Union Tobacco Company," *Business History Review* 56 (Spring 1982): 33–53. See also Patrick Porter, "Origins of the American Tobacco Company," *Business History Review* 43 (Spring 1969): 59–76. Curiously, Chandler (*Visible Hand*, pp. 291–92) treats the organization of American Tobacco in his chapter on vertical integration; as he notes, however, the "desire to control . . . competition" was the sole motive for the merger.

30. Ralph Hidy and Muriel Hidy, *Pioneering in Big Business, 1882–1911* (New York, 1955), esp. pp 9–23, 32–49; but see Chandler, *Scale and Scope*, pp. 24–25.

31. After the Hidys completed their volume, the company apparently destroyed the records upon which their study was based—making it difficult, of course, to develop new evidence on the vital question of the motives for organizing the trust.

32. Chandler, *Scale and Scope*, pp. 47–233. See also Malcolm Burns, "Economies of Scale in Tobacco Manufacture, 1897–1910," *Journal of Economic History* 43 (June 1983): 461–74.

33. Chandler, *Scale and Scope*, pp. 77–78; Richard Edwards, "Stages in Corporate Stability and the Risk of Corporate Failure," *Journal of Economic History* 35 (June 1975): 428–57; see Gabriel Kolko, *The Triumph of Conservatism* (New York, 1963), pp. 26–56, for a different interpretation of the weeding-out process.

34. Hence Chandler is pleased to see lower prices and Scherer is still nervous because allocative efficiency appears to be impaired (as it clearly is, in static terms). Chandler discusses "allocative effectiveness" (*Scale and Scope*, p. 227) but does not meet Scherer head on.

35. Even in those firms with substantial market power, there was considerable pressure on the research laboratories to justify their expenditures in the short term. This was true in both regulated and unregulated firms. See, for example, Leonard Reich, *The Making of American Industrial Research: Science and Business at GE and Bell, 1876–1926* (New York, 1983).

36. Thorelli, *Federal Antitrust Policy*; and Louis Galambos, *The Public Image of Big Business in America, 1880–1940* (Baltimore, 1975).

37. Thomas McCraw, *Prophets of Regulation: Charles Francis Adams, Louis D. Brandeis, James M. Landis, Alfred E. Kahn* (Cambridge, Mass., 1984), pp. 1–152.

38. *U.S. v. American Tobacco*, 221 US 106-93; *The Standard Oil Company of New Jersey et al. v. U.S.*, 221 US 1-106; *U.S. v. E. I. du Pont de Nemours & Co. et al.*, 188 US 127.

39. Joseph Pratt, "The Petroleum Industry in Transition: Antitrust and the Decline of Monopoly Control in Oil," *Journal of Economic History* 40 (Dec. 1980): 815–37.

40. See note 38 above.

41. Vail set forth his position in *Annual Report of the Directors of American Telephone & Telegraph Company to the Stockholders for the Year Ending December 31, 1907*, p. 18. See also Vail's letter to P. Henry Woodward, Feb. 25, 1908, AT&T Archive. The settlement between AT&T and the federal government is set forth in N. C. Kingsbury to the Attorney General, Dec. 19, 1913; J. C. McReynolds to N. C. Kingsbury, Dec. 19, 1913; and Woodrow Wilson to James C. McReynolds, all reprinted in AT&T's *Annual Report . . . 1913*, pp. 24–27. See Gerald Brock, *The Telecommunications Industry: The Dynamics of Market Structure* (Cambridge, Mass., 1981), pp. 155–56.

42. Kolko, *Triumph of Conservatism*, launched this line of reanalysis. See also Stephen Breyer, *Regulation and Its Reform* (Cambridge, Mass., 1982), and more recently, Gary Libecap, "The Political Economy of Crude Oil Cartelization in the United States, 1933–1972," *Journal of Economic History* 49 (Dec. 1989): 833–55.

43. Chandler, *Scale and Scope*, pp. 127–40; Reich, *Making of American Industrial Research*, pp. 42–96; Passer, *Electrical Manufacturers*; W. Bernard Carlson, *Innovation as a Social Process: Elihu Thomson and the Rise of General Electric, 1870–1900* (New York, 1991).

44. Carlson, *Innovation*, p. 329. My discussion here does not do credit to Carlson's penetrating analyses of how the process of innovation changed at GE during the 1890's (see pp. 306–35). The author quotes Thomas Edison's remark: "I can only invent under powerful incentive. No competition means no invention" (p. 292).

45. Ibid., pp. 335–39, 343–50. As Carlson observes (p. 349), GE came to emphasize science in part because its "managers wanted an institution to perform the function of innovation that was as reliable, as controlled, as their new manufacturing and marketing institutions. Consequently, they turned to scientists for new product development because in their rhetoric those scientists spoke of being able to predict and control the forces of nature."

46. Scherer, *Industrial Market Structure*, p. 438.

47. George David Smith, *From Monopoly to Competition: The Transformations of Alcoa, 1888–1896* (New York, 1988); Margaret Graham and Bettye Pruitt, *R&D for Industry: A Century of Technical Innovation at Alcoa* (New York, 1990); and Louis Galambos, "Theodore N. Vail and the Role of Innovation in the Modern Bell System" (forthcoming, *Business History Review*). Alcoa might be considered a special case because in order to increase demand, it had to force its way into markets heretofore dominated by other materials.

48. Scherer, *Industrial Market Structure*, pp. 151–52.

49. I have developed this theme at greater length in "What Have CEOs Been Doing?" *Journal of Economic History* 48 (June 1988): 243–58. The problem this creates for economic theory is akin to the problems associated with the theory of regulation and the experience of deregulation; the theory provides no midpoints at which partial regulation might be judged socially successful, nor does it offer any means of improving performance other than by introducing more competition (that is, by removing regulatory restraints). Historical experience with regulation suggests, to the contrary, that not all regulated industries are unsuccessful, and that even regulated competition can under certain circumstances be successful.

Judging by recent experiences in America with deregulation, we will probably learn more about these theoretically unspecifiable but historically observable midpoints in the next few years.

50. For the distinction between "adaptive" and "formative" innovations, see Louis Galambos, "Theodore N. Vail"; and William Lazonick, *Business Organization and the Myth of the Market Economy* (New York, 1991).

51. Joseph Schumpeter, *Capitalism, Socialism, and Democracy* (New York, 1947), esp. pt. 2, pp. 61–163; and Schumpeter, *The Theory of Economic Development: An Inquiry into Profits, Capital, Credit, Interest, and the Business Cycle* (New York, 1961).

52. David Hounshell and John Kenly Smith, Jr., *Science and Corporate Strategy: Du Pont R&D, 1902–1980* (New York, 1988).

53. Thomas Hughes, *Networks of Power: Electrification in Western Society, 1880–1930* (Baltimore, 1983), esp. pp. 140–74, discusses "technological momentum." For the down side of momentum, see Richard Hirsch, *Technology and Transformation in the American Electric Utility Industry* (New York, 1989), pp. 87–142.

54. Hounshell and Smith, *Science and Corporate Strategy*, pp. 125–89, 210–21.

55. Ibid., pp. 249–74. It seems unlikely that any organization, large or small, bureaucratic or nonbureaucratic, can significantly increase its probability of developing formative innovations in a systematic, predictable fashion over the long term. Thus the problem from the point of view of the firm was that of developing a rational organization to cope with an inherently stochastic process. From the point of view of society, the problem was to ensure that there were a sufficient number of efforts made to devise (but not necessarily to introduce) formative innovations over the long run.

56. Ibid., pp. 331–64.

57. On the monopoly years, see Smith, *From Monopoly to Competition*, pp. 43–190; Graham and Pruitt, *R&D for Industry*, pp. 29–271.

58. See especially Graham and Pruitt, *R&D for Industry*, pp. 275–473; and Smith, *From Monopoly to Competition*, pp. 312–20, 333–63.

59. On fiscal innovations and political skills, see Andrew Butrica, *Out of Thin Air: A History of Air Products and Chemicals, Inc., 1940–1990* (New York, 1990). On distribution, see Richard Tedlow's excellent study *New and Improved: The Story of Mass Marketing in America* (New York, 1990). Most of Tedlow's marketing sagas involve innovative rivals and early movers that failed to remain innovative over the long term. See also Peter Temin, with Louis Galambos, *The Fall of the Bell System: A Study in Prices and Politics* (New York, 1987), which is in part a study of the political capability of MCI, the Bell System's major rival. On "organizational capabilities" in general, see Chandler, *Scale and Scope*. Although the most successful firms appear to sustain innovations across a broad range of their functions, we actually know very little about how these activities interact within the firm.

60. The business schools are discussed in Susan Aaronson, "Without Practice or Practitioners: Graduate Business Education, 1945–1960," *Business and Economic History*, 2d ser., 19 (1990): 262–72; and Aaronson, "Serving American Business" (forthcoming in *Business History*).

61. Jesse Markham, *Conglomerate Enterprise and Public Policy* (Boston, 1973); Milton Leontiades, *Managing the Unmanageable: Strategies for Success Within the Conglomerate* (Reading, Mass., 1986).

62. Alfred D. Chandler, "The Enduring Logic of Industrial Success," *Harvard Business Review* 2 (Mar.-Apr. 1990): 138–40.

63. Galambos and Pratt, *Rise of the Corporate Commonwealth*, pp. 227–55. See also Michael Jensen, "Eclipse of the Public Corporation," *Harvard Business Review* 5 (Sept.-Oct. 1989): 61–74.

64. Paul Lawrence and Davis Dyer, *Renewing American Industry: Organizing for Efficiency and Innovation* (New York, 1983), esp. pp. 11–54, 270–74, 287–88. See also Gilbert Gall, "Labor Relations in the Automobile Industry," in George May, ed., *The Automobile Industry, 1920–1980* (New York, 1989), pp. 284–92; Thomas Kochan, ed., *Challenges and Choices Facing American Labor* (Cambridge, Mass., 1985).

65. Louis Galambos, "Paying Up: The Price of the Vietnamese War," in *Vietnam, 1964–1973: An American Dilemma, Proceedings of the Fourteenth Military History Symposium* (Colorado Springs, forthcoming).

66. See, for instance, Paul Tiffany, *The Decline of American Steel: How Management, Labor, and Government Went Wrong* (New York, 1988), pp. 153–90; Lawrence and Dyer, *Renewing American Industry*, pp. 17–85; Margaret Graham, *RCA and the VideoDisc: The Business of Research* (New York, 1986).

67. The automobile, chemical, and basic metal industries appear to be moving toward this international structure, and the airline industry may follow shortly.

68. Lazonick, *Business Organization*, proposes a more drastic break with neoclassical theory.

69. See, for instance, Harold Livesay, "Entrepreneurial Dominance in Businesses Large and Small, Past and Present," *Business History Review* 63 (Spring 1989): 1–21.

70. Although it is heartening to see the *Journal of Economic Perspectives* (vol. 5 [Spring 1991]: 15–110) publishing a symposium on "Organizations and Economics," it is disappointing to find that none of the participants used any of the recent historical studies of business organizations. The explanation for this oversight is perhaps embodied in Joseph Stiglitz's remark (p. 15) that "most economists have traditionally relegated the study of organizations to business schools, or worse still, to sociologists."

⚹ Index

In this index an "f" after a number indicates a separate reference on the next page, and an "ff" indicates separate references on the next two pages. A continuous discussion over two or more pages is indicated by a span of page numbers, e.g., "57–59." *Passim* is used for a cluster of references in close but not consecutive sequence.

Library of Congress Cataloging-in-Publication Data

American economic development in historical perspective /
  edited by Thomas Weiss and Donald Schaefer.
      p.   cm.
  Includes bibliographical references and index.
  ISBN 0-8047-2084-3
    1. United States—Economic conditions—To 1865.
  2. United States—Economic conditions—1865–1918.
  I. Weiss, Thomas Joseph. II. Schaefer, Donald.
  HC105.A62 1993
  338.973—dc20   92-47404
                                               CIP

♾ This book is printed on acid-free paper.